Brain, Mind, and Developmental Psychopathology in Childhood

Edited by M. Elena Garralda
and Jean-Philippe Raynaud

JASON ARONSON
Lanham • Boulder • New York • Toronto • Plymouth, UK

Published by Jason Aronson
A wholly owned subsidary of The Rowman & Littlefield Publishing Group, Inc.
4501 Forbes Boulevard, Suite 200, Lanham, Maryland 20706
http://www.rowmanlittlefield.com

Estover Road, Plymouth PL6 7PY, United Kingdom

British Library Cataloguing in Publication Information Available

Library of Congress Cataloging-in-Publication Data
Brain, mind, and developmental psychopathology in childhood / edited by M. Elena Garralda and Jean-Philippe Raynaud.
    p. ; cm.—(IACAPAP book series) (IACAPAP book series. The working with children and adolescents series)
  Includes bibliographical references and index.
  Summary: "Brain, Mind, and Developmental Psychopathology in Childhood, part of the International Association of Child and Adolescent Psychiatry and Allied Professions' book series "Working with Children and Adolescents" edited by Elena Garralda and Jean-Philippe Raynaud updates the knowledge about connections between brain, mind, and developmental psychopathology. The volume illuminates our understanding of different types of psychiatric disorders in children including autism, hyperkinetic disorder, obsessive compulsive disorder, and childhood schizopreniaand the effects of child maltreatment and deliberate self harm. This book describes how to integrate physical and psychological treatments for child and adolescent mental health problems and advocacy for the treatment of children and adolescents with mental health problems. "—Provided by publisher.
  ISBN 978-0-7657-0864-9 (cloth : alk. paper)—ISBN 978-0-7657-0865-6 (paper : alk. paper)—ISBN 978-0-7657-0866-3 (electronic)
  I. Garralda, M. Elena. II. Raynaud, Jean-Philippe. III. Series: IACAPAP book series ; v. 19. IV. Series: IACAPAP book series. The working with children and adolescents series.
  [DNLM: 1. Mental Disorders—psychology. 2. Adolescent. 3. Child Development. 4. Child. 5. Mental Disorders—etiology. 6. Psychopathology. WS 350.6]
  618.92'89—dc23   2011046406

Printed in the United States of America

Contents

Part II: Individual Disorders/Problems: Updates

Part III: Treatment and Advocacy

List of Tables and Figures

TABLES

FIGURES

Acknowledgments

We would like to thank the authors for contributing to this volume of the IACAPAP book series and providing some interesting and thought-provoking chapters. At Rowman & Littlefield, Julie Kirsch and Amy King ensured a smooth pathway to publication. Finally, our grateful thanks are due to Nicole Hickey, who conducted all the admin for the editors and produced the final version of the manuscript.

Preface

Just like the theme of the twentieth International Association for Child and Adolescent Psychiatry and Allied Professions (IACAPAP) Congress to be held in Paris, the book for this Congress, "Brain, Mind, and Developmental Psychopathology in Childhood," is timely. This publication reveals that the care of the mind and body of a child is one whole and that it should start before conception and continue through infancy, childhood and adolescence. Important aspects of different professional contributions to the field of child and adolescent mental health (CAMH) are covered in this study of the brain, mind, and development. This book is fuel for our CAMH melting pot.

The book represents IACAPAP's purpose as highlighted in Article 2 of the association's constitution:

> To advocate for the promotion of mental health and development of children and adolescents through policy, practice, and research. To promote the study, treatment, care and prevention of mental and emotional disorders and disabilities involving children, adolescents and their families through collaboration among the professions of child and adolescent psychiatry, psychology, social work, paediatrics, public health, nursing, education, social sciences, and other relevant disciplines.

CAMH is now receiving more attention than it ever has. In 2011, for the very first time, mental health was designated as an area of importance by the United Nations General Assembly. In addition, the World Health Organization's "Ten Facts on Mental Health" highlight the reality that one in five children and adolescents has a mental disorder and that half of all psychiatric disorders start before children reach the age of fourteen years. Attention is also drawn to the greatly uneven distribution of CAMH resources. This is evidenced by the huge treatment gap in resource-poor regions where the majority of the children in the world live and where more than half of the population are children and adolescents.

One way in which CAMH care can be significantly improved all over the world and especially in resource-poor regions is to bridge the divide between physical and mental healthcare that is common in developing regions and to integrate the work of all the healthcare professionals in contact with children and adolescents. Investing early in both the mental and physical healthcare of children is extremely important as this will yield significant benefits for families, communities and countries at large, when the children grow up to be responsible and creative citizens in society. In this way, our care for infants, children, and adolescents is not only holistic but also focused on the critical period of child development in the spirit of "Brain, Mind, and Development."

Olayinka Olusola Omigbodun MBBS (Ibadan), MPH (Leeds), FMCPsych, FWACP.
President of IACAPAP.
Professor of Psychiatry, College of Medicine, University of Ibadan.
Consultant in Child and Adolescent Psychiatry, University College Hospital, Ibadan, Nigeria.

September 2011, Abuja, Nigeria

Editorial Introduction

M. Elena Garralda and Jean-Philippe Raynaud

The IACAPAP book series marks the 2012 IACAPAP Paris Congress with the publication of this volume along the lines of the Congress theme: "Brain, Mind, and Development." As with previous books in the series, it aims to reflect emerging evidence to support clinical work in the field of child and adolescent mental health worldwide.

The first IACAPAP Congress was hosted in Paris in 1937 with Georges Heuyer as Congress President. Seventy-five years later it is fitting for a Congress focusing on links between brain and mind to be based in Paris, as French thinking has left a legacy which is central to our understanding in this field of enquiry. Descartes, as a major exponent of ontological dualism, has been credited with separating bodies from the immaterial thinking mind. As W. H. Auden put it, using an interesting psychological perspective, "Devoid of a mother to love him, Descartes divorced mind and body." Nevertheless, instances of mutual influences where the mind becomes "mixed-up" with the body have always been acknowledged. This book should contribute to "nurturing" and increasing our understanding of the bodily, brain and mental processes that underlie developmental and psychiatric disorders in children and young people.

Authors have been chosen as expert writers in their field with an ability to meet the tight submission time deadlines imposed by the fixed Congress dates! We also chose contributions that open perspectives for clinical practice in child and adolescent mental health. As the Congress takes place in Paris there is a predominance of European contributors, but IACAPAP has a worldwide remit and writers from different continents have been approached to make sure that a broad range of perspectives are represented. There are background conceptual and empirical chapters on biological and psychological influences on developmental psychopathology in childhood, clinical updates with a main focus on the biological underpinnings of individual child neuropsychiatric disorders, as well as a chapter on how to integrate biological and psychological therapies in child mental health. In addition there is discussion on broader psychological/social problems with chapters on the effects of child maltreatment on the developing brain, an update on understanding and managing self-harm, and advocacy papers on learning disorders and child and adolescent mental health.

BIOLOGICAL AND PSYCHOLOGICAL INFLUENCES ON DEVELOPMENTAL PSYCHOPATHOLOGY

The first four chapters address biological models for understanding child development and psychopathology, the interplay between biological and psychological processes as antecedents in infancy for personality disorders, as well as insights into childhood psychiatric disorders derived from new developmental neuro-imagining techniques and genetic findings.

David Cohen discusses the need to consider not just gene-by-environment but gene-environmental-developmental aetiological interactions for psychopathology. He uses mathematical models from cellular network development to describe probabilistic or statistical dimensions. He describes how environmental factors contribute to mental conditions and draws from key animal studies that help us understand how stress and early life adversities impact on development and behavior, and how environment can shape DNA and neural structure. He reviews ways in which genetic factors affect human behavior and how transmission/inheritance occurs during human development and he proposes an integration of these factors in a nonhierarchical developmental model of probabilistic epigenesis, one that (in contrast to the deterministic/vulnerability model) relies on the possibility of accepting bidirectional interactions in the development of psychopathology.

Miri Keren and Sam Tyano cover antecedents in infancy for personality disorders, with a special emphasis on the interplay between biological and psychological processes. They outline neurobiological studies in the context of developmental psychopathology and links between early interpersonal experiences, brain development, and personality organization later in life. They mention links between right brain limbic dominance and attachment experiences in early years. They also point out that exposure to stressful and traumatic experiences at a time when the brain is undergoing enormous change may leave an indelible imprint on the structure and function of the brain, especially for individuals with genetic vulnerability. They comment on the precursors of personality disorders which can be traced to early traumatic attachment experiences and childhood emotional and behavioural disturbance, as well as on concepts of resilience, vulnerability and sensitivity, and on specific "maladaptive personality traits" in childhood and their generational transmission.

Philip Shaw's review focuses on the application of structural longitudinal neuroimaging to our understanding of neurodevelopmental deviations in children. Insights have been made possible due to unprecedented access to the anatomy and physiology of the developing brain afforded by magnetic resonance imaging without the use of ionizing radiation. He examines the complex patterns of structural brain development in healthy children in relation to neurodevelopmental deviations. Using attention deficit hyperactivity disorder (ADHD) as a primary example of the latter he argues that—as with other neuropsychiatric disorders—ADHD can be conceptualized as resulting from perturbations from the trajectory of typical development of brain structure and function. This work shows that much may be learnt from focusing attention on mechanisms which control the timing of postnatal cortical development, anomalies in the developmental sequence of the activation and deactivation of genes that sculpt cortical architecture, and substances such as neurotrophins which are essential for the proliferation, differentiation, and survival of both neuronal and non-neuronal cells. The clinical potential of this approach might inform a move away from a nosology based purely on clinical symptoms to one which incorporates patterns of brain growth, and to the need for longitudinal studies to help unravel the neural bases of differential clinical outcomes and, by implication, lead to more targeted treatments.

Genetic research is changing our outlook on many medical disorders. Marie Christine Mouren, Thomas Bourgeron, and Richard Delorme provide an update on common and rare genetic variants recently identified as risk factors for autism spectrum disorders. These variants point to biological pathways that may be at play in autism through their ability to influence synaptic homeostasis (such as synaptic cell adhesion molecules and scaffolding proteins relevant to synaptic development, proteins related to axonal growth and synaptic identity, and genes regulating synaptic protein levels). They note, however, that beyond technological advances future progress to understand the complex genotype-phenotype relationships in autism and the detection of subtle effects on relative risk will require close research collaborations between clinicians, neurobiologists and molecular geneticists, and large well-characterized clinical samples.

INDIVIDUAL DISORDERS/PROBLEMS: UPDATES

The clinical chapters address obsessive compulsive disorder (OCD), autism and child schizophrenia, and developmental dyslexia. They are complemented by contributions on the effects of traumatic and abusive experiences on brain development and on deliberate self-harm.

Recent years have witnessed an important increase in our understanding of the neuroanatomical and neurophysiological bases of OCD, and Luisa Lazaro and Josep Toro provide an update of biological and clinical knowledge on OCD in children. They note that this work has resulted in OCD being conceptualized as a neurodevelopmental disorder in which psychosocial factors play only a comparatively limited part. Nevertheless, the authors highlight gaps in our knowledge; for example, with regard to the biological underpinnings of the links between OCD and tics and early-onset OCD. They draw attention to areas for future research, such as endophenotypes and possible family biomarkers which may help put into place preventative strategies, and into the study of how psychosocial stress influences the onset and clinical manifestation of OCD.

The empirical basis for links between autism and schizophrenia is addressed by Saskia Palmen and Herman van Engeland. Their historical background makes clear how much of what we know about the relationship between the two disorders has changed over the years. Their review of current evidence leads the authors to conclude that both autism and schizophrenia are neurodevelopmental disorders sharing—on a clinical phenotypic level—deficits in social behaviour, oddness of speech, unusual responsiveness to the environment and inappropriate affect. They make the case for overlapping brain abnormalities, possibly accounted for by shared vulnerability factors both environmental (in-utero disease and stress exposure, pre- and perinatal complications, season of birth, urbanicity and parental age) and genetic (large and rare CNVs). However, there is no explanation for how these shared genetic and environmental risk factors result in quite different illness picture and progressions, differences in age of onset, sex-distribution and co-morbidity with mental retardation. Clarifying this should remain a work in progress.

Early-onset schizophrenia is one of the most devastating and yet comparatively little studied of child psychiatric disorders. Helmut Remschmidt and Frank Theisen draw on their unique experience of researching and managing children with this condition. Their systematic approach to definition, epidemiology, description of clinical features and management is aided by excellent tables and figures, and is a first class resource for clinicians who are unlikely to see affected children very frequently but where their clinical skills as child psychiatrists are pivotal.

Developmental dyslexia is a common co-morbidity amongst children attending child and adolescent mental health services. Its neurobiological correlates have been particularly well studied and Andreas Warnke, Gerd Schulte-Körne and Elena Ise outline recent findings. They provide a detailed description of the deficits involved, the research into underlying neurobiological anomalies, and of treatments that may be put in place—some of these informed by underlying deficits. They also discuss the importance of cultural factors and structural language aspects that influence the development of reading and writing disorders in different countries.

Danya Glaser provides an account of the increasingly compelling empirical evidence for the effects of child maltreatment on brain development and function. The study of sensitive and critical periods in brain development and the response to environmental experiences is central to this work. Deprivation, neglect and abuse are associated with changes in brain function and these changes are either not at all or only partially reversible with improved environments. Significant reductions in the size of the corpus callosum in children who have been maltreated, larger amygdala volumes correlating with longer time spent in institutional care and with difficulty in emotion regulation, and reduced eye contact mediated by increased amygdala activity are all cases in point, as is the growing evidence of both genetic vulnerability and resilience to the effects of maltreatment.

The chapter by Dennis Ougrin, Troy Tranah, Eleanor Leigh, Lucy Taylor and Joan R. Asarnow addresses recent knowledge on self-harm and implications for clinical practice. Whilst biological and psychological correlates (i.e., impulsive aggression, emotional dysregulation, poor problem solving, and impaired selective attention) are likely to reflect gene-environment interactions underpinning the development of self-harm, psychosocial influences undoubtedly play a central part. The authors describe in detail desirable ways of conducting assessments and engaging and treating children and adolescents. They also provide a critical account of existing empirical evidence (or lack of) for treatments currently in use; special mention is made of the SOS (signs of suicide) prevention programme, therapeutic assessment programmes and dialectical and cognitive behaviour therapies. This review will be particularly helpful for clinicians involved in this area of work.

TREATMENT AND ADVOCACY

Duke University has for some time taken a leading role in the evaluation and integration of treatments for child psychiatric disorders, and in the practice of evidence-based child and adolescent psychiatry. Jeffrey Sapyta and John March are therefore in an excellent position to remind us that the combined efforts of molecular neuroscience and cognitive psychology are driving a revolution in how we understand the diagnosis and treatment of mental illness. Empirically supported unimodal treatments for children are now available for most disorders seen in clinical practice and a number of strongly powered and well designed large, multi-centre studies, carried out in the USA predominantly, are all now impacting on clinical interventions. As a result it has become clear that a combination of targeted medication and psychosocial therapies skilfully applied across time will afford the most plausible basis for sustained benefit in children and adolescents with a variety of major mental illnesses. The authors describe how to implement evidence-based medicine in the child psychiatric context with multi-disciplinary practice in child psychiatry—as always—being best, and they outline ways of making research relevant for clinical practice. This chapter is a must-read for clinicians wishing to integrate research into clinical practice.

Daniel Fung and Liying Su have written a thought-provoking essay on the concept of learning disabilities as it applies to the field of child and adolescent mental health from a broad socio-educational and cultural perspective. They highlight the importance of education and schooling for social mobility and prosperity which leads to parents setting high store by the educational progress of their children and also to becoming highly stressed in the presence of learning failure. They discuss the strengths and weaknesses of the concept of intelligence, different models of understanding learning disability —including a critique of learning disorder as a diagnostic entity—cultural and structural language influences and links with mental disorders. They make suggestions for how learning disorder may be helpfully incorporated into current and future medical classification systems and, importantly, they describe carefully applied, sensible, helpful treatment approaches.

The final chapter by Gordon Harper addresses the past and present of child and adolescent mental health advocacy. The child protection movement, recognising the special educational rights of children, the early programmes for children's emotional and behavioural problems and schools for delinquent children were all early advocates. However, attitudinal changes enabled the development of clinics for child and adolescent mental health problems, and current advocacy involves numerous organisations, institutions and voluntary agencies. He points out that advocacy for child and adolescent mental health has become a vast field encompassing patients and families, mental health professionals, lawyers that are experts in rights litigation, professional advocates and researchers from the biological, behavioural and social sciences. The challenge inherent in so rich a field is also its greatest asset; to speak for the historically voiceless using methods not available even a generation ago in a way that still allows the voice of the child to be heard clearly.

Our discipline of child and adolescent psychiatry is fed by its history and ability to evolve and be open to the future and progress while taking into account cultural diversity. We thank all the authors and hope this new IACAPAP book, due to the diversity and richness of its contributions, is a forerunner to a twentieth World Congress of IACAPAP full of exchanges and forged links between researchers and clinicians from all countries.

I

BIOLOGICAL AND PSYCHOLOGICAL INFLUENCES ON DEVELOPMENTAL PSYCHOPATHOLOGY

1

The Developmental Being

Modeling a Probabilistic Approach to Child Development and Psychopathology

David Cohen

INTRODUCTION

Genetic and neuropsychological determinants have recently dominated the debates on the aetiopathological understanding of child and adolescent psychiatric disorders; the archetypal model is one of genetic vulnerability (e.g., Karmiloff-Smith, 1998). The human genome project revealed that there are only approximately 22,000 genes, not the 100,000 previously thought; however, even 100,000 genes cannot sufficiently contain enough information to organize a fully developed social mind (Panksepp, 2007). Furthermore, genetics is not the exclusive mode of inheritance in humans (Jablonka and Lamb, 2007). For example, externalizing behaviors have indeed been associated with a great variety of risk factors that include non-neurobiological factors (Farrington and Loeber, 2000). Even autism, which is regarded as the disorder that carries the strongest genetic determinants still has unresolved questions. To date, no specific gene or genetic abnormality has been associated with autism. Rather, the genetic determinants of autism are shared not only with other intellectual disabilities but also with other psychiatric disorders, including schizophrenia (Guilmatre et al., 2009). Even environmental factors contribute to the autism phenotype. Recently, Grandgeorge et al. (2009) demonstrated in a large sample that better language development was associated with parental socioeconomic status. In some cases, environmental factors may also cause autism, particularly when they occur prenatally (Guinchat et al., in press).

The developmental determinants of psychopathology are less studied because of methodological issues; however, longitudinal studies have demonstrated that early childhood and adolescence are two periods of extreme sensitivity that lead to the concept of sensitive dependence on initial conditions (Breton, 1999). Therefore, one should not only consider gene-by-environment interactions, but also gene-by-environment-by-development interactions (Thompson and Stanwood, 2009). Recent studies have shown that environmental factors can shape brain structures at molecular (McGowan et al., 2009) and structural/functional levels (Vanderwert et al., 2010). These modifications can have pathological consequences by themselves, but can also influence development via adaptive/compensatory mechanisms (Shaw et al., 2010). Therefore, the developmental trajectories of mental conditions in children and adolescents may help understand both psychological and pathological processes that result in certain conditions (Marcelli and Cohen, 2009). Essex et al.'s study (2010) on social anxiety in adolescence and its relationship with severe inhibition in childhood is a remarkable example. Finally, onsets of psychiatric conditions in children and adolescents follow a developmental course in line with the two key periods of development and are summarized in Figure 1.1, showing the major modifications in brain organization.

In an effort to present an integrated view, I will show that another model, one that combines the diversity and complexity of factors that influence the

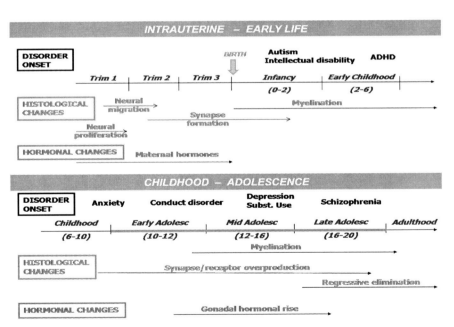

Figure 1.1.   The age of onset in children and adolescents of major psychiatric conditions: A developmental view of histological and hormonal changes in the brain. (Modified from Ernst, 2009; Pardo and Ehberadt, 2007)

development of psychiatric condition, indeed exists. These factors include genetic, neuropsychological and hormonal factors as well as environmental and developmental determinants (Marcelli and Cohen, 2009). The environmental determinants vary greatly, and their impact on a child's development is often not specific (Poulton et al., 2002). They include a large spectrum of events from exposure to drugs and toxins to social and cultural factors (Cohen, 2008). They also include traumatic life experiences (e.g., physical and sexual abuse), which have been studied widely.

The model that best encompasses the complexity of these different factors is a developmental model of probabilistic epigenesis. This model is one of biological development that integrates bidirectional interactions between the different structures and determinants (Gottlieb, 2007). In short, this model assumes that neural structures (or other structures) start to operate before they are completely mature and that this operation is derived either from intrinsic activity or from extrinsic interactions. The pre-activation of neural structures plays a significant role in the developmental process. The coordination of functional influences and formative structures within one factor and between several factors is not perfect; therefore, a probabilistic element is necessary for all developing human systems and the results of those developments (Milgram and Atlan, 1983; Gottlieb, 2007; Cohen, 2010). When the result happens to be a psychiatric condition, this model allows us to involve every known factor and determinant and to determine how their bidirectional interactions lead to strengthening or cumulative effects (Breton, 1999). I will present recent studies that support this model and help to understand the diversity of the aetiopathogenic determinants of psychiatric conditions. Although I will provide examples of many disorders, I will keep externalizing disorders in the forefront. In addition to the categorical approach of psychiatric nosography, I will adopt a dimensional approach of phenomenology. This approach will help to focus on specific pertinent dimensions such as clinical signs, psychological characteristics, and environmental or genetic factors to study their interactions and their possible developmental outcomes (Cohen, 2010).

To better catch the meaning of the model, I first recall some mathematical models from cellular network development that describe the probabilistic or statistical dimensions (Milgram and Atlan, 1983), focusing on an integrative view they offer to development and psychopathology and the recent confirmation of this mathematical model in the field of language learning (e.g., Saffran et al., 1996). The parallel with written language acquisition and mathematical learning offers a unique view of cultural/environmental influences on brain development.

Secondly, I summarize how environmental factors contribute to mental conditions by discussing their biological and psychological impacts. I review key studies, particularly those that have focused on animal models of early life adversities because these help us to understand how stress affects development and behavior (Denenberg, 2000) and how environment can shape DNA and neural structure as well (Hyman, 2009). I will also briefly review how genetic factors affect human behavior (Caspi and Moffit, 2006) and the ways in which transmission/inheritance occurs during human development.

Finally, I propose an integration of all the aforementioned factors in a non-hierarchical developmental model of probabilistic epigenesis. Again, a key issue regarding probabilistic epigenesis (as opposed to the deterministic/vulnerability model) relies on the possibility (1) of accepting (1) bidirectional interactions between all bio-psycho-social levels (Gottlieb, 2007); (2) temporal focus on early interactions that many authors consider crucial in terms of developmental cues (see also Keren and Tyano Chapter in this book).

STATISTICAL LEARNING: FROM THE PROBABILISTIC AUTOMATA OF NEURAL NETWORKS TO LANGUAGE LEARNING AND DEVELOPMENT

Probabilistic Automata as a Model for the Epigenesis of Cellular Networks

Atlan (1979) suggested the theory of adaptive self-organization based on reducing the initial redundancy of partially random, noise producing, and environmental factors. This theory helps us to understand the logic of an "organizing" effect of randomness as a source of biological organization in addition to the deterministic genetic programme. Using mathematical models of growing networks made of dividing, interconnected cells, Milgram and Atlan (1983) compared probabilistic automata to deterministic automata. They showed that the number of necessary states in the initial generating cell automatons was dramatically reduced when the automaton was probabilistic rather than deterministic. They defined an automaton by its sets of 1) internal states, 2) inputs, and 3) transition matrices that represent its various possibilities to go from one state to another upon receiving a given input. Within *deterministic automatons*, transitions are produced in a unique and unambiguous way for each input. Matrices only have one element ("1") in each line. Within *probabilistic automatons*, transitions are produced by probabilities ε, which may take on any value between 0 and 1.

It appears that 1) Probabilistic programming is more efficient than deterministic programming in accounting for the generation of complex networks (i.e., high number of cells or diversity of interactions); 2) Probabilistic automata have self-organizing properties that allow them to account for non-directed learning at both the cellular and multi-cellular levels; and 3) Changes in the structure of a network can come about as a result of its functioning. In their theoretical work, Milgram and Atlan (1983) showed that probabilistic automata could generate networks with some specificity, despite a loss of accuracy, compared to deterministic procedures in which the price for infinite accuracy would be paid by a much larger number of states. In sum, they produced a probabilistic instrument that presented highly superior characteristics compared to predetermined instruments for neural networks. Their model suggested that a more probabilistic model should replace the classic and controversial metaphor of genetic programming (i.e., that DNA has a specific genetic determinism). Their mathematical solution greatly reduced the number of steps necessary to create the chains, rings and structures in trees from an initial cellular instrument generator. Furthermore, this proposal was particularly well adapted for the development of neural networks (Atlan, 1979) and the immune system (Danchin, 1978), given their high level of biological complexity.

Statistical Learning: The Example of Language Development

Empirical evidence for probabilistic or statistical learning has matured in the fields of auditory and visual inputs (Perruchet and Pacton, 2006). In language acquisition, cultural factors are crucial for both oral and written language; however, cultural influences on oral and written language develop in radically different ways. Oral language develops "spontaneously" unless the child is deprived from language exposure. As evidenced by the number of illiterates in countries with poor educational systems, reading acquisition is not spontaneous. Learning to read requires a long process of education. From an evolutionary viewpoint, Homo sapiens have only recently acquired the ability to read.

After Saffran et al.'s seminal study on six-month-olds' attention towards phonological/auditory stimuli (1996), Atlan's intuition was confirmed. Saffran et al. (1996), as well as Kuhl and colleagues (2007; 2004; 1997), showed that 1) infants possess the ability to discriminate the phonemes and prosodic features of all languages from birth; 2) the language areas within the left hemispheres of infants as young as three months old activate when exposed to language stimuli (Dehaene-Lambertz et al., 2006); 3) infants develop a strategy of learning based on input language signs and characteristics and explore language statistical properties, leading to so-called statistical" or "probabilistic learning"; and 4) the language experience involves the perceptual system at a neuronal level, increasing native-language speech perception and decreasing foreign-language speech perception via the "magnet effect" (Kuhl, 2000). This transition usually occurs between six to eight months after birth. Simple exposure, however, does not explain language learning. In both speech production and perception, the presence of an adult interacting with a child strongly influences learning (Goldstein et al., 2003).

In contrast to oral language development, reading acquisition is an extraordinary example of brain plasticity and how education can shape brain structures. Reading acquisition involves visual, auditory, and motor tasks. Establishing links between these tasks requires the ability to differentiate phonemes (i.e., phonological awareness), graphemes, and to distinguish articulatory movements (Goswami and Bryant, 1990). These tasks are unconscious in good readers. In the course of learning to read, two word-identification strategies are settled: first, the grapho-phonologic strategy puts together letters into words; second, the lexical strategy is much faster and allows children to recognise the whole word in a stock of known written words (Humphreys and Evett, 1985). Numerous factors can influence learning to read, including oral abilities, psychosocial context and support, education strategies and cognitive/developmental skills (e.g., attention, phonology, and visual spatial) that result in dyslexia (Plaza et al., 2003; see also Warnke chapter in this book). Despite the fact that restrictive biological views are dominant in the field of reading (e.g., Meng et al., 2005), recent studies have shown that cultural factors constrain the neurobiological abnormalities associated with dyslexia (Siok et al., 2004). This concept is best described using examples from numeration.

NUMERATION DEVELOPMENT: FROM EARLY INTUITION TO NUMBER SYMBOLS CALCULATION

Early Numeration Intuition

In numeration acquisition, distinguishing symbolic from non-symbolic aspects is important. The former deals with understanding and manipulating Arabic numerals such as "2" or "12" and number words such as "two" or "twelve." Non-symbolic arithmetic deals with estimating grandiosity of concrete sets of objects (e.g., visual dots). These three ways of dealing with numeration in adults have lead to the triple code model (Dehaene and Cohen, 1995). Numeration ability appears to be a complex mixture of "natural intuition" and cultural influences during development and education.

In contrast with Piaget, a pioneer in the study of the development of mathematical abilities, numerous behavioral studies have revealed that 4– to 6–month-olds show a clear sensitivity to large numbers (Dehaene, 2009). This core knowledge is mainly non-symbolic and permits the rapid estimation of the number of objects that are present in a scene and how two different quantities can be classified according to grandiosity. This core knowledge is present in humans with no education or mathematical training such as indigenous Amazonian groups (Gordon, 2004; Pica et al., 2004). It follows a logarithmic Weber's law, and is particularly efficient with small numbers. This ability to discriminate numbers is also seen in macaque monkeys, in which number-coding neurons have been identified by two independent groups (Nieder et al., 2002; Sawamara et al., 2002). Are these neurons the evolutionary precursor of human numeration natural ability?

Cultural Influence on Early Numeration Intuition

As previously mentioned, the availability of number symbols varies across cultures. Recent studies have shown that if available during development and education, number symbols become strongly attached to non-symbolic codes, resulting in a "second-order intuition" because the link between symbols and quantities become automated and unconscious (Dehaene, 2009). In Western countries, this second-order intuition follows a linear "base 10" representation. How cultural influences shape early numerical intuition has been shown recently. Deheane et al. (2008) compared the Mundurucu, an indigenous Amazonian group with a reduced numerical lexicon and little or no formal education, to Western-educated participants. They showed that the ability to map numbers onto space is a universal intuition and that this initial intuition of numbers is logarithmic (see Figure 1.2). The concept of a "Base 10" linear number line that dominates Western nations appears to be a cultural invention that fails to develop in the absence of formal education.

In the field of language, the Jerger et al. study (2009) should be mentioned here as it evidenced change in language ability that parallels learning to read. Using a picture naming task with auditory and audiovisual phonological distracters, they showed that the results varied in complex ways as a function of age as well as the type and modality of distracters. Specifically, the results for congruent audiovisual distracters yielded an inverted U-shaped function: they found a significant influence on naming latencies in 4–year-olds and 10– to 14–year-olds but not 5– to 9–year-olds. The authors proposed that the temporary loss of sensitivity to audiovisual distracters reflected the reorganization of brain systems dedicated to relevant processing subsystems—particularly phonology—paralleling (a) formal literacy instruction and (b) developmental changes in multimodal processing and auditory perceptual, linguistic, and cognitive skills.

Integrating knowledge and recent advances in both reading and arithmetic, Dehaene and Cohen (2007) proposed a model called the "cultural recycling" of cortical maps. This mechanism allows a novel cultural object to encroach onto a pre-existing brain system as a result of brain plasticity

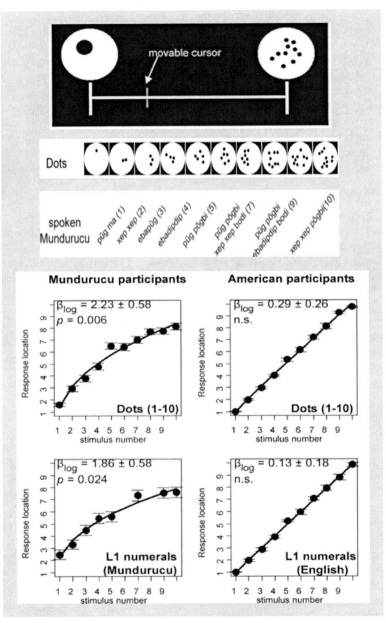

Figure 1.2. Number-space mapping task used in the Mundurucun. In this task each target number is presented as a set of dots or a Mundurucu number-word. Participants pointed to the corresponding location on the number line. The results shown at bottom illustrate that participants in the Mundurucu group understood the task and mapped numbers in a logarithmic scale. This pattern was not seen in control American participants. (*From Dehaene et al., 2008.*)

and human evolution. They proposed this model to explain the tremendous course of knowledge evolution in recent centuries. This proposal is of high interest for our purpose because it supports the idea of bidirectional interactions even at the neuronal level.

THE CONTRIBUTION OF ENVIRONMENTAL FACTORS TO YOUTH PSYCHOPATHOLOGY

Classifying Environmental Factors

The impact of environmental factors on child development is often not specific (Poulton et al., 2002). Environmental factors are multiple and extremely varied (Mealey, 1995). Many longitudinal studies point to the cumulative effects of stressors and suggest that prevention efforts should be directed at multi-problem families (Jaffee et al., 2007). Table 1.1 lists

Table 1.1. Environmental factors associated with psychopathology classified by subject's distance

Toxic and perinatal factors that impact brain development either during pregnancy and/or infancy

  Alcohol and other abuse during pregnancy
  Smoking during pregnancy
  Malnutrition, severe deprivation
  Low birth weight
  Hyperbilirubin

Micro-environmental variables that impact the child and his/her family in a proximal way

  Low socioeconomic status
  Early separation
  Single/disrupted parent (father absence)
  Large number of siblings
  Individual handicap or poor social skills
  Sexual and/or physical abuse
  Family violence and/or alcoholism
  Mentally ill parent (e.g., maternal depression; anti-social personality)
  Parental use of punishment as opposed to reward

Macro-environmental variables that impact at a more general societal level

  Urban residency and high population density
  TV/violence exposure
  Minority in situation of social exclusion or discrimination
  Rejection from school favouring poor education, social disadvantage, poor self-esteem
  Inclusion in at-risk pro-social alternatives (peer grouping: e.g., ganging, drug abuse)
  Competitive and violent culture

Note: From Cohen (2010)

some environmental factors, distinguishing toxins, micro- and macro-level factors, according to their respective major impact level (Cohen, 2010). Sociologists and economists have discussed the distinction between micro- and macro-factors for many years, but recent studies have reinforced their differences with data from experimental and evolutionary psychology (Denenberg, 2000). Other authors insist that distinguishing risk factors from protective factors (Breton, 1999) and moderators from mediators (Baron and Kenny, 1986) may help us to better understand longitudinal psychosocial data. A risk factor (vs. protective factor) is a variable that enhances (vs. decreases) the risk of occurrence of a dependent variable; a moderator is a variable that affects the direction, strength, or both of the relationship between an independent or predictor variable and the dependent variable (e.g., a specific psychopathology); and a mediator is a variable that accounts for the relationship between the predictor variable and the dependant variable. In sum, moderators specify when certain effects will hold, whereas mediators speak to how and why such effects occur (Baron and Kenny, 1986).

For a first estimate, we can isolate the contribution of certain toxins to which a child is exposed during pregnancy or early development (e.g., alcohol, tobacco, and other drugs). In addition to the extreme case of fetal alcohol syndrome, recent studies have shown that a low consumption of alcohol could have long-term consequences as well. Regarding externalizing disorders, environmental variables may be passed on via intermediary variables; for example, the correlation between cigarette consumption during pregnancy and birth weight (Wang et al., 2002). It may also pass on through genetic modulations (e.g., polymorphism of dopamine transporter; Khan et al., 2003). Again, as previously mentioned, non-specificity is the rule when one studies environmental variables. Another example is the similarity between prenatal risk factors of intellectual disabilities and prenatal risk factors of autism (Guinchat et al., in press).

The second type of environmental factors includes individual and familial factors, known as microenvironments. Most studies refer to different microenvironments as precursory, maintenance or prognostic factors (Burke et al., 2002). Regarding externalizing disorders, these include physical or sexual abuse, lack of family discipline, use of extreme punishment, poverty, minority status, an urban environment, a family history of psychiatric disorders, school failure and isolated parents (Burke et al., 2002; Roskam et al., 2007). The E-RISK study contributed to the understanding the role of these variables by studying the development of almost twelve hundred pairs of same-sex twins. In this study, the precursory factor of physical abuse was related to the severity of the abuse and the appearance of antisocial behaviors in children between five and seven years old (Jaffee et al., 2004). Furthermore, early maternal depression had a close relationship to antisocial behaviors; the number of post-partum depression episodes often had a cumulative effect (Kim-Cohen et al., 2005). Interestingly, recent studies such as STAR*D have illustrated how pharmacological treatment of mother depression can improve both parent and child outcomes in terms of reduction of child psychopathology (Weissman et al., 2006). Finally in a representative sample of 1,420 rural children, of which 25 percent were American Indians, Costello et al., (2003) showed that poverty contributed to conduct disorder (CD) and oppositional defiant disorder (ODD). These data support a social causation as opposed to a social selection explanation of childhood externalizing disorders.

Brent et al. (2009) showed that the incidence and course of depression, PTSD and substance use were high in bereaved youths after the loss of a parent and that this increase was even higher when parents died by suicide as opposed to natural or accidental deaths. The same group, in the Brodsky et al. family study on depression (2008) showed that sexual abuse was a risk factor for suicide attempts in both parents and offspring. More interestingly, they found that the transmission of suicide risk across generations was related to the familial transmission of sexual abuse and impulsivity. The victim did not directly transmit sexual abuse to the next generation because an affected parent was rarely a perpetrator; nevertheless, transmission was probably related to family dynamics.

Macro-environmental factors are more difficult to demonstrate with clear evidence because they require cross-cultural or longitudinal studies with a large number of participants to control for confounding factors. However, the numeration example given earlier demonstrates the power of macro-environmental factors. To continue with a previous example, several studies have shown that higher population densities and competitive societies that advocate short-term efficiency encourage externalizing factors (Mealey, 1995). In a prospective study, Lacourse et al. (2006) showed that associating with an antisocial group during adolescence was characterized by (1) a temporal dynamic with two trajectories of group affiliation—one in the beginning of adolescence, the other occurring in the middle of adolescence; and (2) the aggravation of behavioral disorders when a youth joins the group and a decrease when another leaves.

How environmental factors affect development at biological levels and through non-genetic transmission is a complex issue. The impact of environmental variables on stress regulation may be one answer. This will be developed later in this paper. First, let us select some biological effects of environmental exposure that have been discovered.

The Impact of Environmental Factors on the Biological System

Severe deprivation is one of the most documented environmental consequences on biological systems. Interestingly, attempts have been made to understand how genetic-by-environment interactions contribute to child attachment during development. Bakermans-Kranenburg and Ijzendoorn (2007) favor a differential susceptibility model rather than one of classic vulnerability. Genetic factors appear to moderately contribute to attachment styles. The children orphaned in Romania permitted scientists to assess risk and protective factors related to severe deprivation after taking into account many confounding variables. Severe early deprivation of human contact affects early brain development with cases of autism, intellectual disability, or both (Rutter et al., 2007). Despite a large amount of variance across children, IQ was negatively correlated with duration of deprivation. Children who entered the UK after two years of institutionalization had General Cognitive Indices that were twenty-five points lower than those who spent six months or less in a Romanian orphanage, regardless of the degree of malnutrition. The reversibility of the process depends on the age of the child when normal family rearing is restored (Rutter et al., 2004) and suggests the possibility of a sensitive period in cognitive development (Nelson et al., 2007). Besides cognitive development, severe deprivation also increases the risk of mental disorders, with boys being more at risk than girls (Zeanah et al., 2009). Zeanah and colleagues assessed whether the type of rearing influenced child outcomes in the US. Foster care compared to care as usual lowered the risk of internalizing disorders. More important, the cognitive outcomes of children who remained in a US institution were markedly below that of never-institutionalised children and children taken out of the institution and placed into foster care. The same group also showed that EEG brain activity was abnormal in children reared in institutions. Only the children placed in foster care before 24 months of institutionalisation achieved some measure of reversibility (Vanderwert et al., 2010). Interestingly, EEG abnormalities were associated with externalizing behaviors (McLaughlin et al., 2010). Using brain imaging, Mehta et al. (2009) showed that adolescents who had experienced severe early deprivation in Romania had smaller total grey and white matter volumes than non-deprived, non-adopted UK controls. After correcting difference in brain volume, the group who experienced deprivation had greater amygdala volumes. These studies show that deprivation affects emotional development and brain functioning as well as anatomic brain organization.

Other studies have examined the development of children placed under a milder early stress. For example, O'Connor et al. (2002; 2005) showed that prenatal maternal anxiety predicted behavioral and emotional problems by the age of 4 and that problems were linked to individual differences in the cortisol levels of pre-adolescents. Gerardin et al. (2010) showed that neonates (and boys more specifically) of depressed mothers during pregnancy had significant changes in psychomotor regulation as measured using Brazelton assessment. In another study, Van de Bergh and Marcoen (2004) demonstrated that prenatal maternal anxiety was linked to hyperactivity, externalizing problems and increased anxiety in children between 8 and 9 years old. Furthermore, Caspi et al. (2004) demonstrated that, among pairs of monozygotic twins, the child who received the most negative maternal attention and the least amount of warmth more frequently showed antisocial behavior by the age of 7. The mother viewed the other twin as more positive. The maternal view was measured through a subjective questionnaire that mothers responded to before their children were 5 years old. More recently, Teicher et al. (2010) showed that the frequency and severity of peer verbal abuse was correlated with several problems, including depression, anxiety, hostility and somatisation. They also showed that peer verbal abuse was associated with corpus callosum abnormalities.

We now investigate how environmental factors affect the biological system, not only at the level of the exposed organism, but also in offspring and consecutive generations.

The Contribution of Animal Models to the Understanding of Stress in Development

Despite the pioneering efforts of Victor Denenberg, who first showed the non-genomic transmission of behavioral traits in animals in the 1960s (Denenberg and Whimby, 1963; Denenberg and Rosenberg, 1967), the swing towards genetic studies in the 1980s made understanding the importance of stress difficult until the recent work of Michael Meaney and colleagues (Figure 3, second line from the bottom). Using rodent models, these authors showed that early stress, maternal care and stress during the gestation affected the development of future generations of rats through the HPA axis and epigenetic modifications. These modifications could be transferred from generation to generation and were independent of an animal's genetic inheritance.

The following briefly lists the important points learned from these experiments: 1) Early experience has a long-term effect on behavior and the biological system, especially when the mother and offspring are separated or when the quality of maternal care varies dramatically (Denenberg and Rosenberg, 1967; Liu et al., 1997); 2) Certain early experiences can affect future generations, providing a non-genomic mechanism for the transmission of behavioral traits (Denenberg and Whimby, 1963; Francis et al., 1999); and 3) The uterine setting affects development through environmental factors rather than genetic ones (Denenberg et al., 1998; Francis et al., 2003).

Meaney and others completed these general principles by describing how maternal care affected development through a behavioral programme and the future adult's pathological responses to stress. The quality of maternal care influenced the stress response HPA axes of offspring (Liu et al., 1997), cytogenesis and hippocampal synaptic development and memory and spatial development (Liu et al., 2000; Mirescu et al., 2004). Moreover, the quality of maternal care greatly influenced the epigenesis in the following generations. Improving the quality of maternal care by entrusting these pups to more affectionate mothers or blocking histone acetylation shortly after birth (stopping DNA epigenomic marking) reversed this effect (Weaver et al., 2004). Furthermore, naturally occurring variations in maternal behavior (increased pup licking/grooming and arched back nursing) are associated with differences in oestrogen-inducible central oxytocin receptors, which are involved in pro-social behaviors (Champagne et al., 2001). Variation in maternal care also alters $GABA_A$ receptor subunit expression in brain regions associated with fear (i.e., the amygdala, hippocampus, and medial prefrontal cortex; Caldgi et al., 2003; 2004).

On the one hand, these models offer a revolutionary paradigm from the perspective of genetic pre-determinism or genotype shaping of one's environment (Scarr and McCartney, 1983; Karmiloff-Smith, 1998). In effect, a trans-generational transmission independent of genetic heritage must completely modify paradigms to consider not only unidirectional interactions but also bidirectional interactions. On the other hand, these models, which imply a number of early stress factors, help to shed light on early childhood treatment and the importance of the temporality of the aforementioned environmental factors. In these animal models, environmental enrichment during the peripubertal period indeed leads to a functional reversal of the effects of maternal separation (e.g., HPA and behavioral response) through compensation rather than the reversal of early life adversity neural effects (Francis et al., 2002). Therefore, these studies demonstrate the need to consider not only gene-by-environment interactions, but also gene-by-environment-by-development interactions (Thompson and Stanwood, 2009).

Is it possible to extrapolate rodent models to Homo sapiens? Is it valid to "translate" or "parallel" these rodent models with some psychopathological proposals related to impaired infant-mother relationship such as Fraiberg et al. (1975) "Ghosts in the nursery"? or Schechter and Willheim (2009) proposal to relate mother's PTSD to atypical caregiver behavior, atypical maternal behavior to disturbances of attachment, the latter being a risk factor of psychopathology? Let's visit first other studies conducted with monkeys. Barr et al. (2004a; 2004b) recently showed that when chimps are reared separately from their mothers and placed in a situation of emotional deprivation, their adrenocorticotropic (ACTH) levels change as a result of stress. A functional genetic polymorphism that occurs in the serotonin transporter modulates this effect. As adults, only the apes that were both emotionally deprived and had the serotonin transporter allele (s/l) developed alcoholism when alcoholic drinks were included in their diet. In another set of experiments (Kraemer et al., 2008), the same group showed that neonatal consequences of prenatal alcohol exposure to apes was modulated by the same serotonin transporter polymorphism. Interestingly, there are numerous studies on corticosteroid/serotonin interactions in the neurobiological mechanisms of stress-related disorders (Lanfumey et al., 2008).

To test whether this model is valid in humans, one needs to use longitudinal studies with carefully chosen candidate variables that belong to each level of functioning. In the field of human behavior, two studies can be mentioned here. The Kumsta et al. (2010) study belongs to the Romanian adoptee studies. They showed that the effect of early institutional deprivation on emotional problems in adolescence was moderated by a serotonin transporter polymorphism, and also by the number of significant life events encountered during early adolescence. McGowan et al.'s (2009) study on suicide is also notable; as animal models of stress predict, they showed that the markers of epigenetic regulation in the glucocorticoid receptor were present in the brains of suicide victims with a history of child abuse compared to either suicide victims with no history of child abuse or controls. Because childhood abuse alters HPA response to stress and increases the risk of suicide in humans, this report suggests that there is a common effect of parental care on the epigenetic regulation of brain glucocorticoid receptor expression that contributes to individual differences and the risk of psychopathology. Integrative studies of this kind are still lacking in other psychopathologies.

TRANSMISSION AND INHERITANCE

Genetic Inheritance

The idea of genetic determinism has evolved in recent years (Karmiloff-Smith, 1998). To simplify these complex developments, several types of genetic determinants can be distinguished (Figure 3). The first is a "direct" form of determinism. It is found in certain aetiologies of autism and mental retardation (Cohen et al., 2005), although the literature is prevalent with examples of patients with atypical phenotypes (meaning that the genetic abnormality usually associated with autistic disorders or mental retardation is not) (e.g., Cohen et al., 2007). One should keep in mind, however, that animal models of degenerative disease or mental retardation have shown that environmental conditions can dramatically influence the adult phenotype (see Figure 1.3, bottom line; Nithianantharajah and Hannan, 2006).

Despite significant amounts of research, the literature on externalizing disorders, especially conduct disorder (CD), is extremely limited. Brunner

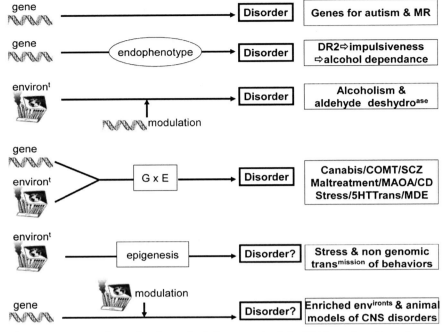

Figure 1.3. Genetic and epigenetic influences (mainly DNA centered) on human behaviors and psychiatric diseases. PHA: Phenylalanine hydroxylase; DR2: Dopamine receptor 2; COMT: Catecholamine O methyl transferase; SCZ: schizophrenia; MAOA: Mono-amine oxydase A; CD: Conduct disorder; 5HTTrans: Serotonin transporter; MDE: Major depressive episode; CNS: Central nervous system. In yellow: specific examples to illustrate each possibility are shown. (*From Cohen, 2010; modified from Caspi and Moffit, 2006.*)

and colleagues targeted a Dutch family with a mild form of mental retardation and severe CD (including aggression, impulsive behavior, and rapes) and found that these disorders were associated with a truncating mutation in monoamine oxydase A (MAOA), which is encoded by a gene on the X chromosome (Brunner et al., 1993). The idea of direct determinism, however, is somewhat limited in externalizing disorders.

The second type of determinism is carried through a variable called an endophenotype which is directly linked to the disorder. A classic example is the link between alcohol and impulsiveness. Numerous studies have shown that a polymorphism of the dopamine D2 receptor is linked to impulsiveness; participants could become dependent on alcohol even if only exposed to it once. Impulsiveness plays an intermediary role between alcohol consumption and genetic determinism (Limosin et al., 2003). In externalizing disorders, this variable can be described as an empathy that is linked to callous unemotional traits (Guile and Cohen, 2010). Clinical samples have found an association between weak empathy and the severity of a child's antisocial behavior in a difficult family context (e.g., Enebrink et al., 2005). The importance of genetic influence on antisocial behavior was well described in a study that tested 3,600 pairs of twins. By comparing the absence of empathy and the presence or absence of antisocial behavior in both monozygotic and dizygotic twins, Viding et al. (2005) found that the heritability of lack of empathy was high (67 percent). What was even more remarkable, however, was the difference between antisocial twins with low empathy (a heritability score of 81 percent) compared to antisocial twins with normal empathy (a heritability score of 30 percent). When weak empathy development is associated with antisocial disorders, genetic influences are much stronger than environmental effects. In contrast, when an antisocial trait is present without empathy impairment, the genetic influence is weaker even though the shared environment is strong.

The last form of genetic determinism is the possibility of a gene-environment interaction (see Figure 1.3, fourth line from top). This form should be distinguished from a genetic modulation of environmental effects on development (see Figure 1.3, 3^d line from top) such as breast-feeding effects on IQ through genetic variation in fatty acid metabolism (Caspi, 2007). For the past twenty years, numerous studies have investigated the possibility of a gene-environment interaction (e.g., depression, schizophrenia). In the field of childhood depression, Kaufman et al. (2004; 2006) showed that the occurrence of depression in maltreated children was moderated by polymorphisms of brain-derived neurotrophic factor and serotonin transporter genes as well as social support that tended to be protective.

Regarding externalizing disorders, Cadoret et al. (1995), using an adoption design, showed that behavioral disorders in adopted children depended not only on their biological parents but also on the environment of their adoptive family. More recently, Caspi et al. (2002) followed a group of 440 young New Zealand males from birth to the age of twenty-six. Violent behavior, CD and antisocial personality disorders were associated with abusive situations that occurred before the age of eleven. A functional polymorphism of MAOA could modify this effect.

Non-Genetic Inheritance

As previously mentioned, genetics is not the exclusive mode of inheritance in humans. At least three other modes—epigenetic, behavioral and symbol based—have been described (Jablonka and Lamb, 2007). Heredity comes from several elements including (i) genes, (ii) cellular epigenetic variations, (iii) developmental legacies transmitted in utero by the mother or (iv) transmitted in early infancy through statistical learning, (v) behavioral legacies transmitted through early interactions or through social learning, and (vi) symbol/cultural-based transmission. Many examples have been mentioned earlier. I now briefly review two datasets that emphasise the power of sociocultural factors. The first example shows how a genetic disease can be transmitted at a higher risk in a defined population according to socio-cultural factors: Using an evolutionary perspective, Nance and Kersey (2004) showed how different cultural factors can influence the frequency of a gene associated with deafness. This gene, DNFB1, occurs more frequently in the United States compared to Mongolia, where its incidence has steadily decreased. This variation may be explained by the thriving U. S. deaf culture, including its specific schools and a two-hundred-year-old sign language that likely encourage marriages between deaf people. A similar phenomenon has been described on the Island of Benkala in Bali with the DN1FB3 gene (Nance and Kersey, 2004). The second example shows how the constraint of social conformity participates, even in animals, in the learning and choice of a new behavior; Whiten et al. (2005) trained two leading female chimpanzees (F1 and F2) from two different groups (G1 and G2) to use a candy distributor. F1 was trained using Technique A; F2 with Technique B. Techniques A and B were equally difficult. When placed back in their groups of origin, F1 transmitted Technique A to her peers in G1 and F2 transmitted Technique B to G2. Because they were motivated to obtain candy, most of the chimps were able to discover the alternative technique (B for G1, A for G2). However, few chimps continued to use the alternative technique during follow-up. By doing so, they showed a social conformity to their group and leader.

PROBABILISTIC EPIGENESIS: AN ALTERNATIVE CAUSAL MODEL FOR MENTAL DISORDERS IN CHILDREN AND ADOLESCENTS

In keeping with the developmental perspective, the determining factors of mental disorders may be impossible to thoroughly translate. This complexity implies factors in which the points of impact are situated across different levels, including genetic, cellular, neurological, behavioral, familial and cultural levels (Cohen, 2010). Models that favor a homogeneous point of view or affect level stratifications based on a unidirectional and predetermined model cannot be supported because of the complexity of the phenomena that put several different levels into play (Atlan, 1979; Gotlieb, 2007).

A probabilistic epigenetic model is the best way to consider the complexity and diversity of so many factors. Such a model takes into account the diversity of determinant factors (e.g., Cohen, 2010), recent developments in longitudinal studies (e.g., Caspi et al., 2004), studies on environmental effects (e.g., Jaffee et al., 2004), animal models of early stress factors (e.g., Liu et al., 1997) and how the quality of maternal care affects child development (e.g., Rutter et al., 2004). Moreover, neural structures (or other structures) in this model begin functioning before they completely mature. This activity, be it intrinsically derived or extrinsically influenced, plays a significant role in developmental processes (Cohen, 2010). This model also necessitates that all different participatory levels (i.e., the genetic level, the level of biological, cerebral and neurological functioning, the conduct and behavioral level and the environmental level including the physical, social and cultural environments) work and interact with each other, not only via unidirectional interactions but constant bidirectional interactions as well. Because the coordination of the formal influences between and within each of these levels of analysis are not perfect, a probabilistic element must be introduced into the systems of development and their evolution, regardless of whether the influences are structural or functional (Gottlieb, 2007). When the result is a psychiatric disorder, this model permits the implication of the different known determinants at each level of analysis and integrates how their interactions often potentiate the effects due to their bidirectional nature (see Figure 1.4).

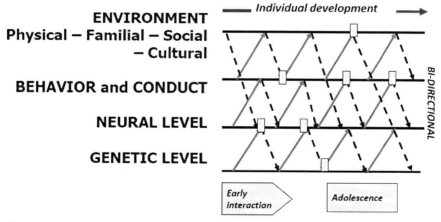

Figure 1.4. Meta-theoretical model of probabilistic epigenesis as a model for child psychopathology. In this view, neural (and other) structures begin to function before they are fully mature. This activity, whether intrinsically derived or extrinsically stimulated, plays a significant role in the developmental process. Because the coordination of formative-functional and structural influences within and between all levels of analysis is not perfect, a probabilistic element is introduced in all developing systems and their outcome. Some tension may occur (e.g., in the case of externalized disorders: early life adversities, cultural influences, callous unemotional traits, genetic factors). In this figure, I describe four levels of functioning from the cellular/genetic (low/micro) to the environmental (high/macro) level. Red arrows reflect influences from lower to higher levels and vice versa for green arrows. Yellow boxes refer to individual commitments that may occur during development and that influence the course of maturation (e.g., maternal language exposure or sexual abuse). Yellow signs refer to the two most important developmental periods of life, infancy and adolescence, in terms of both environmental and biological influences. (*From Cohen, 2010; modified from Gottlieb, 2007.*)

Studies have demonstrated that the first years of childhood and adolescence are sensitive developmental time periods. Each time a potential tension (or a critical moment) at a particular level occurs, there are subsequent downturns that appear on the trajectory. Keeping conduct disorder as the example given at each level, these critical moments include the consequences of genetic polymorphisms (e.g., MAOA), primary or secondary cerebral lesions (e.g., frontal dysfunction, Pincus, 2000), diverse environmental problems (e.g., child's maltreatment) or behaviors and intermediary phenotypes (e.g., hyperactivity) that reflect psychopathological difficulties. This model also questions the categorical logic of the nosographical classifications that should be replaced by a multidimensional perspective. This perspective permits easier monitoring of clinical, psychological, social and genetic aspects and considers their interactions and possible developmental results (Cohen, 2010). This integrative view may help develop prevention and promotion programs for the mental health of children and adolescents (Breton, 1999).

CONCLUSION

Using paradigms such as neural network modeling (Milgram and Atlan, 1983), organism development (Gottlieb, 2007), evolutionary theory (Denenberg, 2000) and infant development (Kuhl, 2004), several researchers have concluded that development and learning are driven by human cultural/environmental dependence. To accurately predict outcomes, this model requires a probabilistic factor. A multidisciplinary approach that integrates all known determinants and risk factors of a given disorder and places them in a probabilistic model appears to yield the most accurate representation of the diversity and complexity of child psychopathology.

REFERENCES

Atlan, H. (1979). *Entre cristal et fumée*. Paris: Le Seuil.
Bakermans-Kranenburg, M. J., and Van Ijzendoorn, M. H. (2007). Research review: Genetic vulnerability or differential susceptibility in child development: The case of attachment. *J Child Psychol Psychiatry*. 48, 1160–73.
Baron, R. M., and Kenny, D. A. (1986). The moderator-mediator variable distinction in social psychological research: Conceptual, strategic, and statistical considerations. *J Personality Social Psychol*. 51, 1173–82.
Barr, C. S., Newman, T. K., Lindell, S., Shannon, C., Champoux, M., Lesch, K. P., Suomi, S. J., Goldman, D., and Higley, J. D. (2004a). Interaction between sero-

tonin transporter gene variation and rearing condition in alcohol preference and consumption in female primates. *Arch Gen Psychiatry*. 61, 1146–52.

Barr, C. S., Newman, T. K., Shannon, C., Parker, C., Dvoskin, R. L., Becker, M. L., Schwandt, M., Champoux, M., Lesch, K. P., Goldman, D., Suomi, S. J., and Higley, J. D. (2004b). Rearing condition and rh5–HTTLPR interact to influence limbic-hypothalamic-pituitary-adrenal axis response to stress in infant macaques. *Biol Psychiatry*. 55, 733–38.

Brent, D., Melhem, N., Donohoe, M. B., and Walker, M. (2009). The incidence and course of depression in bereaved youth 21 months after the loss of a parent to suicide, accident, or sudden natural death. *Am J Psychiatry*. 166, 786–94.

Breton, J. J. (1999). Complementary development of prevention and mental health promotion programs for Canadian children based on contemporary scientific paradigms. *Can J Psychiatry*. 44, 227–34.

Brodsky, B., Mann, J., Stanley, B., Tin, A., Oquendo, M., Birmaher, B., Greenhill, L., Kolko, D., Zelazny, J., Burke, A. K., Melhem, N., and Brent, D. (2008). Familial transmission of suicidal behaviors: Factors mediating the relationship between childhood abuse and offspring suicide attempts. *J Clin Psychiatry*. 69, 584–96.

Brunner, H. G., Nelen, M. R., Breakefield, X. O., Ropers, H. H., and van Oost, B. A. (1993). Abnormal behavior associated with a point mutation in the structural gene for Monoamine Oxidase, A. *Sciences*. 262, 578–80.

Burke, J. D., Loeber, R., and Birmaher, B. (2002). Oppositional defiant disorder and conduct disorder: A review of the past 10 years, part II. *J Am Acad Child Adolesc Psychiatry*. 41, 1275–93.

Cadoret, R. J., Yates, W. R., Troughton, E., Woodworth, G., and Stewart, M. A. (1995). Genetic-environmental interaction in the genesis of aggressivity and conduct disorders. *Arch Gen Psychiatry*. 52, 916–24.

Caldgi, C., Diorio J., Anisman, H., and Meaney, M. J. (2004). Maternal behavior regulates benzodiazepine/GABAA receptor subunit expression in brain regions associated with fear in BALB/c and C57BL/6 mice. *Neuropsychopharmacology*. 29, 1344–52.

Caldgi, C., Diorio, J., and Meaney, M. J. (2003). Variations in maternal care alter GABA(A) receptor subunit expression in brain regions associated with fear. *Neuropsychopharmacology*. 28, 1950–59.

Caspi, A., McClay, J., Moffitt, T. E., Mill, J., Martin, J., Craig, I. W., Taylor, A., and Poulton, R. (2002). Role of genotype in the cycle of violence in maltreated children. *Science*. 297, 851–54.

Caspi, A., and Moffitt, T. E. (2006). Gene-environment interactions in psychiatry: Joining forces with neuroscience. *Nat Rev Neurosci*. 7, 583–90.

Caspi, A., Moffitt, T. E., Morgan, J., Rutter, M., Taylor, A., Arseneault, L., Tully, L., Jacobs, C., Kim-Cohen, J., and Polo-Tomas, M. (2004). Maternal expressed emotion predicts children's antisocial behavior problems: Using monozygotic-twin differences to identify environmental effects on behavioral development. *Dev Psychol*. 40, 149–61.

Caspi, A., Williams, B., Kim-Cohen, J., Craig, I. W., Milne, B. J., Poulton, R., Schalkwyk, Taylor, A., Werts, H., and Moffitt, T. E. (2007). Moderation of breastfeeding effects on the IQ by genetic variation in fatty acid metabolism. *Proc Natl Acad Sci USA*. 104, 18860–65.

Champagne, F., Diorio, J., Sharma, S., and Meaney, M. J. (2001). Naturally occurring variations in maternal behavior in the rat are associated with differences in estrogen-inducible central oxytocin receptors. *Proc Natl Acad Sci USA*. 98, 12736–41.

Cohen, D. (2008). Vers un modèle développemental d'épigenèse probabiliste du trouble des conduites et des troubles externalisés de l'enfant et de l'adolescent. *Neuropsychiatr Enf*. 56, 237–44.

Cohen, D., (2010). Probabilistic epigenesis: An alternative causal model for conduct disorders in children and adolescents. *Neuro Bio-behavioral Reviews*. 34: 119–29.

Cohen, D., Martel, C., Wilson, A., Déchambre, N., Amy, C., Duverger, L., Guile, J. M., Piripas, E., Benzacken, B., Cavé, H., Cohen, L., Héron, D., and Plaza, M. (2007). Visual-Spatial Deficit in a 16-year-old Girl with Maternally Derived Duplication of Proximal 15q. *J Aut Dev Dis*. 37: 1585–92

Cohen, D., Pichard, N., Tordjman, S., Baumann, C., Burglen, L., Excoffier, S., Lazar, G., Mazet, P., Pinquier, C., Verloes, A., and Heron, D. (2005). Specific genetic disorders and autism: Clinical contribution towards identification. *J Aut Dev Dis*. 35, 103–116.

Costello, J., Compton, S. N., Keeler, G., and Angold, A. (2003). Relationships between poverty and psychopathology. *JAMA*. 290, 2023–2029.

Danchin, A. (1978). Ordre et dynamique du vivant. Paris: Le Seuil.

Dehaene, S. (2009). Origins of mathematical intuitions: The case of arithmetic. *Ann NY Acad Sci*. 1156: 232–259.

Dehaene, S., and Cohen, L. (1995). Mathematical Cognition. 1, 83–120.

Dehaene, S., and Cohen, L. (2007). Cultural recycling of cultural maps. *Neuron*. 56, 384–98.

Dehaene, S., Izard, V., Spelke, E., and Pica, P. (2008). Number scale in Western and Amazonian indigene cultures. *Science*. 320, 1217–20.

Dehaene-Lambertz, G., Hertz-Pannier, L., and Dubois, J. (2006). Nature and nurture in language acquisition: Anatomical and functional brain-imaging studies in infants. *Trends in Neurosciences* 29: 367–73.

Denenberg, V. H. (2000). Evolution proposes and ontogeny disposes. *Brain Lang*. 73, 274–96.

Denenberg, V. H., Hoplight, B. J., and Mobraaten, L. E. (1998). The uterine environment enhances cognitive competence. *Neuroreport*. 9, 619–23.

Denenberg, V. H., and Rosenberg, K. M. (1967). Nongenetic transmission of information. *Nature*. 216, 549–50.

Denenberg, V. H., and Whimby, A. E. (1963). Behavior of adult rats is modified by the experiences their mothers had as infants. *Science*. 142, 1192–93.

Enebrink, P., Andershed, H., and Langstrom, N. (2005). Callous-unemotional traits are associated with clinical severity in referred boys with conduct problems. *Nord J Psychiatry*. 59, 431–40.

Essex, M. J., Klein, M. H., Slattery, M. J., Goldsmith, H. H., and Kalin, N. H. (2010). Early risk factors and developmental pathways to chronic high inhibition and social anxiety disorder in adolescence. *Am J Psychiatry*. 167, 40–46.

Farrington, D. P, and Loeber, R. (2000). Epidemiology of juvenile violence. *Child Adol Psychiatric Clin N Am*. 9, 733–49.

Fraiberg, S., Adelson, E., and Shapiro, V. (1975). Ghosts in the nursery. A psycho-analytic approach to the problems of impaired infant-mother relationships. *J Am Acad Child Psychiatry.* 14, 387–421.

Francis, D., Diorio, J., Liu, D., and Meaney, M. J. (1999). Nongenomic transmission across generations of maternal behavior and stress responses in the rat. *Science.* 286, 1155–1158.

Francis, D., Diorio, J., Plotsky, P. M., and Meaney, M. J. (2002). Environmental enrichment reverses the effects of maternal separation on stress reactivity. *J Neurosci.* 22, 7840–43.

Francis, D. D., Szegda, K., Campbell, G., Martin, W. D., and Insel, T. R. (2003). Epigenetic sources of behavioral differences in mice. *Nat Neurosci.* 6, 445–46.

Gerardin, P., Wendland, J., Bodeau, N., Galin, A., Bialobos, S., Tordjman, S., Mazet, Ph., Darbois, Y., Nizard, J., Dommergues, M., and Cohen, D. (2011). Depression during pregnancy: Is the developmental impact earlier on boys? A prospective case-control study. *Journal of Clinical Psychiatry.* 72, 378–80.

Goldstein, M., King, A., and West, M. (2003). Social interaction shapes babbling: Testing parallels between birdsong and speech. *Proc Natl Acad Sci USA.* 100, 8030–35.

Gordon, P. (2004). Numerical cognition without words: Evidence from Amazonia. *Science.* 306, 496–99.

Goswami, U. Bryant, P. (1990). Phonological skills and learning to read. Lawrence Erlbaum, Hillsdale, NJ.

Gottlieb, G. (2007). Probabilistic epigenesis. *Dev Sci.* 10, 1–11.

Grandgeorge, M., Hausberger, M., Tordjman, S., Deleau, M., Lazartigues, A., and Lemonnier, E. (2009). Environmental factors influence language development in children with autism spectrum disorders, *PlosOne.* 4:e4683,1–8.

Guile, J. M., Cohen, D. (2010). Les perturbations de l'empathie sont au cœur des troubles des conduites de l'enfant et de l'adolescent. *Neuropsychiatr Enf.* 58: 241–247.

Guilmatre, A., Dubourg, C., Mosca, A. L., et al. (2009). Recurrent rearrangements in synaptic and neurodevelopmental genes and shared biologic pathways in schizophrenia, autism, and mental retardation. *Arch Gen Psychiatry.* 66, 947–56.

Guinchat, V., Thorsen, P., Laurent, C., Cans, C., Bodeau, N., and Cohen, D. (in press). Pre, peri, and neonatal risk factors for autism. *Acta Obstetrica Scandinavica.*

Humphreys, G. W., and Evett, L. J. (1985). Are there independant lexical and non lexical routes in word processing? An evaluation of the route theory of reading. *Behavior and Brain Sciences,* 8: 689–739

Hyman, S. E. (2009). How adversity gets under the skin. *Nat Neurosci.* 12, 241–43.

Jablonka, E., and Lamb, M. J. (2007). Précis of: Evolution in four dimensions. *Behavioral Brain Sciences.* 30, 353–65.

Jaffee, S. R., Caspi, A., Moffitt, T. E., Polo-Tomas, M., and Taylor, A. (2007). Individual, family, and neighborhood factors distinguish resilient from non-resilient maltreated children: A cumulative stressors model. *Child Abuse Negl.* 31, 231–53.

Jaffee, S. R., Caspi, A., Moffitt, T. E., and Taylor, A. (2004). Physical maltreatment victim to antisocial child: Evidence of an environmentally mediated process. *J Abnorm Psychol.* 113, 44–55.

Jerger, S., Damian, M. K., Spence, M. J., Tye-Murray, N., and Abdi, H. (2009). Developmental shifts in children's sensitivity to visual speech: A new multimodal picture-word task. *J Exp Child Psychology*. 102, 40–59.

Karmiloff-Smith, A. (1998). Development itself is the key to understanding developmental disorders. *Trends Cog Sciences*. 2, 389–98.

Kaufman, J., Yang, B. Z., Douglas-Palumberi, H., Grasso, D., Lipschitz, D., Houshyar, S., Krystal, J. H., and Gelernter, J. (2006). Brain-derived neurotrophic factor-5-HTTLPR gene interactions and environmental modifiers of depression in children. *Biol Psychiatry*. 59, 673–80.

Kaufman, J., Yang, B. Z., Douglas-Palumberi, H., Houshyar, S., Lipschitz, D., Krystal, J. H., et al. (2004). Social supports and serotonin transporter gene moderate depression in maltreated children. *Proc Natl Acad Sci USA*. 101, 17316–21.

Khan, R. S., Khoury, J., Nichols, W. C., and Lanphear, B. P. (2003). Role of dopamine transporter genotype and maternal prenatal smoking in childhood hyperactive-impulsive, inattentive, and oppositional behaviors. *J Pediatr*. 143, 104–10.

Kim-Cohen, J., Moffitt, T. E., Taylor, A., Pawlby, S. J., and Caspi, A. (2005). Maternal depression and children's antisocial behavior: Nature and nurture effects. *Arch Gen Psychiatry*. 62, 173–81.

Kraemer, G. W., Moore, C. F., Newman, T. K., Barr, C. S., and Schneider, M. L. (2008). Moderate level fetal alcohol exposure and serotonin transporter gene promoter polymorphism affect neonatal temperament and limbic-hypothalamic-pituitary-adrenal axis regulation in monkeys. *Biol Psychiatry*. 63, 317–24.

Kuhl, P. K. (2000). A new view of language acquisition. *Proc Natl Acad Sci USA*. 97, 11850–57.

Kuhl, P. K. (2004). Early language acquisition: Cracking the speech code. *Nature Reviews Neuroscience*. 5, 831–43.

Kuhl, P. K. (2007). Is speech learning 'gated' by the social brain? *Developmental Science*. 10, 110–20.

Kuhl, P. K., Andruski, J. E., Chistovich, I. A., Chistovich, L. A., Kozhevnikova, E. V., Ryskina, V. L., Stolyarova, E. I., Sundberg, U., and Lacerda, F. (1997). Cross-language analysis of phonetic units in language addressed to infants. *Science*. 277, 684–86.

Kumsta, R., Stevens, S., Brookes, K., Scholtz, W., Castle, J., Beckett, C., Kreppner, J., Rutter, M., and Sonuga-Barke, E. (2010). 5HTT genotype moderates the influence of early institutional deprivation on emotional problems in adolescence: Evidence from the English and Romanian Adoptee (ERA) study. *J Child Psychol Psychiatry*. 51, 755–62.

Lacourse, E., Nagin, D. S., Vitaro, F., Cote, S., Arseneault, L., and Tremblay, R. E. (2006). Prediction of early-onset deviant peer group affiliation: A 12-year longitudinal study. *Arch Gen Psychiatry*. 63, 562–68.

Lanfumey, L., Mongeau, R., Cohen-Salmon, C., Hamon, M. (2008). Corticosteroid–serotonin interactions in the neurobiological mechanisms of stress-related disorders. *Neuroscience Behavioral Rev*. 32, 1174–84.

Limosin, F., Loze, J. Y., Dubertret, C., Gouya, L., Ades, J., Rouillon, F., and Gorwood, P. (2003). Impulsiveness as the intermediate link between the dopamine receptor D2 gene and alcohol dependence. *Psychiatr Genet*. 13, 127–29.

Liu, D., Diorio, J., Day, J. C., Francis, D. D., Meaney, M. J. (2000). Maternal care, hippocampal synaptogenesis and cognitive development in rats. *Nat Neurosci.* 3, 799–806.

Liu, D., Diorio, J., Tannenbaum, B., Caldji, C., Francis, D., Freedman, A., Sharma, S., Pearson, D., Plotsky, P. M., and Meaney, M. J. (1997). Maternal care, hippocampal glucocorticoid receptors, and hypothalamic-pituitary-adrenal responses to stress. *Science.* 277, 1659–62.

Marcelli, D., and Cohen, D. (2009). *Enfance et psychopathologie* (8ème édition). Paris: Masson.

McGowan, P. O., Sasaki, A., D'Alession, A. C., Dymov, S., Labonté, B., Szyf, M., Turecki, G., and Meaney, M. J. (2009). Epigenetic regulation of the glucocorticoid receptor in human brain associates with childhood abuse. *Nature Neuroscience.* 12, 342–48.

McLaughlin, K. A., Fox, N. A., Zeanah, C. H., Sheridan, M. A., Marshall, P., and Nelson, C. A. (2010) Delayed maturation in brain electrical activity partially explains the association between early environmental deprivation and symptoms of attention-deficit/hyperactivity disorder. *Biol Psychiatry.* 68, 329–36.

Mealey, L. (1995). The sociobiology of sociopathy: An integrated evolutionary model. *Behavioral and Brain Sciences.* 18, 523–99.

Mehta, M. A., Golembo, N. I., Nosarti, C., Colvert, E., Mota, A., Williams, S., Rutter, M., and Sonuga-Barke, E. (2009). Amygdala, hippocampal and corpus callosum size following severe early institutional deprivation: The English and Romanian adoptees study pilot. *J Child Psychol Psychiatry* 50, 943–51.

Meng, H., Smith, S. D., Hager, K., Held, M., Liu, J. et al. (2005). DCDC2 is associated with reading disability and modulates neuronal development in the brain. *Proc Natl Acad Sci USA.* 102, 17053–58.

Milgram, M., and Atlan, H. (1983). Probabilistic automata as a model for epigenesis of cellular networks. *J Theor Biol.* 103, 523–47.

Mirescu, C., Peters, J. D., and Gould, E. (2004). Early life experience alters response of adult neurogenesis to stress. *Nat Neurosci.* 7, 841–46.

Nance, W. E., and Kearsey, M. J. (2004). Relevance of connexin deafness (DFNB1) to human evolution. *Am J Hum Genet.* 74, 1081–87.

Nelson, C. A., Zeanah, C. H, Fox, N. A., Marshall, P. J., Smyke, A. T., and Guthrie, D. (2007). Cognitive recovery in socially deprived young children: The Bucharest Early Intervention Project. *Science.* 318:1937–40.

Nieder, A., Freedman, D. J., Miller, E. K. (2002). Representation of the quantity of visual items in the primate prefrontal cortex. *Science,* 297, 1708–11.

Nithianantharajah, J., and Hannan, A. J. (2006). Enriched environments, experience-dependent plasticity and disorders of the nervous system. *Nat Rev Neurosci.* 7, 697–709.

O'Connor, T. G., Ben-Shlomo, Y., Heron, J., Golding, J., Adams, D., and Glover, V. (2005). Prenatal anxiety predicts individual differences in cortisol in pre-adolescent children. *Biol Psychiatry.* 58, 211–17.

O'Connor, T. G., Heron, J., Golding, J., Beveridge, M., and Glover, V. (2002). Maternal antenatal anxiety and children's behavioral/emotional problems at 4 years. Report from the Avon Longitudinal Study of Parents and Children. *Br J Psychiatry.* 180, 502–8.

Panksepp, J. (2007). Can play diminish ADHD and facilitate the construction of the social brain? *J Can Acad Child Adolesc Psychiatry*. 16, 57–66.

Perruchet, P., and Pacton, S. (2006). Implicit learning and statistical learning: One phenomenon, two approaches. *Trends Cog Sciences*. 10, 233–38.

Pica, P., Lemer, C., Izard, V., and Dehaene, S. (2004). Exact and approximate arithmetic in an Amazonian indigene group. *Science*. 306, 499–503.

Pincus, J. H. (2000). Neurologic evaluation of violent juveniles. *Child Adol Psychiatric Clin N Am*. 9, 777–93.

Plaza, M., and Cohen, H. (2003). The Interaction Between Phonological Processing, Syntactic Awareness and Naming Speed in the Reading and Spelling Performance of First-Grade Children. *Brain and Cognition* 53: 287–92

Poulton, R., Caspi, A., Milne, B. J., Thomson, W. M., Taylor, A., Sears, M. R., and Moffitt, T. E. (2002). Association between children's experience of socioeconomic disadvantage and adult health: A life-course study. *Lancet*. 360, 1640–45.

Roskam, I., Kinoo, P., and Nassogne M-C. (2007). L'enfant avec troubles externalisés du comportement: Approche épigénétique et développementale. *Neuropsychiatr Enf*. 55, 204–13.

Rutter M., Kreppner J., Croft C., Murin M., Colvert E., Beckett C., Castle J., and Sonuga-Barke E. (2007). Early adolescent outcomes of institutionally deprived and non-deprived adoptees. III. Quasi-autism. *J Child Psychol Psychiatry*. 48, 1200–7.

Rutter, M., and O'Connor, T. G. (2004). English and Romanian Adoptees (ERA) study. Are there biological programming effects for psychological development? Findings from a study of Romanian adoptees. *Dev Psychol*. 40, 81–84.

Saffran, J. R., Aslin, R. N., and Newport, E. L. (1996). Statistical learning by 8-month-old infants. *Science*. 274, 1926–28.

Sawamura, H., Shima, K., and Tanji, J. (2002). Numerical representation for action in the parietal cortex of the monkey. *Nature*. 415, 918–22.

Scarr, S., and McCartney, K. (1983). How people make their own environments: A theory of genotype → environment effects. *Child Dev*. 54, 424–35.

Schechter, D. S., and Willheim, E. (2009). Disturbances of attachment and parental psychopathology in early childhood. *Child Adolesc Psychiatric Clin N Am*. 18, 665–86.

Shaw, P., Gogtay, N., and Rapoport, J. (2010). Childhood psychiatric disorders as anomalies in neurodevelopmental trajectories. *Hum Brain Mapp*. 31, 917–25.

Siok, W. T., Perfetti, C. A., Jin, Z., and Tan, L. H. (2004). Biological abnormality of impaired reading is constrained by culture. *Nature*. 431, 71–76.

Teicher, M., Samson, J. A., Sheu, Y. S., Polcari, A., and McGreenery, C. E. (2010). Hurtful words: Association of exposure to peer verbal abuse with elevated psychiatric symptom scores and corpus callosum abnormalities. *Am J Psychiatry*. doi: 10.1176/appi.ajp.2010.10010030

Thompson, B. L., and Stanwood, G. D. (2009). Pleiotropic effects of neurotransmission during development: Modulators of modularity. *J Autism Dev Disord*. 39, 260–68.

Van den Bergh, B. R., and Marcoen, A. (2004). High antenatal maternal anxiety is related to ADHD symptoms, externalizing problems, and anxiety in 8- and 9-year-olds. *Child Dev*. 75, 1085–97.

Vanderwert, R. E., Marshall, P. J., Nelson, C. A. III, Zeanah, C. H., and Fox, N. A. (2010). Timing of intervention affects brain electrical activity in children exposed to severe psychosocial neglect. *PLoS ONE.* 5(7), e11415.

Viding, E., Blair, R. J., Moffitt, T. E., and Plomin, R. (2005). Evidence for substantial genetic risk for psychopathy in 7-year-olds. *J Child Psychol Psychiatry.* 46, 592–97.

Wang, X., Zuckerman, B., Pearson, C., Kaufman, G., Chen, C., Wang, G., Niu, T., Wise, P. H., Bauchner, H., and Xu, X. (2002). Maternal cigarette smoking, metabolic gene polymorphism, and infant birth weight. *JAMA.* 287, 195–202.

Weaver, I. C., Cervoni, N., Champagne, F. A., D'Alessio, A. C., Sharma, S., Seckl, J. R., Dymov, S., Szyf, M., and Meaney, M. J. (2004). Epigenetic programming by maternal behavior. *Nat Neurosci.* 7, 847–54.

Weissman, M. M., Pilowsky, D. J., Wickramaratne, P. J., et al. (2006). Remissions in maternal depression and child psychopathology: A STAR*D-child report. *JAMA.* 295, 1389–98.

Whiten, A., Horner, V., and de Waal, F. B. (2005). Conformity to cultural norms of tool use in chimpanzees. *Nature.* 437, 737–40.

Zeanah, C. H., Egger, H. L., Smyke, A. T., Nelson, C. A., Fox, N. A., Marshall, P. J., and Guthrie, D. (2009). Institutional rearing and psychiatric disorders in Romanian preschool children. *Am J Psychiatry.* 166, 777–85.

2

Antecedents in Infancy of Personality Disorders

The Interplay between Biological and Psychological Processes

Miri Keren and Sam Tyano

INTRODUCTION

The onset of adult psychiatric disorders at a young age has been shown in a large epidemiological study (Egger and Angold, 2006), including important associations between early behavioral, emotional, and/or social problems and adult mental disorders. In spite of the well-known fact that personality disorders are a major mental health problem because of their prevalence, their associated disability, and the cost of treatment (Rey et al., 1995), one may advocate for early preventive interventions, as is the general trend for medical diseases. Hence, longitudinal studies of early childhood antecedents of personality disorders become the main tool for determining what are the risk and the protective factors for the development of personality disorders. A substantial body of data shows that personality disorders do have their origin in the early years of life, at observable, symptomatic, biological, and genetic levels (De Clercq and De Fruvt, 2007). Broadly speaking, recent findings suggest that both temperamental and other genetic traits as well as environmental factors and very early interpersonal experiences contribute to adult personality psychopathology in a complex interplay.

We therefore start this chapter with relevant core concepts of developmental psychopathology, and then we go into the specific studies about the development of personality disorders from infancy to adulthood, from both brain research and developmental psychopathology studies. We end the chapter with a clinical vignette, to illustrate pathways of the development of personality disorders from childhood to motherhood.

CORE CONCEPTS OF DEVELOPMENTAL PSYCHOPATHOLOGY

Developmental psychopathology provides a coherent, interdisciplinary theoretical framework for normal and abnormal development (Cicchetti, 1984; 2006). It is not a single theory, but, rather, an integrated perspective derived from multiple theories, encouraging analysis at all levels from molecular genetics to culture (Cicchetti and Dawson, 2002).

Issues of time and timing are essential in understanding the link between past experience and present circumstances, and in predicting future adaptation. Patterns of developmental continuity and discontinuity are especially interesting; change is always possible, with the caveat that the likelihood and degree of change is constrained by prior history and current context (Sroufe, 1997). Psychiatric disorders can start at a very young age, though the prevalence of specific disorders change over time (Egger and Angold, 2006). Consequently, studies of continuity and discontinuity should start in infancy. Today, as we will see, most of the existing longitudinal studies have started at preschool age (three to six years); only a very few have their starting point in infancy (zero to three years).

MODELS OF DEVELOPMENT CURRENTLY USED

For many years a *linear model* has been used (see Figure 2.1), postulating that a trait, for instance difficult temperament, will turn into a disorder, such as conduct disorder in adolescence and antisocial personality disorder in adulthood (Robins, 1966).

However, this model does not explain how one child might become a well adjusted adult in spite of many adversities, whilst another with a good start in childhood does poorly in adulthood. Sameroff's longitudinal study (Sameroff and Chandler, 1975) of community-sampled children from birth to young adulthood led to the conceptualization of a *transactional model* of normal and abnormal development. This model postulates that the constant in a child's development is not a set of "traits," but the processes by which traits are maintained through the interactions between children and their experiences across time.

While examining continuities and discontinuities in normal and abnormal development, this model takes into account genetic, biological, cultural, and psychological factors and life events. All these factors impact each on the child, on his/her close environment, and on the relationship between the two. Any of these factors may change over time. The implications of this model are two-sided: on one hand, our ability to predict from infancy to adulthood may be quite limited; on the other hand, interventions may promote change at different points in time and ports of entry. While trying to understand the dynamic interplay of all the bio-psycho-social factors that determine the individual's outcome at any point in time one needs to take account of the following processes.

Gene-Environment Correlations (rGE) and Gene-Environment Interplay (GXE)

The concept gene-environment correlations refers to genetic differences in response to specific environments/experiences; Gene-environment interplay relates to genetic differences in the susceptibility to specific environments/experiences (Jaffee and Price, 2007). Three causal mechanisms have been described (Scarr and McCartney, 1983):

1. The *passive* GxE correlation, in which parents provide both genes and environment for their children. An example is the development of antisocial personality disorder as an end result of the inheritance of anti-sociability and the experience of maltreatment.
2. The *evocative (reactive)* GxE correlation, in which children's behavior evokes particular responses from others, such as, for example, the interplay between difficult child's temperament and the parent-infant relationship.
3. The *active* GxE correlation, whereby children actively seek out the environments they prefer; for example, the extroverted child may seek very different environments from those a shy child prefers.

The Mediating Role of Risk and Protective Factors

Sameroff's longitudinal study (Sameroff and Chandler, 1975) defines the risk and protective factors that might have interacted and explains the outcome for each child. According to the transactional model, risk and protective factors can occur either in the infant/child/adolescent, in the parents, or in the social environment. The final impact of risk and protective factors is cumulative.

Risk factors in the child are *biological* (such as severe prematurity, congenital disease, chronic medical illness), *constitutional* (such as vulnerability, difficult temperament) and *experiential* (such as insecure and disorganized attachment relationships, neglect, abuse, trauma, and loss). Risk factors *in the parents* include poor maternal education, low IQ, physical/mental illness, borderline/narcissistic personality disorder, unresolved trauma/loss, past abuse, and disorganized attachment representations. Risk factors *in the environment* include poverty, lack of social support, and adverse life events.

Similarly, protective factors can be identified in the child, the parents, and the environment. Protective factors in the child are *biological* (such as good physical health), *constitutional* (such as resilience, easy temperament, above average IQ), and *experiential* (such as secure attachment and a growth-promoting parent-infant relationship). Protective factors *in the parents* include maternal education, IQ, healthy personality, capacity for reflective functioning, good family instrumental and emotional communication, and a stable marital relationship. Protective factors *in the environment* include social support, high socio-economic status, and positive life events.

Among risk and protective factors, *gender* has a paradoxical role. It has been posited (Eme, 1992) that the sex in which a particular disorder is less prevalent should show higher levels of symptoms and impairment than the sex in which the disorder is more prevalent. For example, ADHD is less common in girls, but is more severe and has a worse outcome than in boys. In other words, gender can convey either protection or risk.

The concepts of *resilience, vulnerability and sensitivity* are especially complex, because they relate to the child as well as to the environment. Resilience is no longer regarded as a characteristic of the child, but rather as a dynamic process of adaptation in spite of adversity (Kim-Cohen, 2007). A favorable outcome may be the result of the impact of a "big resilience" gene (such as the serotonin transporter gene) that buffers against a poor environment, or a "small resilience" gene that is empowered by a good environment (Caspi et al., 2003). Cyrulnik (2006) suggests the term of *"sensitivity"* rather than *"vulnerability"*; for example, a child with a short 5HTT allele will cope with sensitivity if the family environment is calm and stable. In the light of these findings, the nature/nurture debate becomes quite irrelevant. Future studies require consideration of both.

Developmental Nosology

Consequent to the complexity of the interplay between risk and protective factors in the child, the parents and the environment, Sroufe et al. (2005) have proposed a developmental nosology, referring to pathways, rather than syndromes, according to the following rules:

- Multiple pathways can lead to the same outcome.
- The same initial pathway can lead to multiple outcomes.
- Change is possible at many points in development, leading to new challenges and new opportunities.
- Change is constrained by prior development.
- Early caregiving is important. The longer a pathological pathway is pursued, the more difficult change becomes.

In summary, the major difference between the viewpoint of developmental psychopathology and the traditional perspective of psychiatry lies in the conceptualization of mental disorder. The traditional perspective regards disorder as an inherent trait; developmental psychopathology sees it as the end result of a dynamic interplay between individual and environment. This new approach is especially relevant to the understanding of personality disorders, where principles of both multi-finality and equi-finality apply: specific personality risk factors in early childhood may lead to a wide range of adult mental disorders or no disorder at all (multi-finality), while the same clinical picture of adult personality disorder may result from very different sources in early childhood (equi-finality). The various gene-environment patterns we described above are also relevant to the development of personality disorders, especially in light of recent evidence of a genetic basis for psychopathy, as we will review later.

PSYCHOLOGICAL ANTECEDENTS IN INFANCY AND PERSONALITY DISORDERS IN ADULTHOOD

Personality disorders are characterized by persistent maladaptive, rigid defense mechanisms associated with significant distress and poor interpersonal relationships. The object-relations theoretical approach has conceptualized these disturbed defense mechanisms that characterize them, especially in borderline and narcissistic disorders; but only in the last decade have empirical studies explored their source in infancy and early childhood.

The crucial role of early parent-child relationship and secure attachment in the development of a healthy personality (Bowlby, 1988) prompts a search for the antecedents in infancy of personality disorder. Winnicott (1984) was the first to make the clinical link between emotional deprivation and antisocial personality disorder. More recently, Fonagy and his team (Fonagy, Target, Steele and Steele, 1997) provided us with empirical data showing the link between borderline personality disorder and security of attachment.

Attachment relationships are one of the major experiences the child encounters in his first years of life; therefore, more and more links between the attachment system and the development of the brain have been made in recent years. Bowlby argued for the existence of an innate drive throughout the life cycle to look for a protective figure while in distress, especially in emergencies, because its biological function is protection regardless of age. The age range of peak development is within two to seven months, and distress is the trigger of activation of the attachment behaviors.

Attachment behaviors are of two types: Signals behaviors (mainly cry and anticipatory arms rising), and proximity-seeking to attachment figure (such as crawling, climbing on knees, and walking towards caregiver). Based on these definitions, Ainsworth has developed the well-known paradigm of the Strange Situation, where distress in the infant is triggered by separation from caregiver, and attachment behaviors observed during the reunion. The securely attached infant reacts to the separation, greets the parent at reunion, looks for proximity, and returns to his/her baseline level of exploration and play. Two types of insecure attachment have been defined: the avoidant and the ambivalent/resistant type. The avoidant strategy of coping with distress is to dampen the attachment system down, and therefore the infant looks indifferent to the separation. This type of attachment is characteristic of infants who have internalized their caregiver as inefficient in their ability to calm them down while in distress (for instance, depressed or psychotic mothers). The resistant type of attachment is the opposite, meaning the infant's attachment system is overactivated, the infant is very distressed by the separation but the parent's return does not calm him/her down. This pattern is typical of infants of unpredictable caregivers (such as parents with personality disorders). There is a fourth type, the disorganized attachment type, seen in clinical populations, especially where abuse and chaotic family functioning are common. The infant is distressed, but seems frightened by the caregiver, and therefore shows contradictory attachment behaviors. The attachment system is in balance with the exploratory system: the more protected/secure the child feels towards his/her caregiver, the more readily he/she will engage into exploratory behavior of the surroundings. The exploratory system is itself crucial for learning and curiosity development. The securely attached child develops an internal schema of "self-with-attachment figure" (Stern, 1985), and therefore is very much linked to the development of basic trust, one of the pivots of the quality of object relationships. Indeed, longitudinal studies (Sroufe et al., 2005) have shown that infants who were secure at twelve months were cooperative, popular, resilient, and resourceful children at the age of four and a half years; those who were avoidant at twelve months showed a lack of empathy, were hostile towards other children, and looked for the teacher's attention. Those who were resistant/ambivalent at twelve months were tense, impulsive, frustrated or passive and helpless. Finally, those who were disorganized at twelve months had severe behavior problems at the age of four and a half years.

In the light of these, it is not surprising that a strong correlation has been found between personality disorder (especially borderline and narcissistic), and disorganized attachment (Fonagy, 2001). Fonagy suggests to look at the adult classification of attachment as a continuum of structures for affect regulation: on one end, the dismissing type (equivalent to the avoidant type in the infant), whose structures suppress affect by using highly orga-nized but rigid structures. At the other pole is the preoccupied (equivalent to the resistant/ambivalent type in the infant), whose structures "hyper-activate" affective cues to caregivers. There is evidence from controlled studies employing the Adult Attachment Interview (Barone, 2003; Fonagy et al., 1996; Patrick et al., 1994) that women with borderline personality disorders tend to be "enmeshed" in representations of their early attach-ments, and especially prone to fearful, confused and overwhelmed states of mind, as well as being unresolved with respect to trauma. The devel-opmental histories of people with borderline personality disorder are very similar to those with dissociative disorder, especially regarding a history of early abuse. Links were found between childhood abuse and all types of personality disorder (Grover et al., 2007). The infant's psychic envelope is much more vulnerable than the adult's, is almost totally dependent on the adult's protection, and therefore it is not surprising that domestic violence is known as the most long-term adverse type of trauma. In a sample of 524 adult patients with PD, unstable family environment, and parental psycho-pathology, and a history of abuse, all independently predicted borderline personality disorder. Sexual abuse contributed to the prediction of Bor-derline Personality Disorder over and above family environment (Bradley, Jenei, and Westen, 2005). Fonagy (2001) has summarized the common ground between psychoanalytic and attachment theories, and has gradually increased the general awareness of the relevance of attachment processes to the field of developmental psychology, especially in the development of borderline personality disorders. The theory of attachment concepts have been more and more used in the understanding of transferential processes that characterize borderline personality disorders. For instance, Hobson, Patrick, and Valentine (1998) reported a controlled study that showed how psychotherapies with borderline personality disordered patients are characterized with intense locked-in hostility and idealizing or denigrating projections on the therapist, as a reflection of their very insecure early at-tachment representations.

BIOLOGICAL ANTECEDENTS IN INFANCY OF PERSONALITY DISORDERS

The traditional assumption was that the environment determines only the psychological components of development, while brain anatomy matures on its fixed ontogenetic calendar. Environmental experience is now recog-nized to be critical to the differentiation of brain tissue itself; Greenough and Black (1992) have described how experience causes strengthening, pruning out and creation of synaptic connections. Kandel (1998) showed that experience and learning lead to changes in synaptic strength at specific synapses, and memory is associated with the persistence of those changes. In the light of this neurobiological new knowledge, Siegel (2001) has proposed an integrated view of how human development occurs within a social world in transaction with the functions of the *brain*, thus giving rise to the *mind*. His concept of "Interpersonal Neurobiology" is based on the increasing knowledge about the dynamic and complex interplay between experience and brain development that takes place from conception into the first three years of life.

The peak of brain development is in first 3 years, while the child faces experiences within his own body, with his physical environment and with human beings, and records them in "schemas-of being-with" (Stern, 1985). These psychological processes need to be linked with what we have learned from neurobiology studies in the 1990s. For instance, Chiron and colleagues (1997) have shown that the right brain is dominant in human infants, while, in parallel, it has been shown in different studies (Keenan et al., 2000; Schore, 2000) that attachment experiences, also dominant in infancy, specifically impact the development of the infant's right brain limbic system. In addition, it turns out that the mother's right hemisphere is involved in comforting functions (Siegel, 1999). This "coincidence" led to the notion of a "context of resonance," where the self-organization of the developing brain occurs in the context of a relationship with another self, another brain (Schore, 2002). Secure attachments are created within such a mutually resonant form of interpersonal communication. The concept of neural resonance may be the biological basis of the amazing rate of 75 percent concordance found between the infant's pattern of attachment to the parent, and the parent's attachment classification (measured by the Adult Attachment Interview; Hesse, 1999). The parent's internal integration of emotional experiences promotes the infant's interpersonal experience integration. The chain of "events" from childhood to adulthood, leading to healthy personality could be then conceptualized as follows:

Contingent emotional communication that characterizes secure attachments→Coherent interpersonal relationships→Coherent neural integration within the child→Adaptive self-regulation of the growing child→Adult mental health (defined by Bowlby [1988] as a person who can give as well as receive support, and who values intimacy and warmth). The capacity for empathy is a major tenet of a healthy personality. Here again we find an amazing interplay between biological and psychological processes. Young children acquire theory of mind abilities at an earlier age if their parents frequently use expressions referring to mental states ("Parental reflective functioning"). This is the psychological prerequisite for developing empathy. The biological prerequisite is the presence and functioning of mirror neurons in the premotor cortex (first in monkey brains and then in humans') that reflect the actions, sensations and emotions that one observes in others. Lack of empathy, that characterizes many of the personality disordered individuals, may be the result of deficient psychological and/or biological prerequisites.

An additional neurobiological concept relevant to the development of personality disorders is "neural model of coherence," namely the functional links between the two hemispheres: the left hemisphere interpretates the primary emotional processes of the right hemisphere, and produces self-knowledge. The bilateral hemispheric integration permits the individual to engage in spontaneous dyadic communication (which is one of the hallmarks of secure attachments beyond early childhood).

A deficit in this integration may be one of the biological correlates of the link between insecure disorganized attachments in infancy, child abuse, and personality disorders, especially borderline personality disorders. Child maltreatment, indeed, has been repeatedly linked with the development of personality disorders in adolescence and adulthood, especially borderline personality disorders and antisocial personality disorders. Jonson-Reid et al. (2010) have recently shown that child maltreatment exhibits causal influence on antisocial outcome when controlling for inherited liability in both the general population and in a clinical sample. Teicher et al. (2002) reviewed the cascade of neurobiological events triggered by severe psychological stress that may significantly impact brain development and subsequent psychiatric health. These changes operate on multiple levels, such as neurohumoral (mainly the hypothalamic-pituitary-adrenal axis), structural and functional. Structural changes induced by early severe stress include reduced size of the midportions of the corpus callosum and diminished development of the left neocortex, hippocampus, and amygdala. Functional changes include increased electrical irritability in limbic structures and reduced activity of the cerebellar vermis. These changes in neurobiologic systems may result in aggravated responses to subsequent stressors experienced in childhood, rending the survivors more vulnerable to the development of PTSD and related problems (Eth, 2001). This knowledge of the impact of trauma on brain development may explain why early childhood traumatic experiences, such as *abuse and maltreatment*, do not necessarily lead to full, DSM IV based PTSD in childhood (Famularo, Fenton, Kinscherff, et al., 1996), but do lead to anxiety, depression and behavior problems in childhood, and to sensitization to re-traumatization, PTSD in adulthood, and borderline personality disorders (Yehuda et al., 2001).

In the continuation of this line of integrating psychological and neurobiological processes, LeGris and van Reekum (2006) have suggested the existence of an impaired executive functioning and disinhibitory processes, primarily associated with dorsolateral prefrontal cortical regions, among borderline personality disordered patients with suicidal behavior. A more recent review of neurobiological studies (Dell'Osso, Berlin, Serati and Altamura, 2010) has shown that symptoms of Borderline Personality Disorder are partly associated with alterations in glutamatergic, dopaminergic and serotonergic systems, especially the N-methyl-D-aspartate (NMDA) subtype receptor, that plays a major role in neuronal plasticity, cognition and memory. Grosjean and Guochuan (2007) propose that borderline personality disorder may be the result of a combination of biological vulnerability and environmental influences mediated by the NMDA neurotransmission. In parallel, neuroimaging studies in BPD patients indicate differences in the volume and activity of specific brain regions related to emotions and impulse control, including the prefrontal and cingulate cortex, amygdale and hippocampus. Like LeGris, they mention the neurobiological alterations that have been related to cognitive disturbances in these patients, and neuropsychological tests have demonstrated abnormalities in memory, attention, language, and executive functions.

One more step of neuropsychological integration has been taken by Fonagy, who suggests to conceptualize the goals of psychotherapy for personality disorders in an integrated psychological and biological model: psychotherapy for these patients should aim at two major goals, namely to facilitate coherence, or integration of past-present-future interpersonal emotional experiences, and to enhance "reflective functioning," conceptualized as a dialogue between the left hemisphere interpreting functions of right hemisphere perceived experiences.

THE CONCEPT OF "MALADAPTIVE PERSONALITY TRAITS" IN CHILDHOOD

De Clercq, De Fruvt, Van Leeuwen, and Mervielde (2006) have suggested adopting a dimensional, hierarchical approach rather than the DSM categorical one, in relation to personality disorders. Although a categorization of personality disorders facilitates communication among practitioners and helps to establish guidelines regarding appropriate treatment, the accuracy and validity of Axis II diagnoses is in controversy (Trull and Durrett, 2005). The major issues that have been argued include the co-morbidity among personality disorder axis, the extensive co-occurrence between personality disorders and other disorders, and the lack of a clear point of demarcation differentiating normal from abnormal psychological functioning (Widiger and Clark, 2000). Saulsman and Page (2004) have argued that personality disorders do not reflect discrete categories but a continuum of functioning, where the boundaries between adaptive and maladaptive functioning are unclear, thus strengthening the dimensional stance. In a similar process, De Clercq et al. (2006) suggest to adopt the construction of a taxonomy of trait-related symptoms in childhood, that are presumed to be precursors of enduring maladaptive patterns of behavior, thought processes and feelings characterizing adult personality disorders. The challenging task is to delineate the higher and lower level of maladaptive trait structure at young ages. Emotional instability, disagreeableness, introversion, and compulsivity in childhood are the traits that have been clearly linked with personality disorder in adulthood (Caspi, 2000; O'Connor, 2005). The main limitation of these findings is their being cross-sectional. They do not provide us with information on the longitudinal course.

LONGITUDINAL STUDIES OF CHILDHOOD ANTECEDENTS OF PERSONALITY DISORDERS

Two well-controlled studies have supported the continuity of schizoid and borderline symptoms from childhood through adolescence and early adulthood (Aarkrog, 1981; Wolff and Chick, 1980). Their main limitations were the size and the clinical nature of their sample. A community-based sample of 641 children (Bernstein et al., 1996) was assessed between the ages of one and ten years, and again ten years later. Four composite measures of childhood problems were used: *conduct problems, depressive symptoms, anxiety/fear, and immaturity.* All four were found to be associated with a greater risk for personality disorder in adolescence and adulthood. Childhood conduct problems predicted all three clusters of personality disorders, not antisocial PD alone. Childhood depressive symptoms predicted cluster A personality disorders (paranoid, schizoid, and schizotypal) which were found in 6.6 percent of all the cases (more often in boys). Immaturity predicted cluster B personality disorders (antisocial, borderline, narcissistic) and was found in 6.6 percent of all the cases (more in girls). Anxious behavior in childhood did not predict cluster C disorders (anxious, avoidant, obsessive) which were found in 12.8 percent of all cases, particularly girls. A retrospective study (Rettew et al., 2003) has examined the childhood antecedents of avoidant personality disorder (AVPD): Adults with AVPD report inferior athletic performance, less involvement in hobbies, and less popularity in childhood and adolescence than the other personality disorder groups.

From Disruptive Behaviors in Early Childhood to Personality Disorders

Difficult temperament, hyperactivity, aggression in the preschool years, and truancy and stealing in the elementary school years were again found in a more recent longitudinal study of 335 three-year-old children as known antecedents of antisocial personality disorders (Glenn, Raine, Venables, and Mednick, 2007). The study has revealed that children with low fearfulness, high stimulation-seeking and reduced skin conductance responsivity scored high on a psychopathy scale at the age of twenty-eight.

Psychopathy is neither a synonym for conduct disorder (CD) or antisocial personality disorder (APD). Only 25 percent of individuals classified as having either CD or APD show psychopathic tendencies (Hart and Hare, 1996; Kotler and McMahon, 2005). Psychopathy has been conceptualized (Frick et al., 1999) as a developmental disorder because it can be identified during childhood as well as in adulthood. Based on available data, no longitudinal studies have shown that those identified as psychopathic in childhood continue to be psychopathic. Nevertheless, the neurocognitive impairments identified in psychopathic children are seen also in adults with psychopathic tendencies (Blair, 2003ab). A core feature of psychopathy in children as well as in adults is the excessive use of instrumental aggression (purposeful, planned, goal-directed, and affectless). In contrast, reactive aggression (i.e., defensive, impulsive, affective), is usually caused by negative affect, such as frustration, threat, or anger. Psychopaths often have high levels of reactive aggression, but their instrumental aggression is markedly higher than in individuals with CD or APD alone (Blair, 2003b).

Emotional dysfunction is thought to be at the heart of psychopathy (Blair et al., 2006). Psychopathy is genetic and not caused by abuse, trauma, poor parenting, or unemployment, unlike CD and ASP. The main genetically mediated factor is the Callous/Unemotional (C/U) component of psychopathy. In almost 3,500 twin pairs (The Twins Early Development Study [TEDS]), genetic factors accounted for two thirds of the difference between seven-year-old C/U and non-C/U children (Viding, Blair, Moffitt, and Plomin, 2005). Some of these children exhibited C/U traits without conduct disorder. C/U children have a unique "invulnerability" to punishment, possibly due to a constitutionally low-functioning Behavioral Inhibition System (BIS) (Kotler and McMahon, 2005). A core feature of psychopathy (Hare, 1970) is indeed a reduction in the individual's response to threat (as opposed to its elevation in normal and CD and APS individuals without C/U traits). Abuse and/or exposure to extreme trauma enhance neural systems involved in the individual's response to threat, including reactive aggression and consequent CD. Thus, abuse is unlikely to lead to the affective flattening characteristic of psychopathy. It has even been proposed that the neurobiological basis of psychopathy protects the individual from depression, anxiety, and post traumatic stress disorder (Blair et al., 2006). Indeed, in psychopaths anxiety level is inversely correlated with the emotional dimension of psychopathy, but positively associated with the antisocial behavior dimension (Frick et al., 1999). The BIS (Gray, 1987), a neurological system activated by punishment, is thought to produce anxiety, and to inhibit ongoing behavior in the presence of novel stimuli, fear, and signals of punishment. Underactivity of the BIS could lead to low responsivity to punishment, less fearfulness, and less susceptibility to anxiety. The following findings have been reported (Gray, 1987):

- C/U traits predict a reward-dominant response style. Such children tend to become hyper-focused on indicators of reward and less attentive to cues of punishment (a finding with important clinical implications for the choice of intervention).
- Conduct problems without C/U do not show this reward dominant response style.
- Children with CD problems and C/U traits are found to have less trait anxiety than children with conduct problems alone.
- C/U traits are found in both genders, in contrast to CD which is more prevalent in boys.

Ineffective parenting is associated with conduct problems only in children without significant levels of C/U traits. An association has been found between child *abuse* and an increased risk of reactive aggression and conduct disorder (Farrington and Loeber, 2000). Abused children typically react more aggressively to lower-level threats than non-abused children do. Children with C/U traits (i.e., with a psychopathic profile) do not show such an elevation in their responsiveness to threat.

These observations have led to the conceptualization of psychopathy as a clinical entity that has a unique neural basis and is fundamentally distinct from conduct disorder (Blair, 2003c; Blair et al., 2006). Orbital and ventro-lateral frontal cortex dysfunction (i.e., in the regions regulating of the basic response to threat) is a risk factor for reactive aggression, conduct disorder, and psychopathy. In contrast, amygdaloid dysfunction is found only in psychopathy (Blair, 2003b). Functional imaging has shown reduced activation of the amygdala during the processing of emotional memory (Kiehl et al., 2001) and aversive conditioning (Birbaumer et al., 2005). Amygdaloid dysfunction is believed to disrupt the child's socialization, putting him at risk of employing instrumental aggression to achieve his goals. These children have a striking lack of empathy, the link of which to amygdaloid dysfunction has been demonstrated (Blair, 2003a).

An important clinical implication of the different pathways to conduct disorder and psychopathy is that therapeutic interventions aimed at improving parenting skills, including the use of empathy induction to facilitate aversion to antisocial behavior, should not be expected to be effective in psychopathy. It is clearly very important to be aware of this distinct group of children, and to differentiate them in therapeutic planning. The well-known poor prognosis of children with psychopathic traits, regardless of therapy, is now much better understood.

In Bernstein et al.'s longitudinal study of 641 community-based children (Bernstein et al., 1996) who were assessed between the ages of one and ten years, and again ten years later, childhood conduct problems predicted all three clusters of personality disorders, not antisocial PD alone. Among 145 young adults (Rey et al., 1995), 40 percent of those who had disruptive disorder during adolescence have high rates of all types of personality disorder, while only 12 percent of those who had had emotional disorders did. The authors suggest either that treatment is more effective for emotional disorders than for conduct disorders, or that the personality psychopathology of emotionally disturbed adolescents is less severe than in those who have disruptive behavior disorders.

In sum, there is a clear need for prospective (behavioral and genetic) studies to verify how and when childhood predispositions evolve into adult maladaptive trait patterns. Favorable early childhood interpersonal experiences are clearly protective and linked to better outcomes in avoidant and schizotypal personality disorders (Skodol et al., 2007). Artistic talent, superior school performance, above-average intellect, and talents in other areas are also protective (Helgeland and Torgersen, 2004).

We tried to summarize the data presented here in the format of a diagram of antecedents that may lead to the development of personality disorders from infancy to childhood (see Figure 2.1).

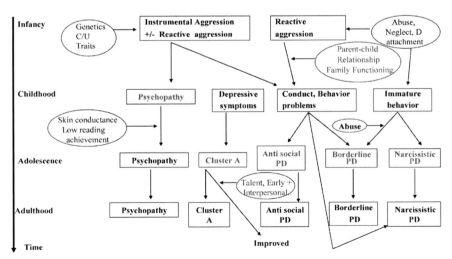

Figure 2.1. Pathways of the antecedents to personality disorders

CLINICAL VIGNETTE

S., a two-month-old baby girl and her mother, A., were referred to our Infant Mental Health unit by a community nurse, who was concerned about the baby's persistent crying and the mother's tense, sad, and at loss look. Nurse suspected the presence of maternal post-partum depression, and referred her, while adding that it is a "hard-to-reach" untruthful family. Indeed, the mother did not come to any of the first appointments we gave her. In the light of a suspected emergency situation, a home visit was set up by therapist (MK). While entering the one-room apartment, she was struck by the chaotic and messy atmosphere: baby was crying, and mother, disheveled and not well groomed, was unsuccessfully trying to breast-feed her. She was so overwhelmed that she did not greet the therapist, and straightly said: "Even breast-feeding does not calm her. I'm really bad at it. She knows it. "

Standard questions about the course of the pregnancy and delivery triggered tears, and mother started to talk for over two hours. A. linked her lack of readiness for motherhood to her own very traumatic attachment experiences. Indeed, she grew up with a drug-addicted and sexually promiscuous mother, her father left home when she was about two years old and ignored her, and she experienced emotional and sexual abuse by her stepfather. Child protection services took her out of home, and placed her in a boarding school, while her younger and only sister stayed at home. She continued to have negative experiences with adult care-givers at the boarding school, and grew up into a very lonely and angry adolescent. The relationship with her sister was very ambivalent, mixed with feelings of responsibility and anger towards her. On the day of the car accident in which her sister was killed, A. was fifteen years old, and her sister was nine, they were both in the back of the car, having a fight, and the accident happened while A.'s sister was trying to reconcile. A. developed a very pathological grief reaction that lasted until the time of the referral; she still would go almost every day to her sister's grave.

A few months before getting pregnant, A. had a dream about her late sister saying "I can't wait anymore," A. felt she had to "get pregnant and have a girl like her sister," in spite of her inner feeling she was not ready for motherhood. Baby's name was identical to her late "little aunt's," except for one letter.

During the following sessions, maternal pathological projections on the infant unfold. In A.'s mind, S. was born in order to replace her late little aunt, and there was an almost total lack of differentiation between the two (like their first names were almost identical). For instance, S.'s cry reminded A. of her sister's crying and clingy behavior, and evoked the same kind of ambivalent reactions, such as either gratifying the baby or becoming harsh and rejecting. Obviously, A.'s pathological grief and own internalized traumatizing parental figures impinged on her ability to be a consistent protective figure for her child. At 9 months, we could already identify the baby's insecure anxious/tense attachment pattern to her mother. Following a session where she talked about the car accident and her guilt feelings, a frightening "missed" accident happened to S.: A. "forgot" to tie the baby in her stroller. Also, her ability to put limits to the infant was very poor, because saying "no" to her child reminded her of saying "no" to her sister just before the car accident. An additional distorted parenting behavior was around sleep times: S. slept with mother because, in A.'s perception, "nights are dangerous to sleep alone" (A. unconsciously perceived her husband as potential harmful to her and to her child). S's father had also a very problematic childhood history, with a physically abusive mother and a passive father. He developed a narcissistic personality disorder, and, unlike his wife, he had absolutely no insight about his own problematic parenting behaviors, and refused treatment. With the transition into parenthood, their marital relationship became very tense, and ended up with separation.

Dyadic mother-infant psychotherapy lasted for three years. Its full description is beyond the scope of this chapter. Our main goals included 1. Providing the mother with a "corrective attachment experience" through establishing a trusting relationship with the therapist; 2. Identifying the parents' distorted thinking projected onto the child; 3. Identifying the maladaptive, frightening/frightened parenting behaviors; 4. Providing developmental guidance to increase knowledge and improve parenting skills. These goals were partially met. Mother took a long time to develop a trusting relationship with the therapist, but became gradually more insightful about the emotional significance of her own and S.'s behaviors, in the light of her past. When S. was one year old S. went to the cemetery and separated "for good" from her sister. On the other hand, Father did not co-operate with therapy, and the child was caught between the parents' intense struggles. S. was able to achieve her developmental milestones and to function normally at the kindergarten. Nevertheless, she remained a vulnerable child.

To conclude, this clinical case illustrates quite vividly how very early traumatic attachment experiences lead to a basic and pervasive lack of trust and unstable close relationships (so characteristic of adults with borderline and narcissistic personality disorders), are transmitted from one generation to another, and how entry into parenthood triggers distorted projections on the infant, who then, may become a dysfunctional infant. Indeed, Hobson et al. (2009) have shown how mothers with borderline personality disorders show disrupted affective communication, and often react with frightening/disoriented behavior to their infant's distress. This, in turn, puts the infant at risk for developing insecure disorganized attachment, and later borderline personality disorder. Thus, early detection of such high risk new parents and implementing psychotherapeutic interventions is crucial if one is trying to prevent the development of personality disorder from childhood into adulthood. In the presented case, parent-infant therapeutic intervention was aimed at preventing the trans-generational transmission of traumatic attachment relationships and promoting a more secure attachment for the child.

CONCLUSIONS

The combination of developmental psychopathology and neurobiological studies has led to the link between early interpersonal experiences, brain development, and personality organization later in life. During the early years of life, a period where the right brain is dominant and attachment experiences specifically impact the development of the infant's right brain limbic system, the basic circuits of the brain are developing and are the substrate of mental processes, involving emotions, memory, behavior and interpersonal relationships. Early interpersonal affective experiences have a critical effect on the early organization of the right limbic system, an area of emotion processing, organization of new learning, and capacity to adapt to a rapidly changing environment. Exposure to stressful and traumatic experience(s) at a time when the brain is undergoing enormous change may leave an indelible imprint on the structure and function of the brain, especially in individuals with genetic vulnerability. There is nowadays a bulk of compelling evidence for the continuity of psychopathology from early life, eventually indicating that underlying trait characteristics play an important role in processes of maladjustment over time.

The availability of a comprehensive taxonomy that specifically describes maladaptive traits in childhood can clarify the long term importance of early personality symptoms in the understanding of adult personality disorders. Personality disorders can be traced from childhood emotional and behavioral disturbances. This approach implies giving up the traditional view that personality disorders should not be diagnosed until after adolescence, and implies the need to identify emerging personality disorder symptoms at younger ages. Specific risks, such as disorganized attachments, domestic violence, and abuse, as well as protective factors, should be identified very early in life, for the planning of intervention.

REFERENCES

Aarkrog, T. (1981). The borderline concept in childhood, adolescence, and adulthood: Borderline adolescents in psychiatric treatment and five years later. *Acta psychiatric Scandinavian Supplement, 293*, 1–30.

Barone, L. (2003). Developmental protective and risk factors in borderline personality disorder: A study using the Adult Attachment Interview. *Attachment and Human Development, 5*, 64–77.

Bernstein, D. P., Cohen, P., Skodol, A., and Bezirganian, Brook, J. S. (1996). Childhood antecedents of adolescent personality disorders. *American Journal of Psychiatry, 153*, 907–13.

Birbaumer, N., Veit, R., Lotze, M., Erb, M., Hermann, C., Grodd, W., and Flor, H. (2005). Deficient fear conditioning in psychopathy: A functional magnetic resonance imaging study. *Archives of General Psychiatry*, *62*, 799–805.

Blair, R. J. R. (2003a). Facial expressions, their communicatory functions, and neuro-cognitive substrates. Philosophical Transactions of the Royal Society London B. *Biological Science*, *358*, 561–72.

Blair, R. J. R. (2003b). Neurobiological basis of Psychopathy. *British Journal of Psychiatry*, *182*, 5–7.

Blair, R. J. R. (2003c). A neurocognitive model of the psychopathic individual. In M. A. Ron and T. W. Robins (Eds.), *Disorders of Brain and Mind* (pp. 400–420). Cambridge: Cambridge University Press.

Blair, R. J. R., Peschardt, K. S, Budhani, S., Mitchell, D. G. V., and Pine, D. S. (2006). The development of Psychopathy. *Journal of Child Psychology and Psychiatry*, *47*, 262–75.

Bowlby, J. (1988). *A secure base.* New York: Basic Books.

Bradley, R., Jenei, J., and Westen, D. (2005). Etiology of borderline personality disorder: Disentangling the contributions of inter correlated antecedents. *Journal of Nervous and Mental Disorder*, *193*, 24–31.

Caspi, A. (2000). The child is father of the man: Personality continuities from childhood to adulthood. *Journal of Personality and Social Psychology*, *78*, 158–72.

Caspi, A., Sugden, K., Moffitt, T. E., Taylor, A., Craig, I. W., Harrington, H., McClay, J., Mill, J., Martin, J., Braithwaite, A., and Poulton, R. (2003). Influence of life stress on depression: Moderation by polymorphism in the 5–HTT gene. *Science*, *301*, 386–89.

Chiron, C., Jambaque, I., Nabbout, R., Lounes, R., Syrota, A., and Dulac, O. (1997). The right brain hemisphere is dominant in human infants. *Brain*, *120*, 1057–65.

Cicchetti, D. (1984).The emergence of developmental psychopathology. *Child Development*, *55*, 1–7.

Cicchetti, D. (2006). Development and psychopathology. In C. Cicchetti and D. J. Cohen (Eds.), *Developmental Psychopathology, Vol 1. Theory and Method* (pp. 1–23). 2nd Edition. Hoboken: Wiley and Sons.

Cicchetti, D., and Dawson, G. (2002). Editorial: Multiple levels of analysis. *Development and Psychopathology*, *14*, 417–20.

Cyrulnik, B. (2006). *De chair et d'âme.* Paris: Odile Jacob.

De Clercq, B., and De Fruvt, F. (2007). Childhood antecedents of personality disorder. *Current Opinion in Psychiatry*, *20*, 57–61.

De Clercq, B., De Fruvt, F., Van Leeuwen, K. and Mervielde, I. (2006). The structure of maladaptive personality traits in childhood: A step toward an integrative developmental perspective for DSM-V. *Journal of Abnormal Psychology*, *115*, 639–57.

Dell'Osso B., Berlin, H. A., Serati, M. and Altamura, A. C. (2010). Neuropsychobiological aspects, comorbidity patterns and dimensional models in borderline personality disorder. *Neuropsychobiology*, *6*(14), 169–79.

Egger, H. L., and Angold, A. (2006). Common emotional and behavioral disorders in preschool children: Presentation, nosology, and epidemiology. *Journal of Child Psychology and Psychiatry*, *47*, 313–37.

Eme, R. F. (1992). Selective female affliction in the developmental disorders of childhood: A review. *Journal of Clinical Child Psychology*, *21*, 354–64.

Eth, S. (2001). *PTSD in Children and Adolescents.* Review of Psychiatry Series, *20*(1). Washington, DC: American Psychiatric Publishing.

Famularo, R., Fenton, T., Kinscherff, R., and Augustyn, M. (1996). Psychiatric co-morbidity in childhood postraumatic stress disorder. *Child Abuse & Neglect, 20,* 953-61.

Farrington, D. P., and Loeber, R. (2000). Epidemiology of juvenile violence. *Child and Adolescent Psychiatry Clinics of North America, 9,* 733-48.

Fonagy, P. (2001). *Attachment theory and psychoanalysis.* New York: Other Press.

Fonagy, P., Leigh, T., Steele, M., Steele, H., Kennedy, R., Mattoon, G., et al. (1996). The relation of attachment status, psychiatric classification, and response to psychotherapy. *Journal of Consulting Clinical Psychology, 64,* 22-31.

Fonagy, P., Target, M., Steele, M. and Steele, H. (1997). Morality, disruptive behavior, borderline personality disorder, crime, and their relationships to security of attachment. In L. Atkinson and K.J. Zucker (Eds.), *Attachment and Psychopathology,* New York: Guilford, pp. 223-74.

Frick, P. J., Lillianfeld, S. O., Ellis, M., Loney, B. and Silverton, P. (1999). The association between anxiety and psychopathy dimensions in children. *Journal of Abnormal Child Psychology, 27,* 383-92.

Glenn, A. L., Raine, A., Venables, P. H. and Mednick, S. A. (2007). Early temperamental and psychophysiological precursors of adult psychopathic personality. *Journal of Abnormal Psychology, 116,* 508-18.

Gray, J. A. (1987). *The Psychology of Fear and Stress.* Cambridge, UK: University of Cambridge Press.

Greenough, W. T., and Black, J. E. (1992). Induction of brain structure by experience: Substrates for cognitive. In M. R. Gunnar and C. A. Nelson (Eds.), *Developmental Behavior Neuroscience,* Hillsdale, NJ: Erlbaum, pp. 155-200.

Grosjean, B., and Guochuan, E. T. (2007). NMDA neurotransmission as a critical mediator of borderline personality disorder. *Journal of Psychiatry and Neuroscience, 32* (2), 103-15.

Grover, K. E., Carpenter, L. L., Price, L. H, Gagne, G. G., Mello, A. F., Mello, M. F., and Tyrka, A. R. (2007). The relationship between childhood abuse and adult personality disorder. *Journal of Personality Disorders, 21:* 442-47.

Hare, R. D. (1970). *Psychopathy: Theory and Research.* New York: Wiley.

Hart, S. D. and Hare, R. D. (1996). Psychopathy and antisocial personality disorder. *Current Opinion in Psychiatry, 9,* 129-32.

Helgeland, M. I., and Torgersen, S. (2004). Developmental antecedents of borderline personality disorder. *Comprehensive Psychiatry, 45,* 138-47.

Hesse, E. (1999). The Adult Attachment Interview: Historical and Current Perspectives. In J. Cassidy and P. R. Shaver (Eds.), *Handbook of Attachment: Theory, Research, and Clinical Applications.* New York: The Guilford Press, pp. 395-434.

Hobson, R. P, Patrick, M. P. H., Hobson, J. A., Crandell, L., Bronfman, E. and Lyons-Ruth K. (2009). How mothers with borderline personality disorder relate to their year-old infants. *The British Journal of Psychiatry, 195,* 325-30.

Hobson, R. P, Patrick, M. P. H., Valentine, J. D. (1998). Objectivity in psychoanalytic judgments. *The British Journal of Psychiatry, 173,* 172-17.

Jaffee, S. R. and Price, T. S. (2007). Gene-environment correlations: A review of the evidence and implications for prevention of mental illness. *Molecular Psychiatry, 12,* 432-42.

Jonson-Reid, M., Presnall, N., Drake, B., Fox, L., Bierut, L., Reich, W., Kane, P., Todd, R. D., and Constantino, J. N. (2010). Effects of Child Maltreatment and Inherited Liability on Antisocial Development: An Official Records Study. *Journal of American Academy of Child and Adolescent Psychiatry, 49,* 321–32.

Kandel, E. R. (1998). A new intellectual framework for psychiatry. *American Journal of Psychiatry, 155,* 457–69.

Keenan, J. P., Wheeler, M. A., Gallup, C. G., Jr., and Pascual-Leone, A. (2001). Self-recognition and the right prefrontal cortex. *Trends in Cognitive Science, 4,* 338–44.

Kiehl, K. A., Smith, A. M., Hare, R. D., Mendrek, A., Forster, B. B., Brink, J., and Liddle, P. F. (2001). Limbic abnormalities in affective processing by criminal psychopaths as revealed by functional magnetic resonance imaging. *Biological Psychiatry, 50,* 677–84.

Kim-Cohen, J. (2007). Resilence and developmental psychopathology. *Child and Adolescent Psychiatry Clinics of North America, 16,* 271–83.

Kotler, J. S. and McMahon, R. J. (2005). Child Psychopathy: Theories, measurement, and relations with the development and persistence of conduct problems. *Clinical Child Family Psychology Review, 8,* 291–325.

LeGris, J., and van Reekum, R. (2006). The neuropsychological correlates of borderline personality disorder and suicidal behavior. *Canadian Journal of Psychiatry, 51*(3), 131–42

O'Connor, B. P. (2005). A search for consensus on the dimensional structure of personality disorders. *Journal of Clinical Psychology, 61,* 323–45.

Patrick, M. Hobson, R. P., Castle, D., Howard, R., and Maughan, B. (1994). Personality disorder and the mental representation of early social experience. *Developmental Psychopathology, 6,* 375–88.

Rettew, D. C., Zanarini, M. C., Yen, S., Grilo, C. M., Skodol, A. E., Shea, M. T., McGlashan, T. H., Morey, L. C., Culhane, M. A., and Gunderson, J. G. (2003). Childhood antecedents of avoidant personality disorder: A retrospective study. *Journal of American Academy Child and Adolescent Psychiatry, 42,* 1122–30.

Rey, J. M., Morris-Yates, A., Singh, M., Andrews, G., Stewart, G. W. (1995). Continuities between psychiatric disorders in adolescents and personality disorders in young adults. *American Journal of Psychiatry, 152,* 895–900.

Robins, L. N. (1966). *Deviant children grown-up.* Baltimore: Williams and Wilkins.

Sameroff, A. J., and Chandler, M. J. (1975). Reproductive risk and the continuum of caretaking casualty. In F. D. Horowitz, M. Hetherington, S. Scarr-Salapatek, G. Siegel (Eds.), *Review of Child Development Research, 4,* 187–244. Chicago: University of Chicago Press.

Saulsman, L. M., and Page, A. C. (2004). The five-factor model and personality disorder empirical literature: A meta-analytic review. *Clinical Psychology Review, 23,* 1055–85.

Scarr, S., and McCartney, K. (1983). How people make their own environments: A theory of genotype-environmental effects. *Child Development, 54,* 424–35.

Schore, A. N. (2000). Attachment and the regulation of the right brain. *Attachment and Human Development, 2,* 23–47.

Schore, A. N. (2002). Dysregulation of the right brain: A fundamental mechanism of traumatic attachment and the psychopathogenesis of post traumatic stress disorder. *Australian and New Zealand Journal of Psychiatry, 36,* 9–30.

Siegel, D. J. (1999). *The developing mind: Toward a neurobiology of interpersonal experience*. New York: The Guilford Press.

Siegel, D. J. (2001). Toward an interpersonal neurobiology of the developing mind: Attachment relationships, "mindsight," and neural integration. *Infant Mental Health Journal, 22*(1–2), 67–94.

Skodol, A. E., Bender, D. S., Pagano, M. E., Shea, M. T., Yen, S., Sanislow, C. A., Gilo, C. M., Daversa, T. M., Stout, R. L., Zanarini, M. C., McGlashen, T. H., and Gunderson, J. G. (2007). Positive childhood experiences: Resilience and recovery from personality disorder in early adulthood. *Journal of Clinical Psychiatry, 68*, 1102–8.

Sroufe, L. A. (1997). Psychopathology as an outcome of development. *Development and Psychopathology, 9*, 251–68.

Sroufe, L. A., Egeland, B., Carlson, E. A. and Collins, W. A. (2005). *The Development of the Person: The Minnesota Study of Risk and Adaptation from Birth to Adulthood.* New York: Guilford Press.

Stern, D. (1985). *The Interpersonal World of the Infant.* New York: Basic Books.

Teicher, M. H., Andersen, S. L., Polcari, A., Anderson, C. M., and Navalta, C. P. (2002). Developmental neurobiology of childhood stress and trauma. *Psychiatry Clinics of North America, 25*: 397–426.

Trull, T. J., and Durrett, C. A. (2005). Categorical and dimensional models of personality disorder. *Annual Review of Clinical Psychology, 1*, 1–26.

Viding, E., Blair, R. J. R., Moffitt, T. E., and Plomin, R. (2005). Genetic risk for psychopathy in 7-year-olds. *Journal of Child Psychology and Psychiatry, 46*, 592–597.

Widiger, T. A., and Clark, L. A. (2000). Toward DSM V and the classification of psychopathology. *Psychological Bulletin, 126*, 946–963.

Winnicott, D. W. (1984). *Deprivation and Delinquency.* In C. Winnicott, R. Shepherd, and M. Davis (Eds.). London: Tavistock publications.

Wolff, S. and Chick, J. (1980). Schizoid personality in childhood: A controlled follow up study. *Psychological Medicine, 10*, 85–100.

Yehuda, R. Spertus, I. L., and Golier, J. Q. (2001). Relationship between childhood traumatic experiences and PTSD in adults. In Eth, S. (Ed.). *PTSD in Children and Adolescents.* Review of Psychiatry Series, Vol. 20. Washington, DC: American Psychiatric Publishing.

3

Insights into Childhood Psychiatric Disorders from Developmental Neuroimaging

Philip Shaw

INTRODUCTION

Childhood psychiatric disorders are rarely static: rather they change over time. Capturing the essence of the neural changes underpinning such dynamic phenomena is hard, particularly when cross-sectional data is used. There has been a recent shift in emphasis towards using longitudinal designs which intuitively appear better suited to delineate neurodevelopmental processes. This review will thus focus on the application of longitudinal neuroimaging to the understanding of childhood neuropsychiatric disorders, arguing that these be can conceptualized as resulting from perturbations away from the trajectory of typical development of brain structure and function. These insights are possible due to unprecedented access to the anatomy and physiology of the developing brain without the use of ionizing radiation afforded by magnetic resonance imaging (MRI).

This selective review focuses on structural neuroimaging of attention deficit hyperactivity disorder (ADHD), chosen partly as it is a common disorder of childhood which represents both a challenge for the affected child and his or her family and a major public health burden. Additionally ADHD is an ideal model for a consideration of how neurodevelopmental disorders can be conceptualized as disruptions to typical neurodevelopmental trajectories. ADHD has a highly variable clinical outcome by adulthood—some remit completely, some have impairing symptoms but not the full syndrome and some have a truly persistent form of the disorder (Faraone, Biederman, and Mick, 2006). Understanding the neural processes which might either reflect or even drive this variable outcome can thus give insights both into processes that perpetuate mental disorders, and also mechanisms of recovery. Other disorders which have been conceptualized as disruptions to neurodevelopmental trajectories will also be considered—specifically autism and very early onset schizophrenia.

Before considering how developmental trajectories can go awry, it is helpful to review briefly the patterns of structural brain development in healthy children. In grey matter development—whether measured by cortical volume or thickness—throughout most of the cerebral cortex there is a phase of early increase, followed by a late childhood/adolescent phase of decrease, before the cortex settles into adult dimensions (J. N. Giedd and Rapoport, 2010; Shaw et al., 2008). Regionally, cortical grey matter appears to mature in a parieto-frontal (back to front) direction, and medially in a centripetal ("top-down") fashion. White matter has a more sustained pattern of expansion persisting through adolescence into adulthood. Given the complexities of these trajectories it is perhaps not surprising that they can go awry, resulting in disturbances in cognition, affect and behavior.

WHY USE LONGITUDINAL DATA?

The theoretical advantages of longitudinal data are well known: they not only separate effects of aging (changes over time within individuals) from cohort effects (differences between subjects at baseline), but also provide more efficient estimates than cross-sectional designs with the same number and pattern of observations, partly by excluding between subject variation from error (Kraemer, Yesavage, Taylor, and Kupfer, 2000). It should still be stressed that cross-sectional studies have been, and will continue to be very valuable, and have led to several fascinating hypotheses about possible developmental anomalies in childhood disorders (McAlonan et al., 2009; Plessen et al., 2006; Stanley et al., 2008), which can then be further tested through longitudinal studies. It should also be noted that longitudinal studies are not without their limitations: foremost are problems with subject retention and the possibility of non-random loss to follow-up. Gaps in data sets can appear, often with poorer coverage of younger age ranges (especially under six) reflecting the challenges associated with acquiring high quality neuroimaging data on the very young—especially those who have problems lying still such as hyperactive, psychotic or very anxious children. In studies conducted over years, continual improvements in technology can lead to the complex, but not insurmountable, problem of integrating data acquired on different scanners over time. Despite these limitations there is little doubt that the benefits of longitudinal approaches for delineating developmental processes outweigh the disadvantages.

ADHD: CURRENT NEUROANATOMIC FINDINGS AND THE CONTRIBUTION OF LONGITUDINAL NEUROIMAGING

Before exploring the insights into ADHD and other neurodevelopmental disorders that can be gained from adopting a longitudinal approach, it is worthwhile to summarize the state of the field. A summary of the main findings of recent studies is given in Table 3.1; several summary points can be made.

First, there have been sufficient studies to allow for quantitative summaries and it emerges that there is an overall reduction in the volume of the cerebrum in ADHD, a deficit of around 3 to 4 percent which affects all lobes and both grey and white matter (FX. Castellanos et al., 2002; Krain and Castellanos, 2006; Valera, Faraone, Murray, and Seidman, 2007). These changes do not appear to be mere epiphenomena of symptoms as similar, attenuated changes are seen in the unaffected first degree relatives of those with ADHD (Durston et al., 2005; Durston et al., 2004). Additionally the neuroanatomic differences do not appear to be secondary to psychostimulant medication used as treatment for ADHD, as several studies have now found that this medication tends to be associated with brain dimensions closer to healthy controls—including white matter (FX. Castellanos et al., 2002) key regions implicated in ADHD such as the anterior cingulate, basal ganglia (Semrud-Clikeman, Pliszka, Lancaster, and Liotti, 2006; Sobel et al., 2010) and portions of the cerebellar vermis (Bledsoe, Semrud-Clikeman, and Pliszka, 2009).

Secondly, advances in neuroimaging techniques and analysis allow us to delineate the exact regions which are most compromised in ADHD. These studies have used metrics which allow an exquisite level of spatial resolution such as voxel based morphometry which estimates grey matter density and volume, and measures of the thickness of the cortex made at thousands of points across the cerebrum. Of note, a recent meta-analysis of eight voxel based morphometric studies found that only right putamen volume loss was significant across studies (Ellison-Wright, Ellison-Wright, and Bullmore, 2008). This is an important finding as region of interest studies have generally not included the putamen, partly as it is a small structure hard to delineate manually, and have focused instead on the caudate with mixed findings of either volume increase or (Mataro, Garcia-Sanchez, Junque, Estevez-Gonzalez, and Pujol, 1997) reduction (F. X. Castellanos et al., 1994; Filipek et al., 1997). It is also an important finding, as while nearly all of the individual studies included in the meta-analysis reported prefrontal cortical (and often parietal) deficits, there was little agreement over precise location and thus the meta-analysis did not find any common points of cortical compromise. The variability in the results for the cortical regions, especially the prefrontal cortex, is usually attributed to differences

Table 3.1. Summary of the main structural neuroimaging studies in ADHD

Study	Metric	N	Mean age (yrs) of patients	Main findings
Corticometrics				
(Makris et al., 2007)	Cortical thickness	24	34.8	ADHD adults had thinner cortex in right dorsolateral prefrontal gyrus, inferior parietal lobule and anterior cingulate cortex.
(Sowell et al., 2003)	Grey matter density and surface shape	27	12	ADHD children had reduced regional brain size in inferior portions of dorsal prefrontal cortices bilaterally and anterior temporal cortices
				Increased grey matter in posterior temporal and inferior parietal cortices bilaterally.
(Shaw et al., 2007)	Cortical thickness	163	8.9	Children with ADHD had global thinning of the cortex (mean reduction, −0.09 mm) most prominently in the medial and superior prefrontal and precentral regions. Children with worse clinical outcome had a thinner left medial prefrontal cortex at baseline than the better outcome group (−0.38 mm; P=.003) and controls (−0.25 mm; P=.002).
(Wolosin, Richardson, Hennessey, Denckla, & Mostofsky, 2009)	Thickness, surface area and gyrification	21	10.8	Decreased cortical folding and surface area in ADHD in all lobes
(Li et al., 2007)	Cortical convolution complexity	12	10.2	ADHD had reduction of the normal left-greater-than-right cortical convolution complexity pattern.
(Narr et al., 2009)	Cortical thickness	22	11.7	Significant cortical thinning (FDR-corrected $p < .0006$) was observed over large areas of frontal, temporal, parietal and occipital association cortices and aspects of motor cortex, but not within primary sensory regions.
(M.-g. Qiu et al., 2010)	Cortical thickness	15	12.6	Bilateral middle prefrontal and right cingulate thinning of the cortex.

Voxel-based morphometry

Study	Method	N	Age	Findings
(Brieber et al., 2007)	VBM- volume	15	13.1	Grey matter reduction in right middle frontal gyrus, left superior temporal gyrus, bilateral caudate and hippocampus and left insula.
				Grey matter increase in bilateral superior parietal and postcentral gryus and left middle cingulate.
(Carmona et al., 2005)	VBM- volume	25	10.9	Grey matter deficits in left fronto-parietal areas (left motor, premotor and somatosensory cortex), left cingulate cortex, parietal lobe (precuneus bilaterally), temporal cortices (right middle temporal gyrus, left parahippocampal gyrus), and the cerebellum (bilateral posterior).
(McAlonan et al., 2007)	VBM- volume	28	9.9	Right sided fronto-pallida-parietal grey deficits
				White matter: deficits in region of the inferior longitudinal fasiculi and occipitofrontal fasiculi, the vicinity of corpus callosal radiation fibers, and temporo-occipital pathways
(McAlonan et al., 2009)	VBM- volume	22	9.9	Anterior cingulate, striatal and cerebellar volumes correlated with a measure of response inhibition and attention-shifting.
(Overmeyer et al., 2001)	VBM- volume	18	10.4	Grey matter deficits in right superior frontal gyrus, posterior cingulate and basal ganglia bilaterally/
				White matter deficits close to precentral cortex and the basal ganglia.
(Wang, Jiang, Cao, & Wang, 2007)	Deformation-based morphometry	12	13.4	Grey matter volume loss in right prefrontal, right medial temporal and right putamen.
				Volume enlargement in right occipital lobe

Table 3.1. *(Continued)*

Subcortical shape

(Plessen et al., 2006)	Volume and shape of hippocampus and amygdala	51	12.3	Larger hippocampus in ADHD, driven by enlarged hippocampal head. Amygdala had reduced size bilaterally over the area of the basolateral complex. Correlations with prefrontal measures suggested abnormal connectivity between the amygdala and prefrontal cortex in the ADHD group.
(A. Qiu et al., 2008)	Volume and shape of basal ganglia	47	10.4	Boys with ADHD showed significantly smaller basal ganglia volumes due to volume compression bilaterally in caudate head and body, the anterior putamen, left anterior globus pallidus and right ventral putamen. Volume expansion seen in the posterior putamen. No volume or shape differences were revealed in girls with ADHD.
(Sobel et al., 2010)	Volume and shape of basal ganglia	47	10.4	Significantly smaller putamen. Significant inward deformations in all basal ganglia which correlated with severity of symptoms and localized primarily to portions of these nuclei that are components of limbic, associative, and sensorimotor pathways in the cortico-striato-thalamo-cortical circuits. All disorder-related changes were less pronounced in those on psychostimulants

in the study populations (e.g., comorbidities, medication status), in equipment and in the neuroimaging sequences used. Another important source of variability may be the age differences in the studies which ranged from a mean age of roughly ten to sixteen years old.

Of particular interest among the new analytic methods, are tools which allow the definition of the thickness, surface area and complexity of the cortex across the entire cerebrum. These studies largely converge to find that the cortex is thinner in ADHD and that compromise is greatest in the prefrontal regions—see Table 3.1 (F. Castellanos, Xavier, and Proal, 2009; Narr et al., 2009; Qiu et al., 2010; Shaw et al., 2006; Wolosin, Richardson, Hennessey, Denckla, and Mostofsky, 2009).

Cross-sectional studies have thus helped establish that the brain is different in ADHD and that at least some of these differences are not epiphenomena of symptoms as they are found in unaffected relatives and do not seem to be due to medication. But what have longitudinal studies added?

At the NIMH we have collected a group of over 250 children and adolescents with ADHD, the majority of whom have had repeated neuroanatomic imaging in tandem with ongoing clinical assessments. This data allows us to define neurodevelopmental trajectories and to relate these to cognitive and clinical variables. We have been particularly interested in cortical development, and compared the change in the thickness of the cortex—estimated at over 40,000 cerebral points using computational techniques—in 223 children and adolescents with ADHD from the cohort against cortical development in 223 age, sex and IQ matched healthy controls (Shaw et al., 2007). The growth trajectory of each cortical point was determined along with the age at which peak cortical thickness was attained—that is the age at which childhood increase in cortical thickness gives way to adolescent decrease. Cortical development in children with ADHD lagged behind that of typically developing children by about three years overall—and the delay was most prominent in the lateral prefrontal cortex (see Figure 3.1). However, the ordered sequence of regional development, with primary sensory and motor areas attaining their peak cortical thickness before high-order association areas, was similar in both groups, suggesting that ADHD is characterized by delay rather than deviation in cortical maturation. The primary motor cortex was the only cortical area in where the ADHD group showed slightly earlier maturation.

This study implies that the relatively narrow age window of about eight to twelve years is a developmental phase characterized by marked difference in the regional trajectories of cortical change in children with and without ADHD: diagnostic differences differ exquisitely with age. This could explain some of the inconsistencies in previous neuroanatomic studies, the majority of which lie within this age range. More importantly the study represents a shift towards thinking of the neuroanatomic signature of ADHD as being dynamic.

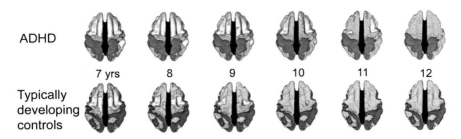

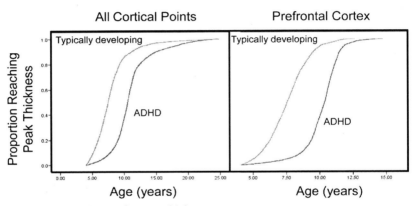

Figure 3.1. Comparisons of cortex thickness

UNPACKING THE TRAJECTORIES

There is a vast amount of information nestling within these neurodevelopmental trajectories, which we have only begun to examine. This is particularly the case when we begin to look at the relationship between developmental trajectories of different brain regions. For example do the right and left hemispheres develop differently in typical development and ADHD and could this be of relevance to our understanding of the disorder? Understanding the development of cortical asymmetries is a pivotal issue in neuroscience, given the links between such asymmetries and the lateralization of motor and cognitive functions in typical development (Galaburda, LeMay, Kemper, and Geschwind, 1978; Toga and Thompson, 2003). Additionally, disruption of asymmetry has been implicated in the pathogenesis of not just ADHD but other childhood neuropsychiatric disorders, including autism and schizophrenia (Crow, 1997; Herbert et al., 2005; Rubia et al., 2000).

The most consistently reported structural asymmetry in typically developing adults is a relative increase in the dimensions of the right frontal and left occipital lobes (Bear, Schiff, Saver, Greenberg, and Freeman, 1986; Bilder et al., 1994; Good et al., 2001; Le May and Kido, 1978; Watkins et al., 2001). However, studies of healthy infant and child populations show different asymmetries. One volumetric study of 46 right handed children reported a complete reversal of adult asymmetries, finding that children showed larger left frontal and right temporo-occipital cortical volumes (Herbert et al., 2005). Other studies find that children only partially demonstrate the adult patterns of asymmetry (Jay N. Giedd et al., 1996; Gilmore et al., 2007; Matsuzawa et al., 2001; Reiss, Abrams, Singer, Ross, and Denckla, 1996). These studies, which were all cross-sectional, imply asymmetry is a dynamic property of the childhood brain which could be further understood using longitudinal neuroanatomic data.

We thus defined the developmental trajectory of cortical asymmetry in both typically developing children and children with ADHD (Shaw et al., 2009). The differences in thickness between homologous points in the right and left hemispheres were defined across development throughout the entire cerebrum using our longitudinal data, which included 223 children with ADHD and 358 typically developing children, with a total of 1,133 neuroanatomic magnetic resonance images. In right-handed, typically developing youth, the left orbitofrontal/inferior frontal gyrus in early childhood was relatively thicker than the right, but by late adolescence this had reversed and this anterior region was relatively thicker in the right hemisphere, resembling the well-established adult pattern of asymmetry. A similar increase with age in relative right hemispheric thickness was found in the medial occipital region, extending superiorly to the medial aspect of the superior parietal lobule and motor cortex, and inferiorly to the medial occipitotemporal junction. The reverse pattern—with a significant increase with age in cortical asymmetry, indicating relative gain in left hemispheric thickness—was seen in the a region centered on the middle occipital and angular gyri, extending from the posterior temporal cortex to the occipital pole. Thus there was a "flip" in cortical asymmetries during typical development: a relatively thicker left anterior and right posterior cortex in childhood develops into the well-established adult asymmetries of a thicker right anterior and left posterior cortex.

Could alterations of these developmental trajectories of cortical asymmetries play a role in the pathogenesis of Attention-Deficit/Hyperactivity Disorder (ADHD) (Rubia et al., 2000)? A loss of typical frontal asymmetry due to right frontal volume loss is one of the more consistently replicated findings in cross sectional neuroimaging studies in ADHD, and abnormal development of prefrontal lateralized processing has been implicated in the disorder (F. X. Castellanos et al., 1996; Filipek et al., 1997; Langleben et al., 2001; Rubia et al., 2000; Rubia, Smith, Brammer, Toone, and Taylor, 2005). We thus defined the change in cortical asymmetry (using cortical thickness difference between homologous points in the hemispheres as the metric) in right-handed children with ADHD. There was marked similarity in the posterior regions: the ADHD group showed a relative increase in left hemispheric thickness in a similar posterior-temporo-occipital region to the typically developing group. However, unlike the typically developing subjects, the ADHD group showed no opposing tendency of increasing relative right hemispheric thickness in the frontal cortex. Rather there was a small region in the anterior superior temporal gyrus which showed this increase in relative right hemispheric thickness with age. Thus the right handed ADHD group showed typical posterior, but atypical anterior evolving asymmetry.

What is the functional significance of this finding? In one of the few functional studies to examine directly anomalous lateralization of activation in ADHD, a SPET study demonstrated decreased right and increased left dorsolateral prefrontal cortical perfusion during response inhibition in those with clinically severe compared to those with mild ADHD (Langleben et al., 2001), suggesting anomalous prefrontal lateralization may characterize the disorder. Disrupted development of prefrontal asymmetry might contribute to the consistent findings of anomalous prefrontal activation in the disorder during tasks of cognitive control (Rubia et al., 2005; Smith, Taylor, Brammer, Toone, and Rubia, 2006). More generally, it demonstrates the insights into developmental processes that can be gained from defining the relationships between developmental trajectories in different cortical regions.

Such findings can inform our search for etiological factors. For example, if ADHD is characterized by anomalous development of cortical asymmetry, then it would be expected that asymmetrically expressed genes would be associated with the disorder. This was indeed confirmed in a recent case control study which found that of six functional candidate genes which showed at least a 1.9-fold differential expression between the hemispheres, one gene was associated with ADHD in two independent large cohorts (Ribases et al., 2009).

This finding of anomalous development of cortical asymmetry in children and adolescents with ADHD would also lead one to expect congruent developmental anomalies of other interconnected structures, such as the corpus callosum. As the development of cortical asymmetry was disrupted in prefrontal and not posterior regions, it would be predicted that there would be a congruent disruption in the growth of the anterior corpus callosum, which contains white matter tracts connecting prefrontal cortical regions. This prediction was confirmed in a study which used a semi-automated method to define the areas of five sub-regions of the corpus callosum, and their growth rates in our cohort (Gilliam et al., 2011). Right-handed ADHD children showed a significantly higher rate of growth in the anterior-most region of the corpus callosum (estimated annual increase in area of 0.97 percent, SEM 0.12 percent) than their typically developing peers (annual increase in area of 0.32 percent SEM 0.13 percent). No significant diagnostic differences in growth rates were found in any other regions of the corpus callosum. This anomalous anterior callosal growth may reflect, or even drive disrupted development of prefrontal cortical asymmetries.

USING LONGITUDINAL DATA TO MAP THE NEURAL BASIS OF VARIABLE CLINICAL OUTCOME

Longitudinal data is also ideal for studying the neuroanatomic correlates of one of most salient features of ADHD —namely its tendency to improve with age in most, but certainly not all, subjects. A recent meta-analysis showed that while only 15 to 20 percent of those with childhood ADHD retained the diagnosis in adulthood, approximately a further 50 percent had residual symptoms which were impairing (Faraone et al., 2006). We found a similar pattern of outcome in our cohort. Using our yoked, prospectively acquired neuroanatomic and clinical data we defined the neuroanatomic trajectories which reflected varying clinical outcome (Shaw et al., 2006). Due to the smaller sample size of those with outcome data and the restricted age range we could only delineate the phase of cortical thinning which characterizes adolescent cortical development. We first examined cortical development in ADHD subjects with full or partial remission at last follow-up. This group differed significantly in the trajectory of cortical change in the right parietal cortex, most prominently in the superior parietal lobule. Here, there was a convergence between the trajectories of the remitted ADHD group and the typically developing cohort, such that by late adolescence there was "normalization" of cortical thickness in those who remit from ADHD. A similar trend held throughout the lateral prefrontal cortex. By contrast, the group of ADHD subjects with persistent combined type ADHD showed either fixed non-progressive cortical deficits or a slight tendency to diverge away from typical trajectories. These deficits localized to the medial prefrontal wall especially the left posterior cingulate and regions in the superior frontal gyri. If compromise of these regions characterizes poor outcome in ADHD then we would expect to find cortical change in these regions in adults with the disorder—which another group indeed recently reported in their study of adult ADHD (Makris et al., 2007).

We found similar links between clinical outcome and developmental trajectories at the cerebellar level (Mackie et al., 2007). Using a semi-automated method to measure ten cerebellar hemispheric and vermal compartments, we found that trajectories of the inferior posterior hemispheres, the largest single cerebellar compartment, differed between the outcome groups as the subjects with persistent ADHD diverged from both their peers with remitting ADHD and typically developing controls. A theme emerges: persistent ADHD may be characterized by progressive deviation away from neurotypical trajectories and a deviant trajectory, whereas remission in ADHD is associated with a normalization of deficits and convergence to typical development.

We can only speculate on cellular events which underlie change in cortical thickness, but these are likely to include alterations in synaptic connections, and changing myelination of the peripheral cortical neuropil (Huttenlocher and Dabholkar, 1997; Sowell et al., 2004; Yakovlev and Lecours, 1967).

APPLICATION TO OTHER NEUROPSYCHIATRIC DISORDERS

This developmental neuroimaging approach has been applied by others to the understanding of disorders including autism and childhood onset schizophrenia. In autism, two longitudinal studies have examined brain volumes as determined by MRI at age two, and related these to head circumference measures (taken as a proxy for brain volume) made at birth and during the early years (Courchesne, Carper, and Akshoomoff, 2003; Hazlett et al., 2005). They found that while head circumference at birth was normal or low-normal in infants who would later be diagnosed with autism, there was an infantile rapid acceleration of brain growth—both in gray and white matter. In one study this spurt started around 6 months, in the other study the acceleration started around one year. The accelerated growth was dysregulated as by two years of age the children with autism had greater brain volumes than typically developing and developmentally delayed comparison subjects. This excessive growth ceases after early childhood and by late childhood brain volumes regress to normal ranges, or fall to below typical levels (Redcay and Courchesne, 2005). A similar pattern in early childhood was found for the amygdalae; at both ages two and four children with autism had large amygdalae—consistent with a pattern of early overgrowth leading to bigger volumes (Mosconi et al., 2009). This enlargement had functional correlates with deficits in the ability to engage in joint attention—a core aspect of social cognition.

We turn finally to a consideration of a very rare disorder, childhood onset schizophrenia, defined by the onset of symptoms before the age of thirteen years. Much of this work has stemmed from a longitudinal study at NIMH of over one hundred patients with childhood onset of schizophrenia, who have had repeated combined neuroimaging and clinical assessments—and is reviewed more fully elsewhere (Gogtay, 2008; Rapoport and Gogtay, 2008). As discussed earlier, in typical development cortical grey matter appears to mature in a parieto-frontal (back-to-front) direction and medially in a centripetal ("top-down") fashion. While the sequence of grey matter development during adolescence in patients with COS resembled that of healthy controls, it had a much higher velocity (Thompson et al., 2001). Both the adolescent parieto-frontal and centripetal medial waves of cortical thinning which characterizes typical development were greatly accentuated in the disorder, occurring at an increased velocity (Vidal et al., 2006). This increased rate of cortical thinning did not persist into adulthood in the parietal cortex, but rather the thinning appeared to "stop" during late adolescence. This leads to a partial normalization of cortical thickness in this region, as during typical adolescence this region continues to thin (Greenstein et al., 2006). However, in the fronto-temporal cortex the anomalous trajectories persisted, resulting in fronto-temporal cortical changes resembling those seen in adult-onset schizophrenia.

In typical development, the trajectories of grey and white matter growth are distinct. It is therefore unsurprising that the nature of the illness-related disruptions to grey and white matter might differ within the same disorder. This is clearly seen in COS. As mentioned earlier, during typical development white matter volumes increase during adolescence (J. N. Giedd et al., 1999). However, this volumetric gain is almost completely absent during adolescence in patients with COS (Gogtay et al., 2008). Instead of steady increase, these patients show a loss of white matter expansion throughout the entire right hemisphere with "growth" rates not differing significantly from zero, and only a trend to white matter growth in the left hemisphere. Thus while grey matter change is characterized by acceleration of typical trajectories, white matter trajectories are characterized by an almost complete arrest of typical development. Such regional heterogeneity can give vital insights into future searches for the genetic and environmental factors which might underpin the different disturbances to different brain compartments seen in COS.

CONCLUSIONS

So, are longitudinal studies worth the effort? The theoretical justification is strong and empirically the initial findings from longitudinal studies are promising. Conceptualizing childhood psychiatric disorders as arising in part due to perturbations in neruodevelopmental trajectories may give us one part of the pathogenic puzzle. It suggests that we should focus attention on mechanisms which control the timing of postnatal cortical development. Genetic factors will certainly play a role, with a perturbation in the developmental sequence of the activation and deactivation of genes that sculpt cortical architecture. In this context, neurotrophins, essential for the proliferation, differentiation, and survival of neuronal and nonneuronal cells, emerge as promising candidates, and, indeed, polymorphisms within the brain-derived neurotrophic factor and nerve growth-factor three genes have already been tentatively linked with ADHD and other neuropsychiatric disorders (Syed, Dudbridge, and Kent, 2007).

This approach has clinical potential. Could the different trajectories we find in each disorder represent diagnostic signals, which might allow us to move away from a nosology based purely on clinical symptoms, to one which incorporates features such as patterns of brain growth? The difference in trajectories between different disorders is illustrated in Figure 3.2. It should be stressed that this is a hypothetical figure and much work remains to be done to confirm the trajectory differences suggested. Additionally, diagnostic use of such trajectories will require the reliable identification at the individual level of diagnostic signals in neurodevelopmental trajectories—a goal which will undoubtedly require new technologies, novel combinations of existing ones and advances in statistical analysis. Finally, longitudinal studies may help us unravel neural bases of differential clinical outcome in disorders, which promises better, more targeted treatments.

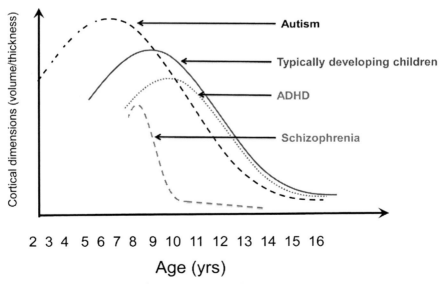

Figure 3.2.   Comparisons of disorder trajectories

REFERENCES

Bear, D., Schiff, D., Saver, J., Greenberg, M., and Freeman, R. (1986). Quantitative analysis of cerebral asymmetries. Fronto-occipital correlation, sexual dimorphism and association with handedness. *Archives of Neurology, 43*(6), 598–603.

Bilder, R. M., Wu, H., Bogerts, B., Degreef, G., Ashtari, M., Alvir, J. M., et al. (1994). Absence of regional hemispheric volume asymmetries in first-episode schizophrenia. *American Journal of Psychiatry, 151*(10), 1437–47.

Bledsoe, J., Semrud-Clikeman, M., and Pliszka, S. R. (2009). A Magnetic Resonance Imaging Study of the Cerebellar Vermis in Chronically Treated and Treatment-Naïve Children with Attention-Deficit/Hyperactivity Disorder Combined Type. *Biological Psychiatry.*

Castellanos, F., Lee, P., Sharp, W., Jeffries, N., Greenstein, D., Clasen, L., et al. (2002). Developmental trajectories of brain volume abnormalities in children and adolescents with attention-deficit/hyperactivity disorder. *JAMA, 288,* 1740–48.

Castellanos, F., Xavier, M. D., and Proal, E. M. S. (2009). Location, Location, and Thickness: Volumetric Neuroimaging of Attention-Deficit/Hyperactivity Disorder Comes of Age. *Journal of the American Academy of Child and Adolescent Psychiatry, 48*(10), 979–81.

Castellanos, F. X., Giedd, J. N., Eckburg, P., Marsh, W. L., Vaituzis, A. C., Kaysen, D., et al. (1994). Quantitative morphology of the caudate nucleus in attention deficit hyperactivity disorder. *American Journal of Psychiatry, 151*(12), 1791–96.

Castellanos, F. X., Giedd, J. N., Marsh, W. L., Hamburger, S. D., Vaituzis, A. C., Dickstein, D. P., et al. (1996). Quantitative brain magnetic resonance imaging in attention-deficit hyperactivity disorder. *Archives of General Psychiatry, 53*(7), 607–16.

Courchesne, E., Carper, R., and Akshoomoff, N. (2003). Evidence of brain overgrowth in the first year of life in autism. [see comment]. *JAMA, 290*(3), 337–44.

Crow, T. J. (1997). Schizophrenia as failure of hemispheric dominance for language. [see comment]. *Trends in Neurosciences, 20*(8), 339–343.

Durston, S., Fossella, J. A., Casey, B. J., Hulshoff Pol, H. E., Galvan, A., Schnack, H. G., et al. (2005). Differential effects of DRD4 and DAT1 genotype on fronto-striatal gray matter volumes in a sample of subjects with attention deficit hyperactivity disorder, their unaffected siblings, and controls. *Molecular Psychiatry, 10*(7), 678–85.

Durston, S., Hulshoff Pol, H. E., Schnack, H. G., Buitelaar, J. K., Steenhuis, M. P., Minderaa, R. B., et al. (2004). Magnetic resonance imaging of boys with attention-deficit/hyperactivity disorder and their unaffected siblings. *Journal of the American Academy of Child and Adolescent Psychiatry, 43*(3), 332–40.

Ellison-Wright, I., Ellison-Wright, Z., and Bullmore, E. (2008). Structural brain change in Attention Deficit Hyperactivity Disorder identified by meta-analysis. *BMC Psychiatry, 8,* 51.

Faraone, S. V., Biederman, J., and Mick, E. (2006). The age-dependent decline of attention deficit hyperactivity disorder: A meta-analysis of follow-up studies. *Psychological Medicine, 36*(2), 159–65.

Filipek, P. A., Semrud-Clikeman, M., Steingard, R. J., Renshaw, P. F., Kennedy, D. N., and Biederman, J. (1997). Volumetric MRI analysis comparing subjects having attention-deficit hyperactivity disorder with normal controls. *Neurology, 48*(3), 589–601.

Galaburda, A. M., LeMay, M., Kemper, T. L., and Geschwind, N. (1978). Right-left asymmetrics in the brain. *Science, 199*(4331), 852–56.

Giedd, J. N., Blumenthal, J., Jeffries, N. O., Castellanos, F. X., Liu, H., Zijdenbos, A., et al. (1999). Brain development during childhood and adolescence: A longitudinal MRI study. *Nature Neuroscience, 2*(10), 861–63.

Giedd, J. N., and Rapoport, J. L. (2010). Structural MRI of Pediatric Brain Development: What Have We Learned and Where Are We Going? *Neuron, 67*(5), 728–34.

Giedd, J. N., Snell, J. W., Lange, N., Rajapakse, J. C., Casey, B. J., Kozuch, P. L., et al. (1996). Quantitative Magnetic Resonance Imaging of Human Brain Development: Ages 4–18. *Cereb. Cortex, 6*(4), 551–59.

Gilliam, M., Stockman, M., Malek, M., Sharp, W., Greenstein, D., Lalonde, F., et al. (2011). Developmental Trajectories of the Corpus Callosum in Attention-Deficit/ Hyperactivity Disorder. *Biological Psychiatry, 69*(9), 839–46.

Gilmore, J. H., Lin, W., Prastawa, M. W., Looney, C. B., Vetsa, Y. S. K., Knickmeyer, R. C., et al. (2007). Regional Gray Matter Growth, Sexual Dimorphism, and Cerebral Asymmetry in the Neonatal Brain. *J. Neurosci., 27*(6), 1255–60.

Gogtay, N. (2008). Cortical brain development in schizophrenia: Insights from neuroimaging studies in childhood-onset schizophrenia. *Schizophrenia Bulletin, 34*(1), 30–36.

Gogtay, N., Lu, A., Leow, A. D., Klunder, A. D., Lee, A. D., Chavez, A., et al. (2008). Three-dimensional brain growth abnormalities in childhood-onset schizophrenia visualized by using tensor-based morphometry. *Proceedings of the National Academy of Sciences of the United States of America, 105*(41), 15979–84.

Good, C. D., Johnsrude, I. S., Ashburner, J., Henson, R. N., Friston, K. J., and Frackowiak, R. S. (2001). A voxel-based morphometric study of ageing in 465 normal adult human brains. *Neuroimage, 14*(1 Pt 1), 21–36.

Greenstein, D., Lerch, J., Shaw, P., Clasen, L., Giedd, J., Gochman, P., et al. (2006). Childhood onset schizophrenia: Cortical brain abnormalities as young adults. *Journal of Child Psychology & Psychiatry & Allied Disciplines, 47*(10), 1003–1012.

Hazlett, H. C., Poe, M., Gerig, G., Smith, R. G., Provenzale, J., Ross, A., et al. (2005). Magnetic resonance imaging and head circumference study of brain size in autism: Birth through age 2 years. *Archives of General Psychiatry, 62*(12), 1366–76.

Herbert, M. R., Ziegler, D. A., Deutsch, C. K., O'Brien, L. M., Kennedy, D. N., Filipek, P. A., et al. (2005). Brain asymmetries in autism and developmental language disorder: a nested whole-brain analysis. *Brain, 128*(Pt 1), 213–26.

Huttenlocher, P. R., and Dabholkar, A. S. (1997). Regional differences in synaptogenesis in human cerebral cortex. *Journal of Comparative Neurology, 387*(2), 167–78.

Kraemer, H. C., Yesavage, J. A., Taylor, J. L., and Kupfer, D. (2000). How Can We Learn About Developmental Processes From Cross-Sectional Studies, or Can We? *Am J Psychiatry, 157*(2), 163–71.

Krain, A. L., and Castellanos, F. X. (2006). Brain development and ADHD. *Clinical Psychology Review, 26*(4), 433–444.

Langleben, D. D., Austin, G., Krikorian, G., Ridlehuber, H. W., Goris, M. L., and Strauss, H. W. (2001). Interhemispheric asymmetry of regional cerebral blood flow in prepubescent boys with attention deficit hyperactivity disorder. *Nuclear Medicine Communications, 22*(12), 1333–40.

Le May, M., and Kido, D. K. (1978). Asymmetries of the cerebral hemispheres on computed tomograms. *Journal of Computer Assisted Tomography, 2*(4), 471–76.

Mackie, S., Shaw, P., Lenroot, R., Pierson, R., Greenstein, D. K., Nugent, T. F., 3rd, et al. (2007). Cerebellar development and clinical outcome in attention deficit hyperactivity disorder.[see comment]. *American Journal of Psychiatry, 164*(4), 647–55.

Makris, N., Biederman, J., Valera, E. M., Bush, G., Kaiser, J., Kennedy, D. N., et al. (2007). Cortical thinning of the attention and executive function networks in adults with attention-deficit/hyperactivity disorder. *Cerebral Cortex, 17*(6), 1364–75.

Mataro, M., Garcia-Sanchez, C., Junque, C., Estevez-Gonzalez, A., and Pujol, J. (1997). Magnetic resonance imaging measurement of the caudate nucleus in adolescents with attention-deficit hyperactivity disorder and its relationship with neuropsychological and behavioral measures. *Archives of Neurology, 54*(8), 963–68.

Matsuzawa, J., Matsui, M., Konishi, T., Noguchi, K., Gur, R. C., Bilker, W., et al. (2001). Age-related volumetric changes of brain gray and white matter in healthy infants and children. *Cerebral Cortex, 11*(4), 335–42.

McAlonan, G. M., Cheung, V., Chua, S. E., Oosterlaan, J., Hung, S.-f., Tang, C.-p., et al. (2009). Age-related grey matter volume correlates of response inhibition and shifting in attention-deficit hyperactivity disorder. *The British Journal of Psychiatry, 194*(2), 123–29.

Mosconi, M. W., Cody-Hazlett, H., Poe, M. D., Gerig, G., Gimpel-Smith, R., and Piven, J. (2009). Longitudinal study of amygdala volume and joint attention in 2- to 4-year-old children with autism. *Archives of General Psychiatry, 66*(5), 509–16.

Narr, K. L. P. D., Woods, R. P. M. D., Lin, J. B. S., Kim, J. B. A., Phillips, O. R. B. S., Del'Homme, M. P. D., et al. (2009). Widespread Cortical Thinning Is a Robust Anatomical Marker for Attention-Deficit/Hyperactivity Disorder. *Journal of the American Academy of Child & Adolescent Psychiatry, 48*(10), 1014–22.

Plessen, K. J., Bansal, R., Zhu, H., Whiteman, R., Amat, J., Quackenbush, G. A., et al. (2006). Hippocampus and amygdala morphology in attention-deficit/hyperactivity disorder. *Archives of General Psychiatry, 63*(7), 795–807.

Qiu, M.-g., Ye, Z., Li, Q.-y., Liu, G.-j., Xie, B., and Wang, J. (2010). Changes of Brain Structure and Function in ADHD Children. *Brain Topography*, 1–10.

Rapoport, J. L., and Gogtay, N. (2008). Brain neuroplasticity in healthy, hyperactive and psychotic children: Insights from neuroimaging. *Neuropsychopharmacology, 33*(1), 181–97.

Redcay, E., and Courchesne, E. (2005). When is the brain enlarged in autism? A meta-analysis of all brain size reports. *Biological Psychiatry, 58*(1), 1–9.

Reiss, A. L., Abrams, M. T., Singer, H. S., Ross, J. L., and Denckla, M. B. (1996). Brain development, gender and IQ in children: A volumetric imaging study. *Brain, 119*(5), 1763–1774.

Ribases, M., Bosch, R., Hervas, A., Ramos-Quiroga, J. A., Sanchez-Mora, C., Bielsa, A., et al. (2009). Case-control study of six genes asymmetrically expressed in the two cerebral hemispheres: Association of BAIAP2 with attention-deficit/hyperactivity disorder. *Biological Psychiatry, 66*(10), 926–34.

Rubia, K., Overmeyer, S., Taylor, E., Brammer, M., Williams, S. C., Simmons, A., et al. (2000). Functional frontalisation with age: Mapping neurodevelopmental trajectories with fMRI. *Neuroscience & Biobehavioral Reviews, 24*(1), 13–19.

Rubia, K., Smith, A. B., Brammer, M. J., Toone, B., and Taylor, E. M. D. (2005). Abnormal Brain Activation During Inhibition and Error Detection in Medication-Naive Adolescents With ADHD. *American Journal of Psychiatry, 162*(6), 1067–75.

Semrud-Clikeman, M., Pliszka, S. R., Lancaster, J., and Liotti, M. (2006). Volumetric MRI differences in treatment-naive vs chronically treated children with ADHD. [erratum appears in *Neurology.* 2006 Dec 12;67(11):2091]. *Neurology, 67*(6), 1023–27.

Shaw, P., Eckstrand, K., Sharp, W., Blumenthal, J., Lerch, J. P., Greenstein, D., et al. (2007). Attention-deficit/hyperactivity disorder is characterized by a delay in cortical maturation. *Proceedings of the National Academy of Sciences of the United States of America, 104*(49), 19649–54.

Shaw, P., Kabani, N. J., Lerch, J. P., Eckstrand, K., Lenroot, R., Gogtay, N., et al. (2008). Neurodevelopmental trajectories of the human cerebral cortex. *Journal of Neuroscience, 28*(14), 3586–94.

Shaw, P., Lalonde, F., Lepage, C., Rabin, C., Eckstrand, K., Sharp, W., et al. (2009). Development of Cortical Asymmetry in Typically Developing Children and Its Disruption in Attention-Deficit/Hyperactivity Disorder. *Arch Gen Psychiatry, 66*(8), 888–96.

Shaw, P., Lerch, J., Greenstein, D., Sharp, W., Clasen, L., Evans, A., et al. (2006). Longitudinal mapping of cortical thickness and clinical outcome in children and adolescents with attention-deficit/hyperactivity disorder. *Archives of General Psychiatry, 63*(5), 540–49.

Smith, A. B., Taylor, E., Brammer, M., Toone, B., and Rubia, K. (2006). Task-specific hypoactivation in prefrontal and temporoparietal brain regions during motor inhibition and task switching in medication-naive children and adolescents with attention deficit hyperactivity disorder. [see comment]. *American Journal of Psychiatry, 163*(6), 1044–51.

Sobel, L. J., Bansal, R., Maia, T. V., Sanchez, J., Mazzone, L., Durkin, K., et al. (2010). Basal Ganglia Surface Morphology and the Effects of Stimulant Medications in Youth With Attention Deficit Hyperactivity Disorder. *Am J Psychiatry, 167*(8), 977–86.

Sowell, E. R., Thompson, P. M., Leonard, C. M., Welcome, S. E., Kan, E., and Toga, A. W. (2004). Longitudinal mapping of cortical thickness and brain growth in normal children. *Journal of Neuroscience, 24*(38), 8223–31.

Stanley, J. A., Kipp, H., Greisenegger, E., MacMaster, F. P., Panchalingam, K., Keshavan, M. S., et al. (2008). Evidence of developmental alterations in cortical and subcortical regions of children with attention-deficit/hyperactivity disorder: A multivoxel in vivo phosphorus 31 spectroscopy study. *Archives of General Psychiatry, 65*(12), 1419–28.

Syed, Z., Dudbridge, F., and Kent, L. (2007). An investigation of the neurotrophic factor genes GDNF, NGF, and NT3 in susceptibility to ADHD. *American Journal of Medical Genetics Part B: Neuropsychiatric Genetics, 144B*(3), 375–78.

Thompson, P. M., Vidal, C., Giedd, J. N., Gochman, P., Blumenthal, J., Nicolson, R., et al. (2001). Mapping adolescent brain change reveals dynamic wave of accelerated gray matter loss in very early-onset schizophrenia. *Proceedings of the National Academy of Sciences of the United States of America, 98*(20), 11650–55.

Toga, A. W., and Thompson, P. M. (2003). Mapping brain asymmetry. *Nature Reviews Neuroscience, 4*(1), 37–48.

Valera, E. M., Faraone, S. V., Murray, K. E., and Seidman, L. J. (2007). Meta-analysis of structural imaging findings in attention-deficit/hyperactivity disorder. *Biological Psychiatry, 61*(12), 1361–69.

Vidal, C. N., Rapoport, J. L., Hayashi, K. M., Geaga, J. A., Sui, Y., McLemore, L. E., et al. (2006). Dynamically spreading frontal and cingulate deficits mapped in adolescents with schizophrenia. *Archives of General Psychiatry, 63*(1), 25–34.

Watkins, K. E., Paus, T., Lerch, J. P., Zijdenbos, A., Collins, D. L., Neelin, P., et al. (2001). Structural asymmetries in the human brain: A voxel-based statistical analysis of 142 MRI scans. *Cerebral Cortex, 11*(9), 868–77.

Wolosin, S. M., Richardson, M. E., Hennessey, J. G., Denckla, M. B., and Mostofsky, S. H. (2009). Abnormal Cerebral Cortex Structure in Children with ADHD. *Human Brain Mapping, 30*(1), 175–84.

Yakovlev, P. I., and Lecours, A. R. (1967). The myelinogenetic cycles of regional maturation of the brain. In A. Minokowski (Ed.), *Regional development of the brain in early life.* Oxford: Blackwell Scientific.

4

Common and Rare Genetic Variants as Risk Factors for Autism Spectrum Disorders

Marie Christine Mouren, Thomas Bourgeron,
and Richard Delorme

CHAPTER SYNOPSIS

Autism spectrum disorders (ASD) are characterized by impaired reciprocal social communication (both verbal and nonverbal) and stereotyped behavior. In the last few years, several independent studies have identified a growing number of rare and common genetic variants associated with ASD. The rare variants seem to be highly penetrative conferring high risk for ASD in a subset of patients. Common risk variants are associated with very low risk of having ASD and have not always been replicated. In this review, we present the main rare variants associated with idiopathic ASD as well as early findings on the identification of common variants as risk factors. These results indicate that a set of mechanisms such as abnormal synaptic homeostasis could increase the risk of having ASD. The epistasis (whereby the effects of one gene is modified by one or several other genes) between the rare and common variants will remain difficult to understand without a better characterization of the genetic and phenotypic heterogeneity of ASD.

INTRODUCTION

Autism spectrum disorders (ASD) (OMIM 209850) are characterized by impaired reciprocal social communication (both verbal and nonverbal) and stereotyped behavior. ASD include typical autism, Asperger syndrome and pervasive developmental disorders not otherwise specified (PDD-NOS). The prevalence of ASD overall is about 1/100, but closer to 1/300 for typical autism (Fernell and Gillberg, 2010). Impairments in reciprocal social inter-action range from major social withdrawal to difficulties in interpersonal relationships. Compromised nonverbal communication varies from a lack of eye contact with poor communicative gestures to a slightly diminished nonverbal expression of emotions. Cognitive rigidity and repetitive behav-iors can result in the reiterative, invasive motor symptoms and obsessive behavioral patterns that are often observed in children with intellectual disability (ID).

ASD are considered as the most genetic of neuropsychiatric disorders. Family-based studies have shown that recurrence risk in siblings of affected children is twenty times higher than the risk in the general population (Fombonne, 2005). Among the ASD patient siblings, 12 to 20 percent, show autistic traits (Bolton et al., 1994). Also, twin studies have confirmed that familial aggregation of autistic traits is the consequence of its high heritability (h^2:0.8) (Freitag, 2007; Lichtenstein et al., 2010). Two coexist-ing genetic models have been proposed for ASD. In the first model, ASD are considered as a polygenic trait (i.e., a group of patients with a relatively homogeneous phenotype produced by multiple genes, each of low effect), also referred to as the common disease-common variant (CD-CV) hypoth-esis (Altshuler et al., 2008). Although the absence of strong linkage and/or association loci replication by whole genome scans does not support the CD-CV model, the latter has not been excluded. Specifically, the identifica-tion of low risk alleles requires large groups of patients. In ASD, the number of subjects included in the most recent GWAS (Genome Wide Association Study) was less than three thousand cases (Anney et al., 2010). The second model proposes that ASD could result from the effect of a single highly penetrative variation that would be sufficient to produce the disorders. This common disease-rare variant (CD-RV) model of ASD was recently sup-ported by the identification of apparently monogenic forms, each affecting a limited number of patients, approximately 1 to 2 percent for the most replicated genes.

In this review, we present the main rare variants associated with idio-pathic ASD (i.e., in the absence of a known genetic syndrome or clear evi-dence of a monogenic disorder) as well as early findings on the implication of common variants as risk factors for ASD.

RARE VARIANTS ASSOCIATED WITH ASD

Whole genome analyses have revealed that genomic imbalances also called copy number variants (CNVs) are an important source of human genetic variability (Redon et al., 2006). Many studies have searched for specific CNVs in patients with ASD. The differences in patient inclusion criteria, genotyping methodologies and algorithms to detect CNVs make comparison of these studies difficult. Nevertheless, a significant increase in rare inherited and *de novo* CNVs in ASD patients compared with controls has been observed. For example, Pinto et al. (Pinto et al., 2010), comparing 996 ASD individuals of European ancestry to 1,287 matched controls, reported a higher global burden of rare, genetic CNVs (1.19 fold), especially for loci previously implicated in either ASD and/or ID (1.69 fold). The presence of dysmorphic features in patients could increase the odds of detecting a rare or *de novo* CNV in up to 27.5 percent (Jacquemont et al., 2006). Surprisingly, the difference in the frequency of rare and *de novo* CNVs between simplex and multiplex families appears to be the same according to a recent investigation (5.6 percent) (Sebat et al., 2007; Pinto et al., 2010), in contrast to previous reports (Sebat et al., 2007). The reasons for the variability observed have not yet been clarified, although the increasing resolution of array platforms might obscure some differences between groups. Although the role of rare CNVs in ASD has been collectively demonstrated, the bulk of the published ASD associated CNV regions are composed of unique events, with minimal overlap between studies. It is therefore extremely difficult to pinpoint which CNVs are specific risk factors for ASD, since most of them represent also risk factors for ID, epilepsy or schizophrenia. This overlap suggests that a large range of neuropsychiatric disorders may share common genetic mechanisms (Gauthier et al., 2010). (See also the chapter in this book by Saskia Palmen and Herman van Engeland).

Deletions/Duplications at 1q21.1

Two large screens of patients with ID and/or ASD lead to the detection of a recurrent CNV at 1q21.1 (Brunetti-Pierri et al., 2008; Mefford et al., 2008). Mefford et al. studied 5,218 patients with ID (a small fraction also had a comorbid ASD) and 4,737 controls, and detected twenty-five deletions of 1q21.1 (only in patients) and seven duplications of the same region (one in a control) (Mefford et al., 2008). The clinical phenotype of patients carrying the genomic imbalances ranged from mild to severe ID, absence to severe autistic symptoms, and normal head circumference to macrocephaly. Brunetti-Pierri et al. reported similar results, detecting twenty-one deletions and fifteen duplications in 16,577 patients suffering from ID, ASD or congenital abnormalities, but not in 550 controls (Brunetti-Pierri et al., 2008). The authors also reported that the CNVs were preferentially observed in subjects with micro or macrocephaly. The functional impact of genes located in the CNV remains unclear. *HYDIN* located on 16q22.2, implicated in cerebral cortex size, has a paralog inserted onto 1q21.1 that could probably be linked to head-size abnormalities (Brunetti-Pierri et al., 2008).

Deletions/Duplications at 15q11-q13

Prader-Willi syndrome is characterized by paternal chromosome 15q11-13 deletions (70–80 percent) and Angelman syndrome is caused by a maternal deletion (70-80 percent). In a few groups of patients, these syndromes are secondary to a uniparental disomy (20–30 percent) or mutations of the footprint center (1–2 percent). Patients with Prader-Willi syndrome often display moderate ID, hypotonia, neonatal growth retardation, marked hyperphagia, obesity, and autistic features in 25 percent of the cases (Veltman et al., 2005). Patients with Angelman syndrome are characterized by microcephaly, ataxia, seizures, severe ID and abnormal speech development. Some symptoms mimic those observed in patients with ASD. Maternally derived duplication of the same 15q11-q13 region is associated with autistic-like behavior. This duplication seems to be relatively frequent in patients with ASD, accounting for approximately 1 to 3 percent of cases (Bucan et al., 2009). The associated phenotype is characterized by epilepsy, hypotonia, muscle coordination problems, motor delay, moderate to severe ID as well as lack of language and severe hyperactivity.

Deletions/Duplications at 15q13.3

Sharp et al. were the first to describe a *de novo* 1.5Mb deletion in 15q13.3 in 2/757 individuals with mild to moderate ID and dysmorphic features (Sharp et al., 2008). Later, additional studies found the variation in 0.2 percent of patients with schizophrenia (Stefansson et al., 2008) but also in 1 percent of patients with idiopathic epilepsy (Helbig et al., 2009). Further studies reported recurrent deletions and duplications involving the 15q13.2-q13.3 region in multiple patients with ASD (Miller et al., 2009; Pagnamenta et al., 2009; Shen et al., 2010). Among the genes present in the critical region, *APBA2* plays a role in synaptic transmission and interacts directly with neurexins, which are neuronal cell adhesion molecules previously associated with autism (Szatmari et al., 2007). However, Babatz et al. were unable to detect any enrichment of nonsynonymous variants of *APBA2* in ASD patients compared with controls (Babatz et al., 2009). The *CHRNA*, coding for an alpha7 subunit of the nicotinic receptor could also be involved, specifically in patients with comorbid epilepsy. Cholinergic pathways have several important functions in the brain, and nicotinic acetylcholine receptors containing the alpha7 subunit are localized both pre- and post synaptically and are thought to modulate excitatory and inhibitory pathways (Steinlein and Bertrand, 2008).

Deletions/Duplications at 16p11.2

Deletions/duplications at 16p11.2 could be one of the most frequent CNVs associated with ASD (Kumar et al., 2008; Marshall et al., 2008; Weiss et al., 2008). Two groups nearly simultaneously found a significant association of recurrent *de novo* CNVs, including both microdeletion and duplication (Kumar et al., 2008; Weiss et al., 2008) at 16p11.2 in idiopathic ASD, reporting on partially overlapping samples. Marshall et al. confirmed these results, and found 16p11.2 chromosomal rearrangements in 4/427 ASD families but not in 1,762 controls (Marshall et al., 2008). Among the three other recent large-scale CNV studies, the 16p11.2 findings were not replicated due to a relative higher rate of 16p11.2 CNV in controls (Glessner et al., 2009), or were biased by an extensive sample overlap with the previously reported cases (Bucan et al., 2009; Pinto et al., 2010). Interestingly, a recent study a 4284 individuals with ID and multiple congenital anomalies found 16p11.2 CNVs in 0.3 percent of cases, consistent with that seen previously among ASD cohorts (Bijlsma et al., 2009), and providing further evidence for wide-ranging phenotypic manifestations emerging from 16p11.2 variations.

Deletions/Duplications at 22q11.2

Deletion at 22q11.2 occurs mostly *de novo* and encompasses 1.5-3 Mb of genomic DNA including 24 to 30 genes. With an incidence of approximately 1/4,000, this deletion is the underlying cause of the velocardiofacial syndrome (Oskarsdottir et al., 2004). This syndrome is characterized by congenital heart defects, velopharyngeal insufficiency, hypoparathyroidism, thymic aplasia or hypoplasia, craniofacial dysmorphism, learning difficulties and psychiatric disorders. A restricted number of patients with 22q11 deletions meet criteria for schizophrenia (2 percent) or ASD (1 percent) (Niklasson et al., 2009) (Karayiorgou et al., 2010). The reciprocal duplications of the 22q11 region could also represent a risk for autism (Chudley et al., 1998; Ogilvie et al., 2000) since 20 percent of patients carrying a 22q11 duplication have autism and the percentage rises to 40 percent if the complete autistic spectrum is considered (Fine et al., 2005; Vorstman et al., 2006; Niklasson and Gillberg, 2010).

The Neuroligins

NLGN3 and *NLGN4X* are X-linked genes that code for cell adhesion molecules at the postsynaptic side of the synapse and are mutated in rare cases of ASD. Neuroligins are major organizers of excitatory glutamatergic and inhibitory GABAergic synapses, contributing to the activity-dependent formation of neuronal circuits in mice (Sudhof, 2008). A frame-shift mutation in the *NLGN4X* has been identified in two brothers, one with autism and the other with Asperger syndrome (Jamain et al., 2003). In the same study, a non-synonymous mutation (R451C) of the X-linked *NLGN3*, was transmitted by their mothers to two affected boys. This mutation affected a highly conserved amino acid in the esterase domain. Both mutations were found to alter the function of the *NLGN3* and *NLGN4*, namely their ability to trigger synapse formation in cultured neuronal cells (Chih et al., 2004). Several laboratories replicated the original findings and identified new *NLGN* point mutations (Laumonnier et al., 2004) or deletions (Lawson-Yuen et al., 2008). In addition, a *de novo* mutation in the promoter of *NLGN4X*, increasing the transcript level of *NLGN4X*, has been reported in a boy with ASD (Daoud et al., 2009). Although independent mutations in *NLGN3* and *NLGN4X* have been identified and functionally validated as susceptibility factors for ASD, these mutations only concern a limited number of patients (less than 1 percent) (Vincent et al., 2004; Gauthier et al., 2005; Blasi et al., 2006). Mutations within *NLGN4X* have also been associated with ID (Laumonnier et al., 2004) and with Gilles de la Tourette syndrome (Lawson-Yuen et al., 2008).

SHANK2, SHANK3 Variants and Deletions/Duplications at 22q13

The deletion of the terminal region of the long arm of chromosome 22 has been found in 3 percent to 6 percent of cases of ASD (Phelan, 2008). The phenotype associated with these deletions is variable, generally characterized by global developmental delay, normal to accelerated growth, absent to severely delayed speech, and minor dysmorphic features (Cusmano-Ozog et al., 2007; Phelan, 2008). Up to 44 percent of these children meet ASD criteria. Reciprocal duplication of the same region has also been reported in a patient with Asperger syndrome, another with ADHD, and in several patients with schizophrenia (Durand et al., 2007; Gauthier et al., 2010). *SHANK3*, located in the deletion and coding for a scaffolding protein at the postsynaptic density of glutamatergic synapses, has been reported to be the causative gene. *De novo* deleterious mutations affecting *SHANK3* have been repeatedly reported in ASD (Gauthier et al., 2010; Durand et al., 2007; Moessner et al., 2007; Pinto et al., 2010) and could affect more than 1 to 2 percent of ASD patients (Durand et al., 2007; Berkel et al., 2010). Functional experiments in cultured neurons indicate that both *de novo* and inherited mutations are associated with a reduction of synaptic density at dendrites (Durand et al., 2007). Recently, *de novo SHANK3* mutations have been associated with schizophrenia (Gauthier et al., 2010) and *de novo* deletions of *SHANK2* located at 11q13 reported in patients with ID or ASD (Berkel et al., 2010; Pinto et al., 2010).

CNTNAP2 Variants

CNTNAP2 variants were originally identified in Amish individuals diagnosed with recessive cortical dysplasia-focal epilepsy syndrome (CDFE) and language regression (Strauss et al., 2006). Notably, two-thirds of the affected individuals also met criteria for ASD. Especially when the carboxy-terminal of *CNTNAP2* is truncated, *CNTNAP2* mutations are associated with severe autism with medication-insensitive temporal lobe seizures, language regression and low IQ. Following this initial report, several independent studies showed that chromosomal alterations, rare single base-pair mutations, as well as common variation in *CNTNAP2*, all might contribute to ASD. Bakkaloglu et al. reported a *de novo* 7q35 inversion that disrupted *CNTNAP2* in a child with autistic features (Bakkaloglu et al., 2008). They also sequenced the coding part of this gene in 635 patients with ASD and 942 control individuals. Thirteen rare variants were identified in affected cases and of these eight were predicted to be deleterious. These variants were roughly twice as frequent in patients as in control subjects. One variant (I869T) was found in four affected individuals from three different families, but was not present in two thousand controls. In mice *CNTNAP2* is differentially expressed in distinct neuronal structures, including the soma and dendrites, and in specific short-segmented pairs along myelinated axons (Coman et al., 2006). Its expression in myelinated nerves is mostly confined to the axon at the juxtaparanodal region and to some isolated paranodal loops. Therefore, patients carrying mutations in *CNTNAP2* might have slight to severe alterations of neurotransmission velocity. In addition to their scaffolding roles at the nodes of Ranvier, *CNTNAP2* could also be involved in cortical histogenesis and may mediate intercellular interactions during latter phases of neuroblast migration, laminar organization or axonal pathfinding (Abrahams et al., 2007).

NRXN1 Variants

Another susceptibility protein which was identified within the Neuroligin pathway is *NRXN1*, the pre-synaptic binding partner of NLGNs. *NRXN1* is located in chromosome 2p16 and codes for the long Neurexin α and the short Neurexin β forms. In humans, the first *NRXN1* alteration was identified in a seven-year-old boy with an IQ of 74 and a complex psychiatric phenotype including attention deficit disorder and Asperger syndrome (Zahir et al., 2008). The patient carried a *de novo* 320kb deletion of *NRXN1* that removes the promoter and first exon of *NRXN1a*, but apparently does not affect *NRXN1b*. The second *NRXN1* genetic alteration was detected using a whole genome approach performed by the Autism Genome Project Consortium that investigated 1168 multiplex families for the presence of small genomic alterations or copy number variants (CNV) (Szatmari et al., 2007). This analysis detected a *de novo* deletion in the *NRXN1* gene, removing several exons from both the *NRXN1α* and *NRXN1β*, in two sisters with typical ASD. More recently, two cases with ASD harbouring translocations within or near *NRXN1* have been identified (Kim et al., 2008). The first was a female with ASD carrying a paternally inherited translocation that directly disrupts *NRXN1α* within intron 5. The second case was a male patient carrying a *de novo* translocation with a breakpoint at about 750 kb of the *NRXN1* gene. Following these reports, a mutation screening of the *NRXN1* coding sequence was performed in two cohorts of ASD subjects (Kim et al., 2008). A number of rare variants altering evolutionary conserved residues were identified. However, as for some translocations, these point mutations were inherited from healthy parents, indicating that other factors are also involved in producing ASD. In addition, like *NLGN4X*, the phenotypes associated with *NRXN1* mutations are not specific to ASD. Indeed, one deletion which partially overlaps with the first deletion described in an ASD patient, was identified in two siblings with schizophrenia and in their asymptomatic mother (Kirov et al., 2009).

COMMON VARIANTS AS RISK FACTORS FOR ASD

GWAS detect disease-related alleles that are relatively common (more than 5 percent). Thus, the effect sizes conferred by such common alleles are typically small, with odds ratios mainly in the range of 1.1 to 1.5 (Altshuler et al., 2008). Detection of low-risk alleles requires large samples, and the statistical significance needs to be corrected for the large number of tests performed (Consortium, 2007). Three independent large scale GWAS in ASD have been conducted each one in 1000–3000 cases in a family-based analysis. The absence of strong replication of the results in the three large GWAS makes these genetic associations difficult to interpret. However, the susceptibility genes could be of interest for understanding the risk of ASD conferred by common variants present in the general population.

Cadherin 9 (CDH9) and Cadherin 10 (CDH19), at 5q14.1

Wang et al. genotyped 550,000 SNPs in an initial group of 780 independent families with ASD (3,101 subjects) and a second cohort of 1,204 patients with ASD and 6,491 controls (Wang et al., 2009). Using both a transmission disequilibrium test (TDT) and a case control study, a significant association was observed between ASD and rs4307059 located in the 5p14.1 region reaching GWAS significance (p=3.4 x 10^{-8}; OR=1.19), but also with five additional SNPs in the same locus (p < 10^{-4}). These results were replicated, but with higher statistical significance P values, in two additional cohorts of 447 families with ASD and of 108 patients with ASD and their 540 genetically matched controls. Closer examination of the 5p14.1 region indicated that all these SNPs were located in the same LD block, in an intergenic region between *CDH9* and *CDH10*. Both genes code for transmembrane proteins that modulate Ca^{2+} dependant cell-cell adhesion. Finally, Wang et al. tried to compare their data with the two GWAS previously mentioned (see above), despite a low power to replicate them. They did not obtain additional evidence for either of the top findings from the two previous GWAS.

SEMA5A and TAS2R1, at 5p15.2

Weiss et al. performed a high throughput analysis by using Affymetrix 5.0 and Affymetrix 500K platforms allowing them to explore more than 500,000 SNPs (Weiss et al., 2009). The study was performed on a large set of patients including 1,031 multiplex ASD families with 4,233 subjects. The authors were unable to detect any associations reaching the GWAS significance. Also, looking at the allele reported to be associated with ASD in the Wang et al. article (see above); they were again unable to replicate the finding. However, genotyping of top hits in an additional sample of 90 unrelated ASD cases and 1,476 controls revealed a suggestive association (p < 2.5 x 10^{-7}) with SNP (rs10513025) located in chromosome 5p15, in the intergenic region between *SEMA5A* and *TAS2R1* genes. A decrease of *SEMA5A* mRNA level was observed in the brain of patients with ASD compared with controls (Weiss et al., 2009) as previously shown for B lymphoblastoid cell lines (Melin et al., 2006; Weiss et al., 2009). Semaphorins are membrane or secreted proteins that regulate axon outgrowth and pruning, synaptogenesis and the density and maturation of dendritic spines (Pasterkamp and Giger, 2009).

MACROD2, at 20p12.1

Anney et al. performed a family-based association study on 1,369 families with ASD (Anney et al., 2010). They detected a cluster of SNPs falling in a 300kb intronic region of *MACROD2*, with the strongest association occurring for rs4141463 (p=2.1x10^{-8}). Using additional cases and control samples, the estimated odds ratio ranged from 0.56 to 0.65 (95 percent CI, 0.57-0.75) with a p=4.7x10^{-8}. The function of *MACROD2* is largely unknown, but it contains a MACRO domain, which is a high-affinity

ADP-ribose-binding domain of important for multiple biological processes. In addition, CNVs in *MACROD2* have also been recently reported in schizophrenia (Bradley et al., 2010).

CONCLUSIONS AND PERSPECTIVES

Many problems have strongly hampered the identification of causative genes in ASD: a high degree of genetic heterogeneity, a polygenic or oligogenic mode of inheritance and the presence of significant gene-gene and gene-environment interactions. Despite these difficulties, several genes have been identified providing significant information on this complex spectrum. The recent identification of rare variants that confer a high risk for ASD has shed a new light in the field. Indeed, they delineate biological pathways that could be altered in patients with ASD (Toro et al., 2010). For example, genetic mutations seem to affect synaptic development. As mentioned previously, synaptic cell adhesion molecules such as *NLGNs* and *NRXNs* and scaffolding proteins (e.g. *SHANK2* and *SHANK3*) contribute to the development of neuronal circuits (Graf et al., 2004; Sudhof, 2008; Bourgeron, 2009). In addition, proteins related to axonal growth and synaptic identity, (e.g. *CNTNAP2, SEMA5A, CDH*), are suspected of having a role in ASD. Finally, genes regulating synaptic protein levels (e. g. *FMR1, MECP2, PTEN, TSC1/2, NF1*) could also be involved in the etiology of ASD (Glessner et al., 2009). Taken together, this large number of genes associated with ASD suggests that ASD could result from an alteration of synaptic homeostasis (Ramocki and Zoghbi, 2008). Indeed, neurons are under especially tight homeostatic constraints, and have to keep an optimal level of activity despite the global changes in the overall activity of the network.

In summary, the improvement in genomic technologies, such as exomes or whole genome sequence, will certainly shed light on new genes/pathways associated with ASD and on the epistasis between rare and common variants. The recent one thousand genome project estimates that around fifteen to two hundred deleterious mutations are present in one genome (Durbin et al., 2010). Furthermore, the occurrence of *de novo* mutations could explain an additional proportion of ASD cases, as shown recently for ID (Vissers et al., 2010). Beyond technology, only a tight collaboration between clinicians, neurobiologists and molecular geneticists will allow us to understand the complex genotype-phenotype relationship in ASD. Specifically, larger and well-characterized samples will be required to detect subtle effects on relative risk.

REFERENCES

Abrahams, B. S., Tentler, D., Perederiy, J. V., Oldham, M. C., Coppola, G., and Geschwind, D. H. (2007) Genome-wide analyses of human perisylvian cerebral cortical patterning. *Proceedings of the National Academy of Sciences of the United States of America, 104,* 17849–54.

Altshuler, D., Daly, M. J., and Lander, E. S. (2008) Genetic mapping in human disease. *Science, 322,* 881–88.

Anney, R., et al. (2010) A genome-wide scan for common alleles affecting risk for autism. *Human molecular genetics, 19,* 4072–82.

Babatz, T. D., Kumar, R. A., Sudi, J., Dobyns, W. B., and Christian, S. L. (2009) Copy number and sequence variants implicate APBA2 as an autism candidate gene. *Autism Res, 2,* 359–64.

Bakkaloglu, B., O'Roak, B. J., Louvi, A., Gupta, A. R., Abelson, J. F., Morgan, T. M., Chawarska, K., Klin, A., Ercan-Sencicek, A. G., Stillman, A. A., Tanriover, G., Abrahams, B. S., Duvall, J. A., Robbins, E. M., Geschwind, D. H., Biederer, T., Gunel, M., Lifton, R. P., and State M. W. (2008) Molecular cytogenetic analysis and resequencing of contactin associated protein-like 2 in autism spectrum disorders. *American journal of human genetics, 82,* 165–73.

Berkel, S., Marshall, C. R., Weiss, B., Howe, J., Roeth, R., Moog, U., Endris, V., Roberts, W., Szatmari, P., Pinto, D., Bonin, M., Riess, A., Engels, H., Sprengel, R., Scherer, S. W., and Rappold, G. A. (2010) Mutations in the SHANK2 synaptic scaffolding gene in autism spectrum disorder and mental retardation. *Nature genetics, 42,* 489–91.

Bijlsma, E. K. et al. (2009) Extending the phenotype of recurrent rearrangements of 16p11.2: deletions in mentally retarded patients without autism and in normal individuals. *European journal of medical genetics, 52,* 77–87.

Blasi, F., Bacchelli, E., Pesaresi, G., Carone, S., Bailey, A. J., Maestrini, E. (2006) Absence of coding mutations in the X-linked genes neuroligin 3 and neuroligin 4 in individuals with autism from the IMGSAC collection. *Am J Med Genet B Neuropsychiatr Genet, 141B,* 220–21.

Bolton, P., Macdonald, H., Pickles, A., Rios, P., Goode, S., Crowson, M., Bailey, A., Rutter, M. (1994) A case-control family history study of autism. *Journal of child psychology and psychiatry, and allied disciplines, 35,* 877–900.

Bourgeron, T. (2009) A synaptic trek to autism. Current opinion in neurobiology 19, 231–234.

Bradley, W. E., Raelson, J. V., Dubois, D. Y., Godin, E., Fournier, H., Prive, C., Allard, R., Pinchuk, V., Lapalme, M., Paulussen, R. J., Belouchi, A. (2010) Hotspots of large rare deletions in the human genome. *PloS one, 5,*e9401.

Brunetti-Pierri, N., et al. (2008) Recurrent reciprocal 1q21.1 deletions and duplications associated with microcephaly or macrocephaly and developmental and behavioral abnormalities. *Nature genetics, 40,* 1466–71.

Bucan, M., et al. (2009) Genome-wide analyses of exonic copy number variants in a family-based study point to novel autism susceptibility genes. *PLoS genetics, 5,* e1000536.

Chih, B., Afridi, S. K., Clark, L., Scheiffele, P. (2004) Disorder-associated mutations lead to functional inactivation of neuroligins. *Human molecular genetics, 13,* 1471–77.

Chudley, A. E., Gutierrez, E., Jocelyn, L. J., Chodirker, B. N. (1998) Outcomes of genetic evaluation in children with pervasive developmental disorder. *J Dev Behav Pediatr, 19,* 321–25.

Coman, I., Aigrot, M. S., Seilhean, D., Reynolds, R., Girault, J. A., Zalc, B., and Lubetzki, C. (2006) Nodal, paranodal and juxtaparanodal axonal proteins during demyelination and remyelination in multiple sclerosis. *Brain, 129,* 3186–95.

Consortium WTCC (2007) Genome-wide association study of 14,000 cases of seven common diseases and 3,000 shared controls. *Nature, 447,* 661–78.

Cusmano-Ozog, K., Manning, M. A., and Hoyme, H. E. (2007) 22q13.3 deletion syndrome: a recognizable malformation syndrome associated with marked speech and language delay. *Am J Med Genet C Semin Med Genet, 145C,* 393–98.

Daoud, H., Bonnet-Brilhault, F., Vedrine, S., Demattei, M. V., Vourc'h, P., Bayou, N., Andres, C. R., Barthelemy, C., Laumonnier, F., and Briault, S. (2009) Autism and nonsyndromic mental retardation associated with a de novo mutation in the NLGN4X gene promoter causing an increased expression level. *Biological psychiatry, 66,* 906–10.

Durand, C. M., et al. (2007) Mutations in the gene encoding the synaptic scaffolding protein SHANK3 are associated with autism spectrum disorders. Nature genetics 39, 25–27.

Durbin, R. M., Abecasis, G. R., Altshuler, D. L., Auton, A., Brooks, L. D., Durbin, R. M., Gibbs, R. A., Hurles, M. E., and McVean, G. A. (2010) A map of human genome variation from population-scale sequencing. *Nature, 467,* 1061–73.

Fernell, E., and Gillberg, C. (2010) Autism spectrum disorder diagnoses in Stockholm preschoolers. *Research in developmental disabilities, 31,* 680–85.

Fine, S. E., Weissman, A., Gerdes, M., Pinto-Martin, J., Zackai, E. H., McDonald-McGinn, D. M., Emanuel, B. S. (2005) Autism spectrum disorders and symptoms in children with molecularly confirmed 22q11.2 deletion syndrome. *Journal of autism and developmental disorders, 35,* 461–70.

Fombonne, E. (2005) Epidemiology of autistic disorder and other pervasive developmental disorders. *The Journal of clinical psychiatry, 66,* Suppl 10, 3–8.

Freitag, C. M. (2007) The genetics of autistic disorders and its clinical relevance: a review of the literature. *Molecular psychiatry, 12,* 2–22.

Gauthier, J., Bonnel, A., St-Onge, J., Karemera, L., Laurent, S., Mottron, L., Fombonne, E., Joober, R., and Rouleau, G. A. (2005) NLGN3/NLGN4 gene mutations are not responsible for autism in the Quebec population. *Am J Med Genet B Neuropsychiatr Genet, 132B,* 74–75.

Gauthier, J., et al. (2010) De novo mutations in the gene encoding the synaptic scaffolding protein SHANK3 in patients ascertained for schizophrenia. *Proceedings of the National Academy of Sciences of the United States of America, 107,* 7863–68.

Glessner, J. T., et al. (2009) Autism genome-wide copy number variation reveals ubiquitin and neuronal genes. *Nature, 459,* 569–73.

Graf, E. R., Zhang, X., Jin, S. X., Linhoff, M. W., and Craig, A. M. (2004) Neurexins induce differentiation of GABA and glutamate postsynaptic specializations via neuroligins. *Cell, 119,* 1013–26.

Helbig, I., et al. (2009) 15q13.3 microdeletions increase risk of idiopathic generalized epilepsy. *Nature genetics, 41*, 160–62.

Jacquemont, M. L., Sanlaville, D., Redon, R., Raoul, O., Cormier-Daire, V., Lyonnet,
S., Amiel, J., Le Merrer, M., Heron, D., de Blois, M. C., Prieur, M., Vekemans, M.,
Carter, N. P., Munnich, A., Colleaux, L., and Philippe, A. (2006) Array-based comparative genomic hybridisation identifies high frequency of cryptic chromosomal
rearrangements in patients with syndromic autism spectrum disorders. *Journal of
medical genetics, 43*, 843–849.

Jamain, S., Quach, H., Betancur, C., Rastam, M., Colineaux, C., Gillberg, I. C.,
Soderstrom, H., Giros, B., Leboyer, M., Gillberg, C., and Bourgeron, T. (2003)
Mutations of the X-linked genes encoding neuroligins NLGN3 and NLGN4 are
associated with autism. *Nature genetics, 34*, 27–29.

Karayiorgou, M., Simon, T. J., and Gogos, J. A. (2010) 22q11.2 microdeletions:
linking DNA structural variation to brain dysfunction and schizophrenia. *Nat Rev
Neurosci, 11*, 402–16.

Kim, H. G., et al. (2008) Disruption of neurexin 1 associated with autism spectrum
disorder. *American journal of human genetics, 82*, 199–207.

Kirov, G., Rujescu, D., Ingason, A., Collier, D. A., O'Donovan, M. C., and Owen, M.
J. (2009) Neurexin 1 (NRXN1) deletions in schizophrenia. *Schizophrenia bulletin,
35*, 851–54.

Kumar, R. A., KaraMohamed, S., Sudi, J., Conrad, D. F., Brune, C., Badner, J. A.,
Gilliam, T. C., Nowak, N. J., Cook, E. H., Jr., Dobyns, W. B., and Christian, S. L.
(2008) Recurrent 16p11.2 microdeletions in autism. *Human molecular genetics,
17*, 628–38.

Laumonnier, F., Bonnet-Brilhault, F., Gomot, M., Blanc, R., David, A., Moizard, M.
P., Raynaud, M., Ronce, N., Lemonnier, E., Calvas, P., Laudier, B., Chelly, J., Fryns,
J. P., Ropers, H. H., Hamel, B. C., Andres, C., Barthelemy, C., Moraine, C., and
Briault, S. (2004) X-linked mental retardation and autism are associated with a
mutation in the NLGN4 gene, a member of the neuroligin family. *American jour-
nal of human genetics, 74*, 552–57.

Lawson-Yuen, A., Saldivar, J. S., Sommer, S., Picker, J. (2008) Familial deletion
within NLGN4 associated with autism and Tourette syndrome. *Eur J Hum Genet,
16*, 614–18.

Lichtenstein, P., Carlstrom, E., Rastam, M., Gillberg, C., and Anckarsater, H. (2010)
The genetics of autism spectrum disorders and related neuropsychiatric disorders
in childhood. *The American journal of psychiatry, 167*, 1357–63.

Marshall, C. R., et al. (2008) Structural variation of chromosomes in autism spectrum disorder. *American journal of human genetics, 82*, 477–88.

Mefford, H. C., et al. (2008) Recurrent rearrangements of chromosome 1q21.1 and
variable pediatric phenotypes. *The New England journal of medicine, 359*, 1685–99.

Melin, M., Carlsson, B., Anckarsater, H., Rastam, M., Betancur, C., Isaksson, A.,
Gillberg, C., and Dahl, N. (2006) Constitutional downregulation of SEMA5A
expression in autism. *Neuropsychobiology, 54*, 64–69.

Miller, D. T. et al. (2009) Microdeletion/duplication at 15q13.2q13.3 among individuals with features of autism and other neuropsychiatric disorders. *Journal of
medical genetics, 46*, 242–48.

Moessner, R., Marshall, C. R., Sutcliffe, J. S., Skaug, J., Pinto, D., Vincent, J., Zwaigenbaum, L., Fernandez, B., Roberts, W., Szatmari, P., and Scherer, S. W. (2007) Contribution of SHANK3 mutations to autism spectrum disorder. *Am J Hum Genet, 81*, 1289–97.

Niklasson, L., and Gillberg, C. (2010) The neuropsychology of 22q11 deletion syndrome. A neuropsychiatric study of 100 individuals. *Research in developmental disabilities, 31*, 185–94.

Niklasson, L., Rasmussen, P., Oskarsdottir, S., and Gillberg, C (2009) Autism, ADHD, mental retardation and behavior problems in 100 individuals with 22q11 deletion syndrome. *Research in developmental disabilities, 30*, 763–73.

Ogilvie, C. M., Moore, J., Daker, M., Palferman, S., and Docherty, Z. (2000) Chromosome 22q11 deletions are not found in autistic patients identified using strict diagnostic criteria. IMGSAC. International Molecular Genetics Study of Autism Consortium. *American journal of medical genetics, 96*, 15–17.

Oskarsdottir, S., Vujic, M., and Fasth, A. (2004) Incidence and prevalence of the 22q11 deletion syndrome: a population-based study in Western Sweden. *Archives of disease in childhood, 89*, 148–51.

Pagnamenta, A. T., Wing, K., Sadighi Akha, E., Knight, S. J., Bolte, S., Schmotzer, G., Duketis, E., Poustka, F., Klauck, S. M., Poustka, A., Ragoussis, J., Bailey, A. J., and Monaco, A. P. (2009) A 15q13.3 microdeletion segregating with autism. *Eur J Hum Genet, 17*, 687–92.

Pasterkamp, R. J., and Giger, R. J. (2009) Semaphorin function in neural plasticity and disease. *Current opinion in neurobiology, 19*, 263–74.

Phelan, M. C. (2008) Deletion 22q13.3 syndrome. Orphanet journal of rare diseases 3, 14.

Pinto, D. et al. (2010) Functional impact of global rare copy number variation in autism spectrum disorders. *Nature, 466*, 368–72.

Ramocki, M. B., and Zoghbi, H. Y. (2008) Failure of neuronal homeostasis results in common neuropsychiatric phenotypes. *Nature, 455*, 912–918.

Redon, R. et al. (2006) Global variation in copy number in the human genome. *Nature, 444*, 444–54.

Sebat, J. et al. (2007) Strong association of de novo copy number mutations with autism. *Science, 316*, 445–49.

Sharp, A. J. et al. (2008) A recurrent 15q13.3 microdeletion syndrome associated with mental retardation and seizures. *Nature genetics, 40*, 322–28.

Shen, Y. et al. (2010) Clinical genetic testing for patients with autism spectrum disorders. *Pediatrics, 125*, e727–35.

Stefansson, H. et al. (2008) Large recurrent microdeletions associated with schizophrenia. *Nature, 455*, 232–36.

Steinlein, O. K., and Bertrand, D. (2008) Neuronal nicotinic acetylcholine receptors: from the genetic analysis to neurological diseases. *Biochemical pharmacology, 76*, 1175–83.

Strauss, K. A., Puffenberger, E. G., Huentelman, M. J., Gottlieb, S., Dobrin, S. E., Parod, J. M., Stephan, D. A., and Morton, D. H. (2006) Recessive symptomatic focal epilepsy and mutant contactin-associated protein-like 2. *The New England journal of medicine, 354*, 1370–77.

Sudhof, T. C. (2008) Neuroligins and neurexins link synaptic function to cognitive disease. *Nature, 455*, 903–11.

Szatmari, P., et al. (2007) Mapping autism risk loci using genetic linkage and chromosomal rearrangements. *Nature genetics, 39*, 319–28.

Toro, R., Konyukh, M., Delorme, R., Leblond, C., Chaste, P., Fauchereau, F., Coleman, M., Leboyer, M., Gillberg, C., and Bourgeron, T. (2010) Key role for gene dosage and synaptic homeostasis in autism spectrum disorders. *Trends Genet, 26*, 363–72.

Veltman, M. W., Thompson, R. J., Craig, E. E., Dennis, N. R., Roberts, S. E., Moore, V., Brown, J. A., and Bolton, P. F. (2005) A paternally inherited duplication in the Prader-Willi/Angelman syndrome critical region: a case and family study. *Journal of autism and developmental disorders, 35*, 117–27.

Vincent, J. B., Kolozsvari, D., Roberts, W. S., Bolton, P. F., Gurling, H. M., and Scherer, S. W. (2004) Mutation screening of X-chromosomal neuroligin genes: no mutations in 196 autism probands. *Am J Med Genet B Neuropsychiatr Genet, 129B*, 82–84.

Vissers, L. E., de Ligt, J., Gilissen, C., Janssen, I., Steehouwer, M., de Vries, P., van Lier, B., Arts, P., Wieskamp, N., Del Rosario, M., van Bon, B. W., Hoischen, A., de Vries, B. B., Brunner, H. G., and Veltman, J. A. (2010) A de novo paradigm for mental retardation. *Nature genetics, 42*, 1109–12.

Vorstman, J. A., Morcus, M. E., Duijff, S. N., Klaassen, P. W., Heineman-de Boer, J. A., Beemer, F. A., Swaab, H., Kahn, R. S., and van Engeland, H. (2006) The 22q11.2 deletion in children: high rate of autistic disorders and early onset of psychotic symptoms. *Journal of the American Academy of Child and Adolescent Psychiatry, 45*, 1104–13.

Wang, K., et al. (2009) Common genetic variants on 5p14.1 associate with autism spectrum disorders. *Nature, 459*, 528–33.

Weiss, L. A., Arking, D. E., Daly, M. J., and Chakravarti, A. (2009) A genome-wide linkage and association scan reveals novel loci for autism. *Nature, 461*, 802–8.

Weiss, L. A. et al. (2008) Association between microdeletion and microduplication at 16p11.2 and autism. *The New England journal of medicine, 358*, 667–75.

Zahir, F. R., Baross, A., Delaney, A. D., Eydoux, P., Fernandes, N. D., Pugh, T., Marra, M. A., and Friedman, J. M. (2008) A patient with vertebral, cognitive and behavioural abnormalities and a de novo deletion of NRXN1alpha. *Journal of medical genetics, 45*, 239–43.

II

INDIVIDUAL DISORDERS/PROBLEMS

Updates

5

Obsessive-Compulsive Disorder

Luisa Lázaro and Josep Toro

INTRODUCTION

Obsessive-compulsive disorder (OCD) is a heterogeneous disorder characterized by the presence of distressing intrusive thoughts, impulses, fears or images (obsessions), and/or repetitive behaviours or mental rituals (compulsions). Epidemiological studies indicate that it affects between 1 percent and 4 percent of children and adolescents (Douglass et al., 1995; Flament et al., 1998; Nestadt et al., 2000; Rapoport et al., 2000). Although the median age at OCD onset is 19 years, around 21 percent of cases are diagnosed around the age of ten (Kessler et al., 2005). At least one-third of adults with OCD report that their symptoms began during childhood or adolescence (Rassmussen and Eisen, 1990).

OCD often has a chronic course and the long-term prognosis is poor. One meta-analysis found a persistence rate of 41 percent for full OCD and 60 percent for full or sub-threshold OCD (Stewart et al., 2004). A more recent nine-year follow-up study confirmed the persistence rate of 41 percent, and also highlighted that 40 percent of patients presented other psychiatric disorders in addition to OCD (Micali et al., 2010). Functional impairment and quality of life were reported to be mildly to moderately affected, with approximately 50 percent of patients still receiving treatment and about 50 percent saying they felt a need for further treatment. Thus, although around half the cases of OCD that onset in childhood or adolescence tend to remit, a high percentage of individuals continue to suffer into adulthood. The most severe cases are highly dysfunctional and incapacitating.

The dysfunctions and maladaptive behaviour of children with OCD are produced or aggravated by the high rate of comorbidity with tic disorders, including Tourette's syndrome (TS), and attention deficit hyperactivity disorder (ADHD). Longitudinally the presence of tics in childhood usually predicts the subsequent appearance and/or aggravation of OCD in adolescence and young adulthood (Peterson et al., 2001). These three diagnoses, i.e., OCD, TS and ADHD, correspond to three neurodevelopmental disorders whose aetiology shares a common denominator, namely anomalies in cortical-striatal-thalamic-cortical circuitry. The association between the three disorders can be explained by the genetic correlation between OCD and TS, on the one hand, and between OCD and ADHD on the other; however, it should be noted that the latter two disorders also share environmental factors (Mathews and Grados, 2011). In this context, one latent class analysis showed that the comorbid class Tourette's syndrome + OCD + ADHD presents high heritability (0.65), suggesting a genetic determinant for a neuropsychiatric vulnerability (Grados and Mathews, 2008).

The association with tic disorders significantly differentiates childhood-onset from adult-onset OCD (Geller et al., 1998; Rosario-Campos et al., 2001). Other significant differences have also been described, since childhood OCD is associated with a predominance of males, shows high familial aggregation (for both OCD and tics), and is frequently comorbid with externalizing disorders; furthermore, children with OCD have more compulsions that resemble tics and respond less well to anti-obsessional psychoactive drugs. These findings led Geller et al. (1998) to suggest that juvenile OCD could be a developmental subtype of the disorder. This question remains open to debate.

GENETICS OF OBSESSIVE-COMPULSIVE DISORDER

Genetic research in relation to OCD has made significant advances over the last ten years.

Family History

Family aggregation studies of OCD provided the first evidence of a genetic component to the pathogenesis of the disorder. Pauls et al. (1995) found a significantly higher rate of OCD (10.3 percent vs. 1.9 percent) and subclinical OCD (7.9 percent vs. 2.0 percent) among first-degree relatives of subjects with OCD than among relatives of control subjects. The first controlled family study to be conducted in Europe also revealed significant differences between relatives of probands and controls: 10.3 percent vs. 5.6 percent in OCD and 15.4 percent vs. 4.1 percent in subclinical OCD (Grabe et al., 2006). An earlier meta-analysis had already indicated an aggregate risk of 8.3 percent and an odds ratio of 4.0 for first-degree relatives of probands with OCD (Hettema et al., 2001).

Studies of twins with OCD have found significant differences in the concordance rates of monozygotic and dizygotic twins: 80 percent vs. 20 percent (Inouye, 1965) and 87 percent vs. 47 percent (Carey and Gottesmann, 1981). Of particular interest in this regard is the role played by genetics and the environment in relation to the presence of obsessive-compulsive symptoms during childhood and adolescence. Using the Obsessive-Compulsive Scale of the Child Behaviour Checklist in twins aged seven, ten, and twelve years, the genetic influence has been estimated to be between 45 percent and 58 percent, while non-shared environmental influences were between 42 percent and 55 percent; shared environmental influences only became significant (16 percent) at twelve years of age (Hudziak et al., 2004). Genetic factors contribute significantly to obsessive-compulsive symptoms at twelve, fourteen, and sixteen years of age, although the variation in symptom liability rises from 27 percent at age twelve to 57 percent and 54 percent at ages fourteen and sixteen, respectively (van Grootheest et al., 2008). Therefore, the heritability of obsessive-compulsive symptoms was estimated to be around 55 percent, but it was lower at around age twelve. It is worth noting that in the study by Hudziak et al. (2004) shared environmental influences only became significant (16 percent) at twelve years of age, their influence being weaker at younger and older ages. This raises the question as to whether this phenomenon is related to the onset of puberty that usually occurs around this age.

In cases of compulsive hoarding, genetic factors explain approximately 50 percent of the variance, the remainder being explained almost entirely by nonshared environmental influences (Iervolino et al., 2009). However, this is only the case in male patients, despite the fact that the rate of hoarding among females tends to be twice as high.

A poor therapeutic response to a treatment of proven efficacy is indicative of a severe disorder. It has been shown that youths with a family history of OCD are unlikely to benefit from cognitive behavioural therapy (CBT), when compared with patients without such a family history, the effect size being six-fold lower (Garcia et al., 2010). This suggests that the genetic load increases the severity of paediatric OCD.

Possible Familial Biomarkers

Over the last decade various studies have sought to detect possible functional or anatomical brain anomalies in the relatives of OCD patients, the aim being to trace the familial transmission of predisposition to the disorder. In patients with OCD research has shown white matter anomalies, especially in parietal and frontal regions, which are similar to those found in unaffected first-degree relatives, thereby suggesting that they could be considered as white matter endophenotypes for OCD (Menzies et al., 2008). The oligodendrocytes are responsible for the production of white matter (myelin) and the OLIG2 gene is required for the development of oligodendrocytes. A study in a sample of relatives of OCD patients demonstrated an association between the OLIG2 gene and OCD, suggesting a link between these two factors and the white matter anomalies observed in OCD (Stewart et al., 2007).

Research using reversal learning tasks has shown, in both patients with OCD and their unaffected first-degree relatives, reduced activation in various cortical regions including the lateral orbitofrontal cortex, indicating the possible existence of an underlying endophenotype (Chamberlain et al., 2008).

Molecular Genetics

Studies have been conducted of numerous candidate genes associated with different neurotransmitters: serotonin (SERT, HTR1D, HTR2A and HTR2C), dopamine (DRD4), glutamate (SLC1A1, GRIN2B and *Sapap3*), those involved in metabolism (COMT, MAOA and TPH1), and those involved in neurodevelopment (BDNF, OLIG2 and MOG). For almost all these genes there are studies which have reported an association with OCD, although these are counterbalanced by other studies showing dissimilar results (see the reviews by Grados, 2010; Walitza et al., 2010). Special mention should be made of SLC1A1, a glutamate transporter gene that plays a key role in brain development. In relation to OCD there are six studies that propose it to be a significant positional candidate gene, as well as a positive candidate gene (Grados, 2010). However, some variants of SLC1A1 associated with OCD seem to be transmitted to male but not to female offspring (Arnold et al., 2006). Furthermore, the 3' region of SCL1A1 may contain a susceptibility allele associated precisely with early-onset OCD, with differential effects in males and females (Dickel et al., 2006). Taken together, these findings seem to support a role for dysfunctions of the glutamatergic system in the pathogenesis of OCD, especially as regards early-onset OCD.

As regards the compulsive hoarding phenotype, research has identified a region on chromosome 14 that is linked to this compulsion in families with OCD (Samuels et al., 2007).

After reviewing the available evidence Walitza et al. (2010) suggested that the gene-environment interaction in the pathogenesis of OCD may include moderation by a functional polymorphism of the risk for developing OCD following exposure to a traumatic event, or an effect of a functional polymorphism on the development of a personality/neurocognitive profile that may predispose a person to OCD following environmental stress.

It should be noted that the majority of molecular genetic studies regarding family aggregation and history in relation to OCD have been conducted with adult probands. If childhood-onset OCD does indeed constitute a genetically distinct variant, then any conclusions reached will not be fully generalizable.

CEREBRAL SUBSTRATES

Structural Abnormalities

Neuroanatomical models of OCD propose that frontal-striatal and limbic circuits are involved in the mediation of symptoms. Structural studies have examined different regions of interest (ROIs). Research in adult OCD patients has shown significant reductions in the orbitofrontal cortex and amygdala (Szeszko et al., 1999), reduced (Robinson et al., 1995) or increased (Scarone et al., 1992) caudate nucleus, and no changes in regional brain volume (Kellner et al., 1991). These inconsistent results may, in part, be accounted for by clinical variables such as the heterogeneity of the patients included, differences in illness duration, exposure to psychoactive medication, and methodological differences between studies. When voxel-based morphometry (VBM) is used to investigate structural differences in the whole brain, adult studies have reported reduced grey matter (GM) in orbitofrontal regions, increased GM in striatal areas and the thalamus, and structural changes in the left inferior parietal lobe and the right supramarginal and angular gyri (Kim et al., 2001; Pujol et al., 2004; Valente et al., 2005; Gilbert et al., 2008; Yoo et al., 2008). These findings indicate that the frontal-subcortical circuitry is dysfunctional in OCD, but also the parietal cortex may play a role in the pathophysiology of this disease.

In children and adolescents with OCD, Rosenberg and Keshavan (1998) reported an increased volume of the anterior cingulate but not of the posterior cingulate cortex or the dorsolateral prefrontal cortex. There was also a correlation with obsession severity but not with compulsions. Later, with drug-naïve paediatric OCD patients, the same researchers reported increased GM in the anterior cingulate gyrus compared with controls, but found no differences in frontal regions. Therefore, it is possible that structural alterations in the anterior cingulate gyrus are specific to GM, at least at the gross anatomical level (Szeszko et al., 2004). These results support the hypothesis that abnormalities in the ventral prefrontal cortical-striatal anatomy may be associated with the clinical presentation of OCD.

As regards the striatum, a reduction in volume of the putamen but not the caudate nucleus was reported in paediatric patients with OCD (Rosenberg et al., 1997a). There was also an inverse correlation between symptom severity of obsessions (but not compulsions) and putamen volume. As a possible explanation the authors suggested an abnormality in the pruning of frontostriatal structures in OCD patients. Thus, the reductions in striatal volumes in early-onset OCD patients could represent an exaggeration of pruning or a reduction of neural brain elements.

Within the basal ganglia the globus pallidum has also been implicated in OCD neuroimaging. Smaller globus pallidum volumes were found in drug-naïve paediatric OCD patients than in healthy subjects, but there were no differences in the striatum (Szeszko et al., 2004). The globus pallidum has afferent connections from other regions implicated in the pathophysiology of OCD, such as the thalamus and striatum. Moreover, the orbital frontal lobe has connections with the ventromedial caudate and nucleus accumbens, which also project to the ventromedial globus pallidus. In a later longitudinal study, greater thalamic volumes were reported in treatment-naïve OCD paediatric patients (Gilbert et al., 2000). In addition to this, a decrease in thalamic volume was associated with a reduction in OCD symptom severity. It should also be noted that treatment studies using antidepressant drugs, specifically, selective serotonin reuptake inhibitors (SSRIs), have reported normalization of structural abnormalities in child and adolescent OCD patients, especially in the basal ganglia and thalamus.

Other studies have discussed different cerebral structures in early-onset OCD. For instance, one study showed that all of the corpus callosum regions except the isthmus were significantly associated with OCD symptom severity but not illness duration. The age-related increase in corpus callosum size seen in normal subjects was absent in OCD patients (Rosenberg et al., 1997b). In addition, the pituitary gland was significantly smaller in treatment-naïve paediatric OCD patients compared with controls, especially in males. There was also an inverse correlation between severity of compulsions (but not obsessions) and decreased volume (MacMaster et al., 2006). Decreased pituitary volume associated with increased OCD symptom severity in paediatric OCD patients suggests a potential effect of this dysregulation on pituitary volume. Reduced pituitary volume might therefore represent an early neurobiological marker of OCD, or may simply be an epiphenomenon of the underlying psychopathology of the illness (MacMaster et al., 2006).

When using VBM techniques with child and adolescent OCD patients, Carmona et al. (2007) found a statistically significant decrease in GM volume in frontal cortex but no increase in the basal ganglia region. The VBM analysis revealed decreased bilateral GM in frontal and cingulate regions, as well as decreased white matter (WM) in bilateral frontal and right parietal regions. This study also detected a significant negative correlation between scores on the Child Yale-Brown Obsessive-Compulsive Scale (CY-BOCS) and bilateral GM volumes in the parahippocampal region. The authors suggest that smaller bilateral hippocampi are more likely the result of neurodevelopmental damage than an illness-specific abnormality. It should be noted that this study differs from previous OCD structural studies in that it failed to observe basal ganglia deficits, possibly due to the shorter duration of illness in this sample. In another study of paediatric OCD patients Szeszko et al. (2008) showed significantly more GM in regions predicted to differ a priori between groups, including the right putamen and orbital frontal cortex. Among patients, more GM in the left putamen and right lateral orbital frontal cortex correlated significantly with greater OCD symptom severity, but not with anxiety or depression.

Lázaro et al. (2009), in an optimized VBM study, found lower GM volume in the parietal regions in the OCD group compared with control subjects. WM was also lower in the parietal lobe in the OCD group. In this longitudinal study, after six months of pharmacological treatment that revealed a clear clinical improvement, the authors observed increased GM volume in the OCD group in the areas which had previously been different (parietal lobes). The lateral parietal regions are involved in attention and dynamic aspects of executive functioning, inhibition, and visuo-spatial and non-verbal networks. Research has shown impairment in some of these functions in both adult and paediatric OCD patients (Andres et al., 2008). It may be that the parietal dysfunction interacts with frontal-subcortical circuits through an anatomical connection between parietal associative areas and the lateral orbitofrontal cortex, the striatum and the thalamic nucleus (Valente et al., 2005). As such, the parietal lobe should be a focus for further exploration of structural abnormalities in OCD, and these findings can be added to the growing body of evidence implicating parietal lobe dysfunction in the pathophysiology of OCD.

Functional Abnormalities

Some of the initial studies with 1H-MRI spectroscopy in OCD adult patients found lower N-acetyl-aspartate (NAA) levels related to the anterior cingulate and striatum (Ebert et al., 1997; Bartha et al., 1998), suggesting reduced neuronal density in these regions. More recently, it has been reported that adult patients with OCD showed reduced levels of neuronal NAA in the dorsal anterior cingulate region, which was negatively correlated with their blood oxygen level-dependent activation of the region (Yucel et al., 2007). Moreover, lower NAA concentrations in the anterior cingulate were also found but only in a subgroup of patients, namely responders to an SSRI in combination with an atypical antipsychotic (Sumitaki et al., 2007). In addition, after twelve weeks of SSRI treatment, the NAA level in the prefrontal cortex and frontal WM was found to have increased (Jang et al., 2006).

Studies that employed 1H-MRS techniques in OCD paediatric samples have reported contradictory results. A significant reduction in NAA was observed in both right and left medial thalami (Fitzgerald et al., 2000), and in the left medial thalamus this reduction was inversely correlated with increased OCD symptom severity. A later study observed a significant increase in NAA in the left but not the right dorsolateral prefrontal cortex in OCD patients versus control subjects (Russell et al., 2003), although no significant differences were found in choline (Cho) or creatine (Cr) levels in the left or right dorsolateral prefrontal cortex (Smith et al., 2003). Moreover, anterior cingulate glutamatergic concentrations were significantly reduced in OCD patients (and in patients with major depressive disorder) compared to controls (Rosenberg et al., 2004), and medial thalamic creatine-phosphocreatine concentrations were increased in untreated OCD patients (Mirza et al., 2006).

Possible metabolic changes after OCD treatments have also been studied in paediatric treatment-naïve OCD patients. Caudate glutamatergic concentrations were significantly greater compared to controls, but declined significantly after paroxetine treatment to levels comparable with those of controls. A decrease in caudate glutamate was associated with a decrease in OCD symptom severity (Rosenberg et al., 2000a). However, in a later study using a similar methodology no significant changes in caudate metabolites were observed in treatment-naïve children before and after twelve weeks of CBT (Benazon et al., 2003).

Functional neuroimaging studies have shown hyperactivity in the orbitofrontal and cingulate cortices, basal ganglia and thalamus (Whiteside et al., 2004). Interestingly, some functional neuroimaging studies have reported increased activation of these brain areas during the provocation of obsessive-compulsive symptoms (Rauch et al., 1994; Breiter et al., 1996; Adler et al., 2000; Hendler et al., 2003; Shapira et al., 2003; Mataix-Cols et al., 2004) and reduced activation in frontal, striatal, temporal and parietal regions during tasks of inhibitory and cognitive control (Nakao et al., 2005; Roth et al., 2007; Woolley et al., 2008; Page et al., 2009). Treatment effect on brain activation has mainly been investigated in adult OCD patients. The most replicated finding is the presence of hyperactivity in the orbitofrontal cortex in nontreated patients, which then decreases after pharmacological treatment (Rubin et al., 1995; Saxena et al., 1999, 2002; Kang et al., 2003). Some authors have reported an inverse relationship between brain activity in these areas and the response to SSRIs (Swedo et al., 1992; Brody et al., 1998; Saxena et al., 1999; Rauch et al., 2002).

Functional neuroimaging studies in paediatric OCD patients also support a dysregulation of the orbitofrontal and parietal cortex, thalamus and basal ganglia (Lazaro et al., 2008; Wooley et al., 2008) that could contribute to the inhibitory mechanisms observed in OCD. One study involving a symptom provocation experiment found that paediatric OCD subjects had reduced activity in neural regions underlying emotional and cognitive processing and motor performance, as compared with healthy controls (Gilbert et al., 2009). Less amygdala/hippocampus activation in response to facial expression relative to fixation was also found in a paediatric OCD sample compared to controls (Britton et al., 2010a). Amygdala activation was less in response to positive, negative and neutral facial expressions, and this reduced activation could potentially be explained by differences in amygdala structure. Activation during a cognitive task was also studied by the same researchers (Britton et al., 2010b). Activation of the left interior frontal gyrus during set-shifting was greater in controls than in the paediatric OCD group. The latter also showed behavioural deficits in set-shifting, evidenced by the tendency to have a greater shift cost. This study therefore suggests that the OCD group may have difficulty shifting cognitive sets because of a failure to activate the left interior frontal gyrus.

Finally, two follow-up functional studies have been conducted in child and adolescent OCD patients. One study showed that cerebral activation decreases after pharmacological treatment and clinical improvement (Lázaro et al., 2008), while the other showed longer mean reaction times but similar accuracy during planning, this being associated with decreased recruitment of frontal-parietal areas that ceased to be significant after cognitive-behavioural treatment (Huyser et al., 2010).

Connectivity

Recent diffusion tensor imaging (DTI) studies in OCD adult patients have shown abnormalities in fractional anisotropy (FA), a measure of WM connectivity; specifically, this was decreased in the cingulate and parietal regions and corpus callosum, and increased in the corpus callosum and internal capsule and bilateral semioval centre to the subinsular WM (Szeszko et al., 2005; Menzies et al., 2008; Saito et al., 2008; Yoo et al., 2007; Canistrato et al., 2007; Nakamae et al., 2008). These findings could reflect possible abnormalities in the WM tracts that connect the prefrontal cortex with the basal ganglia within the frontal-striatal model of OCD, which would also support a role for the parietal cortex in the pathophysiology of the disorder. Unaffected first-degree relatives exhibited significant FA abnormalities in parietal and frontal regions, which might suggest WM endophenotypes for OCD (Menzies et al., 2008).

Another technique, resting state functional connectivity, analyses the temporal correlation of spontaneous low-frequency blood oxygen level-dependent signal fluctuations, which are believed to represent neuronal activity intrinsically generated by the brain. OCD patients had significantly increased functional connectivity along a ventral cortico-striatal axis (Harrison et al., 2009) and less functional connectivity within the anterior cingulate cortex, middle frontal gyrus and putamen compared with controls (Jang et al., 2010). As yet there are no published DTI studies that evaluate WM integrity in child and adolescent OCD patients. However, the first functional connectivity study to use resting state techniques in a paediatric OCD population recently reported greater activation of the dorsal anterior cingulate cortex (dACC), which predicted worse performance, as well as increased connectivity between the dACC and the ventral medial frontal cortex during a task. These findings suggest that altered function and connectivity in these networks may represent early markers of OCD (Fitzgerald et al., 2010).

In summary, although neurobiological models have implicated the frontal-striatal-thalamic cortical network, there is also evidence for involvement of the parietal cortex, as well as of the corpus callosum, limbic circuitry and the pituitary gland. The hypothesis of a developmentally-mediated network dysplasia due to differential patterns of pruning and myelinization within fronto-striatal networks in child and adolescent OCD patients can probably be extended to other cortical areas (temporo-parietal), as well as to other subcortical regions including the thalamus and limbic structures.

NEUROTRANSMISSION SYSTEMS

Serotonin System

There are three complementary approaches that suggest a role for serotonin (5HT) neurotransmission in OCD. The strongest evidence for the putative role of the 5HT system comes from the increasing number of clinical studies that point to the efficacy of 5HT reuptake inhibitors (SRIs) in the pharmacological treatment of OCD. The initial investigations were performed with clomipramine, a tricyclic antidepressant which has a preferential serotoninergic profile. It has extensively been shown that clomipramine reduces OC symptomatology, and a positive correlation has been found between plasma clomipramine levels and the anti-obsessional response (Mavissakalian et al., 1990). Subsequently, many studies have also documented the anti-obsessional effect of SSRIs. The central role of 5HT neurotransmission is illustrated by the change in peripheral markers of 5HT function that is associated with the improvement in OCD symptoms after treatment with SRIs. Treatment with clomipramine was also reported to reduce the concentrations of 5–HIAA, the major central metabolite of 5HT, in the lumbar cerebrospinal fluid (CSF) of OCD patients. This progressive decline in CSF levels of 5–HIAA was positively correlated with an improvement in OCD symptoms (Thoren et al., 1980). Thus, it can be postulated that an enhanced availability of 5HT at the synapse, due to presynaptic reuptake inhibition, may be a central factor in the clinical efficacy of anti-depressant agents in OCD.

The second approach, based on the direct analysis of peripheral and central markers of 5HT neurotransmission, suggests that OCD could be associated with decreased availability of extracellular 5HT. The hypothesis is that OCD may involve a specific abnormality of 5HT release and/or 5HT receptors. From this perspective, a reduction in 5HT reuptake capacity could be considered as a compensatory mechanism in the attempt to maintain the availability of extracellular 5HT.

The third approach explores the relationship between various pharmacological agents, related to a variety of 5HT receptors, and the production of OC symptoms. Research has found that OC symptoms worsened with m-CPP, which acts as an agonist to 5HT1A, 5HT1D, 5HT2C receptors, and as an antagonist to the 5HT3 receptor. Oral sumatriptan, a selective 5HT1D receptor agonist, produced a transient and significant aggravation of OC symptoms. These observations support the hypothesis that 5HT1D and/or 5HT3 receptor subtypes may be involved in the production of OC symptoms.

Dopaminergic System

Among the putative neurotransmitter systems that are thought to play a major role in the expression of OC symptoms, the dopamine system, with which 5HT interacts, probably represents the most likely candidate. Results from pharmacological challenge studies with dopamine receptor agonists in OCD are as yet inconsistent, but there are indications that OC symptoms may be related to increased dopamine neurotransmission. Cocaine, a DAT blocker, elevates synaptic dopamine levels and increases DAT density. It has been reported that chronic use of cocaine may be associated with stereotyped examining and an exacerbation of obsessive-compulsive symptoms. Methylphenidate and amphetamine have also been reported to exacerbate or induce, as well as to improve, OCD symptoms. Conversely, anti-dopaminergic agents have favourable effects on the management of SRI-resistant forms of OCD with and without comorbid tics. One intriguing finding is why antipsychotics in monotherapy lack efficacy in OCD, whereas they are capable of inducing *de novo* OCD symptoms in patients with psychotic disorders, and are efficacious in combination with SSRIs in OCD patients without psychotic features. It has been proposed that $5-HT^{2A}$ receptor antagonism exacerbates OC symptoms by increasing the firing rate of dopamine neurons, whereas D_2 receptor antagonism reduces OC symptoms through inhibition of dopamine neurons.

Glutamate

The first reports of *in vivo* differences in glutamate (Glx) levels between paediatric OCD patients and healthy subjects were published by Rosenberg and Keshavan (1998). In OCD patients the authors found a lower concentration of glutamate in the anterior cingulate (Rosenberg et al., 2004), while greater Glx/Cr levels have been observed in orbital frontal white matter (Whiteside et al., 2006). These neuroimaging reports gain further support from genetic studies that noted an increased susceptibility to OCD in subjects expressing alterations in the neuronal glutamate transporter gene (Arnold et al., 2006; Dickel et al., 2006) and certain glutamate receptor genes (Arnold et al., 2004). A study by our group found that CSF glutamate levels were significantly raised in OCD patients compared to normal controls, and that the difference was unrelated to age or gender of the subjects.

Peripheral markers and animal models have provided additional support for glutamate dysfunction in OCD. McGrath et al. (2000) showed that MK-801, a non-competitive NMDA receptor antagonist that indirectly stimulates cortical-limbic glutamate output, aggravated a transgene-dependent abnormal behaviour (repetitive climbing and leaping) in a transgenic mouse model of comorbid Tourette syndrome and OCD; this occurred at doses which were insufficient to induce stereotypes, whereas at higher doses MK-801 more readily induced stereotypes and limbic seizure behaviours.

Finally, a number of glutamate-modulating agents are now showing promise as potential treatments for OCD.

PHYSICO-CHEMICAL CAUSAL FACTORS

Perinatal Disorders

All the studies of family genetics, including those of twin concordance, point to the influence of environmental factors, especially non-shared ones, in the pathogenesis of OCD. For many years the tendency has been to identify environmental risk factors with interpersonal and psychosocial experiences. While the potential role of such experiences should not be ignored it is reasonable to assume that in a neurodevelopmental disorder such as OCD the possible contact between the individual and the physical and chemical environment may affect the development of the central nervous system (CNS). This possible effect could be more harmful the younger the individual—and the less mature the CNS. As such, what occurs during pregnancy, birth and the first stages of life, when interpersonal relationships barely impact, may be important in relation to subsequent psychopathology. While this aspect has been widely studied and verified in the context of other neurodevelopmental disorders, especially schizophrenia, ADHD, autism and eating disorders, there has been scant research of this kind in relation to OCD. However, this lack of information has recently been overcome through an interesting study conducted by a team of researchers at the University of São Paulo (Vasconcelos et al., 2007). They found that a series of prenatal, perinatal and postnatal anomalies were significantly more common ($p \leq 0.001$) among individuals with OCD than in controls. These anomalies were oedema of the hands, feet or face and excessive weight gain during gestation, hyperemesis gravidarum, prolonged labour, preterm birth and jaundice. After controlling for the possible effects of socioeconomic status, two anomalies, prolonged labour and oedema during pregnancy, remained statistically significant. Protracted delivery may be related to primiparity, dystocia, obstetric trauma, hypoxia, and foetal distress, while oedema during pregnancy is often a first sign of pre-eclampsia.

Given that they precede several disorders, including those which are most comorbid with OCD (i.e. TS and ADHD), these early environmental risk factors probably lack causal specificity in relation to OCD. It has been suggested that such environmental factors may exert their influence by contributing to the expression of phenocopies (Kano et al., 2001). However, since we are dealing here with genuine neurodevelopmental disorders it seems reasonable to assume that any noxa which has a functional or structural effect on the CNS during its process of maturation could, via these alterations, play a role in the pathogenesis of various disorders. In this context it should be noted that the possible influence of smoking during pregnancy has not been studied in relation to OCD, whereas it has been shown to be a risk factor in other neurodevelopmental disorders, namely ADHD.

Infections by Streptococcus Bacteria: PANDAS

In one study, over 70 percent of children with Sydenham's chorea reported that they had experienced an abrupt onset of repetitive, unwanted thoughts and behaviours two-to-four weeks before the onset of their chorea (Swedo, 2001). In 1998 Swedo et al. proposed that infection by Group A β-haemolytic streptococcus (GABHS) may give rise not only to Sydenham's chorea but also to a set of neurobehavioural disorders that they termed *paediatric autoimmune neuropsychiatric disorders associated with streptococcus* (PANDAS). PANDAS are characterized by the abrupt appearance or exacerbation of OCD and/or tic disorders, accompanied by emotional lability, separation anxiety, nighttime fears and bedtime rituals, cognitive deficits, oppositional behaviours, and motoric hyperactivity. The fifty cases included in the first report corresponded to pre-pubertal children with a mean age at onset of 6.3 years.

The rate of exacerbations has recently been studied in children with PAN-DAS and in controls with OCD or chronic tic disorder with no known temporal relationship to GABHS infection (Kurlan et al., 2008). This research showed that cases had a higher clinical exacerbation rate and a higher bona fide GABHS infection rate than the control group. However, 75 percent or more of the clinical exacerbations in cases had no observable temporal relationship to GABHS. The authors concluded that PANDAS seem to represent a subgroup of patients with chronic tic disorders and OCD who may be vulnerable to GABHS infections as a precipitant of neuropsychiatric symptom exacerbations. However, these infections are not the most frequent antecedent of exacerbations.

In both PANDAS and Sydenham's chorea the cross-reactive antibodies seem to recognize epitopes on basal ganglia neurons, particularly in the caudate, putamen and globus pallidus. The resulting inflammation alters the basal ganglia, giving rise to choreic and/or neuropsychiatric disorders. However, this anti-neuronal antibody model is insufficient to explain PANDAS, not least because 20 to 40 percent of healthy children present similar antibodies in serum. Swedo (2001) suggested that the initial model be modified, highlighting that the immune response is not limited to the anti-neuronal antibodies. The proposed model includes the streptococcus bacteria, host susceptibility and abnormal immune responsivity. The host susceptibility would result from a combination of genetic, developmental and immunological factors.

A GABHS infection may precipitate tics and obsessive symptoms in PAN-DAS. However, a family history of tics and OCD has a similar prevalence rate in children with and without PANDAS (Lougee et al., 2000). This suggest that children with PANDAS may simultaneously inherit a susceptibility to post-streptococcal sequelae, similar to that reported for children with Sydenham's chorea, and a susceptibility to OCD and tic disorders.

Since the first description of PANDAS their nature and characteristics have been subject to controversy. Indeed, the relationship between GABHS infections and OCD and tics appears debatable in the light of some findings. For example, Luo et al. (2004) found no clear relationship between new GABHS infections and symptom exacerbations in an unselected group of patients with TS. However, when, instead of investigating possible exacerbations of already diagnosed disorders, the focus of study is the existence of streptococcal infections prior to the initial diagnosis of OCD, TS or tic disorders the association between these infections and the diagnosis seems to be sufficiently well established (Leslie et al., 2008; Mell et al., 2005). Therefore, the exacerbation of existing disorders may not have the same relationship to GABHS as do the precipitation of these disorders. In this context the results of the study by Leslie et al. (2008) are also of interest: streptococcal infections were significantly frequent antecedents not only of OCD and TS but also of ADHD and even major depressive disorder. These findings cast doubt on the pathogenic specificity of GABHS and highlight the existence of shared biological risk factors among developmental disorders.

In contrast to what was assumed in the first studies of PANDAS there are at present no biological markers of these disorders. It was initially suggested that the D8/17 monoclonal antibody could be a marker of susceptibility to PANDAS (Murphy et al., 1997; Swedo et al., 1997). However, subsequent research has shown it to lack specificity, and studies with paediatric OCD patients found that the expression of D8/17 in B cells was very low, with the great majority of patients being negative for the (supposed) D8/17 marker (Morer et al., 2005). In children with OCD and/or tic disorder who presented considerable symptom changes, positive correlations have been found between GABHS titres, especially carbohydrate A, and changes in OCD severity ratings (Murphy et al., 2004).

Many aspects of PANDAS require further clarification. In terms of developmental psychopathology it is very important to note the childhood onset, i.e. they are pre-pubertal disorders. One question raised by this concerns the role played by the neurohormonal changes associated with puberty, such that puberty seems to act as a protective factor. Given that genetic and environmental factors interact in the pathogenesis of OCD and, therefore, of PANDAS, it also has be asked whether what occurs in these disorders is similar to what happens in eating disorders, where the genetic influence seems to act mainly after puberty, interacting with ovarian activation in girls (Klump et al., 2003). The fact that PANDAS almost always occur in childhood, and that they have the manifestations they do, also raises the question as to whether they are related to the apparent subtype of childhood-onset OCD. In summary, this is a field characterized by more questions than answers, although what is clear is that PANDAS appear after damage to the fronto-striatal circuits, especially the basal ganglia, caused by a streptococcus infection.

DIMENSIONAL AND CATEGORICAL APPROACHES

Obsessive-compulsive disorder (OCD) is phenomenologically and aetiologically heterogeneous. In recent years, considerable attention has been paid to the symptomatic heterogeneity of OCD in an attempt to find biological markers, genetic transmission mechanisms or ways of predicting treatment response (Mataix-Cols et al., 2005). Factor analytic studies have found similar symptom structures and four reliable dimensions have been described: Factor I (aggressive, sexual and religious obsessions, and checking compulsions); Factor II (symmetry obsessions and repeating, counting and ordering compulsions); Factor III (contamination obsessions and cleaning compulsions); and Factor IV (hoarding obsessions and compulsions). Moreover, recent brain-imaging and genetic studies have provided evidence for the biological validity of these dimensions. Factor analyses of obsessive-compulsive symptoms have also been conducted in children and adolescents with OCD, and almost all of them have confirmed the existence of the four symptom dimensions previously described in adults (Delorme et al., 2006; Stewart et al., 2008; Mataix-Cols et al., 2008). In addition, one follow-up study found that the symptom dimensions identified remained essentially unmodified (Delorme et al., 2006).

Another promising approach in relation to reducing phenotypic heterogeneity involves the identification of homogeneous subtypes of OCD based on clinical characteristics. The aim here is to define mutually exclusive subgroups of patients based on demographic and clinical characteristics (Millet et al., 2004), and research has highlighted the importance of gender, age at onset, clinical course and comorbidity.

Gender

Various studies in adults have shown differences between male and female OCD patients. Using a classification based on OCD symptom factor scores it was found that women were more represented on Factor III (contamination obsessions and cleaning compulsions), whereas men were more represented on Factor I (aggressive, sexual, religious and somatic obsessions, and checking compulsions) (Mataix-Cols et al., 1999; Denys et al., 2004; Hasler et al., 2005).

Age at Onset

Early onset of OCD is a putative and distinct phenotypic expression. Early age at onset has been associated with familial forms of OCD (Pauls et al., 1995). Alsobrook et al. (1999), using segregation analysis in a large OCD family sample, confirmed these findings and showed that OCD inheritance in families loading high on aggressive, sexual and checking symptoms was best explained by a polygenic model, whereas an inheritance model involving a major gene locus was indicated in families loading high on the symmetry and ordering factor. Hasler et al. (2005) reported significant positive associations between early age at OCD onset (before age 16) and Factors I and II. This is in line with previous reports on differences in OCD symptoms between early and later age at OCD onset (Denys et al., 2004; Millet et al., 2004).

Clinical Course

Some authors have found differences between episodic and chronic courses of OCD. In childhood the only factor that predicted a poor outcome was severity of OCD at this age, measured by the duration of the obsessive-compulsive symptoms. Both females and males also had OCD in adulthood, either chronically or episodically (Thomsen et al., 1995). The episodic course, which is less common, is associated with a family history of mood disorders, comorbidity with bipolar II and panic disorders, and later onset of obsessive-compulsive symptoms (Perugi et al., 1998).

COMORBID PSYCHIATRIC DISORDERS

It is very common for patients with OCD to be diagnosed with other psychiatric disorders, some of which may be specifically related to OCD (LaSalle et al., 2004). Findings that certain disorders occur more frequently in the relatives of OCD subjects provide compelling evidence for an aetiological relationship (Pauls et al., 1995; Nestadt et al., 2003). Specifically, there is evidence from family studies that tic disorders, generalized anxiety disorder, panic disorder, agoraphobia, and recurrent major depression aggregate with OCD, suggesting shared aetiological elements between these disorders and OCD. Nestadt et al. (2003), using latent class analysis in an OCD family sample, identified a specific OCD subtype associated with major depression and generalized anxiety disorder, and a distinct OCD subtype associated with panic disorder, agoraphobia and tic disorders. Hasler et al. (2005) found specific factor profiles for these combinations of comorbid disorders: both major depression and generalized anxiety disorder were modestly associated with Factor I, a finding also reported by Moritz et al. (2004), while both panic disorder and agoraphobia were strongly associated with Factors I and II. In addition, Factor III was positively associated with eating disorders (including anorexia, bulimia and binge-eating disorder) and negatively associated with Tourette disorder.

An important comorbidity in childhood and adolescence is attention deficit-hyperactivity disorder (ADHD). Up to 30 percent of children and adolescents with OCD also satisfy the diagnostic criteria for ADHD (Geller et al., 2002), while the rate of OCD among children with ADHD is estimated to be 8 to 11 percent (Geller et al., 2000; Arnold et al., 2005). The high prevalence of ADHD and OCD in childhood and the high degree of comorbidity between these disorders suggest that they share genetic factors (Geller et al., 2007). Molecular genetic studies have also shown significant associations of variants in dopaminergic and serotonergic candidate genes in ADHD and OCD (Walitza et al., 2005). Recently, Walitza et al. (2008) investigated the influence of comorbid ADHD on early-onset OCD and compared twenty OCD patients with ADHD and 20 randomly selected OCD patients without ADHD. OCD with ADHD patients tended to show an earlier age at OCD onset, a greater severity of symptoms and a higher persistence rate than did OCD patients without ADHD.

Some forms of OCD may be aetiologically related to tic disorders (Miguel et al., 2005; Leckman et al., 1995). OCD patients with tic disorders are more likely to report compulsions that are not preceded by obsessions and more often experience what are known as *sensory phenomena*, a subjective feeling that precedes or accompanies the obsessive-compulsive symptoms. These sensory phenomena usually include mental and sensory experiences, such as pressure or the need to repeat the behaviour until achieving a specific sensation or a "just right" feeling (Leckman et al., 1995; Miguel et al., 1995, 2001). This form is usually present in patients with an earlier age at onset (Holzer et al., 1994; Leckman et al., 1995; Diniz et al., 2006) and has a higher genetic load (Rosario-Campos et al., 2005) and higher frequencies of comorbid body dysmorphic disorder, trichotillomania and bipolar disorders (Coffey et al., 1998; Diniz et al., 2004). Genetic family and molecular studies have also shown higher rates of obsessive-compulsive symptoms and OCD in relatives of Tourette syndrome (TS) patients, as well as higher rates of tics or TS in first-degree relatives of OCD patients. Molecular studies in OCD patients with tics have focused on candidate genes from the serotoninergic and dopaminergic systems (Nicolini et al., 1996; Cruz et al., 1997; Millet et al., 2003). Neurological evidence has also been reported. For example, structural MRI studies in OCD patients and TS have shown volumetric abnormalities in basal ganglia volumes and orbitofrontal cortices (Scarone et al., 1992; Peterson et al., 1993; Robinson et al., 1995; Rosenberg et al., 1998; Szeszko et al., 1999, 2004), while functional MRI studies have revealed abnormal metabolic activity in similar areas in both disorders (Stern et al., 2000).

Tic-related and early-onset are therefore two types of sub-classification that seem to overlap and should not be considered as mutually exclusive. Rather, it appears that they refer to a group of patients with the following features: early age at onset, male predominance, higher prevalence of tic disorders and high family load. These patients also have more symmetry and ordering compulsions, which are usually not preceded by obsessions but by sensory phenomena, such as a "just right" sensation (de Mathis et al., 2006).

As has been seen, dimensional and categorical approaches can be used in combination. Thus, the identified symptom dimensions have been found to relate to variables such as gender and age at onset, to genetic factors, to comorbid disorders such as chronic tics, or to the response to serotonin reuptake inhibitors or behaviour therapy.

TREATMENT AND THE BRAIN

The therapeutic effect of clomipramine and selective serotonin reuptake inhibitors (SSRIs) is well documented in relation to OCD. Current neuroimaging techniques and neuropsychological assessments have confirmed that the clinical improvement shown by OCD children and adolescents who are treated with these drugs is significantly associated with relevant changes in brain structures involved in the disorder.

Research published in 2000 demonstrated that paroxetine not only reduced thalamic volume but also produced a significant decrease in the glutamatergic (GLx) concentrations of the left caudate nucleus in OCD patients, bringing them within normal limits (Gilbert et al., 2000; Rosenberg et al., 2000a). This decrease in left caudate GLx was positively correlated with a reduction in OCD symptom severity. In 2001, Bolton et al. published a case study in which the normalization of caudate GLx achieved by paroxetine treatment was maintained several months after the medication was discontinued. A subsequent study demonstrated that paroxetine also produced reductions in left amygdala volume that were correlated with the drug dose administered (Szeszko et al., 2004). Obviously, these changes and normalizations are not regarded as the specific consequence of paroxetine itself, but rather as mediated by the brain changes it induces. Indeed, another study with paediatric OCD patients showed that six months of treatment with fluoxetine led to the normalization of previously elevated brain activation in the left insula and left putamen (Lázaro et al., 2008). In other words, the therapeutic response of SSRIs is associated with a tendency to normalize the brain circuits that mediate the symptomatic expression of OCD.

Other research has shown that compared with controls, paediatric OCD patients presented significantly less grey matter volume in the right and left parietal lobes and in right parietal white matter. However, after six months of treatment, and with a clear clinical improvement, the differences between OCD patients and controls in parietal grey and white matter were no longer statistically significant (Lázaro et al., 2009).

Neuropsychological assessments have also shown that the therapeutic response is accompanied by the normalization of cognitive functions that are altered in paediatric OCD. Children and adolescents with OCD have been observed to perform worse on certain tests of memory, speed of information processing and executive functions, similarly to what is found among adult patients. However, six months after effective treatment the cognitive profile of patients was normalized and many of the significant differences with respect to controls in the first assessment had disappeared (Andrés et al., 2008).

In adults with OCD positron emission tomography (PET) has revealed that after treatment with SSRIs or CBT, those patients whose symptoms had improved tended to normalize their neurophysiological functioning, showing reductions in caudate glucose metabolism associated with a reduction in symptom severity (Baxter et al., 1992; Brody et al., 1998;

Saxena et al., 1999; Schwartz et al., 1996). However, Benazon et al. (2003) failed to observe a significant pre- to post-treatment change in left caudate GLx in medication-naïve paediatric OCD patients treated with CBT. This suggests that the reduction in caudate GLx may be specific to the improvements achieved through administration of SSRIs. It could also be the case, however, that children and adults who are treated and improve with CBT respond differently in neurophysiological terms.

Research has progressively shown that the metabolic reduction associated with the therapeutic response takes place in a wide range of brain areas. For example, in adult OCD patients treated with paroxetine, significant metabolic decreases were found in the right caudate nucleus, right ventrolateral prefrontal cortex, bilateral orbitofrontal cortex and thalamus, whereas such changes were not observed in depressed patients treated with the same drug (Saxena et al., 2002).

When psychotherapy, such as CBT, is effective in treating OCD, one also observes modifications of brain functioning. Medication-free paediatric patients with OCD were scanned using a self-paced pseudo-randomized event-related functional magnetic resonance imaging version of the Tower of London in order to study planning, a key executive function (Huyser et al., 2010). At baseline the patients had longer mean reaction times but similar accuracy compared to healthy controls, this being associated with decreased recruitment of frontal-parietal areas during the planning task. With increasing task load the OCD patients compared to controls were found to activate additional brain regions, in particular the dorsomedial prefrontal cortex, dorsal anterior cingulate cortex and insula. However, after CBT these differences between patients and controls ceased to be significant. In addition, changes in symptom severity were correlated with changes in the blood oxygenation level-dependent signal and, after treatment, in the dorsolateral prefrontal cortex and parietal cortex. Notwithstanding potential limitations of this study it was the first to show slower performance and decreased neurophysiological responsiveness in unmedicated paediatric patients with OCD during a planning task, and to demonstrate that this could be reversed after successful CBT.

It appears, however, that CBT does not reduce the volume of the thalamus, which is usually increased in OCD (Rosenberg et al., 2000b). Given that paroxetine does reduce thalamic volume it has been suggested that this is a specific effect of this drug (and of SSRIs in general).

In summary, the brain modifications that result from the effective treatment of OCD constitute the foundation of clinical improvements and highlight the role of the central nervous system in both the pathogenesis and the remission of the disorder.

FINAL CONSIDERATIONS

Recent years have witnessed an important increase in our understanding of the neuroanatomical and neurophysiological bases of OCD. Current knowledge about the aetiopathogenesis of the disorder has rendered obsolete the strictly or purely environmentalist, psychoanalytic and behaviourist notions that predominated throughout much of the twentieth century. OCD can thus be regarded as a neurodevelopmental disorder in which psychosocial factors appear to have only a comparataively limited relevant role. Much remains to be understood, however, and the gaps in knowledge are greater in relation to paediatric as opposed to adult OCD. Continued research is therefore required to address the doubts, uncertainties and questions that remain. Perhaps some of the most important are as follows:

- Is paediatric OCD, especially when accompanied by tic disorders and, as is often the case, ADHD, really a subtype of OCD?
- Is the apparent reduction in striatal volumes observed in early-onset OCD patients really a consequence of an exaggeration of pre-pubertal pruning? Might this be a process associated with the supposed subtype of paediatric OCD?
- In children and adolescents are there significant differences between the OCD dimensions associated with simple OCD, OCD + tics, and OCD + tics + ADHD?
- Do pubertal changes play a role in the change of OCD "subtype" and in those cases where the shared environment has a greater causal influence?
- Research into endophenotypes, possible family biomarkers, such as the OLIG2 gene is of interest in relation to the prevention of OCD.
- Molecular genetics needs to define not only the general genetic profile of OCD but also the genetic factors that have a differential influence in males and females, as well as those that likely contribute to an early or later onset of the disorder.
- Are there situations of psychosocial stress that could predispose the individual to develop OCD, even though it onsets years later, as can occur, for example, in the association between childhood abuse and depression in adolescence or adulthood? If this proved to be the case, would it also be more prevalent among females? If so, why?

REFERENCES

Adler, C. M., McDonough-Ryan, P., Sax, K. W., Holland, S. K., Arndt, S., and Strakowski, S. M. (2000). "fMRI of neuronal activation with symptom provocation in unmedicated patients with obsessive-compulsive disorder." *Journal of Psychiatry Research, 343*, 17–24.

Alsobrook, I. J., Leckman, J. F., Goodman, W. K., Rasmussen, S. A., and Pauls, D. L. (1999) "Segregation analysis of obsessive–compulsive disorder using symptom based factor scores." *American Journal of Medical Genetics, 88*, 669–75.

Andrés, S., Lázaro, L., Salamero, M., Boget, T., Penadés, R et al. (2008) "Changes in cognitive dysfunction in children and adolescents with obsessive-compulsive disorder after treatment." *Journal of Psychiatric Research, 42*, 507–14.

Arnold, P. D., Ickowicz, A., Chen, S., and Schachar, R. (2005) "Attention-deficit hyperactivity disorder with and without obsessive-compulsive behaviours: clinical characteristics, cognitive assessment, and risk factors." *Canadian Journal of Psychiatry, 50*, 59–66.

Arnold, P. D., Rosenberg, D. R., Mundo, E., Tharmalingam, S., Kennedy, J. L., Richter, M. A. (2004) Association of a glutamate (NMDA) subunit receptor gene (GRIN2B) with obsessive-compulsive disorder: a preliminary study. *Psychopharmacology, 174*, 530–38.

Arnold, P. D., Sicard, T., Burroughs, E., Richter, M. A., and Kennedy, J. L. (2006) "Glutamate transporter gene SLC1A1 associated with obsessive-compulsive disorder." *Archives General Psychiatry, 63*, 769–76.

Bartha, R., Stein, M. B., Williamson, P. C., Drost, D. J., Neufeld, R. W., et al. (1998) "A short 1H Spectroscopy and volumetric MRI study of the corpus striatum in patients with obsessive-compulsive disorder and comparison subjects." *The American Journal of Psychiatry, 155*, 1584–91.

Baxter, L. R., Schwartz, J. M., Bergman, K. S., Szuba, M. P., Guze, B. H. et al. (1992) "Caudate glucose metabolic rate changes with both drug and behavior therapy for obsessive-compulsive disorder." *Archives of General Psychiatry, 49*, 681–89.

Benazón, N. R., Moore, G. J., and Rosenberg, D. R. (2003) "Neurochemical analyses in pediatric obsessive-compulsive disorder in patients treated with cognitive behavioral therapy." *Journal of the American Academy of Child and Adolescent Psychiatry, 42*, 1279–85.

Bolton, J., Moore, G. J., MacMillan, S., Stewart, C. M., and Rosenberg, D. R. (2001) "Case study: caudate glutamatergic changes with paroxetine persist after medication discontinuation in pediatric OCD." *Journal of American Academy of Child and Adolescent Psychiatry, 40*, 903–6.

Breiter, H. C., Rauch, S. L., Kwong, K. K., Baker, J. R., Weisskoff, R. M., et al. (1996) "Functional magnetic resonance imaging of symptom provocation in obsessive-compulsive disorder." *Archives of General Psychiatry, 53*, 595–606.

Britton, J. C., Rauch, S. L., Rosso, I. M., Killgore, W. D., Price, L. M., et al. (2010b) "Cognitive inflexibility and frontal-cortical activation in pediatric obsessive-compulsive disorder." *Journal of American Academy of Child and Adolescent Psychiatry, 49*, 944–53.

Britton, J. C., Stewart, S. E., Killgore, W. D., Rosso, I. M., Price, L. M., et al. (2010a) "Amygdala activation in response to facial expressions in pediatric obsessive-compulsive disorder." *Depression and Anxiety, 27*, 643–51.

Brody, A. L., Saxena, S., Schwartz, J. M., Stoessel, P. W., Maidment, K., and Phelps, M. E. (1998) "FDG-PET predictors of response to behavioral therapy versus pharmacotherapy in obsessive-compulsive disorder." *Psychiatry Research, 84*, 1–6.

Cannistraro, P. A., Makris, N., Howard, J. D., Wedig, M. M., Hodge, S. M., et al. (2007) "A diffusion tensor imaging study of white matter in obsessive-compulsive disorder." *Depression and Anxiety, 24*, 440–46.

Carey, G., and Gottesman, I. I. (1981) "Twin and family studies of anxiety, fobic, and obsessive disorders." In Klein, D. F., Rabkin, J. G. (eds.) *Anxiety: new research and changing concepts* (pp 117–36). New York: Raven.

Carmona, S., Bassas, N., Rovira, M. Gispert, J. D., Soliva, J. C., et al. (2007) "Pediatric OCD structural brain deficits in conflict monitoring circuits: a voxel-based morphometric study." *Neuroscience Letters, 421*, 218–23.

Chamberlain, S. R., Menzies, L., Hampshire, A., Suckling, J., Fineberg, N. A., et al. (2008) "Orbitofrontal dysfunction in patients with obsessive-compulsive disorder and their unaffected relatives." *Science, 321*, 421–22.

Coffey, B. J., Miguel, E. C., Biederman, J., Baer, L., Rauch, S. L., et al. (1998) "Tourette's disorder with and without obsessive-compulsive disorder in adults: are they different?" *The Journal of Nervous Mental Disease, 186*, 201–6.

Cruz, C., Camarena, B., King, N., Paez, F., Sidenberg, D., et al. (1997) "Increased prevalence of the seven-repeat variant of the dopamine D4 receptor gene in patients with obsessive-compulsive disorder with tics." *Neurosciences Letters, 231*, 1–4.

de Mathis, M. A., Diniz, J. B., do Rosario, M. A., Torres, A. R., Hoexter, M., et al. (2006) "What is the optimal way to subdivide Obsessive-Compulsive Disorder?" *CNS Spectrum, 11*, 762–79.

Delorme, R., Bille, A., Betancur, C., Mathieu, F., Chabane, N., et al. (2006) "Exploratory analysis of obsessive-compulsive symptom dimensions in children and adolescents: a prospective follow-up study." *BMC Psychiatry, 6*, 1–10.

Denys, D., de Geus, F., van Megen, H. J., Westenberg, H. G. (2004) "Use of factor analysis to detect potential phenotypes in obsessive–compulsive disorder." *Psychiatry Research, 128*, 273–80.

Dickel, D. E., Veenstra-VanderWeele, J., Cox, N. J., Wu, X., Fischer, D. J., et al. (2006) "Association testing of the positional and functional candidate gene SLC1A1/ EAAC1 in early-onset obsessive-compulsive disorder." *Archives of General Psychiatry, 63*, 778–85.

Diniz, J. B., Rosario-Campos, M. C., Hounie, A. G., Curi, M., Shavitt, R. G., et al. (2006) "Chronic tics and Tourette syndrome in patients with obsessive–compulsive disorder." *Journal of Psychiatric Research, 40*, 487–93

Diniz, J. B., Rosario-Campos, M. C., Shavitt, R. G., Curi, M., Hounie, A. G., et al. (2004) "Impact of age at onset and duration of illness on the expression of comorbidities in obsessive-compulsive disorder." *The Journal Clinical of Psychiatry, 65*, 22–27.

Douglass, H. M., Moffitt, T. E., Dar, R., McGee, R., and Silva, P. (1995) "Obsessive-compulsive disorder in a birth cohort of 18–year-olds: Prevalence and predictors." *Journal of the American Academy of Child and Adolescent Psychiatry, 34*, 1424–31.

Ebert, D., Speck, O., König, A., Berger, M., Hennigs, J., Hohagen, F., et al. (1997) "1H-magnetic resonance spectroscopy in obsessive-compulsive disorder: evidence for neuronal loss in the cingulate gyrus and right striatum." *Psychiatry Research, 74*, 173–76.

Fitzgerald, K. D., Moore, G. J., Paulson, L. A., Steward, C. M., Rosenberg, D. R., et al. (2000) "Proton spectroscopy imaging of the thalamus in treatment-naïve pediatric obsessive-compulsive disorder." *Biological Psychiatry, 47,* 174–82.

Fitzgerald, K. D., Stern, E. R., Angstadt, M., Nicholson-Muth, K. C., Maynor M. R., et al. (2010) "Altered function and connectivity of the medial frontal cortex in pediatric obsessive-compulsive disorder." *Biological Psychiatry, 68,* 1039–47.

Flament, N. F., Whitaker, A., Rapoport, J. L., Davies, M., Berg, C. Z., et al. (1988) "Obsessive compulsive disorder in adolescence: An epidemiological study." *Journal of the American Academy of Child and Adolescent Psychiatry, 27,* 764–71.

García, A. M., Sapyta, J. J., Moore, P. S., Freeman, J. B., Franklin, M. E., et al. (2010) "Predictors and moderators of treatment outcome in the Pediatric Obsessive Compulsive Treatment Study (POTS I)." *Journal of the American Academy of Child and Adolescent Psychiatry, 49,* 1024–33.

Geller, D. A., Biederman, J., Faraone, S. V., Cradock, K., Hagermoser, L., et al. (2002) "Attention-deficit hyperactivity disorder in children and adolescents with obsessive-compulsive disorder: fact or artifact?" *Journal of the American Academy of Child and Adolescent Psychiatry, 41,* 52–58.

Geller, D., Biederman, J., Faraone, S. V., Frazier, J., Coffey, B. J., et al. (2000) "Clinical correlates of obsessive compulsive disorder in children and adolescents referred to specialized and non-specialized clinical settings." *Depression and Anxiety, 11,* 163–68.

Geller, D., Biederman, J., Jones, J., Park, K., Schwartz, S., et al. (1998) "Is juvenile obsessive-compulsive disorder a developmental subtype of the disorder? A review of the pediatric literature." *Journal of the American Academy of Child and Adolescent Psychiatry, 37,* 420–27.

Geller, D., Petty, C., Vivas, F., Johnson, J., Pauls, D., Biederman, J. (2007) "Further evidence for co-segregation between pediatric obsessive compulsive disorder and attention-deficit hyperactivity disorder: a familial risk analysis." *Biological Psychiatry, 15,* 1388–94.

Gilbert, A. R., Akkal, D., Almeida, J. R., Mataix-Cols, D., Kalas, C., et al. (2009) "Neural correlates of symptom dimensions in pediatric obsessive-compulsive disorder: a functional magnetic resonance imaging study." *Journal of American Academy of Child and Adolescent Psychiatry, 48,* 936–44.

Gilbert, A. R., Mataix-Cols, D., Almeida, J. R., Lawrence, N., Nutche, J., et al. (2008) "Brain structure and symptom dimension relationship in obsessive-compulsive disorder: A voxel-based morphometric study." *Journal of Affective Disorders, 109,* 117–26.

Gilbert, A. R., Moore, G. J., Keshavan, M. S., Paulson, L. A. D., Narula, V., et al. (2000) "Decrease in thalamic volumes of pediatric patients with obsessive-compulsive disorder who are taking paroxetine." *Archives of General Psychiatry, 57,* 449–56.

Grados, M. A. (2010) "The genetics of obsessive-compulsive disorder and Tourette syndrome: An epidemiological and pathway-based approach for gene discovery." *Journal of the American Academy of Child and Adolescent Psychiatry, 49,* 810–19.

Grados, M. A., and Mathews, C. A. (2008) "Latent class analysis of Gilles de la Tourette syndrome using comorbidities: clinical and genetic implications." *Biological Psychiatry, 64,* 219–25.

Harrison, B. J., Soriano-Mas, C., Pujol, J., Ortiz, H., López-Solà, M., et al. (2009) "Altered corticostriatal functional connectivity in obsessive-compulsive disorder." *Archives of General Psychiatry, 66,* 1189–200.

Hasler, G., LaSalle-Ricci, V. H., Ronquillo, J. G., Crawley, S. A., et al. (2005) "Obsessive–compulsive disorder symptom dimensions show specific relationships to psychiatric comorbidity." *Psychiatry Research, 135,* 121–32.

Hendler, T., Goshen, E., Tzila Zwas, S., Sasson, Y., Gal, G., and Zohar, J. (2003) "Brain reactivity to specific symptom provocation indicates prospective therapeutic outcome in OCD." *Psychiatry Research, 124,* 87–103.

Hettema, J. M., Neale, M. C., and Kendler, K. S. (2001) "A review and meta-analysis of the genetic epidemiology of anxiety disorders. *American Journal of Psychiatry, 158,* 1568–78.

Holzer, J. C., Goodman, W. K., McDougle, C. J., Baer, L., Boyarsky, B. K., et al. (1994) "Obsessive-compulsive disorder with and without a chronic tic disorder. A comparison of symptoms in 70 patients." *British Journal of Psychiatry, 164,* 469–73.

Hudziak, J. J., van Beijsterveldt, C. E. M., Althoff, R. R., Stanger, C., Rettew, D. C., Nelson, E. C., Todd, R. D., Bartels, M.., and Boomsma, D. I. (2004) "Genetic and environmental contributions to the Child Behavior Checklist Obsessive-Compulsive scale: A cross-cultural twin study." *Archives of General Psychiatry, 61,* 608–16.

Huyser, C., Veltman, D. J., Wolters, L. J., de Haan, E., and Boer, F. (2010) "Functional magnetic resonance imaging during planning before and after cognitive-behavioral therapy in pediatric obsessive-compulsive disorder." *Journal of American Academy of Child and Adolescent Psychiatry, 49,* 1238–48.

Iervolino, A. C., Perroud, N., Fullana, M. A., Guipponi, M., Cherkas, L., et al. (2009) "Prevalence and heretability of compulsive hoarding: A twin study." *American Journal of Psychiatry, 166,* 1156–61.

Inouye, E. (1965) "Similar and dissimilar manifestations of obsessive-compulsive neurosis in monozygotic twins." *American Journal of Psychiatry, 121,* 1171–75.

Jang, J. H., Kim, J. H., Jung, W. H., Choi, J. S., Jung, M. H., et al. (2010) "Functional connectivity in fronto-subcortical circuitry during the resting state in obsessive-compulsive disorder." *Neuroscience Letters, 474,* 158–62.

Jang, J. H., Kwon, J. S., Jang, D. P., Moon, W. J., Lee, J. M., et al. (2006) "A proton MRSI Study of brain N-Acetylaspartate level after 12 weeks of citalopram treatment in drug-naïve patients with obsessive-compulsive disorder." *The American Journal of Psychiatry, 163,* 1202–7.

Kang, D. H., Kwon, J. S., Kim, J. J., Youn, T., Park, H. J., et al. (2003) "Brain glucose metabolic changes associated with neuropsychological improvements after 4 months of treatment in patients with obsessive-compulsive disorder." *Acta Psychiatrica Scandinavica, 107,* 291–97.

Kano, Y., Ohta, M., Nagai, Y., Pauls, D., and Leckman, J. (2001) "A family study of Tourette syndrome in Japan," *American Journal of Medical Genetics, 105* (2001), 414–421.

Kellner, C. H., Jolley, R. R., and Holgate, R. C. (1991) "Brain MRI in obsessive-compulsive disorder." *Psychiatry Research, 36,* 45–49.

Kessler, R. C., Berglund, P., Demler, O., Jin, R., Merikangas, K. R., and Walters, E. E. (2005) "Lifetime prevalence and age-at-onset distributions of DSM-IV disorders in the National Comorbidity Survey Replication." *Archives of General Psychiatry,* 62, 593–602.

Kim, J. J., Lee, M. C., Kim, J., Kim, I. Y., Kim, S. I., et al. (2001) "Grey matter abnormalities in obsessive-compulsive disorder. Statistical parametric of segmented magnetic resonance images." *British Journal of Psychiatry, 179,* 330–34.

Klump, K. L., McGue, M., and Iacono, W. G. (2003) "Differential heretability of eating attitudes and behaviors in prepubertal versus pubertal twins." *International Journal of Eating Disorders, 8,* 11–23.

Kurlan, R., Johnson, D., Kaplan, E. L., and the Tourette Syndrome Study Group. (2008) "Streptococcal infection and exacerbation of childhood tics and obsessive-compulsive symptoms: a prospective blinded cohort study." *Pediatrics, 121,* 1188–97.

LaSalle, V. H., Cromer, K. R., Nelson, K. N., Kazuba, D., Justement, L., and Murphy, D. L. (2004) "Diagnostic interview assessed neuropsychiatric disorder comorbidity in 334 individuals with obsessive–compulsive disorder." *Depression and Anxiety, 19,* 163–73.

Lázaro, L., Bargalló, N., Castro-Fornieles, J., Falcón, C., Andrés, S., et al. (2009) "Brain changes in children and adolescents with obsessive-compulsive disorder before and after treatment: a voxel-based morphometric MRI study." *Psychiatry Research, 172,* 140–46.

Lázaro L., Caldú, X., Junqué, C., Bargalló, N., Andrés, S., et al. (2008) "Cerebral activation in children and adolescents with obsessive-compulsive disorder before and after treatment: a functional MRI study." *Journal of Psychiatric Research, 42,* 1051–59.

Leckman, J. F., Goodman, W. K., Anderson, G. M., Riddle, M. A., Chappell, P. B., et al. (1995) "Cerebrospinal fluid biogenic amines in obsessive compulsive disorder, Tourette's syndrome, and healthy controls." *Neuropsychopharmacology, 12,* 73–86.

Leslie, D. L., Kozma, L., Martin, A., Landeros, A., Katsovich, L., et al. (2008) "Neuropsychiatric disorders associated with streptococcal infections: a case-control study among privately insured children." *Journal of the American Academy of Child and Adolescent Psychiatry, 47,* 1166–72.

Lougee, L., Perlmutter, S. J., Nicolson, R., Garvey, M. A., and Swedo, S. E. (2000) "Psychiatric disorders in first-degree relatives of children with pediatric autoimune neuropsychiatric disorders associated with streptococcal infections (PANDAS)." *Journal of the American Academy of Child and Adolescent Psychiatry, 39,* 1120–26.

Luo, F., Leckman, J. F., Katsovich, L., Findley, D., Grantz, H., et al. (2004) "Prospective longitudinal study of children with tic disorders and/or obsessive-compulsive disorder: relationship of symptom exacerbations to newly acquired streptococcal infections." *Pediatrics, 113,* e578–85.

Mataix-Cols, D., Nakatani, E., Micali, N., and Heyman, I. (2008) "Structure of obsessive–compulsive symptoms in pediatric OCD." *Journal of the American Academy of Child and Adolescent Psychiatry, 47,* 773–78.

Mataix-Cols, D., Rauch, S. L., Manzo, P. A., Jenike, M. A, and Baer, L. (1999) "Use of factor-analyzed symptom dimensions to predict outcome with serotonin reuptake inhibitors and placebo in the treatment of obsessive–compulsive disorder." *The American Journal of Psychiatry, 156,* 1409–16.

Mataix-Cols, D., Rosario-Campos, M. C., and Leckman, J. F. (2005) "A multidimensional model of obsessive compulsive disorder." *The American Journal of Psychiatry, 162,* 228–38.

Mataix-Cols, D., Wooderson, S., Lawrence, N., Brammer, M. J., Speckens, A., and Phillips, M. L. (2004) "Distinct neural correlates of washing, checking, and hoarding symptoms dimensions in obsessive-compulsive disorder." *Archives of General Psychiatry, 61,* 564–76.

Mathews, C. A., and Grados, M. A. (2011) "Familiality of Tourette syndrome, obsessive-compulsive disorder, and attention-deficit/hyperactivity disorder: Heritability analysis in a large sib-pair simple." *Journal of the American Academy of Child and Adolescent Psychiatry, 50,* 46–54.

Mavissakalian, M. R., Jones, B., Olson, S., and Perel, J. M. (1990) Clomipramine in obsessive-compulsive disorder: clinical response and plasma levels. *Journal of Clinical Psychopharmacology, 10,* 261–68.

MacMaster, F. P., Russell, A., Mirza, Y., Keshavan, M. S., Taormina, S. P., et al. (2006) "Pituitary volume in pediatric obsessive-compulsive disorder." *Biological Psychiatry, 59,* 252–57.

McGrath, M. J., Campbell, K. M., Parks, C. R., and Burton, F. H. (2000) Glutamatergic drugs exacerbate symptomatic behavior in a transgenic model of comorbid Tourette's syndrome and obsessive-compulsive disorder. *Brain Research, 877,* 23–30.

Mell, L. K., Davis, R. L., and Owens, D. (2005) "Association between streptococcal infections and obsessive compulsive disorder, Tourette's syndrome, and tic disorder." *Pediatrics, 116,* 56–60.

Menzies, L., Williams., G. B., Chamberlain, S. R., Ooi, C., Fineberg, N., et al. (2008) "White latter abnormalities in patients with obsessive-compulsive disorder and their first-degree relatives." *American Journal of Psychiatry, 165,* 1308–15.

Micali, N., Heyman, I., Pérez, M., Hilton, K., Nakatani, E., et al. (2010) "Long-term outcomes of obsessive-compulsive disorder: follow-up of 142 children and adolescents." *The British Journal of Psychiatry, 197,* 128–34.

Miguel, E. C., Coffey, B. J., Baer, L., Savage, C. R., Rauch, S. L., Jenike, M. A. (1995) "Phenomenology of intentional repetitive behaviors in obsessive-compulsive disorder and Tourette's disorder." *Journal of Clinical of Psychiatry, 56,* 246–55.

Miguel, E. C., Leckman, J. F., Rauch, S., do Rosario-Campos, M. C., Hounie, A. G., et al. (2005) "Obsessive-compulsive disorder phenotypes: implications for genetic studies." *Molecular Psychiatry, 10,* 258–75.

Millet, B., Chabane N., Delorme, R., Leboyer, M., Leroy, S., et al. (2003) "Association between the dopamine receptor D4 (DRD4) gene and obsessive-compulsive disorder." *American Journal of Medical Genetics B Neuropsychiatry Genetics, 116,* 55–59.

Millet, B., Kochman, F., Gallarda, T., Krebs, M. O., Demonfaucon, F., et al. (2004) "Phenomenological and comorbid features associated in obsessive–compulsive disorder: influence of age of onset." *Journal of Affective Disorders, 79,* 241–46.

Mirza, Y., O'Neill, J., Smith, E. A., Russell, A., Smith, J. M., et al. (2006) "Increased medial thalamic creatine-phosphocreatine found by proton magnetic resonance spectroscopy in children with obsessive-compulsive disorder versus major depression and healthy controls." *Journal of Child Neurology, 21,* 106–111.

Morer, A., Viñas, O., Lázaro, L., Bosch, J., Toro, J., and Castro, J. (2005) "D8/17 monoclonal antibody: an unclear neropsychiatric marker." *Behavioural Neurology,* 16, 1–8.

Moritz, S., Meier, B., Hand, I., Schick, M., and Jahn, H. (2004) "Dimensional structure of the Hamilton Depression Rating Scale in patients with obsessive–compulsive disorder." *Psychiatry Research, 125,* 171–80.

Murphy, T. K., Goodman, W. K., Fudge, M. W., Williams, R. C., Ayoub, E. M., et al. (1997) "B lymphocyte antigen D8/17: a peripheral marker for childhood-onset obsessive-compulsive disorder and Tourette's syndrome?." *American Journal of Psychiatry, 154,* 402–7.

Murphy, T. K., Sajid, M., Soto, O., Shapira, N., Edge, P., et al. (2004) "Detecting pediatric autoimmune neuropsychiatric disorders associated with streptococcus, (PANDAS) in children with OCD and tics." *Biological Psychiatry, 55,* 61–68.

Nakamae, T., Narumoto, J., Shibata, K., Matsumoto, R., Kitabayashi, Y., et al. (2008) "Alteration of fractional anisotropy and apparent diffusion coefficient in obsessive-compulsive disorder: a diffusion-tensor imaging study." *Progress in Neuro-psychopharmacology & Biological Psychiatry, 35,* 1221–26.

Nakao, T., Nakagawa, A., Yoshiura, T., Nakatani, E., Nabeyama, M., et al. (2005) "Brain activation of patients with obsessive-compulsive disorder during neuropsychological and symptom provocation tasks before and after symptom improvement: a functional magnetic resonance imaging study." *Biological Psychiatry, 57,* 901–10.

Nestadt, G., Addington, A., Samuels, J., Liang, K. Y., Bienvenu, O. J., et al. (2003) "The identification of OCD-related subgroups based on comorbidity." *Biological Psychiatry, 53,* 914–20.

Nestadt, G., Samuels, J., Riddle, M., Bienvenu, O. J., Liang, K. Y. et al. (1996) "A family study of obsessive-compulsive disorder." *Archives of General Psychiatry, 57,* (2000) 358–63.

Nicolini, H., Cruz, C., Camerena, B., Orozco, B., Kennedy, J. L., et al. "DRD2, DRD3 and 5HT2A receptor genes polymorphisms in obsessive-compulsive disorder." *Molecular Psychiatry, 1,* 461–65.

Page, L. A., Rubia, K., Deeley, Q., Daly, E., Toal, F., et al. (2009) "A functional magnetic resonance imaging study of inhibitory control in obsessive-compulsive disorder." *Psychiatry Research, 174,* 202–9

Pauls, D. L., Alsobrook, J. P., Goodman, W., Rasmussen, S., and Leckman, J. F. (1995) "A family study of compulsive-obsessive disorder." *American Journal of Psychiatry, 152,* 76–84.

Perugi, G., Akiskal, H. S., Gemignani, A., Pfanner, C., Presta, S., et al. (1998) Episodic course of obsessive-compulsive disorder. *European Archives of Psychiatry and Clinical Neurosciences, 248,* 240–44.

Peterson, B. S., Pine, D. S., Cohen, P., and Brooks, J. S. (2001) "Prospective, longitudinal study of tic, obsessive-compulsive and attention-deficit/hyperactivity disorder in an epidemiological simple." *Journal of the American Academy of Child and Adolescent Psychiatry, 40,* 685–95.

Peterson, B., Riddle, M. A., Cohen, D. J., Katz, L. D., Smith, J. C., et al. "Reduced basal ganglia volumes in Tourette's syndrome using three-dimensional reconstruction techniques from magnetic resonance images." *Neurology*, 43, (1993) 941–949.

Pujol, J., Soriano-Mas, C., Alonso, P., Cardoner, M., Menchón, J. M., et al. (2004) "Mapping structural brain alterations in obsessive-compulsive disorder." *Archives of General Psychiatry*, 61, 720–30.

Rapoport, J. L., Inoff-Germain, G., Weissman, M. M., Greenwald, S., Narrow, W. E., et al. (2000) "Childhood obsessive-compulsive disorder in the NIMH MECA study: parent versus child identification of cases. Methods for the epidemiology of child and adolescent mental disorders." *Journal of Anxiety Disorders*, 14, 535–48.

Rasmussen, S. A., and Eisen, J. L. (1990) "Epidemiology of obsessive compulsive disorder." *Journal of Clinical Psychiatry*, 53, (suppl) 10–14.

Rauch, S. L., Jenike, M. A., Alpert, N. M., Baer, L., Breiter, H. C., et al. (1994) "Regional cerebral blood flow measured during symptom provocation in obsessive-compulsive disorder using oxygen 15–labeled carbon dioxide and positron emission tomography." *Archives of General Psychiatry*, 51, 62–70.

Rauch, S. L., Shin, L. M., Dougherty, D. D., Alpert, N. M., Fischman, A. J., and Jenike, M. A. (2002) "Predictors of fluvoxamine response in contamination-related obsessive compulsive disorder: A PET symptom provocation study." *Neuropsychopharmacology*, 27, 782–91

Robinson, D., Wu, H., Munne, R A., Ashtari, M., and Alvir, J. M. (1995) "Reduced caudate nucleus volume in obsessive-compulsive disorder." *Archives of General Psychiatry*, 52, 393–98.

Rosario-Campos, M. C., Leckman J. F., Curi M., Quatrano, S., Katsovitch, L., et al. (2005) "A family study of early-onset obsessive-compulsive disorder." *American Journal Medical Genetics. Part B., Neuropsychiatric Genetics*, 136, 92–97.

Rosario-Campos, M. C., Leckman, J. F., Mercadante, M. T., Shawitt, R. G., Prado, H. S., et al. (2001) "Adult with early-onset obsessive-compulsive disorder." *American Journal of Psychiatry*, 158, 1899–1903.

Rosenberg, D. R., Benazon, N. R., Gilbert, A., Sullivan, A., and Moore, G. J. (2000b) "Thalamic volumen in pediatric obsessive-compulsive disorder patients before and after cognitive behavioral therapy." *Biological Psychiatry*, 48, 294–300.

Rosenberg, D. R., Keshavan, M. S. (1998) "Toward a neurodevelopmental model of obsessive-compulsive disorder." *Biological Psychiatry*. 43, 623–40.

Rosenberg, D. R., Keshavan, M. S., Dick, E. L., Bagwell, W. W., MacMaster, F. P., Birmaher, B. (1997b) "Corpus callosal morphology in treatment naïve pediatric obsessive-compulsive disorder." *Progress in Neuro-psychopharmacology & Biological Psychiatry*, 21, 1269–83.

Rosenberg, D. R., Keshavan, M. S., O'Hearn, K. M., Dick, E. L., Bagwell, W. W., et al. (1997a) "Frontostriatal measurement in treatment-naïve children with obsessive-compulsive disorder." *Archives of General Psychiatry*, 54, 824–30.

Rosenberg, D. R., MacMaster, F. P., Keshavan, M. S., Fitzgerald, K. D., Stewart, C. M., and Moore, G. J. (2000a) "Decrease in caudate glutamatergic concentrations in pediatric obsessive-compulsive disorder patients taking paroxetine." *Journal of the American Academy of Child and Adolescent Psychiatry*, 39, 1096–1103.

Rosenberg, D. R., Mirza, Y., Russell, A., Tang, J., Smith, J. M., et al. (2004) "Reduced anterior cingulated glutamatergic concentrations in childhood OCD and major depression versus healthy controls." *Journal of American Academy Child and Ado-lescent Psychiatry, 43,* 1146–53.

Roth, R. M., Saykin, A. J., Flashman, L. A., Pixley, H. S., West, J. D., and Mamourian, A. C. (2007) "Event-related functional magnetic resonance imaging of response inhibition in obsessive-compulsive disorder." *Biological Psychiatry, 62,* 901–9.

Rubin, R. T., Ananth, J., Villanueva-Meyer, J., Trajmar, P. G., Mena, I. (1995) "Regional 133xenon cerebral blood flow and cerebral 99mTc-HMPAO uptake in patients with obsessive-compulsive disorder before and during treatment." *Biological Psychiatry, 38,* 429–37.

Russell, A., Cortese, B., Lorch, E., Ivey, J., Banerjee, S. P., et al. (2003) "Localized functional neurochemical marker abnormalities in dorsolateral prefrontal cortex in pediatric obsessive-compulsive disorder." *Journal of Child and Adolescent Psychopharmacology, 13,* S31–38.

Saito, Y., Nobuhara, K., Okugawa, G., Takase, K., Sugimoto, T., et al. (2008) "Corpus callosum in patients with obsessive-compulsive disorder: diffusion-tensor imaging study." *Radiology, 246,* 536–42.

Samuels, J., Shugart, Y. Y., Grados, M. A., Willour, V. L., Bienvenu, O. J., et al. (2007) "Significant linkage to compulsive hoarding on chromosome 14 in families with obsessive-compulsive disorder: Results from the OCD Collaborative Genetics Study." *American Journal of Psychiatry, 164,* 493–99.

Saxena, S., Brody, A. L., Colgan, M. E., Maidment, K. M., Dunkin, J. J., et al. (1999) "Localized orbitofrontal and subcortical metabolic changes and predictors of response to paroxetine treatment in obsessive-compulsive disorders." *Neuropsychopharmacology, 21,* 683–93.

Saxena, S., Brody, A. L., Ho, M. L., Alborzian, S., Maidment, K. M., et al. (2002) "Differential cerebral metabolic changes with paroxetine treatment of obsessive-compulsive disorder vs major depression." *Archives of General Psychiatry, 59,* 250–61.

Scarone S., Colombo C., Livian S., Abbruzeese, M., Ronchi, P., et al. (1992) "Increased right caudate nucleus size in obsessive-compulsive disorder: detection with magnetic resonance imaging." *Psychiatry Research, 45,* 115–21.

Schwartz, J. M., Stoessel, P. W., Baxter, L. R., Martin, K. M., Phelps, M. E. (1996) "Systematic changes in cerebral glucose metabolic rate after successful behavior modification treatment of obsessive-compulsive disorder." *Archives of General Psychiatry, 53,* 109–13.

Shapira, N. A., Liu, Y., He, A. G., Bradley, M. M., Lessing, M. C., et al. (2003) "Brain activation by disgust-inducing pictures in obsessive-compulsive disorder." *Biological Psychiatry, 54,* 751–56.

Smith, E. A., Russell, A., Lorch, E., Banerjee, S. P., Rose, M., Ivey, J., Bhandari, R., Moore, G. J., and Rosenberg, D. R. (2003) "Increased medial thalamic choline found in pediatric patients with obsessive-compulsive disorder versus major depression or healthy control subjects: a magnetic resonance spectroscopy study." *Biological Psychiatry, 54,* 1399–1405.

Stern, E., Silbersweig, D. A., Chee, K. Y., Holmes, A., Robertson, M. M., et al. (2000) "A functional neuroanatomy of tics in Tourette syndrome." *Archives of General Psychiatry, 57,* 741–48.

Stewart, S. E., Geller, D. A., Jenike, M., Pauls, D., Shaw, D., et al. (2004) "Long-term outcome of pediatric obsessive-compulsive disorder: a meta-analysis and qualitative review of the literature. *Acta Psychiatrica Scandinavica, 110*, 4–13.

Stewart, S. E., Platko, J., Fagerness, J., Birns, J., Jenike, E., et al. (2007) "A genetic family-based association study of OLIG2 in obsessive-compulsive disorder." *Archives of General Psychiatry, 64*, 209–15.

Stewart, S. E., Rosario, M. C., Baer, L., Carter, A. S., Brown, T. A., et al. (2008) "Four-factor structure of obsessive–compulsive disorder symptoms in children, adolescents, and adults." *Journal of the American Academy of Child and Adolescent Psychiatry, 47*, 763–72.

Sumitaki, S., Harada, M., Kubo, H., Ohmori, T. (2007) "Proton magnetic resonance spectroscopy reveals an abnormality in the anterior cingulated of a subgroup of obsessive-compulsive disorder patients." *Psychiatry Research, 154*, 85–92.

Swedo, S. E. (2001) "Genetic of childhood disorders: XXXIII. Autoimmunity, Part 6: Poststreptococcal autoimmunity." *Journal of the American Academy of Child and Adolescent Psychiatry, 40*, 1479–82.

Swedo, S. E., Leonard, E., Garvey, M., Mittelman, B., Allen, A. J., et al. (1998) "Pediatric auto-inmune neuropsychiatric disorders associated with streptococcal infections: clinical descriptions of the first 50 cases." *American Journal of Psychiatry, 152*, 264–71.

Swedo, S. E., Leonard, HL, Mittelman, A. J., Allen, A. J., Rapoport, J. L., et al. (1997) "Identification of children with pediatric autoinmune neuropsychiatric disorders associated with streptococcal infections by a marker associated with rheumatic fever." *American Journal of Psychiatry, 154*, 110–12.

Swedo, S. E., Pietrini, P., Leonard, H. L., Shapiro, M. B., Rettew, D. C., et al. "Cerebral glucose metabolism in childhood-onset obsessive-compulsive disorder. Revisualization during pharmacotherapy." *Archives of General Psychiatry, 49*, (1992) 690–94.

Szeszko, P. R., Ardekani, B. A., Ashtari, M., Malhotra, A. K., Robinson, D. G., et al. (2005) "White matter abnormalities in obsessive-compulsive disorder." *Archives of General Psychiatry, 62*, 782–90.

Szeszko, P. R., Christian, C., MacMaster, F., Lencz, T., Mirza, Y., Taormina, S. P., Easter, P., Rose, M., Michalopoulou, G. A., and Rosenberg, D. R.. (2008) "Gray matter structural alterations in psychotropic drug-naive pediatric obsessive-compulsive disorder: an optimized voxel-based morphometry study." *American Journal of Psychiatry, 165*, 1299–1307.

Szeszko, P. R., MacMillan, S., McMeniman, M., Chen, S., Baribault, K., et al. "Brain structural abnormalities in psychotropic drug-naive pediatric patients with obsessive-compulsive disorder." *American Journal of Psychiatry, 161*, (2004) 1049–56.

Szeszko, P. R., Robinson, D., Alvir, J. M., Bilder, R. M., Lencz, T., et al. (1999) "Orbital frontal and amygdala volume reductions in obsessive-compulsive disorder." *Archives of General Psychiatry, 56*, 913–19.

Thomsen, P. H. (1995) "Obsessive-compulsive disorder in children and adolescents: predictors in childhood for long-term phenomenological course." *Acta Psychiatrica Scandinava, 92*, 255–59.

Thóren, P., Asberg, M., Bertilsson, L., Mellström, B., Sjöqvist, F., and Träskman, L. (1980) "Clomipramine treatment of obsessive-compulsive disorder. II. Biochemical aspects." *Archives of General Psychiatry*, 37, 1289–94.

Vaasconcelos, M. S., Sampaio, A. S., Hounie, A. G., Akkerman, F., Curi, M., et al. (2007) "Prenatal, perinatal, and postnatal risk factors in obsessive-compulsive disorder." *Biological Psychiatry*, 61, 301–7.

Valente, A. A., Miguel, E. C., Castro, C. C., Amarao, E. Jr, Duran, F. L., et al. (2005) "Regional grey matter abnormalities in obsessive-compulsive disorder: A voxel-based morphometric study." *Biological Psychiatry*, 58, 479–87.

Van Grootheest, D. S., Bartels, M., van Beijsterveldt, C. E. M., Cath, D., Beekman, A. T., et al. (2008) "Genetic and environmental contributions to self-report obsessive-compulsive symptoms in Dutch adolescents at ages 12, 14, and 16." *Journal of the American Academy of Child and Adolescent Psychiatry*, 47, 1182–88.

Walitza S., Renner T., Dempfle A., Konrad K., Wewetzer C. H., et al. (2005) "Transmission disequilibrium of polymorphic variants in the tryptophan hydroxylase-2 gene in attention-deficit hyperactivity disorder." *Molecular Psychiatry*, 10, 1126–32.

Walitza, S., Wendland, J. R., Gruenblatt, E., Warnke, A., Sontag, T. A., et al. (2010) "Genetics of early-onset obsessive, compulsive disorder." *European Child and Adolescent Psychiatry*, 19, 227–35.

Walitza, H., Zellmann B. Irblich, K. W. Lange, O. Tucha, O., et al. (2008) "Children and adolescents with obsessive-compulsive disorder and comorbid attention-deficit hyperactivity disorder: preliminary results of a prospective follow-up study." *Journal of Neural Transmission*, 115, 187–90.

Whiteside, S. P., Port, J. D., and Abramowitz, J. S. "A meta-analysis of functional neuroimaging in obsessive-compulsive disorder." *Psychiatry Research*, 15, 69–79.

Whiteside, S. P., Port, J. D., Deacon, B. J., and Abramowitz, J. S. (2004) "A magnetic resonance spectroscopy investigation of obsessive-compulsive disorder and anxiety." *Psychiatry Research*, 146, (2006) 137–47.

Woolley, J., Heyman, I., Brammer, M., Frampton, I., McGuire, P. K., and Rubia, K. (2008) "Brain activation in paediatric obsessive compulsive disorder during tasks of inhibitory control." *British Journal of Psychiatry*, 192, 25–31.

Yoo, S. Y., Jang, J. H., Shin, Y. W., Kim, D. J., Park, H. J., et al. (2007) "White matter abnormalities in drug-naïve patients with obsessive-compulsive disorder: a diffusion-tensor imaging study before and after citalopram treatment." *Acta Psychiatrica Scandinavica,*, 116, 211–19.

Yoo, S. Y., Roh, M. S., Choi, J. S., Kang, D. H., Ha, T. H., et al. (2008) "Voxel-based morphometric study of gray matter abnormalities in obsessive-compulsive disorder." *Journal of Korean Medical Science*, 23, 24–30.

Yucel, M., Harrison, B. J., Wood, S. J., Fornito, A., Wellard, R. M., et al. (2007) "Functional and biochemical alterations of the medial frontal cortex in obsessive-compulsive disorder." *Archives of General Psychiatry*, 64, 946–55.

6

The Relationship between Autism and Schizophrenia

A Reappraisal

Saskia Palmen and Herman van Engeland

HISTORICAL INTRODUCTION

Maudsley was one of the first who paid attention to children with remarkable and deviant behaviour which he called *insanity of childhood*: a mixture of organic states, mental retardation and psychotic symptoms (Maudsley 1879). However, entities were not clearly defined and psychoses were named after the most prominent feature such as dementia, mental retardation, delirium and mania. Although the term childhood psychosis was defined in many different ways, the common divider was the loss of integrative capabilities, a disturbance in the development of self-awareness, a loss of contact with reality, and disturbed affective contact.

At the end of the nineteenth century, Kraepelin tried to organize psychopathology by grouping diseases with similar causes, courses and final states (Kraepelin 1896). He believed that hebephrenia, catatonia and paranoid dementia belonged to one and the same disease: *dementia praecox*. Studying over one thousand cases with dementia praecox, Kraepelin found that 3.5 percent developed symptoms before the age of ten. However, these diagnoses of childhood onset were made retrospectively. The first description of childhood psychosis as a specific entity appeared attributable to De Sanctis, who coined the term *dementia precocissima* (De Sanctis 1906). He described children who, after a period of typical development, developed mannerisms, negativism and catatonia. Likewise, Heller described a group of children with rapid loss of language abilities, motor agitation and regression of intellectual performances after a period of typical development: *dementia infantilis* (Heller 1908).

Bleuler, disapproving of the term dementia, introduced the term schizophrenia (split brain) as he believed the disintegration of one's personality was the core of the disease (Bleuler 1911). He spoke of *a group of schizophrenias* in which partial recovery was possible. According to Bleuler, essential characteristics of schizophrenia were disturbances of thought, impairments in affect and withdrawal from/disturbed (emotional) contact with the outer world, which he called autism. Lutz analysed reports of sixty-six children who became psychotic before the age of ten, applying Bleuler's criteria for schizophrenia (Lutz 1937). Twenty of these children fulfilled the criteria for childhood schizophrenia. The remaining children were reported to have organic psychoses. Of the twenty cases with childhood schizophrenia, five were younger than three years and ten were older than 6 years when psychosis revealed. In one of the first papers appearing in the American literature, Potter, also applying the Bleulerian concept of schizophrenia, described the clinical symptomatology of childhood psychosis as follows: generalized retraction of interest from the environment, dereistic thinking, feeling and acting, disturbances of thought, defect in emotional rapport, diminution and distortion of affect and alterations in behaviour (Potter 1933).

In 1942, Bender described children with a pandevelopmental disorder, which she called childhood schizophrenia (Bender 1942; Fish et al. 1968). Bender stated that childhood schizophrenia represented a lag in maturation within the embryological level of development in all the areas that are prerequisite of future behaviours in all fields. Disturbances could be detected in the temporal organization of maturation (unevenness in longitudinal development, with regressions, accelerations and retardation), physical growth, vaso-vegetative functioning, activity level, motor function, disturbed organization of perceptual impression, body image and orientation in space. Physiological immaturity would be primary, anxiety and identity difficulties were considered secondary in schizophrenic children (Fish 1957). Bender also emphasized the importance of age of onset, delineating three subtypes of childhood schizophrenia: (a) pseudodefective, appearing within the first two to three years of life, dominated by severe mental retardation, (b) pseudoneurotic, appearing between three and five years of age, dominated by pan-anxiety and obsessions and (c) pseudopsychopathic, appearing around the age of twn to eleven years, dominated by paranoid symptomatology (Bender 1947).

In 1943 Kanner borrowed the term autism, coined by Bleuler, to characterize a developmental disorder of childhood in which *"the outstanding pathognomonic fundamental disorder is the children's inability to relate themselves in the ordinary way to people and situations from the beginning of life"* (Kanner 1943). He reported on eleven children with *"extreme autistic aloneness"* and with *"an obsessive desire for sameness."* Five of these children had macrocephaly. Half a year later, Asperger used the term autism in a similar way in his publication *Die Autistischen Psychopathen im Kindesalter* [The autistic psychopaths of childhood] in which he reported on highly intelligent boys in whom the ability to relate to others is severely disturbed (Asperger 1944). Although Kanner and Asperger introduced the term autism into the field of child psychiatry, children with autism were described earlier, although under different names. The first and probably most famous is *Victor, the wild boy of Aveyron* (1798) (Malson 1972) (but see also De Sanctis 1906; Heller 1908; Ssucharewa 1926; Lutz 1937).

Due to lack of universal, circumscribed diagnostic criteria, it remained elusive whether autism and childhood schizophrenia were different names for one and the same disorder, or whether autism and childhood schizophrenia represented different, possible partly overlapping, entities with differential symptomatology, onset and course. Unfortunately Kanner contributed to this confusion as on the one hand he underscored the difference between "his autism" and Potter's and Lutz's childhood schizophrenia as "his children with autism" were born with an inability to form the usual, biologically provided affective contact with people, whereas children with childhood schizophrenia displayed typical development for some period of time before developing psychotic symptoms. However, on the other hand, he emphasized that autism was a psychotic phenomenon, possibly the earliest manifestation of a schizophrenic process.

The issue of heterogeneity was approached in different ways. The British Working Party on Schizophrenic Syndrome in Childhood tried to define the common factors of psychotic children (Creak et al. 1961), whereas the World Health Organisation (WHO)-task force, led by M. Rutter, tried to distinguish separate entities (Rutter 1968). Both through M. Rutter's work and I. Kolvin's (Kolvin 1972), it became clear that autism was not a psychotic disorder but a neurodevelopmental disorder. In accordance with this the *Journal of Autism and Childhood Schizophrenia* changed its name in 1979 to *Journal of Autism and Developmental Disorders*. Ironically, however, since the 1980s schizophrenia itself has come to be thought of as a neurodevelopmental disorder (Murray and Lewis 1987; Fatemi and Folsom 2009).

The discussion about the relationship between autism and schizophrenia has been further complicated by diagnostic classification systems (as in DSM). It was not in fact until the appearance of DSM-III in 1980 that autistic disorder became a valid diagnosis. Both in DSM-I (1952) and in DSM-II (1968) a diagnosis of autistic disorder was lacking. In DSM-I, children with autistic symptoms were diagnosed as schizophrenic reaction, childhood type. In DSM-II, symptoms of seclusiveness, detachment, sensitivity, shyness, timidity, and general inability to form close interpersonal relationships were fitted in the diagnosis "withdrawing reaction of childhood."

In the present article, we will outline the existing evidence for a (partly) shared aetiology, looking at symptomatology, epidemiology, environmental risk factors, (dis)morphology, neuroimaging and genetics.

SYMPTOMATOLOGY

Although it was not until 1980 that autistic disorder was incorporated into the DSM, previous reports of symptomatology in childhood psychosis show clear resemblance with the criteria used for autistic disorder in the present DSM-IV. Potter defined six diagnostic pointers to childhood psychosis: (1) generalized retraction of interest from environment, (2) dereistic thinking, feeling and acting, (3) disturbances of thought, (4) defect in emotional rapport, (5) diminution and distortion of affect and (6) alterations in behaviour (Potter 1933) and Creak et al. (1961) issued a memorandum outlining nine diagnostic points to promote clarification of the diagnosis of childhood psychosis: (1) gross and sustained impairment of emotional relationships with people, (2) a background of serious retardation in which islets of normal, near normal, or exceptional intellectual function or skill may appear, (3) apparent unawareness of his own personal identity, (4) pathological preoccupation with particular objects or certain characteristics of them, (5) sustained resistance to change, (6) abnormal perceptual experience, (7) acute, excessive and illogical anxiety, (8) speech either never acquired, lost, or inappropriate for age and (9) distortion in motility patterns (Creak et al. 1961).

In 1980, autistic disorder was described for the first time in the DSM-III and was defined by six criteria, clearly overlapping with those used by Potter and Creak to describe childhood psychosis: (1) onset before 30 months of age, (2) pervasive lack of responsiveness to other people, (3) gross deficits in language development, (4) if speech was present, peculiar speech patterns such as immediate and delayed echolalia, metaphorical language, pronominal reversal, (5) bizarre responses to various aspects of the environment, e.g., resistance to change, peculiar interest in or attachments to animate or inanimate objects and (6) absence of delusions, hallucinations, loosening of associations, and incoherence as in schizophrenia. Schizoid disorder of childhood was defined in DSM-III as (1) having no close relationships (although may have close relationship with relative), (2) no interest in making friends, (3) no pleasure in interacting with peers, (4) avoidance of social contacts outside nuclear family, (5) no interest in activities involving other children and (6) duration of at least three months.

Recently, Barneveld et al. have reported significantly more schizotypal traits in twenty-seven adolescents with pervasive developmental disorder (PDD) compared to thirty typically developing adolescents using the AQ

(Autism Questionnaire) and the SPQ (Schizotypal Personality Question-naire-Revised) (Barneveld et al. 2010). Besides high levels of negative symptoms, adolescents with PDD also displayed high levels of positive and disorganized symptoms.

In conclusion, autism and schizophrenia share at a clinical phenotypic level deficits in social behaviour, oddness of speech, unusual responsiveness to the environment and inappropriate affect.

EPIDEMIOLOGY

Apart from the problems arisen from absent or changing diagnostic criteria for autism and schizophrenia, views on the relationship between autism and schizophrenia have changed dramatically over the years. As already touched upon in the previous paragraph, Kanner did not originally believe that autism and schizophrenia were related. Children with autism were born with an inability to form the usual, biologically provided affective contact with people, whereas children with childhood schizophrenia displayed typical development for some period of time before developing psychotic symptoms However, on the other hand, he emphasized that autism was a psychotic phenomenon, possibly the earliest manifestation of a schizophrenic process (Kanner 1968), an opinion shared by Bender (Bender 1947). In the 1960s and 1970s Kolvin, Rutter and Eisenberg suggested that the two disorders were unrelated (Kolvin 1971a; Rutter 1972; Eisenberg 1972). Kolvin reported that children who became psychotic before the age of five (early onset) did not have hallucinations and delusions and the familial loading in these children was not comparable to the familial loading of families with adult patients with schizophrenia. These children did not have childhood schizophrenia, but infantile psychosis, also called autistic syndrome (Kolvin 1971a, 1971b). Eisenberg strongly supported the three main categories of childhood psychosis suggested by Rutter: schizophrenia, disintegrative psychosis and infantile autism (Eisenberg 1972).

Although in the DSM-III (1980) a diagnosis of autism specifically excluded individuals with schizophrenia, case reports showed cases of autism associated with schizophrenia (Petty et al. 1984). However, other investigators stated that having autism would act to protect an individual from subsequently developing schizophrenia (Volkmar 1987). It was only in DSM-III-R (1987) that autism and schizophrenia were no longer mutually exclusive, implicating that from then on prevalence studies could be performed looking at comorbidity between the two disorders. Although some studies did not find increased frequency of schizophrenia among autistic adolescents and adults (Volkmar and Cohen 1991; Ghaziuddin,

Weidmer-Mikhail, and Ghaziuddin 1998; Leyfer et al. 2006), the majority of studies in the last decades of the twentieth century showed premorbid developmental abnormalities in childhood onset schizophrenia (COS), including PDD (17 percent to 40 percent) (Asarnow and Ben-Meir 1988; Watkins, Asarnow, and Tanguay 1988; Russell, Bott, and Sammons 1989; Green et al. 1992; Alaghband-Rad et al. 1995; Hollis 1995). In the present century, Sporn et al. showed that 25 percent of seventy-five children with COS had a lifetime diagnosis of PDD (Sporn et al. 2004). As there were no differences between those children with COS with comorbid PDD and those with COS without PDD with respect to age of onset, IQ, response to medications and rate of familial schizotypy, the authors concluded that premorbid PDD in COS is more likely to be a nonspecific marker of severe early abnormal neurodevelopment. However, two PDD-COS children had a sibling with nuclear autism, a prevalence of 4.9 percent, similar to that seen for probands with nuclear autism. Five years later, the same group reported that in 30 percent to 50 percent, COS is preceded and comorbid with PDD (Rapoport et al. 2009).

Besides evidence of increased prevalence of PDD in COS, an increasing body of evidence showed increased prevalence of pervasive developmental disorder (PDD) in *adult* patients with schizophrenia compared to the general population. Stahlberg et al. showed that 7.8 percent of 129 adults who received a PDD diagnosis in childhood were diagnosed with schizophrenia or another psychotic disorder in adulthood (Stahlberg et al. 2004). Although the PDD-psychosis group did not differ from the PDD without psychosis group concerning IQ, the PDD subjects with comorbid psychosis had considerable poorer global functioning, as measured with the GAF (global assessment of functioning) score. In line with the percentage of comorbid psychotic disorders in PDD reported by Stahlberg et al. (2004), Mouridsen et al. (2008) found that 6.8 percent of 118 adults with childhood diagnosis of autism developed a psychotic disorder, compared with 0.9 percent of 336 controls from the general population (Mouridsen et al. 2008). In another study, Mouridsen et al. reported on eighty-nine patients, diagnosed as children with atypical autism. 34.8 percent were also diagnosed with a schizophrenia spectrum disorder (Mouridsen, Rich, and Isager 2008). Finally, a very recent study reported that twenty-two of twenty-six (84.6 percent) adult patients with PDD manifested psychotic symptoms and sixteen (72.7 percent) had a concurrent diagnosis of schizophrenia (Raja and Azzoni 2010). Patients with PDD and comorbid schizophrenia were characterized by a higher prevalence of male gender, younger age and higher susceptibility to motor side effects of antipsychotic treatment compared to patients affected by schizophrenia only. The authors suggested that the high comorbidity rate between PDD and schizophrenia could be related to a shared neurobiology.

Finally, a specific subtype of PDD, MCDD (multiple complex developmental disorder), although not incorporated in DSM-IV, is clearly associated with an increased risk of developing psychosis, with risk between 22 percent and 64 percent (Sprong et al. 2008; Van Engeland and Van der Gaag 1994).

In 2010, two reviews appeared on comorbidity of PDD and psychosis/schizophrenia (Padgett, Miltsiou, and Tiffin 2010; Skokauskas and Gallagher 2010). The overall conclusion of these reviews is that there is conflicting evidence regarding the frequency of schizophrenia in PDD, although there is some evidence for elevated rates of comorbid PDD in individuals with childhood-onset psychosis. Prevalence rates of psychosis in PDD vary between 0 to 53 percent. Vice versa, surveys of juvenile onset of non-affective psychosis showed incidences of PDD ranging from 18 to 56 percent. Both methodological shortcomings (for example referral and screening/surveillance biases) and nosological confusion (the use of categories where dimensions might be more appropriate, overlapping diagnostic criteria, artificial subdivision of syndromes) are a potential source of confounding variables.

Lastly, several studies report an increased prevalence of schizophrenia and other psychotic disorders in parents of children diagnosed with PDD (Larsson et al. 2005; Daniels et al. 2008).

In summary, there is an increasing body of evidence suggesting overlapping prevalence of PDD and schizophrenia, but no prospective longitudinal studies looking at the developmental trajectories of symptomatology from infancy onwards have been performed as yet.

ENVIRONMENTAL RISK FACTORS

Both in PDD and in schizophrenia, an increased prevalence of in-utero disease and stress exposure (Cannon, Dean, and Jones 2004; Landrigan 2010; Kinney et al. 2008), characteristic season of birth (Davies et al. 2003; Stevens, Fein, and Waterhouse 2000), urbanicity (Williams, Higgins, and Brayne 2006; Sundquist, Frank, and Sundquist 2004) and increased rate of pre- and perinatal complications (Cannon, Jones, and Murray 2002; Kolevzon, Gross, and Reichenberg 2007) have been reported. Moreover, paternal age is positively associated with the risk of both PDD and schizophrenia (Petersen, Mortensen, and Pedersen 2011; Reichenberg et al. 2010; Grether et al. 2009; Croen et al. 2007; Malaspina et al. 2001). Increased maternal age has been consistently implicated in PDD (Reichenberg et al. 2010; Grether et al. 2009; Croen et al. 2007), although results in schizophrenia have been equivocal (Dalman and Allebeck 2002; Malaspina et al. 2001).

IMAGING

Since the first quantitative MRI study on autism was performed (Filipek et al. 1992), the quality of brain imaging has improved dramatically. In the last decades several reviews on structural brain abnormalities in PDD have appeared (for example (Palmen and van Engeland 2004; Stanfield et al. 2008). Overall, the majority of studies have found increased brain volume due to larger cerebral, grey matter and cerebellar size– and increased ventricular volume but a decrease in the corpus callosum area in PDD.

Likewise, several reviews of structural brain imaging studies in schizophrenia have been published (for example, Cahn et al. 2009; Hulshoff Pol and Kahn 2008; Wright et al. 2000). As in PDD, increased ventricular volume and decreased corpus callosum area have been consistently found, but, contrary to PDD, there is a decrease in brain volume. Interestingly, Sporn et al. showed that the rate of grey matter loss was greater in the group of children with both COS and PDD, compared to COS without comorbid PDD (Sporn et al. 2004). The authors hypothesised that both PDD and COS have evidence of accelerated trajectories of anatomic brain development at ages near disorder onset. In autism there is an acceleration or excess of early postnatal brain development (one to three years), whereas in COS, there is exaggeration of the brain maturation process of childhood and early adolescence (ten to sixteen years). Both patterns could be seen as an abnormal "shift to the left" with respect to age compared with normal brain development, with autism showing initial overgrowth and COS showing greater "pruning down" of the cortex in early and middle parts of the trajectory, both accelerations normalizing with age. Recently, Toal et al. investigated brain anatomy in a group of adults with PDD, half of whom had a history of psychosis, and controls (Toal et al. 2009). Compared with controls both PDD with and without psychosis had significantly less grey matter bilaterally in the temporal lobes and the cerebellum. In contrast, they had increased grey matter in striatal regions. However, those with psychosis also had a significant reduction in grey matter content of frontal and occipital regions. Within the PDD group, psychosis was associated with a reduction in grey matter of the right insular cortex and bilaterally in the cerebellum extending into the fusiform gyrus and the lingual gyrus. The authors concluded that the abnormalities usually associated with PDD might represent an alternative "entry-point" into a final common pathway of psychosis. Recently, Cheung et al. performed a meta-analysis on twenty-five voxel-based studies comprising 308 patients with PDD, 352 with first-episode schizophrenia and 801 controls (Cheung et al. 2010). Using a novel modification of Anatomical Likelihood Estimation (ALE) 313 foci were extracted. Lower grey matter volumes within limbic basal ganglia loop system were common to both PDD and schizophrenia, while lower grey matter volume in left putamen (PDD) and left fronto-striatal-temporal regions (schizophrenia) appear to distinguish the disorders in terms of grey matter circuitry. These findings support the position that autism and schizophrenia are related. Moreover, Gilmore et al. showed some brain overgrowth in very young male infants at high risk for schizophrenia (Gilmore et al. 2010).

In the last decade, a new technique, DTI (diffusion tensor imaging), visualizing brain connectivity, was introduced into the field of psychiatry. The first DTI study in PDD, reported reduced fractional anisotropy (FA) in those regions in the brain implicated in social functioning in children and adolescents with PDD compared to control children and adolescents (Barnea-Goraly et al. 2004). Numerous DTI studies in PDD followed, mostly focussing on long-distance tracts. Overall, these studies showed microstructural abnormalities in the corpus callosum (Alexander et al. 2007; Shukla et al. 2010; Brito et al. 2009; Keller, Kana, and Just 2007; Kumar et al. 2010), arcuate fasciculus (Fletcher et al. 2010), inferior fronto-occipital and superior longitudinal fasciculi (Sahyoun, Belliveau, and Mody 2010), as well as limbic (Pugliese et al. 2009), hippocampal and amygdalo-fusiform pathways (Conturo et al. 2008), internal capsule (Keller, Kana, and Just 2007; Shukla et al. 2010; Cheng et al. 2010), cerebellar peduncle (Brito et al. 2009; Shukla et al. 2010; Catani et al. 2008) and corticospinal tract (Brito et al. 2009).

Previously, high local connectivity developing in tandem with low long-range connectivity was suggested in the autistic brain (Belmonte et al. 2004; Herbert et al. 2004; Just et al. 2004). Two studies specifically investigated these short, local association fibres and found reduced FA for short association fibres in frontal (Sundaram et al. 2008) and frontal, temporal and parietal lobes (Shukla et al. 2011) in children with PDD compared to typically developing children, arguing against selective sparing of short-distance fibres in PDD. Interestingly, Shukla et al. also found positive correlations between age and FA in typically developing children, but not in children with PDD, which may reflect altered maturation of short-distance tracts in PDD. Of interest is the recently published study of Barnea-Goraly et al. reporting no difference in white matter structure between children with PDD and their unaffected siblings, whereas both groups differed from the control group (Barnea-Goraly, Lotspeich, and Reiss 2010). It was suggested that white matter structure may represent a marker of genetic risk for autism or vulnerability to development of the disorder.

As in DTI studies in PDD subjects, DTI studies in chronic schizophrenia indicate widespread microstructural abnormalities of the corpus callosum (Agartz, Andersson, and Skare 2001; Foong et al. 2000; Kubicki et al. 2005), arcuate fasciculus (Burns et al. 2003; Kubicki et al. 2005), amygdala (Kalus et al. 2005), hippocampus (Kalus et al. 2004), internal capsule

(Buchsbaum et al. 1998; Kubicki et al. 2005) and cerebellar peduncle (Okugawa et al. 2004), but also in the cingulum (Kubicki et al. 2003; Wang et al. 2004; Kubicki et al. 2005) (for review, see (Konrad and Winterer 2008). Peters et al. reviewed the existing literature on DTI studies in (ultra) high risk individuals and first-episode schizophrenia or recent onset patients, and reported similar, but less robust findings compared to chronic schizophrenia patients (Peters, Blaas, and de Haan 2010). They concluded that DTI abnormalities convey a liability for psychosis and additional abnormalities occur around the onset of psychosis. Several lines of evidence point to myelin dysfunction (Davis et al. 2003), reduced oligodendrocyte number or integrity (Segal et al. 2007) or possibly hyperglutamatergic state (Matute et al. 1999; Chang et al. 2007) as causes of the reported white matter pathology, although the exact underlying pathology of DTI abnormalities remains elusive. In addition, Innocenti et al. concluded that, although most evidence favours hypoconnectivity in schizophrenia, in some patients there may be hyperconnectivity between brain regions (Innocenti, Ansermet, and Parnas 2003).

Interestingly, Gilmore et al. were the first to report on prenatal and neonatal brain structure and white matter maturation in children at high risk for schizophrenia (Gilmore et al. 2010). Prenatal ultrasound scans and neonatal MRI and DTI were made of twenty-six offspring of mothers with schizophrenia or schizoaffective disorder (i.e. high risk) and twenty-six comparison mothers. No prenatal differences in lateral ventricle width or head circumference were found between the offspring of the two groups. In addition, male, but not female, neonates at genetic risk for schizophrenia had several larger than normal brain volumes (intracranial, CSF, grey matter and lateral ventricles). The authors conclude that schizophrenia-associated brain alterations may be detectable at birth and may be sex-specific. As increased brain volume is consistently found in autism (although not at birth), the authors also suggest similar early developmental trajectories in autism en schizophrenia. It would be of utmost interest to follow up on these neonates to see if they develop PDD and/or schizophrenia later in life. In an editorial, Ross suggested two critical windows: a foetal and early infancy period, during which vulnerability is established, and a later, often adolescent or young adult period, during which conversion from vulnerability to psychosis occurs (Ross 2010).

In summary, imaging studies on PDD and psychosis/schizophrenia suggest partial overlap in brain abnormalities.

GENETICS

Autism and schizophrenia are estimated to have the highest genetic load among neuropsychiatric disorders. Both common single-nucleotide polymorphisms and rare copy number variants (CNVs) have been implicated in the underlying genetics of autism and schizophrenia (Abrahams and Geschwind 2008). Rzhetsky et al. hypothesize that autism, bipolar disorder and schizophrenia share significant genetic overlap (Rzhetsky et al. 2007). Using a modelling approach, it was estimated that 20 to 75 percent of autism-predisposing variations also predispose the bearer to schizophrenia (and 20 to 60 percent of autism-predisposing variations also predispose the bearer to bipolar disorder). Indeed, the same chromosomal rearrangements and several single genes have emerged as genetic risks in autism and schizophrenia. These findings raise the possibility that autism and schizophrenia share pathogenic mechanisms and that similar defect in biological pathways of brain development might underlie the phenotypic spectrum of these disorders (Burbach and van der Zwaag 2009). Guilmatre et al. investigated CNVs in 247 patient with mental retardation, 260 with autism, 236 with schizophrenia and 236 controls and found recurrent or overlapping CNVs in patients at 40 percent of the selected loci (Guilmatre et al. 2009). Recently, Crespi et al. used data from CNVs, single gene associations, growth-signalling pathways and intermediate phenotypes associated with brain growth to evaluate the genomic and developmental relationships between autism and schizophrenia (Crespi, Stead, and Elliot 2010). The authors hypothesize that autism reflects a bias towards paternally expressed genes, brain overgrowth and underdevelopment of social brain systems, whereas schizophrenia is said to involve maternally expressed genes, brain undergrowth and maladaptive "hyperdevelopment" of social systems (Crespi and Badcock 2008). Of forty-five genes evaluated for association with both autism and schizophrenia and with replicated positive associations, twenty genes exhibit one or more positive associations with both conditions. Rare CNVs at seven loci were analysed for frequencies of deletions versus duplications in autism and schizophrenia. One locus (16q13.1) supported a model of overlap, whereas four loci supported the diametric hypothesis. In accordance with this diametric hypothesis, Bruining et al. reported on the differential effect of the parent of origin of the extra X chromosome in seventy-six patients with Klinefelter syndrome (XXY karyotype) (Bruining et al. 2010). The authors showed that significantly higher scores in schizotypal traits were associated with maternal origin of the extra X chromosome, whereas impairments in social interaction and impairments in communication, but not repetitive and stereotyped behaviours, were associated with paternal origin of the extra X chromosome. However, contrary to the diametric hypothesis, several other studies have reported specific deletions associated both with PDD (Miller et al. 2009; Ben-Shachar et al. 2009; Pagnamenta et al. 2009; Sharp et al. 2008; Mefford et al. 2008) and schizophrenia (Consortium 2008; Stefansson et al. 2008).

In summary, although definitive genetic epidemiological studies of the relationship between PDD and schizophrenia are lacking, there is evidence for shared genetic factors (Rzhetsky et al. 2007), especially genes encoding interacting synaptic proteins, i.e., neuroligins and neurexins, essential for synapse function (Sudhof 2008; Szatmari et al. 2007; Kim et al. 2008; Kirov et al. 2009). Moreover, both in PDD and schizophrenia, contrary to bipolar disorder, the burden of large, rare CNVs is increased and partly overlapping (Consortium 2008; Guilmatre et al. 2009; Stefansson et al. 2008).

OVERALL CONCLUSION

Looking at the existing literature, both PDD and schizophrenia are considered to be neurodevelopmental disorders, sharing, on a clinical phenotypic level, deficits in social behaviour, oddness of speech, unusual responsiveness to the environment and inappropriate affect. It has been shown that there is a substantial overlap in prevalence, most likely explained by shared vulnerability factors. These shared factors include environmental data, such as in utero disease and stress exposure, pre- and perinatal complications, season of birth, urbanicity and parental age, but also genetic data, such as large and rare CNVs (Carroll and Owen 2009). These shared risk factors lead to overlap in (structural) brain abnormalities. However, it is not understood how shared genetic and environmental risk factors in PDD and schizophrenia result in quite different illness progression: difference in age of onset, difference in sex-distribution (Zahn-Waxler, Shirtcliff, and Marceau 2008; Abel, Drake, and Goldstein 2010) and difference of comorbidity with mental retardation.

Up to date studies have been hampered by current categorical diagnostic systems. Future studies should explore the relationship between genes and other biological variables and dimensional measures of key domains of psychopathology across current diagnostic categories. Furthermore, prospective, longitudinal studies looking at the developmental trajectories of symptomatology starting from infancy are crucial.

But, as Bender and Fish already stated, the evidence is overwhelming for PDD and schizophrenia being pan-developmental disorders.

REFERENCES

Abel, K. M., R. Drake, and J. M. Goldstein. (2010). Sex differences in schizophrenia. *International review of psychiatry 22*(5), 417–28.
Abrahams, B. S., and D. H. Geschwind. (2008). Advances in autism genetics: on the threshold of a new neurobiology. *Nature reviews. Genetics, 9*(5), 341–55.

Agartz, I., J. L. Andersson, and S. Skare. (2001). Abnormal brain white matter in schizophrenia: a diffusion tensor imaging study. *Neuroreport 12*(10), 2251–4.

Alaghband-Rad, J., K. McKenna, C. T. Gordon, K. E. Albus, S. D. Hamburger, J. M. Rumsey, J. A. Frazier, M. C. Lenane, and J. L. Rapoport. (1995). Childhood-onset schizophrenia: the severity of premorbid course. *Journal of the American Academy of Child and Adolescent Psychiatry 34*(10), 1273–83.

Alexander, A. L., J. E. Lee, M. Lazar, R. Boudos, M. B. DuBray, T. R. Oakes, J. N. Miller, J. Lu, E. K. Jeong, W. M. McMahon, E. D. Bigler, and J. E. Lainhart. (2007). Diffusion tensor imaging of the corpus callosum in autism. *Neuroimage 34*(1), 61–73.

Asarnow, J. R., and S. Ben-Meir. (1988). Children with schizophrenia spectrum and depressive disorders: a comparative study of premorbid adjustment, onset pattern and severity of impairment. *Journal of child psychology and psychiatry, and allied disciplines 29*(4), 477–88.

Asperger, H. 1944. Die Autistischen Psychopathen im Kindesalter. *Archiv für Psychiatrie und Nervenkrankheiten*, 117, 76–136.

Barnea-Goraly, N., H. Kwon, V. Menon, S. Eliez, L. Lotspeich, and A. L. Reiss. (2004). White matter structure in autism: preliminary evidence from diffusion tensor imaging. *Biological psychiatry 55*(3), 323–6.

Barnea-Goraly, N., L. J. Lotspeich, and A. L. Reiss. (2010). Similar white matter aberrations in children with autism and their unaffected siblings: a diffusion tensor imaging study using tract-based spatial statistics. *Arch Gen Psychiatry 67*(10), 1052–60.

Barneveld, P. S., J. Pieterse, L. de Sonneville, S. van Rijn, B. Lahuis, H. van Engeland, and H. Swaab. (2010). Overlap of autistic and schizotypal traits in adolescents with Autism Spectrum Disorders. *Schizophr Res*.

Belmonte, M. K., G. Allen, A. Beckel-Mitchener, L. M. Boulanger, R. A. Carper, and S. J. Webb. (2004). Autism and abnormal development of brain connectivity. *The Journal of neuroscience: The official journal of the Society for Neuroscience 24*(42), 9228–31.

Ben-Shachar, S., B. Lanpher, J. R. German, M. Qasaymeh, L. Potocki, S. C. Nagamani, L. M. Franco, A. Malphrus, G. W. Bottenfield, J. E. Spence, S. Amato, J. A. Rousseau, B. Moghaddam, C. Skinner, S. A. Skinner, S. Bernes, N. Armstrong, M. Shinawi, P. Stankiewicz, A. Patel, S. W. Cheung, J. R. Lupski, A. L. Beaudet, and T. Sahoo. (2009). Microdeletion 15q13.3, a locus with incomplete penetrance for autism, mental retardation, and psychiatric disorders. *Journal of medical genetics 46*(6), 382–8.

Bender, L. (1942). Schizophrenia in childhood. *The Nervous child* 1, 138–140.

———. 1947. Childhood schizophrenia; clinical study on one hundred schizophrenic children. *Am J Orthopsychiatry 17*(1), 40–56.

Bleuler, E. 1911. *Dementia preacox oder Gruppe der Schizophrenien*. : Leipzig und Wien: Franz Deuticke.

Brito, A. R., M. M. Vasconcelos, R. C. Domingues, L. C. Hygino da Cruz, Jr., S. Rodrigues Lde, E. L. Gasparetto, and C. A. Calcada. (2009). Diffusion tensor imaging findings in school-aged autistic children. *Journal of neuroimaging: official journal of the American Society of Neuroimaging 19*(4), 337–43.

Bruining, H., S. van Rijn, H. Swaab, J. Giltay, W. Kates, M. J. Kas, H. van Engeland, and L. de Sonneville. (2010). The parent-of-origin of the extra X chromosome may differentially affect psychopathology in Klinefelter syndrome. *Biological psychiatry 68*(12), 1156–62.

Buchsbaum, M. S., C. Y. Tang, S. Peled, H. Gudbjartsson, D. Lu, E. A. Hazlett, J. Downhill, M. Haznedar, J. H. Fallon, and S. W. Atlas. (1998). MRI white matter diffusion anisotropy and PET metabolic rate in schizophrenia. *Neuroreport 9*(3), 425–30.

Burbach, J. P., and B. van der Zwaag. (2009). Contact in the genetics of autism and schizophrenia. *Trends Neurosci 32*(2), 69–72.

Burns, J., D. Job, M. E. Bastin, H. Whalley, T. Macgillivray, E. C. Johnstone, and S. M. Lawrie. (2003). Structural disconnectivity in schizophrenia: a diffusion tensor magnetic resonance imaging study. *The British journal of psychiatry: the journal of mental science* 182, 439–43.

Cahn, W., M. Rais, F. P. Stigter, N. E. van Haren, E. Caspers, H. E. Hulshoff Pol, Z. Xu, H. G. Schnack, and R. S. Kahn. (2009). Psychosis and brain volume changes during the first five years of schizophrenia. *Eur Neuropsychopharmacol 19*(2), 147–51.

Cannon, M., K. Dean, and P.B. Jones. (2004). Early environmental risk factors for schizophrenia. In *Neurodevelopment and Schizophrenia*, edited by C. U. Press. Cambridge.

Cannon, M., P. B. Jones, and R. M. Murray. (2002). Obstetric complications and schizophrenia: historical and meta-analytic review. *The American journal of psychiatry* 159(7), 1080–92.

Carroll, L. S., and M. J. Owen. (2009). Genetic overlap between autism, schizophrenia and bipolar disorder. *Genome medicine 1*(10), 102.

Catani, M., D. K. Jones, E. Daly, N. Embiricos, Q. Deeley, L. Pugliese, S. Curran, D. Robertson, and D. G. Murphy. (2008). Altered cerebellar feedback projections in Asperger syndrome. *Neuroimage 41*(4), 1184–91.

Chang, L., J. Friedman, T. Ernst, K. Zhong, N. D. Tsopelas, and K. Davis. (2007). Brain metabolite abnormalities in the white matter of elderly schizophrenic subjects: implication for glial dysfunction. *Biological psychiatry 62*(12), 1396–404.

Cheng, Y., K. H. Chou, I. Y. Chen, Y. T. Fan, J. Decety, and C. P. Lin. (2010). Atypical development of white matter microstructure in adolescents with autism spectrum disorders. *Neuroimage 50*(3), 873–82.

Cheung, C., K. Yu, G. Fung, M. Leung, C. Wong, Q. Li, P. Sham, S. Chua, and G. McAlonan. (2010). Autistic disorders and schizophrenia: related or remote? An anatomical likelihood estimation. *PLoS One 5*(8), e12233.

Conturo, T. E., D. L. Williams, C. D. Smith, E. Gultepe, E. Akbudak, and N. J. Minshew. (2008). Neuronal fiber pathway abnormalities in autism: an initial MRI diffusion tensor tracking study of hippocampo-fusiform and amygdalo-fusiform pathways. *Journal of the International Neuropsychological Society: JINS 14*(6), 933–46.

Creak, M., K. Cameron, V. Cowie, S. Ini, R. MacKeith, G. Mitchell, G. O'Gorman, F. Orford, W. Rogers, A. Shapiro, F. Stone, G. Stroh, and S. Yudkin. 1961. Schizophrenic syndrome in childhood: Progress report of a working party. *British Medical Journal* 2, 889–890.

Crespi, B., and C. Badcock. (2008). Psychosis and autism as diametrical disorders of the social brain. *The Behavioral and brain sciences 31*(3), 241–61; discussion 261–320.

Crespi, B., P. Stead, and M. Elliot. (2010). Evolution in health and medicine Sackler colloquium: Comparative genomics of autism and schizophrenia. *Proc Natl Acad Sci U S A* 107 Suppl 1, 1736–41.

Croen, L. A., D. V. Najjar, B. Fireman, and J. K. Grether. (2007). Maternal and paternal age and risk of autism spectrum disorders. *Archives of pediatrics & adolescent medicine 161*(4), 334–40.

Dalman, C., and P. Allebeck. (2002). Paternal age and schizophrenia: further support for an association. *The American Journal of Psychiatry 159*(9), 1591–2.

Daniels, J. L., U. Forssen, C. M. Hultman, S. Cnattingius, D. A. Savitz, M. Feychting, and P. Sparen. (2008). Parental psychiatric disorders associated with autism spectrum disorders in the offspring. *Pediatrics 121*(5), e1357–62.

Davies, G., J. Welham, D. Chant, E. F. Torrey, and J. McGrath. (2003). A systematic review and meta-analysis of Northern Hemisphere season of birth studies in schizophrenia. *Schizophrenia bulletin 29*(3), 587–93.

Davis, K. L., D. G. Stewart, J. I. Friedman, M. Buchsbaum, P. D. Harvey, P. R. Hof, J. Buxbaum, and V. Haroutunian. (2003). White matter changes in schizophrenia: evidence for myelin-related dysfunction. *Archives of general psychiatry 60*(5), 443–56.

De Sanctis, S. (1906). Sopra alcune varieta della demenza precoc [Concerning various kinds of precocious dementia]. *Rivista Sperimentale di Freniatria e di Medicina Legale* 32, 141–165.

Eisenberg, L. (1972). The classification of childhood psychosis reconsidered. *Journal of autism and childhood schizophrenia 2*(4), 338–42.

Fatemi, S. H., and T. D. Folsom. (2009). The neurodevelopmental hypothesis of schizophrenia, revisited. *Schizophrenia bulletin 35*(3), 528–48.

Filipek, P. A., C. Richelme, D. N. Kennedy, J. Rademacher, D.A. Pitcher, S. Zidel, and V. S. Caviness. (1992). Morphometric analysis of the brain in developmental language disorders and autism. *Ann Neurol* 32, 475.

Fish, B. (1957). The detection of schizophrenia in infancy; a preliminary report. *J Nerv Ment Dis 125*(1), 1–24.

Fish, B., T. Shapiro, M. Campbell, and R. Wile. (1968). A classification of schizophrenic children under five years. *Am J Psychiatry 124*(10), 1415–23.

Fletcher, P. T., R. T. Whitaker, R. Tao, M. B. DuBray, A. Froehlich, C. Ravichandran, A. L. Alexander, E. D. Bigler, N. Lange, and J. E. Lainhart. (2010). Microstructural connectivity of the arcuate fasciculus in adolescents with high-functioning autism. *Neuroimage 51*(3), 1117–25.

Foong, J., M. Maier, C. A. Clark, G. J. Barker, D. H. Miller, and M. A. Ron. (2000). Neuropathological abnormalities of the corpus callosum in schizophrenia: a diffusion tensor imaging study. *Journal of neurology, neurosurgery, and psychiatry 68*(2), 242–4.

Ghaziuddin, M., E. Weidmer-Mikhail, and N. Ghaziuddin. (1998). Comorbidity of Asperger syndrome: a preliminary report. *Journal of intellectual disability research: JIDR 42*(Pt 4), 279–83.

Gilmore, J. H., C. Kang, D. D. Evans, H. M. Wolfe, J. K. Smith, J. A. Lieberman, W. Lin, R. M. Hamer, M. Styner, and G. Gerig. (2010). Prenatal and neonatal brain structure and white matter maturation in children at high risk for schizophrenia. *Am J Psychiatry* 167(9), 1083–91.

Green, W. H., M. Padron-Gayol, A. S. Hardesty, and M. Bassiri. (1992). Schizophrenia with childhood onset: a phenomenological study of 38 cases. *Journal of the American Academy of Child and Adolescent Psychiatry* 31(5), 968–76.

Grether, J. K., M. C. Anderson, L. A. Croen, D. Smith, and G. C. Windham. (2009). Risk of autism and increasing maternal and paternal age in a large north American population. *American journal of epidemiology* 170(9), 1118–26.

Guilmatre, A., C. Dubourg, A. L. Mosca, S. Legallic, A. Goldenberg, V. Drouin-Garraud, V. Layet, A. Rosier, S. Briault, F. Bonnet-Brilhault, F. Laumonnier, S. Odent, G. Le Vacon, G. Joly-Helas, V. David, C. Bendavid, J. M. Pinoit, C. Henry, C. Impallomeni, E. Germano, G. Tortorella, G. Di Rosa, C. Barthelemy, C. Andres, L. Faivre, T. Frebourg, P. Saugier Veber, and D. Campion. (2009). Recurrent rearrangements in synaptic and neurodevelopmental genes and shared biologic pathways in schizophrenia, autism, and mental retardation. *Archives of general psychiatry* 66(9), 947–56.

Heller, T. (1908). Über Dementia infantilis. *Zeitschrift für die Enforschung und Behandlung des Jugendlichen Schwachsinns* 2, 141–165.

Herbert, M. R., D. A. Ziegler, N. Makris, P. A. Filipek, T. L. Kemper, J. J. Normandin, H. A. Sanders, D. N. Kennedy, and V. S. Caviness, Jr. (2004). Localization of white matter volume increase in autism and developmental language disorder. *Annals of neurology* 55(4), 530–40.

Hollis, C. (1995). Child and adolescent (juvenile onset) schizophrenia. A case control study of premorbid developmental impairments. *The British journal of psychiatry : the journal of mental science* 166(4), 489–95.

Hulshoff Pol, H. E., and R. S. Kahn. (2008). What happens after the first episode? A review of progressive brain changes in chronically ill patients with schizophrenia. *Schizophr Bull* 34(2), 354–66.

Innocenti, G. M., F. Ansermet, and J. Parnas. (2003). Schizophrenia, neurodevelopment and corpus callosum. *Molecular psychiatry* 8(3), 261–74.

International Schizophrenia. Consortium (2008). Rare chromosomal deletions and duplications increase risk of schizophrenia. *Nature* 455(7210), 237–41.

Just, M. A., V. L. Cherkassky, T. A. Keller, and N. J. Minshew. (2004). Cortical activation and synchronization during sentence comprehension in high-functioning autism: evidence of underconnectivity. *Brain: a journal of neurology* 127 (Pt 8), 1811–21.

Kalus, P., C. Buri, J. Slotboom, J. Gralla, L. Remonda, T. Dierks, W. K. Strik, G. Schroth, and C. Kiefer. (2004). Volumetry and diffusion tensor imaging of hippocampal subregions in schizophrenia. *Neuroreport* 15(5), 867–71.

Kalus, P., J. Slotboom, J. Gallinat, R. Wiest, C. Ozdoba, A. Federspiel, W. K. Strik, C. Buri, G. Schroth, and C. Kiefer. (2005). The amygdala in schizophrenia: a trimodal magnetic resonance imaging study. *Neuroscience letters* 375(3), 151–6.

Kanner, L. (1943). Autistic disturbances of affective contact. *Nervous Child* 2, 217–250.

———. 1968. Autistic disturbances of affective contact. *Acta paedopsychiatrica* 35(4), 100–36.

Keller, T. A., R. K. Kana, and M. A. Just. (2007). A developmental study of the structural integrity of white matter in autism. *Neuroreport* 18(1), 23–7.

Kim, H. G., S. Kishikawa, A. W. Higgins, I. S. Seong, D. J. Donovan, Y. Shen, E. Lally, L. A. Weiss, J. Najm, K. Kutsche, M. Descartes, L. Holt, S. Braddock, R. Troxell, L. Kaplan, F. Volkmar, A. Klin, K. Tsatsanis, D. J. Harris, I. Noens, D. L. Pauls, M. J. Daly, M. E. MacDonald, C. C. Morton, B. J. Quade, and J. F. Gusella. (2008). Disruption of neurexin 1 associated with autism spectrum disorder. *American journal of human genetics 82*(1), 199–207.

Kinney, D. K., K. M. Munir, D. J. Crowley, and A. M. Miller. (2008). Prenatal stress and risk for autism. *Neuroscience and biobehavioral reviews 32*(8), 1519–32.

Kirov, G., D. Rujescu, A. Ingason, D. A. Collier, M. C. O'Donovan, and M. J. Owen. (2009). Neurexin 1(NRXN1) deletions in schizophrenia. *Schizophrenia bulletin 35*(5), 851–4.

Kolevzon, A., R. Gross, and A. Reichenberg. (2007). Prenatal and perinatal risk factors for autism: a review and integration of findings. *Archives of pediatrics & adolescent medicine 161*(4), 326–33.

Kolvin, I. (1971a). Studies in the childhood psychoses. I. Diagnostic criteria and classification. *The British journal of psychiatry : the journal of mental science 118*(545), 381–4.

———. (1971b). Psychosis in childhood: A comparative study. In *Infantile autism: Concepts, characteristics and treatment*, edited by M. L. Rutter. Edinburg: Churchill Livingstone.

———. (1972). Infantile autism or infantile psychoses. *British Medical Journal 3*(5829), 753–5.

Konrad, A., and G. Winterer. (2008). Disturbed structural connectivity in schizophrenia primary factor in pathology or epiphenomenon? *Schizophrenia bulletin 34*(1), 72–92.

Kraepelin, E. 1896. Die psychologische Versuche in der Psychiatrie. *Psychol Arbeiten 1*, 1–91.

Kubicki, M., H. Park, C. F. Westin, P. G. Nestor, R. V. Mulkern, S. E. Maier, M. Niznikiewicz, E. E. Connor, J. J. Levitt, M. Frumin, R. Kikinis, F. A. Jolesz, R. W. McCarley, and M. E. Shenton. (2005). DTI and MTR abnormalities in schizophrenia: analysis of white matter integrity. *Neuroimage 26*(4), 1109–18.

Kubicki, M., C. F. Westin, P. G. Nestor, C. G. Wible, M. Frumin, S. E. Maier, R. Kikinis, F. A. Jolesz, R. W. McCarley, and M. E. Shenton. (2003). Cingulate fasciculus integrity disruption in schizophrenia: a magnetic resonance diffusion tensor imaging study. *Biological psychiatry 54*(11), 1171–80.

Kumar, A., S. K. Sundaram, L. Sivaswamy, M. E. Behen, M. I. Makki, J. Ager, J. Janisse, H. T. Chugani, and D. C. Chugani. (2010). Alterations in frontal lobe tracts and corpus callosum in young children with autism spectrum disorder. *Cerebral cortex 20*(9), 2103–13.

Landrigan, P. J. (2010). What causes autism? Exploring the environmental contribution. *Current opinion in pediatrics 22*(2), 219–25.

Larsson, H. J., W. W. Eaton, K. M. Madsen, M. Vestergaard, A. V. Olesen, E. Agerbo, D. Schendel, P. Thorsen, and P. B. Mortensen. (2005). Risk factors for autism: perinatal factors, parental psychiatric history, and socioeconomic status. *American journal of epidemiology 161*(10), 916–25; discussion 926–8.

Leyfer, O. T., S. E. Folstein, S. Bacalman, N. O. Davis, E. Dinh, J. Morgan, H. Tager-Flusberg, and J. E. Lainhart. (2006). Comorbid psychiatric disorders in children with autism: interview development and rates of disorders. *Journal of autism and developmental disorders 36*(7), 849–61.

Lutz, J. (1937). Über die Schizophrenie im Kindesalter. *Schweitzer Archiv für Neurologie und Psychiatrie 39*, 335–372.

Malaspina, D., S. Harlap, S. Fennig, D. Heiman, D. Nahon, D. Feldman, and E. S. Susser. (2001). Advancing paternal age and the risk of schizophrenia. *Archives of general psychiatry 58*(4), 361–7.

Malson, L. (1972). *Wolf children and the problem of human nature.* New York: Monthly Review Press.

Matute, C., M. Domercq, D. J. Fogarty, M. Pascual de Zulueta, and M. V. Sanchez-Gomez. (1999). On how altered glutamate homeostasis may contribute to demyelinating diseases of the CNS. *Advances in experimental medicine and biology 468*, 97–107.

Maudsley, H. 1879. *The phychiology and pathology of mind.* 3rd ed: London, UK: MacMillian.

Mefford, H. C., A. J. Sharp, C. Baker, A. Itsara, Z. Jiang, K. Buysse, S. Huang, V. K. Maloney, J. A. Crolla, D. Baralle, A. Collins, C. Mercer, K. Norga, T. de Ravel, K. Devriendt, E. M. Bongers, N. de Leeuw, W. Reardon, S. Gimelli, F. Bena, R. C. Hennekam, A. Male, L. Gaunt, J. Clayton-Smith, I. Simonic, S. M. Park, S. G. Mehta, S. Nik-Zainal, C. G. Woods, H. V. Firth, G. Parkin, M. Fichera, S. Reitano, M. Lo Giudice, K. E. Li, I. Casuga, A. Broomer, B. Conrad, M. Schwerzmann, L. Raber, S. Gallati, P. Striano, A. Coppola, J. L. Tolmie, E. S. Tobias, C. Lilley, L. Armengol, Y. Spysschaert, P. Verloo, A. De Coene, L. Goossens, G. Mortier, F. Speleman, E. van Binsbergen, M. R. Nelen, R. Hochstenbach, M. Poot, L. Gallagher, M. Gill, J. McClellan, M. C. King, R. Regan, C. Skinner, R. E. Stevenson, S. E. Antonarakis, C. Chen, X. Estivill, B. Menten, G. Gimelli, S. Gribble, S. Schwartz, J. S. Sutcliffe, T. Walsh, S. J. Knight, J. Sebat, C. Romano, C. E. Schwartz, J. A. Veltman, B. B. de Vries, J. R. Vermeesch, J. C. Barber, L. Willatt, M. Tassabehji, and E. E. Eichler. (2008). Recurrent rearrangements of chromosome 1q21.1 and variable pediatric phenotypes. *The New England journal of medicine 359*(16), 1685–99.

Miller, D. T., Y. Shen, L. A. Weiss, J. Korn, I. Anselm, C. Bridgemohan, G. F. Cox, H. Dickinson, J. Gentile, D. J. Harris, V. Hegde, R. Hundley, O. Khwaja, S. Kothare, C. Luedke, R. Nasir, A. Poduri, K. Prasad, P. Raffalli, A. Reinhard, S. E. Smith, M. M. Sobeih, J. S. Soul, J. Stoler, M. Takeoka, W. H. Tan, J. Thakuria, R. Wolff, R. Yusupov, J. F. Gusella, M. J. Daly, and B. L. Wu. (2009). Microdeletion/duplication at 15q13.2q13.3 among individuals with features of autism and other neuropsychiatric disorders. *Journal of medical genetics 46*(4), 242–8.

Mouridsen, S. E., B. Rich, and T. Isager. (2008). Psychiatric disorders in adults diagnosed as children with atypical autism. A case control study. *Journal of neural transmission 115*(1), 135–8.

Mouridsen, S. E., B. Rich, T. Isager, and N. J. Nedergaard. (2008). Psychiatric disorders in individuals diagnosed with infantile autism as children: a case control study. *J Psychiatr Pract 14*(1), 5–12.

Murray, R. M., and S. W. Lewis. (1987). Is schizophrenia a neurodevelopmental disorder? *British Medical Journal 295*(6600), 681–82.

Okugawa, G., K. Nobuhara, T. Minami, C. Tamagaki, K. Takase, T. Sugimoto, S. Sawada, and T. Kinoshita. (2004). Subtle disruption of the middle cerebellar peduncles in patients with schizophrenia. *Neuropsychobiology 50*(2), 119–23.

Padgett, F. E., E. Miltsiou, and P. A. Tiffin. (2010). The co-occurrence of nonaffective psychosis and the pervasive developmental disorders: a systematic review. *J Intellect Dev Disabil 35*(3), 187–98.

Pagnamenta, A. T., K. Wing, E. Sadighi Akha, S. J. Knight, S. Bolte, G. Schmotzer, E. Duketis, F. Poustka, S. M. Klauck, A. Poustka, J. Ragoussis, A. J. Bailey, and A. P. Monaco. (2009). A 15q13.3 microdeletion segregating with autism. *European journal of human genetics : EJHG 17*(5), 687–92.

Palmen, S. J., and H. van Engeland. (2004). Review on structural neuroimaging findings in autism. *J Neural Transm 111*(7), 903–29.

Peters, B. D., J. Blaas, and L. de Haan. (2010). Diffusion tensor imaging in the early phase of schizophrenia: what have we learned? *Journal of psychiatric research 44*(15), 993–1004.

Petersen, L., P. B. Mortensen, and C. B. Pedersen. (2011). Paternal age at birth of first child and risk of schizophrenia. *The American Journal of Psychiatry 168*(1), 82–8.

Petty, L. K., E. M. Ornitz, J. D. Michelman, and E. G. Zimmerman. (1984). Autistic children who become schizophrenic. *Archives of general psychiatry 41*(2), 129–35.

Potter, H. W. (1933). Schizophrenia in children. *The American Journal of Psychiatry 12*, 1253.

Pugliese, L., M. Catani, S. Ameis, F. Dell'Acqua, M. Thiebaut de Schotten, C. Murphy, D. Robertson, Q. Deeley, E. Daly, and D. G. Murphy. (2009). The anatomy of extended limbic pathways in Asperger syndrome: a preliminary diffusion tensor imaging tractography study. *Neuroimage 47*(2), 427–34.

Raja, M., and A. Azzoni. (2010). Autistic spectrum disorders and schizophrenia in the adult psychiatric setting: diagnosis and comorbidity. *Psychiatr Danub 22*(4), 514–21.

Rapoport, J., A. Chavez, D. Greenstein, A. Addington, and N. Gogtay. (2009). Autism spectrum disorders and childhood-onset schizophrenia: clinical and biological contributions to a relation revisited. *J Am Acad Child Adolesc Psychiatry 48*(1), 10–8.

Reichenberg, A., R. Gross, S. Sandin, and E. S. Susser. (2010). Advancing paternal and maternal age are both important for autism risk. *American journal of public health 100*(5), 772–3; author reply 773.

Ross, R. G. (2010). Neuroimaging the infant: the application of modern neurobiological methods to the neurodevelopmental hypothesis of schizophrenia. *The American journal of psychiatry 167*(9), 1017–9.

Russell, A. T., L. Bott, and C. Sammons. (1989). The phenomenology of schizophrenia occurring in childhood. *Journal of the American Academy of Child and Adolescent Psychiatry 28*(3), 399–407.

Rutter, M. (1968). Concepts of autism: a review of research. *Journal of child psychology and psychiatry, and allied disciplines 9*(1), 1–25.

———. (1972). Childhood schizophrenia reconsidered. *Journal of autism and childhood schizophrenia 2*(4), 315–37.

Rzhetsky, A., D. Wajngurt, N. Park, and T. Zheng. (2007). Probing genetic overlap among complex human phenotypes. *Proc Natl Acad Sci U S A 104*(28), 11694–9.

Sahyoun, C. P., J. W. Belliveau, and M. Mody. (2010). White matter integrity and pictorial reasoning in high-functioning children with autism. *Brain and cognition 73*(3), 180–8.

Segal, D., J. R. Koschnick, L. H. Slegers, and P. R. Hof. (2007). Oligodendrocyte pathophysiology: a new view of schizophrenia. *The international journal of neuro-psychopharmacology / official scientific journal of the Collegium Internationale Neuro-psychopharmacologicum* 10(4), 503–11.

Sharp, A. J., H. C. Mefford, K. Li, C. Baker, C. Skinner, R. E. Stevenson, R. J. Schroer, F. Novara, M. De Gregori, R. Ciccone, A. Broomer, I. Casuga, Y. Wang, C. Xiao, C. Barbacioru, G. Gimelli, B. D. Bernardina, C. Torniero, R. Giorda, R. Regan, V. Murday, S. Mansour, M. Fichera, L. Castiglia, P. Failla, M. Ventura, Z. Jiang, G. M. Cooper, S. J. Knight, C. Romano, O. Zuffardi, C. Chen, C. E. Schwartz, and E. E. Eichler. (2008). A recurrent 15q13.3 microdeletion syndrome associated with mental retardation and seizures. *Nature genetics* 40(3), 322–8.

Shukla, D. K., B. Keehn, A. J. Lincoln, and R. A. Muller. (2010). White matter compromise of callosal and subcortical fiber tracts in children with autism spectrum disorder: a diffusion tensor imaging study. *Journal of the American Academy of Child and Adolescent Psychiatry* 49(12), 1269–78, 1278 e1–2.

Shukla, D. K., B. Keehn, D. M. Smylie, and R. A. Muller. (2011). Microstructural abnormalities of short-distance white matter fiber tracts in autism spectrum disorder. *Neuropsychologia*.

Skokauskas, N., and L. Gallagher. (2010). Psychosis, affective disorders and anxiety in autistic spectrum disorder: prevalence and nosological considerations. *Psychopathology* 43(1), 8–16.

Sporn, A. L., A. M. Addington, N. Gogtay, A. E. Ordonez, M. Gornick, L. Clasen, D. Greenstein, J. W. Tossell, P. Gochman, M. Lenane, W. S. Sharp, R. E. Straub, and J. L. Rapoport. (2004). Pervasive developmental disorder and childhood-onset schizophrenia: comorbid disorder or a phenotypic variant of a very early onset illness? *Biol Psychiatry* 55(10), 989–94.

Sprong, M., H. E. Becker, P. F. Schothorst, H. Swaab, T. B. Ziermans, P. M. Dingemans, D. Linszen, and H. van Engeland. (2008). Pathways to psychosis: a comparison of the pervasive developmental disorder subtype Multiple Complex Developmental Disorder and the "At Risk Mental State." *Schizophrenia research* 99(1–3), 38–47.

Ssucharewa, G.E. 1926. Die Schizoiden Psychopathien im Kindesalter. *Monatschrift für Psychiatrie und Neurologie* 6, 235–261.

Stahlberg, O., H. Soderstrom, M. Rastam, and C. Gillberg. (2004). Bipolar disorder, schizophrenia, and other psychotic disorders in adults with childhood onset AD/HD and/or autism spectrum disorders. *J Neural Transm* 111(7), 891–902.

Stanfield, A. C., A. M. McIntosh, M. D. Spencer, R. Philip, S. Gaur, and S. M. Lawrie. (2008). Towards a neuroanatomy of autism: a systematic review and meta-analysis of structural magnetic resonance imaging studies. *Eur Psychiatry* 23(4), 289–99.

Stefansson, H., D. Rujescu, S. Cichon, O. P. Pietilainen, A. Ingason, S. Steinberg, R. Fossdal, E. Sigurdsson, T. Sigmundsson, J. E. Buizer-Voskamp, T. Hansen, K. D. Jakobsen, P. Muglia, C. Francks, P. M. Matthews, A. Gylfason, B. V. Halldorsson, D. Gudbjartsson, T. E. Thorgeirsson, A. Sigurdsson, A. Jonasdottir, A. Bjornsson, S. Mattiasdottir, T. Blondal, M. Haraldsson, B. B. Magnusdottir, I. Giegling, H. J. Moller, A. Hartmann, K. V. Shianna, D. Ge, A. C. Need, C. Crombie, G. Fraser, N. Walker, J. Lonnqvist, J. Suvisaari, A. Tuulio-Henriksson, T. Paunio, T. Toulopoulou, E. Bramon, M. Di Forti, R. Murray, M. Ruggeri, E. Vassos, S. Tosato, M. Walshe, T. Li, C. Vasilescu, T. W. Muhleisen, A. G. Wang, H. Ullum, S. Djurovic, I. Melle, J. Olesen, L. A. Kiemeney, B. Franke, C. Sabatti, N. B. Freimer, J. R. Gulcher, U. Thorsteinsdottir, A. Kong, O. A. Andreassen, R. A. Ophoff, A. Georgi, M. Rietschel, T. Werge, H. Petursson, D. B. Goldstein, M. M. Nothen, L. Peltonen, D. A. Collier, D. St Clair, and K. Stefansson. (2008). Large recurrent microdeletions associated with schizophrenia. *Nature 455*(7210), 232–6.

Stevens, M. C., D. H. Fein, and L. H. Waterhouse. (2000). Season of birth effects in autism. *Journal of clinical and experimental neuropsychology 22*(3), 399–407.

Sudhof, T. C. (2008). Neuroligins and neurexins link synaptic function to cognitive disease. *Nature 455*(7215), 903–11.

Sundaram, S. K., A. Kumar, M. I. Makki, M. E. Behen, H. T. Chugani, and D. C. Chugani. (2008). Diffusion tensor imaging of frontal lobe in autism spectrum disorder. *Cerebral cortex 18*(11), 2659–65.

Sundquist, K., G. Frank, and J. Sundquist. (2004). Urbanisation and incidence of psychosis and depression: follow-up study of 4.4 million women and men in Sweden. *The British journal of psychiatry: the journal of mental science 184*, 293–8.

Szatmari, P., A. D. Paterson, L. Zwaigenbaum, W. Roberts, J. Brian, X. Q. Liu, J. B. Vincent, J. L. Skaug, A. P. Thompson, L. Senman, L. Feuk, C. Qian, S. E. Bryson, M. B. Jones, C. R. Marshall, S. W. Scherer, V. J. Vieland, C. Bartlett, L. V. Mangin, R. Goedken, A. Segre, M. A. Pericak-Vance, M. L. Cuccaro, J. R. Gilbert, H. H. Wright, R. K. Abramson, C. Betancur, T. Bourgeron, C. Gillberg, M. Leboyer, J. D. Buxbaum, K. L. Davis, E. Hollander, J. M. Silverman, J. Hallmayer, L. Lotspeich, J. S. Sutcliffe, J. L. Haines, S. E. Folstein, J. Piven, T. H. Wassink, V. Sheffield, D. H. Geschwind, M. Bucan, W. T. Brown, R. M. Cantor, J. N. Constantino, T. C. Gilliam, M. Herbert, C. Lajonchere, D. H. Ledbetter, C. Lese-Martin, J. Miller, S. Nelson, C. A. Samango-Sprouse, S. Spence, M. State, R. E. Tanzi, H. Coon, G. Dawson, B. Devlin, A. Estes, P. Flodman, L. Klei, W. M. McMahon, N. Minshew, J. Munson, E. Korvatska, P. M. Rodier, G. D. Schellenberg, M. Smith, M. A. Spence, C. Stodgell, P. G. Tepper, E. M. Wijsman, C. E. Yu, B. Roge, C. Mantoulan, K. Wittemeyer, A. Poustka, B. Felder, S. M. Klauck, C. Schuster, F. Poustka, S. Bolte, S. Feineis-Matthews, E. Herbrecht, G. Schmotzer, J. Tsiantis, K. Papanikolaou, E. Maestrini, E. Bacchelli, F. Blasi, S. Carone, C. Toma, H. Van Engeland, M. de Jonge, C. Kemner, F. Koop, M. Langemeijer, C. Hijmans, W. G. Staal, G. Baird, P. F. Bolton, M. L. Rutter, E. Weisblatt, J. Green, C. Aldred, J. A. Wilkinson, A. Pickles, A. Le Couteur, T. Berney, H. McConachie, A. J. Bailey, K. Francis, G. Honeyman, A. Hutchinson, J. R. Parr, S. Wallace, A. P. Monaco, G. Barnby, K. Kobayashi, J. A. Lamb, I. Sousa, N. Sykes, E. H. Cook, S. J. Guter, B. L. Leventhal, J. Salt, C. Lord, C. Corsello, V. Hus, D. E. Weeks, F. Volkmar, M. Tauber, E. Fombonne, A. Shih, and K. J. Meyer. (2007). Mapping autism risk loci using genetic linkage and chromosomal rearrangements. *Nature genetics 39*(3), 319–28.

Toal, F., O. J. Bloemen, Q. Deeley, N. Tunstall, E. M. Daly, L. Page, M. J. Brammer, K. C. Murphy, and D. G. Murphy. (2009). Psychosis and autism: magnetic resonance imaging study of brain anatomy. *Br J Psychiatry 194*(5), 418–25.

Van Engeland, H. , and R.-J. Van der Gaag. (1994). Mcdd in childhood: A precursor of schizophrenic spectrum disorder? . *Schizophrenia Research 11*(2), 197.

Volkmar, F. R. (1987). Diagnostic issues in the pervasive developmental disorders. *Journal of child psychology and psychiatry, and allied disciplines 28*(3), 365–69.

Volkmar, F. R., and D. J. Cohen. (1991). Comorbid association of autism and schizophrenia. *Am J Psychiatry 148*(12), 1705–7.

Wang, F., Z. Sun, L. Cui, X. Du, X. Wang, H. Zhang, Z. Cong, N. Hong, and D. Zhang. (2004). Anterior cingulum abnormalities in male patients with schizophrenia determined through diffusion tensor imaging. *The American journal of psychiatry 161*(3), 573–75.

Watkins, J. M., R. F. Asarnow, and P. E. Tanguay. (1988). Symptom development in childhood onset schizophrenia. *Journal of child psychology and psychiatry, and allied disciplines 29,*(6), 865–78.

Williams, J. G., J. P. Higgins, and C. E. Brayne. (2006). Systematic review of prevalence studies of autism spectrum disorders. *Archives of disease in childhood, 91*(1), 8–15.

Wright, I. C., S. Rabe-Hesketh, P. W. Woodruff, A. S. David, R. M. Murray, and E. T. Bullmore. (2000). Meta-analysis of regional brain volumes in schizophrenia. *The American journal of psychiatry, 157*(1), 16–25.

Zahn-Waxler, C., E. A. Shirtcliff, and K. Marceau. (2008). Disorders of childhood and adolescence: gender and psychopathology. *Annual review of clinical psychology,* 4, 275–303.

7

Early-Onset Schizophrenia

Helmut Remschmidt and Frank Theisen
(Translated from the original German by Ethan Taub)

THE HISTORY OF THE DISORDER

From Psychotic Disorders to Schizophrenia

Schizophrenic psychoses in childhood and adolescence are an important group of diseases within the broader spectrum of the psychoses. They were first recognized in the late 1930s as independent disease entities distinct from other types of psychosis. In this chapter, the term "psychotic disorders" refers to psychopathological syndromes of whatever etiology that are characterized by the following features: (1) a marked disturbance of the patient's link to reality, (2) the presence of productive manifestations such as delusions and hallucinations (positive manifestations) or affective disturbances and cognitive impairment (negative manifestations), and (3) a fluctuating temporal course, through which the disease interrupts the continuity of the patient's development, experience, and behavior.

Psychoses in childhood and adolescence were originally classified according to the nosological categories of adult psychiatry (Griesinger 1845; Maudsley 1867). These historic conceptions and descriptions of psychiatric disorders, developed largely through the observation of adult patients, reflected an essentially static view of disease, in which an organic etiology was usually assumed and little attention was paid to phase-specific and developmental psychopathological aspects (albeit with a few exceptions).

Within a few decades, however, the textbooks of childhood psychopathology by Emminghaus (1887), Strohmayer (1910), Ziehen (1915/1926), and Homburger (1926) already highlighted dynamic, rather than biological aspects as well as the phase-specific features of these disorders.

The specialized literature on childhood psychoses up to 1954 was compiled in an extensive bibliography by Goldfarb and Dorsen (1956). Bryson and Hintgen (1971) prepared another bibliography extending into the 1970s, which was followed by the monograph of Kanner (1973a,b) and the historical review "Childhood Psychosis in Schizophrenia" by Parry-Jones (2001).

Over the course of the 1950s, especially in the USA, the term "schizophrenia" came to be applied to a much wider group of disorders than before, including some affecting children and adolescents. Indeed, most behavioral abnormalities of children and adolescents were subsumed under the diagnostic heading of schizophrenia. Harms, a psychiatric historian, remarked in 1952 that any attempt to describe childhood schizophrenia based on the publications of the last 15 years would surely lead to the classification of any and all psychopathological manifestations as schizophrenic. Similarly, Rutter spoke in 1972 of the "astoundingly heterogeneous mixture of disorders" grouped together under the heading of schizophrenia. In contrast, European psychiatry continued to maintain the strict diagnostic criteria of Kraepelin, as further developed by Kurt Schneider (1939).

In the 1950s and 1960s, more or less in parallel with the inflationary use of the diagnosis "schizophrenia," it gradually came to be accepted that the patient's age and developmental state are important criteria for the diagnostic classification of childhood psychoses (Group for the Advancement of Psychiatry 1966; Stutte 1969). This view found support in a number of empirical studies (Rutter et al. 1967; Kolvin et al. 1971a, b, c, d).

Special Types of Childhood Psychosis with a Characteristic Course and their Relation to Schizophrenia

Three distinct types of historically recognized psychotic disorders seem likely to be closely related to schizophrenia.

Schizophrenia of Late Childhood (Late-Onset Psychoses)

The schizophrenic psychoses of late childhood can arise up to the age of puberty. The older the child is at onset, the more likely it is that he or she will go on to have schizophrenia as an adult. These disorders are characterized by cognitive disturbances, hallucinations (mainly auditory), and delusional elements, prominently including so-called transitivistic depersonalization experiences.

Pre-Pubertal Schizophrenia

Children with pre-pubertal schizophrenia, as distinct from schizophrenia arising earlier in childhood, commonly suffer from systematic delusions whose "material" is drawn from phase-specific difficulties. In the affective sphere, the prevailing mood is often abnormal, frequently characterized by marked suspiciousness, affect lability or blunted affect, inappropriate affect, parathymia, and regression to infantile patterns of behavior, also with regard to language (Stutte, 1969). The term "pre-pubertal schizophrenia" has fallen out of use, because the timing of puberty is highly variable and often not precisely determinable. The current term, "childhood-onset schizophrenia," is based on the child's chronological age at onset (twelve years or younger), independently of the timing of puberty.

Early Infantile Catatonia

Karl Leonhard (1986), in the sixth edition of his well-known book entitled *Die Aufteilung der endogenen Psychosen* (The Classification of the Endogenous Psychoses), classified early childhood catatonia as a special type of psychosis in childhood. The idea that this is a distinct entity related to schizophrenia can be traced back to Kraepelin's stated opinion (1913) that many so-called "idiotic" children were actually suffering from schizophrenia from early childhood onward, resulting in an arrest of their mental development. Leonhard's findings have yet to be replicated. It is unclear whether some of the children he described were actually suffering from autistic disorders.

Positive and Negative Schizophrenia

The dichotomous classification of manifestations of schizophrenic diseases as either positive or negative represents an attempt to systematize these multifarious phenomena in an overarching scheme that can be useful both for treatment and for prediction of the course of the disease. Various instruments have been developed to assess positive and negative manifestations. As classified by the Positive and Negative Syndrome Scale (Kay et al. 1987), the following are positive manifestations: delusions, conceptual disorganization, hallucinatory behavior, excitement, grandiosity, suspiciousness, and hostility. The negative manifestations, on the other hand, are blunted affect, withdrawal, poor rapport, passive/apathetic withdrawal, difficulty in abstract thinking, lack of spontaneity, and stereotyped thinking. Neither the positive nor the negative manifestations are stable features of schizophrenic diseases: both are subject to frequent fluctuations over the patient's developmental course and over the course of the illness. The following valid statements can be made:

1. Positive and negative manifestations may represent different psychiatric conditions with different underlying causes (Crow, 1980).
2. The two types of manifestation may be associated with different stages in the course of schizophrenia. Negative manifestations seem to be more closely associated with the advanced stages of the disease.
3. The clinical manifestations may vary depending on the patient's individual characteristics and the demands of the environment.
4. The positive and negative manifestations are not specific to schizophrenia: they are also found outside the schizophrenic spectrum of diseases.

Despite these limitations, the concept of positive and negative manifestations can still be usefully applied to schizophrenic disorders in children and adolescents (cf. Bettes and Welker, 1987).

Remschmidt et al. (1991, 1994) studied positive and negative manifestations in two groups of children and adolescents with schizophrenic

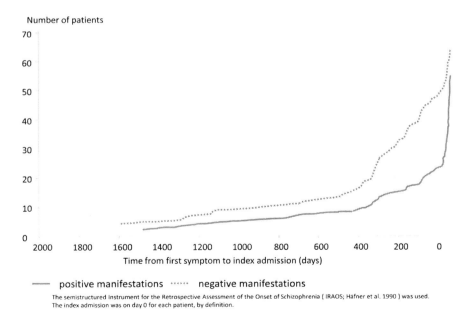

positive manifestations ······ negative manifestations

The semistructured Instrument for the Retrospective Assessment of the Onset of Schizophrenia (IRAOS; Häfner et al. 1990) was used. The index admission was on day 0 for each patient, by definition.

Figure 7.1.   Retrospectively assessed positive and negative manifestations in sixty-one children and adolescents with schizophrenia

disorders, both in the premorbid stage and over the course of the disease. Positive and negative manifestations were both found to arise months or even years before the overt clinical onset of the disease. Moreover, a majority of patients underwent a transition from mostly positive to mostly negative manifestations over the course of their disease (and there were no transitions in the reverse direction).

The first of these two findings is shown in Figure 7.1, taken from a study of 61 children and adolescents with schizophrenic disease. The manifestations of disease were ascertained retrospectively with the aid of IRAOS, an instrument that we specifically adapted for use in children and adolescents (Häfner et al., 1990).

DEFINITION, CLASSIFICATION, AND EPIDEMIOLOGY

Definition and Classification

The following terms relating to schizophrenia in childhood and adolescents, based on the age of onset, are now in general use (Werry et al. 1991):

- Very-early-onset schizophrenia (VEOS), defined as beginning before the child's thirteenth birthday.
- Early-onset schizophrenia (EOS), defined as beginning before the patient's eighteenth birthday (VEOS is thus a subtype of EOS).

Alongside these overlapping designations, there are also non-overlapping ones that are used in parallel:

- Childhood-onset schizophrenia (COS), also called "prepubertal" schizophrenia, even though it is defined not in relation to developmental stage, but rather in relation to the patient's chronological age at onset (twelve years or younger).
- Adolescent-onset schizophrenia (AOS), defined as beginning between the ages of thirteen and seventeen years (inclusive).

These four designations have not been incorporated into the classification systems to be discussed further below, yet we mention them here because it is very useful, both in clinical practice and in research, to have terms that are precisely related to the age of onset. The course of schizophrenia can take one of two forms, in childhood just as in adulthood: an insidious, hebephrenia-like course and a course characterized rather by acute onset and episodic progression, occasionally involving catatonic states as well.

The following classification systems provide the basis for classifying schizophrenic disorders in childhood and adolescence:

- the tenth revision of the International Classification of Diseases (ICD-10) of the World Health Organization (WHO), and
- The Diagnostic and Statistical Manual of Mental Disorders (DSM-IV) of the American Psychiatric Association (APA).

The definitions of schizophrenic disorders in the ICD-10 and DSM-IV have much in common, but also a few differences. The latter relate to the sub-types of schizophrenia and to the classification of organic and substance-induced disorders, which are listed in different chapters in the ICD-10 and the DSM-IV.

Epidemiology

Prevalence and Incidence

The lifetime prevalence of schizophrenia is about 1 percent (Regier et al. 1993). In adulthood, the incidence (rate of new onset) of schizophrenia has remained stable over the last fifty years, across many different countries and cultures, at one to two cases per ten thousand persons per year (Häfner and an der Heiden 1997).

The frequency of schizophrenia as a function of age is shown in Table 7.1. About 4 percent of all cases of schizophrenia arise before age fifteen, and about 1 percent before age ten. Among patients in child and adolescent psychiatric clinics, the rate of schizophrenic disease in children is 1 to 2 percent, while that among adolescents is about 5 percent. There is a mild predominance of boys. Studies of sample clinical populations have revealed that about 10 percent of cases of schizophrenia arise between the ages of fourteen and twenty, and 42 percent between the ages of twenty-one

Table 7.1. The frequency of schizophrenia as a function of age

Designation	Age	Frequency[a]	Sex ratio
Very-early-onset schizophrenia (VEOS)	< 13 years	P = 1.6-1.9 / 100,000 (0.0019%)	Boys more than girls
Adolescent-onset schizophrenia (AOS)	13-19 years[b]	P = 0.23%	Boys about as commonly as girls
Schizophrenia	Adulthood	LP = 1%	Men earlier than women

Note: [a] P = prevalence; LP = lifetime prevalence; [b] The definitions of Gillberg (2001) and Werry (1991) differ.

and thirty. About two-thirds of all patients with schizophrenia are between twenty and forty years old.

Sex Differences

Boys and girls are about equally represented among children and adolescents with schizophrenia. One study determined that, among fifteen-to-nineteen-year-olds, boys develop schizophrenia more frequently (cf. Häfner 2007). In another study, however, a higher incidence was found among boys under age thirteen and between the ages of fifteen and seventeen; yet, among thirteen-to-fifteen-year-olds, the incidence was higher in girls (Mehler-Wex and Warnke 2004).

ETIOLOGY

The major etiological factors include genetic, neurobiological, and neuropsychological characteristics. These are listed in Table 7.2. The importance of genetic factors has been clearly demonstrated by family studies, twin studies, and adoption studies (for a review see Schourfield and McGuffin, 2001). Molecular genetic studies have identified a number of replicated candidate-gene regions. We are, however, still far away from a convincing

Table 7.2. Schizophrenia in childhood and adolescence: Biological components of etiology

1.	Genetic factors (all in adult patients):	6 replicated candidate gene regions on chromosomes 6, 8, 10, 13, 18, 22.
2.	Neurobiological factors:	
	Brain morphology:	Reduced total cerebral volume (correlated with negative manifestations).
	Biochemical changes:	Changes in the glutamatergic, dopaminergic, serotonergic, and noradrenergic systems.
	Electrophysiological changes:	Skin conductance: high baseline activity, slow habituation.
		Evoked potentials: controversial findings.
3.	Neuropsychological factors:	
	Cognitive impairment:	Low IQ, attention deficits, reduced language perception, disturbances in the organization of perception.
	Neurointegrative deficits:	Pandysmaturation (PDM). (Fish 1975)
	Attention deficits:	Possibly correlated with deficits in understanding social relationships.
	Communication deficits:	Poor speech production, incoherent language, unclear and ambiguous way of referring to surroundings, formal thought disorders.

genetic explanation of the disorder. Schizophrenia is presumably a complex disorder that is caused by a large number of genes, and also affected to a considerable extent by environmental factors.

Some interesting biological and neuropsychological findings in early-onset schizophrenia are summarized in Table 7.2. The developmental perspective is a major component of our current understanding of schizophrenic disorders (Remschmidt, 2002). This can be seen, for example, both in biochemistry and in neuropsychology. Studies in animals have revealed developmental changes of the glutamatergic system occurring in adolescence, including sensitization of the adolescent rat brain to glutamate antagonists such as phencyclidine and dysfunction of the N-methyl-D-aspartate (NMDA) receptor (Keshevan and Hogarty, 1999). Such changes may be related to the well-known clinical phenomenon of phencyclidine-induced psychosis.

In developmental neuropsychology, so-called pandysmaturation (PDM) has recently again attracted much attention. The term, coined by Fish (1975), denotes a neurointegrative deficit operationalized by three criteria: (1) transient retardation of motor and/or visual motor development, (2) an abnormal functional profile revealed by a developmental examination, and (3) skeletal growth retardation. Multiple studies (Fish et al., 1992; Done et al., 1994; Jones et al., 1994; Hollis, 2003) have shown delayed development in the children of schizophrenic or pre-schizophrenic parents, and certain types of developmental delay seem to be precursors of early-onset schizophrenia. Moreover, declining IQ in childhood (from the ages of four to seven years) has been found to predict psychotic manifestations, but no other psychiatric manifestations, at age twenty-three (Kremen et al., 1998).

Very-early-onset schizophrenia seems to differ in some respects from schizophrenic disorders beginning in adolescence or later. We consider very-early-onset schizophrenia to be a progressively worsening developmental disorder (Remschmidt, 2002), for the following reasons:

- Over the course of this disorder, the cerebral ventricles enlarge and the cerebellum becomes progressively smaller (Keller et al., 2003; Rapoport et al., 1997). Progressive gray-matter loss in adolescence has also been found to be specific to schizophrenia (Gogtay et al., 2003).
- Intellectual function deteriorates over the course of the disorder (Jacobsen and Rapoport, 1998).
- The outcome is highly unfavorable, worse than that of adolescent-onset or adult-onset schizophrenia (Remschmidt et al., 2005).
- The transition from positive to negative manifestations begins during inpatient treatment and later stabilizes over the long-term course (Remschmidt et al., 1994; 2005).

DIAGNOSIS AND DIFFERENTIAL DIAGNOSIS

Clinical Presentation

- Both VEOS and EOS present with cognitive dysfunction, emotional abnormalities, changes in social functioning, disturbances of speech and language, and motor disturbances.
- The cognitive manifestations of VEOS and EOS include thought distortions, delusions, and hallucinations. There are different types of thought distortion, including thought insertions, breaks and interpolations in the train of thought, thought echoes, and vague and incoherent thinking that patient may not be able to express verbally in an intelligible way.
- There are different types of delusion too in VEOS and EOS including ideas of reference, the belief that one is being persecuted, bodily change delusions, delusions of control, and various other types. Systematized delusions are very rare in children under age twelve but more common in adolescence.
- Hallucinations are usually auditory, consisting either of threatening voices giving comments or commands to the patient, or of non-verbal sounds such as laughter, humming, or whistling. Visual, olfactory, gustatory, and somatosensory hallucinations are rare. The visual hallucinations that do arise are typically in children under age thirteen. The differential diagnosis of visual hallucinations in a child must include an intoxication.
- In VOES and EOS, there are also emotional manifestations and alterations of social functioning, including blunted affect, mood disturbances such as irritability, fearfulness, and suspicion, negative manifestations such as marked apathy and paucity of speech, and incongruous emotional responses impairing social competence and leading to social withdrawal.
- Typical speech and language disturbances include paucity of speech or logorrhoea, perseverations, and speech stereotypies, sometimes also echolalia and phonographism. Neologisms can also be produced. When such manifestations are present, autism is an important differential diagnosis, particularly in children under age eight.
- Motor disturbances come in many kinds, ranging from clumsiness and motor disharmony to bizarre postures, stupor, and catatonia. Bizarre movements and motor stereotypies, e.g., of the fingers, are common. Compulsive behaviors or rituals with strange and unexpected movements may also be seen, both at the onset of the disease and later on in its course.

- The distinction between positive and negative manifestations, which is long established in adult psychiatry, applies just as well to childhood and adolescent schizophrenia. Negative as well as positive manifestations have been found to arise in both VEOS and EOS, sometimes long before the disease becomes clinically overt and leads to hospitalization. Many patients have both positive and negative manifestations before their index admission; manifestations of both types become more frequent and converge around the time of the index admission.

Diagnostic Procedures

Psychotic disorders in children and adolescents, and schizophrenic disorders in particular, are generally diagnosed by the ICD-10 and DSM-IV criteria. The diagnosis is usually based on meticulous history-taking about the patient and his or her family by interview of the parents and the patient, as well as a thorough clinical examination including psychological and neuropsychological testing. Psychological testing should include cognitive assessment of intelligence, concentration, memory, language, and motor function. The patient's emotional state must also be assessed. Depressive manifestations are often either a precursor of adolescent schizophrenia or a component of its initial phase. Some 20 percent of adolescents with schizophrenia have a depressive episode as their first manifestation of the disorder (Remschmidt et al. 1973).

There are more or less standardized clinical interviews and scales for the diagnosis of schizophrenia in childhood and adolescence; these are mostly used for research purposes. The ones most commonly used are listed in Table 7.3.

Differential Diagnosis

A number of disorders enter into the differential diagnosis of schizophrenia in childhood and adolescence. These will be briefly discussed in what follows.

(i) Autism

Autism is currently regarded as a pervasive developmental disorder with onset in the first thirty months of life. Its typical manifestations differ from, but overlap with, those of schizophrenia. As an aid to differential diagnosis, it is worth keeping in mind that hallucinations and delusions are not found in autism, and that schizophrenia does not arise in the first thirty months of life. The correct diagnosis can usually be inferred from the history taken from the parents, clinical observation, and the course of the disorder. Some children have only one type of psychotic state that may be

Table 7.3. Instruments for the diagnosis of schizophrenic disorders in childhood and Adolescence

	Completed by	*Age range*
Clinical Interviews		
K-SADS-E	Parents/Child	age 6-17
(Schedule for Affective Disorder and Schizophrenia for School-Age Children) (Orvaschel & Puig-Antich, 1987)		
ICDS	Parents/Child	age 6-18
(Interview for Childhood Disorders and Schizophrenia) (Russell et al., 1989)		
CAPA	Parents/Child	age 8-18
(Child and Adolescent Psychiatric Assessment) (Angold et al., 1995)		
DICA	Parents/Child	age 6-17
(Diagnostic Interview for Children and Adolesents) (Herjanic & Reich, 1982)		
NIMH DISC	Parents/Child	age 9-17
(NIMH, 1992)		
Scales		
KIDDIE-PANSS	Interviewer/Parents/Child	age 6-16
(Fields et al., 1994)		
CPRS	Interviewer/Child	age ≤5
(Children's Psychiatric Rating Scale) (Fish, 1985)		
TDS	Child	age 5-13
(Thought Disorder Scales) (Caplan et al., 1989)		

difficult to distinguish from schizophrenia: this condition is early infantile catatonia, as described by Karl Leonhard (1986). It is still unclear whether early infantile catatonia is really the first manifestation of schizophrenia or whether at least some of Leonhard's cases may have been suffering from a kind of atypical autism.

(ii) Disintegrative Disorder (Heller's syndrome)

This syndrome is characterized by normal development until age three or four, followed by progressive deterioration and loss of abilities that have already been acquired. It is much rarer than autism, and also rarer than early-onset schizophrenia. The affected children typically lose already acquired functions, such as language, and have characteristic types of social, communicative, and behavioral dysfunction. They are often irritable, anxious, and overactive before the full clinical picture of the disease becomes apparent. This disorder, too, can be distinguished from schizophrenia by at least two distinct criteria: (a) the early loss of acquired skills, and (b) the early onset of the disorder.

(iii) Multiple Complex Developmental Disorders (MCDD) and Multiple Developmental Impairment (MDI)

These disorders are not yet included in the ICD-10 or DSM-IV classification systems. MCDD was first described by Towbin et al. (1993) as a syndrome involving "disturbances in affect modulation, social relatedness and thinking." In contrast, MDI (McKenna et al., 1994) involves brief transient psychotic manifestations, age-inappropriate fantasies, magical but not obviously delusional thinking, social withdrawal, emotional lability, and impaired information processing. The criteria for childhood schizophrenia are not fulfilled. Compared to schizophrenic children, children with MDI have fewer negative manifestations and less severe social impairment.

MCDD and MDI are overlapping syndromes, although the MCDD construct seems to fit more closely into the category of pervasive developmental disorders, while the MDI construct has a greater affinity to schizophrenia. The relationship of either syndrome to schizophrenia is not fully clear. In one follow-up study, 20 percent of children with MCDD were found to develop schizophrenia later on in their lives (van der Gaag, 1993). In contrast, another follow-up study of nineteen children with MDI did not reveal any later development of schizophrenia. It thus seems questionable whether MDI is really a precursor of schizophrenia (Jacobsen and Rapoport, 1998).

(iv) Affective Psychoses (psychotic depression, bipolar disorder)

As stated above, adolescent schizophrenia often begins with a depressive episode. Conversely, studies have shown that bipolar disorders are very often initially diagnosed as schizophrenia (Werry et al., 1991). Nonetheless, schizophrenia and affective disorders can usually be distinguished from each other in the first six months of observation, as they each manifest a typical cluster of disease manifestations.

In most cases, however, a differentiation is possible during the first half year of observation. This can be done by the typical symptom clusters that are different between schizophrenia and bipolar disorder.

(v) Asperger Syndrome

The main features that distinguish Asperger syndrome from schizophrenia are to be found in the patient's past history (manifestations of autistic spectrum disorder, very early language acquisition), the clinical observations on presentation, and the further course of the disorder. Patients with Asperger syndrome generally have no positive manifestations, nor do they suffer from a deterioration of schoolwork or social functioning. Nonetheless, some persons with Asperger syndrome go on to become schizophrenic (Wolff, 1995).

(vi) Drug-Induced Psychosis

Drug-induced psychosis is currently the main differential diagnosis of schizophrenia in adolescence (but not in childhood). Many adolescents presenting with psychosis have taken illicit drugs, and it can be difficult to determine whether they are actually suffering from schizophrenia or from a psychotic state due to an organic brain disorder. Even if the clinical manifestations meet all criteria for schizophrenia, one can still ask whether schizophrenia was triggered or caused by the substances that were consumed. Many drugs are known to induce psychotic states, among them marijuana, LSD, cocaine, amphetamines, alcohol, hypnotics, and anxiolytics. Drug-induced psychosis can be distinguished from schizophrenia through meticulous history-taking, including an inquiry about all substances taken during the last year, along with laboratory testing for drugs. A tentative diagnosis of schizophrenia is confirmed if the manifestations persist for several months after drug withdrawal.

(vii) Organic Brain Disorders

A number of organic brain disorders are associated with psychotic states, including temporal lobe epilepsy and neurodegenerative diseases such as Wilson's disease, Huntington's disease, and juvenile metachromatic leukodystrophy. These disorders can be diagnosed and delineated from schizophrenia by a thorough neurological evaluation, including ancillary testing. Their clinical picture very often involves disturbances of movement and progressive deterioration of cognitive function.

TREATMENT AND REHABILITATION

The main components of treatment and rehabilitation for schizophrenia in children and adolescents are neuroleptic drugs, psychotherapy, family-oriented interventions, and specific rehabilitation measures.

Neuroleptic Antipsychotic Drugs

The pharmacotherapy of schizophrenia in childhood and adolescence (as in adulthood) now mainly involves atypical neuroleptic drugs with the following properties:

- a different receptor-binding profile from conventional neuroleptics (weaker binding to dopamine receptors, higher affinity for $5-HT_{2A}$ and a1 receptors) which accounts for their different clinical effects,

- few extrapyramidal side effects (EPS) in consequence of this receptor-binding profile,
- efficacy not only against positive manifestations, but also against negative ones (unlike most conventional neuroleptics),
- only rare side effects, and absence of hyperprolactinemia as a side effect.

An overview of the most commonly used antipsychotic (neuroleptic) medications is given in Table 7.4, and a decision tree for the selection of antipsychotics in childhood and adolescent schizophrenia is provided in Figure 7.2. The three main goals of pharmacotherapy are to manage acute psychotic states, prevent relapses, and minimize side effects.

Acute psychotic states usually require hospitalization for a treatment whose most important component is antipsychotic medication. Currently, the treatment of severely agitated patients and patients with aggressive

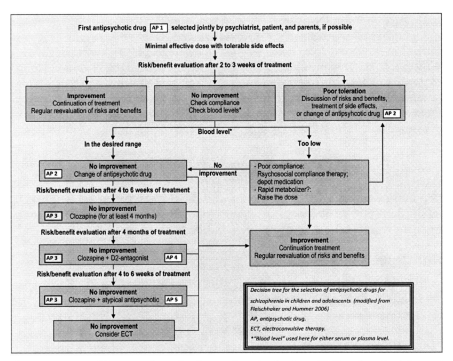

Figure 7.2. Decision tree for selecting antipsychotics for childhood and adolescent schizophrenia

outbursts begins with an atypical antipsychotic drug, possibly with the addition of a benzodiazepine or a typical neuroleptic of moderate or low potency, such as levomepromazine. A strategy for the continuation of pharmacotherapy is shown in the flowchart of Figure 7.2. At each decision point, the current medication is maintained or switched depending on its observed beneficial and adverse effects. In most countries, clozapine can only be given after two different other drugs have been tried unsuccessfully (i.e., without benefit or with intolerable adverse effects). The usual oral and, for depot neuroleptics, intramuscular dosages are given in Table 7.4.

Antipsychotic medication must be given over the long term to prevent relapse (the second goal of pharmacotherapy). Relapses are frequently triggered by emotional stress and adverse life events, but they can also be triggered by positive emotional experiences. When any of these factors are present, anticipatory relapse prevention is very important and can be achieved either by maintaining low-dose oral medication or by switching to a depot neuroleptic. The latter is recommended in case of problematic compliance.[1]

The third goal of pharmacotherapy is the minimization of side effects. Typical neuroleptics induce extrapyramidal manifestations more frequently in children and adolescents than they do in adults. Atypical neuroleptics are usually preferred, because they induce extrapyramidal manifestations only rarely, if at all. Some of them, however, induce other bothersome side effects, e.g., extreme weight gain (most pronounced when clozapine or olanzapine is given). Newer compounds, such as aripiprazole, cause less weight gain but have not yet been extensively used to treat childhood and adolescent-onset schizophrenia. Weight gain is one of the more common causes of non-compliance, especially among adolescents. Various antipsychotic medications have other adverse effects that will not be described here (for a review, cf. Remschmidt et al., 2001).

Psychotherapy

Psychotherapy has four main components:

1. Meticulous and thorough information of the patient and parents about the disorder from a psychoeducational approach,
2. cognitive psychotherapy and other behavioral measures,
3. emotional management therapy,
4. group programs.

Patient information about the disorder is essential and should include the family as well. All explanations should be appropriate to the phase of the disorder that the patient is currently in and should be adapted to his or her cognitive and emotional level.

Table 7.4. The most frequently used antipsychotic medications in child- and adolescent-onset schizophrenia

	Sedation	Positive manifestations	Negative manifestations	Neuroleptic potency	Usual oral dose (or usual IM depot dose)
Typical high-potency neuroleptics					
Benperidol	+	++	++	100	1-6 mg/d
Flupenthixol (*decanoate*)	+	++	++	50	2-10 mg/d (*20-100mg/2-4 wk*)
Fluphenazine (*decanoate*)	+(+)	+++	++	30	5-20 mg/d (*12.5-100mg/2-4 wk*)
Fluspirilene[a]	+	+++	++	300	(*2-10 mg/wk*)[a]
Haloperidol (*decanoate*)	+	+++	++	60	2-20 mg/d (*50-300mg/2-4 wk*)
Perphenazine (*enanthate*)	++	+++	++	8	12-64 mg/d (*50-200mg/2 wk*)
Pimozide	+	+++	++	50	4-20mg/d
Typical moderate- and low-potency neuroleptics					
Chlorpromazine	+++	+++	++	1	150-600 mg/d
Chlorprothixene	+++	++	++	0.8	150-600 mg/d
Levomepromazine	+++	++	++	0.8	75-600 mg/d
Perazine	++	++	++	0.5	75-600 mg/d
Pipamperone	++			0.2	120-360 mg/d
Promethazine	+++			-	50-400 mg/d
Sulpiride	+	++	+++	0.5	100-800 mg/d
Thioridazine	+++	++	++	0.7	200-700 mg/d
Tiapride	+				300-600 mg/d
Zuclopenthixol	+++	++	++		20-150 mg/d

Atypical neuroleptics

Amisulpiride	+	+++	+++		50-300 (400) mg/d[1]
					200-800 (1200) mg/d[2]
Aripiprazol	+	+++	+++		10-30 mg/d
Clozapine	+++	+++	+++	(0.5-2)	25-6001mg/d
Olanzapine (*Zypadhera 150/210/300/405 mg*)[b]	++	+++	+++	(8-20)	10-20mg/d (150 or 210 mg/2 wk; 300 or 405mg/4 wk)
Quetiapine	+	+++	+++		150-750 mg/d
Risperidone (*Risperdal Consta®* 25/37.5/50mg)[b]	+	+++	+++	(50)	1-12 mg/d (25-50 mg/2 wk)
Sertindole	+	+++	+++		16-24 mg/d
Ziprasidone	++	+++	+++		80-160 mg/d
Zotepine	++	+++	+++	(2)	75-300 mg/d

Note: The neuroleptic potency of typical neuroleptics is expressed in relation to chlorpromazine (=1).

The neuroleptic potency of atypical neuroleptics is estimated on the basis of the average clinically effective dose.

+= none or low, ++=moderate, +++=high.

[a] Available only as depot neuroleptic. [b] Currently the only atypical neuroleptics in depot form in Germany.

[1] If negative manifestations predominate; [2] if positive manifestations predominate.

Psychotherapeutic measures based on *cognitive interventions* include various strategies such as distraction treatment, rationale responding, belief modification, and the enhancement of coping strategies. All of these treatment approaches are intended to give the patient an active role and to enhance his or her specific abilities to cope with the manifestations of the disorder, as well as with the related distress and anxiety. There are also integrated approaches that incorporate multiple components simultaneously. One of these, which has been successfully applied to adolescent schizophrenia, is the "Integrative Psychological Therapy Program for Schizophrenic Patients (IPT)," developed in Switzerland (Brenner et al., 1980:1993). This program consists of five standardized therapeutic components: cognitive differentiation, social perception, verbal communication, social skills, and interpersonal problem solving. It originated from the classical social skills training technique, which was extended to the area of communication. It can be administered individually to patients with different profiles of schizophrenic manifestations. Most of the tasks that are assigned in the different therapeutic components of this program of this program are realistic and oriented to everyday situations, and they can be presented in slides and videoclips. IPT was originally developed for young adults and was adapted later for adolescents (Kienzle et al., 1997). Although it seems to be a promising approach, it has not yet been evaluated systematically.

Emotional management therapy has not yet been demonstrated to be effective in young patients with schizophrenia. The emotional sphere is undoubtedly very important in the course of the disorder, but to our knowledge there has not been any study to date evaluating the efficacy of this approach. *Group programs* have been considered helpful in the treatment of young patients with schizophrenia, and have been applied with emphasis on the improvement of skills (e.g. social skills training, problem-solving, communication) and education (e.g. information about the disease and its treatment, management of medication, and relapses). The IPT program described above has often been successfully applied as a group program.

Family-Oriented Measures

It is evident that the families of children and adolescents with schizophrenia have to be included in the conception and planning of treatment. Empirical research, however, has revealed that the ambitious family therapy concepts propagated in recent decades have not brought the benefits that were originally hoped for. It is now quite clear that there is no "typical psychotic family," nor is there any "schizophrenogenic mother." On the other hand, the important concept of expressed emotions that demonstrates the major role of the family in relation to relapses. Therefore, in every case of child and adolescent schizophrenia, one must decide to what extent the family should be integrated into the therapeutic process. This depends mainly on the patient, the disorder, the structure and stability of the family, and the therapist's experience. Family-oriented approaches in the treatment of schizophrenia can have any or all of the following components (Remschmidt et al., 2001):

- *Family counseling and psychoeducational approaches*: The main aim of this type of intervention is to develop a stable therapeutic alliance in which the patient and the family can be given detailed information about the disorder, its treatment, and its course and prognosis. A major component of family education concerns medications (the various substances used and their main beneficial and adverse effects).
- *Supportive and structural family therapy*: The main objective of this approach is to neutralize and control the disease manifestations, particularly by addressing the secondary problems, conflicts, and vicious circles that often arise in the course of the psychotic disorder. Family counseling, which is the first level of family intervention, is carried out separately with the parents and with the patient, while supportive and structural family therapy are carried out in joint sessions with the active participation of the patient, parents, and sometimes siblings and other family members. This kind of intervention is possible only when the disease manifestations have already improved to some extent and good cooperation with the family has been achieved.
- *Extended development-oriented family therapy*: This third level of family intervention can only be carried out in a minority of families with a psychotic child or adolescent. Its main focus is on the pattern of relationships between family members and on the typical family conflicts that are inhibiting the patient's development. This type of intervention can only be performed by highly experienced therapists and only with cooperative families.

Specific Rehabilitation Measures

Some 40 percent of children and adolescents with schizophrenia do not maintain their prepsychotic functional levels regarding school, professional work, communication, and social integration. When these patients begin rehabilitation, their condition is marked by mainly negative manifestations, deficits in social skills, problem-solving, decision-making, and coping skills, interrupted schooling, disrupted social relations, and a high risk of relapse. They may need residential rehabilitation because of either the nature or the course of their illness. In particular, patients who have marked negative manifestations after their acute episode has been treated may not be able to be reintegrated into their families right away. A rehabilitation program for such patients has been developed jointly by the Department of Child and Adolescent Psychiatry of the Philipps University, Marburg (Germany), and the Leppermühle rehabilitation center near Marburg. Patients undergo this program for an average of two years. It includes the following components (Martin, 1991; Remschmidt et al., 2001):

1. a well-structured educational facility with expertise in dealing with these adolescents' special needs;
2. helping the adolescents live up to their educational potential and acquire relevant skills as an integral component of rehabilitation;
3. individual supportive psychotherapy and additional group work for social skills training;
4. occupational therapy as an important rehabilitation measure, and, for older adolescents, integration into appropriate work activities;
5. individually tailored medication to minimize the risk of relapse.

These general principles have been effectuated in an integrated rehabilitation program whose main components are shown in Figure 7.3.

As shown in Figure 7.3, the program aims to reintegrate patients into five main areas of occupational and social life: health, education and work,

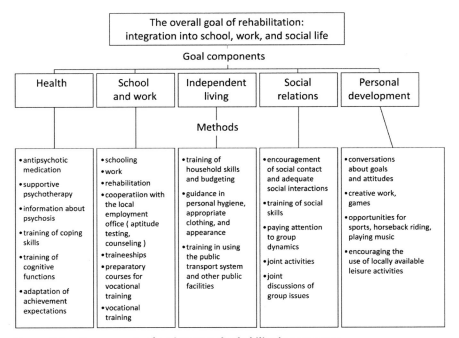

Figure 7.3. Components of an integrated rehabilitation program

independent living, social relations, and personal development. The main methods of reaching each of these goals are also presented in Figure 7.3. Thus, patients can reach and maintain a state of better health by continuing to take antipsychotic medication, receiving supportive psychotherapy and information about the disorder, being trained in coping skills and cognitive functions, and being trained to adapt to the demands of the environment that they live in. Evaluation of this program to date has shown that it is successful after one year of follow-up, and a longer-term evaluation is now in progress. For a more detailed description see Remschmidt et al. (2001).

COURSE AND PROGNOSIS

Predictors of Disease Course

There have been studies of a number of potential predictive factors for a favorable or unfavorable long-term course in schizophrenia beginning in childhood or adolescence. It was already mentioned above that the presence of depressive manifestations affects the probability of therapeutic success of rehabilitation (Martin, 1991; Remschmidt et al., 2001). Table 7.5 contains a list of predictors for the long-term course of schizophrenia beginning in childhood or adolescence that have been identified in various studies.

Interestingly, a correlation has been found between the *extent of premorbid impairment* of psychosocial adaptation in childhood and adolescence and later impairment of social and cognitive abilities (executive functions) in schizophrenic patients examined in adulthood (Silverstein et al. 2002).

The significance that *young age at the onset of the disease* has for its later course is revealed not just by comparisons across age groups in each of the relevant studies on this subject, but also by comparisons of patient groups across studies: the studies that included only patients who had developed schizophrenia before age thirteen (Asarnow et al. 1994, Eggers and Bunk 1997, Trott et al. 1999, Remschmidt et al. 2007) all revealed a highly unfavorable course of disease in comparison to other studies of patients whose onset of disease was later.

CONCLUSIONS

The available study findings on the course and outcome of schizophrenia beginning in childhood or adolescence can be summarized as follows (cf. Remschmidt und Theisen 2005; 2011):

> Schizophrenic psychoses that arise before age thirteen have a very poor prognosis. The disease usually continues to progress in adolescence and adulthood. It can be diagnosed with the same criteria that are used in adults (Asarnow et al. 1994).

Table 7.5. Predictors of a chronic course of schizophrenia beginning in childhood or adolescence (from Bihlmaier, 2008, with additions)

Predictors of a chronic course	Studies
Family history of schizophrenic psychoses[a]	Werry and McClellan 1992; Jarbin et al. 2003; Fleischhaker et al. 2005
Young age at onset of disease*	Werry and McClellan 1992; Eggers and Bunk 1997; Schulz 1998; Fleischhaker et al. 2005; Bihlmaier 2008
Insidious onset	Eggers and Bunk 1997; Schulz 1998; Röpcke and Eggers 2005; Fleischhaker et al. 2005; Bihlmaier 2008
Low premorbid level of psychosocial adaptation	Werry and McClellan 1992; Maziade et al. 1996; Schulz 1998 (internalizing manifestations); Röpcke und Eggers 2005; Fleischhaker et al. 2005 (externalizing manifestations); Bihlmaier 2008 (confirmed manifestations of multiple developmental disorder, but not for internalizing and externalizing manifestations)
Developmental delays[b]	Schulz 1998; Fleischhaker et al. 2005; Remschmidt et al. 2007
Long duration of first episode[c]	Schmidt et al. 1995; Lay et al. 2000; Fleischhaker et al. 2005; Bihlmaier 2008
Large number of episodes	Schmidt et al. 1995
Poor psychosocial adaptation at the time of discharge from the initial hospitalization	Werry and McClellan 1992; Schmidt et al. 1995; Lay et al. 2000
High load of disease manifestations at the time of discharge from the initial hospitalization	Werry and McClellan 1992; Schmidt et al. 1995; Maziade et al. 1996 (positive and negative manifestations); Schulz 1998; Lay et al. 2000 (positive manifestations)

Note: [a] This factor was not confirmed by Maziade et al. (1996b). [b] These factors were not confirmed by Bihlmaier (2008). [c] This factor was not confirmed by Röpcke and Eggers (2005).

Patients whose disease has an acute onset, with productive schizophrenic manifestations such as hallucinations and delusions (i.e., positive manifestations), have a better prognosis than those whose disease begins insidiously and takes an unfavorable course, with depressive states and continually worsening impairment of cognitive function (Remschmidt et al. 1991).

The patient's premorbid personality plays a major role. Patients who were described as socially active, intelligent, and integrated children and adolescents before they became ill have a better prognosis than those who were intellectually impaired, timid, introverted, and uncommunicative before they became ill (Martin 1991; Werry et al. 1991, 1994).

The prognosis seems to be better for patients who have no family history of schizophrenia, those whose families cooperate well, and those whose condition improves rapidly during inpatient treatment (Martin 1991, Remschmidt et al. 1991).

The few available studies on the course and outcome of schizophrenia beginning in childhood and early adolescence confirm that they are much worse than in adult-onset schizophrenia.

A forty-two-year longitudinal study of patients with childhood-onset schizophrenia revealed their suicide rate to be higher than that of patients with adult-onset schizophrenia (Remschmidt et al. 2007). No further longitudinal studies are available to confirm this finding.

NOTE

1. As far as the authors are aware, Risperdal-Consta is the only atypical neuroleptic that is available as a depot preparation, at least in Germany.

REFERENCES

Angold, A., Prendergast, M., Cox, A., Harrington, R., Simonoff, E., and Rutter, M. (1995) The Child and Adolescent Psychiatric Assessment (CAPA). *Psychological Medicine, 25* , 739–53

Asarnow, J.R., M.C. Tompson, and M.J. Goldstein. Childhood-Onset Schizophrenia: A Follow-up Study. *Schizophrenia Bulletin* 20, no. 4 (1994): 599–617.

Bettes, B.A., and E. Walker. Positive and Negative Symptoms in Psychotic and Other Psychiatrically Disturbed Children. *Journal of Child Psychology and Psychiatry* 28, no. 4 (1987): 555–68.

Bihlmaier, K. 8–Jahres-Katamnese von Kindern und Jugendlichen mit einer schizophrenen Psychose, psychosoziale Entwicklung und Rehabilitation. Inaugural-Dissertation zur Erlangung des Doktorgrades, Albert-Ludwigs-Universität, 2008.

Brenner, H.D., V. Roder, and M.C.G. Merlo. Verhaltenstherapeutische Verfahren bei Schizophrenen Erkrankungen. In *Therapie Psychiatrischer Erkrankungen*, edited by H.J. Möller, 222–30. Stuttgart: Enke 1993.

Brenner, H.D., W.G. Stramke, J. Mewes, F. Liese, and G. Seeger. Erfahrungen mit einem spezifischen Therapieprogramm zum Training kognitiver und kommunikativer Fähigkeiten in der Rehabilitation chronisch schizophrener Patienten. *Nervenarzt* 51 (1980): 106–12.

Bryson, C.Q., and Hintgen, J.N. *Early Child and Psychosis: Infantile Autism, Childhood Schizophrenia and Related Disorders.* Maryland: Rockville, 1971.

Caplan, R., Guthrie, D., Tanguay, P., Fish, B., and David-Lando, G. The Kiddie Formal Thought Disorder Scale (K-FTDS): clinical assessment, reliability and validity. *Journal of the American Academy of Child Psychiatry*, 28 (1989): 408–16

Crow, T. J. Molecular Pathology of Schizophrenia: More Than One Disease Process? *British Medical Journal* 280, no. 6207 (1980): 66–68.

Done, D. J., Crow, T. J., Johnstone, E. C., and A. Sacker. Childhood Antecedents of Schizophrenia and Affective Illness: Social Adjustment at Ages 7 and 11. *British Medical Journal* 309, no. 6956 (1994): 699–703.

Eggers, C., and D. Bunk. The Long-Term Course of Childhood-Onset Schizophrenia: A 42-Year Followup. *Schizophrenia Bulletin* 23, no. 1 (1997): 105–17.

Emminghaus. *Die Psychischen Störungen des Kindesalters*. Tübingen: Laupp, 1887.

Fields, J., Grochowski, S., Linenmayer, J., Kay, S., Grosz, D., Hyman, R. and Alexander, G. Assessing positive and negative symptoms in children and adolescents. *American Journal of Psychiatry*, 151 (1994): 249–53

Fish, B. Biological Antecedents of Psychosis in Children. In *The Biology of Major Psychosis*, edited by D. Friedmann, 49–80. New York: Raven Press, 1975.

Fish, B. Children's Psychiatric Rating Scale. *Psychopharmacological Bulletin*, 21 (1985): 753–65

Fish, B, J., Marcus, S. L., Hans, J. G., Auerbach, and Perdue, S. Infants at Risk for Schizophrenia: Sequelae of a Genetic Neurointegrative Deficit. *Archives of General Psychiatry* 49, no. 3 (1992): 221–35.

Fleischhaker, C., E., Schulz, K., Tepper, M., Martin, K., Hennighausen, and Remschmidt, H. Long-Term Course of Adolescent Schizophrenia. *Schizophrenia Bulletin* 31, no. 3 (2005): 769–80.

Gillberg, C. Epidemiology of Early Onset Schizophrenia. In *Schizophrenia in Children and Adolescents*, edited by Remschmidt H, 43–59: Cambridge University Press, 2001.

Gogtay, N., Giedd, J.N., Lusk, L., Hayashi, K.M., Greenstein, D., Vaituzis, A.C., Nugent, T.F. III, Herman, D.H., Clasen, L.S., Toga, A.W., Rapoport, J.L., and Thompson, P.M. Dynamic Mapping of Human Cortical Development During Childhood through Early Adulthood. *Proceedings of the National Academy of Sciences* 101, no. 21 (2003): 8174–8179.

Goldfarb, W., and Dorsen, M. *Annotated Bibliography of Childhood Chizophrenia and Related Disorders*. New York: Basic books, 1956.

Griesinger, W. *Die Pathologie und Therapie der Psychischen Krankheiten*. Berlin: August Hirschwald, 1845.

Group for the Advancement of Psychiatry. *Psychopathological Disorders in Childhood: Theoretical Considerations and a Proposed Classification*. New York: Group for the Advancement of Psychiatry, 1966.

Häfner, H. Die Rolle von Geschlecht und Gehirn bei Schizophrenie. In *Gehirn und Geschlecht. Neurowissenschaft des kleinen Unterschieds zwischen Mann und Frau*, edited by Hausmann M, 297–330. Heidelberg: Springer, 2007.

Häfner, H., and an der Heiden, W. Epidemiology of Schizophrenia. *Canadian Journal of Psychiatry* 42 (1997): 139–51.

Häfner, H., A. Riecher, K. Maurer, S. Meissner, A. Schmidtke, B. Fätkenheuer, W. Löffler, and W. Heiden. Ein Instrument zur retrospektiven Einschätzung des Erkrankungsbeginns bei Schizophrenie. *Zeitschrift für Klinische Psychologie* 19, no. 3 (1990): 230–55.

Harms, E. Essential Problems Regarding Our Present Knowledge of Childhood Schizophrenia. *Nervous Child* 10, no. 1 (1952): 7–8.

Herjanic, B. and Reich, W. Development of a structured psychiatric interview for children: agreement between child and parent on individual symptoms. *Journal of Abnormal Child Psychology*, 10 (1982): 307–24

Hollis, C. Developmental Precursors of Child- and Adolescent-Onset Schizophrenia and Affective Psychoses: Diagnostic Specificity and Continuity with Symptom Dimensions. *British Journal of Psychiatry* 182 (2003): 37–44.

Homburger, A. *Vorlesungen Über Psychopathologie Des Kindesalters.* Berlin: Springer 1926.

Jacobsen, L. K., and Rapoport, J. L. Research Update: Childhood-Onset Schizophrenia: Implications of Clinical and Neurobiological Research. *Journal of Child and Psychology and Psychiatry* 39, no. 1 (1998): 101–13.

Jarbin, H., Y. Ott, and A. L. Von Knorring. Adult Outcome of Social Function in Adolescent-Onset Schizophrenia and Affective Psychosis. *Journal of the American Academy of Child and Adolescent Psychiatry* 42, no. 2 (2003): 176–83.

Jones, P., B. Rodgers, R. Murray, and M. Marmot. Child Development Risk Factors for Adult Schizophrenia in the British 1946 Birth Cohort. *Lancet* 344, no. 8934 (1994): 1398–402.

Kanner, L. *Childhood Psychosis: Initial Studies and New Insights.* New York: Wiley, 1973.

Kanner, L. The Birth of Early Infantile Autism. *Journal of Autism and Childhood Schizophrenia* 3, no. 2 (1973): 93–95.

Kay, S. R., A. Fiszbein, and L. A. Opler. The Positive and Negative Syndrome Scale (Panss) for Schizophrenia. *Schizophrenia Bulletin* 13, no. 2 (1987): 261–76.

Keller, A., F. X. Castellanos, A. C. Vaituzis, N. O. Jeffries, J. N. Giedd, and J. L. Rapoport. Progressive Loss of Cerebellar Volume in Childhood-Onset Schizophrenia. *American Journal of Psychiatry* 160, no. 1 (2003): 128–33.

Keshavan, M. S., and G. E. Hogarty. Brain Maturational Processes and Delayed Onset in Schizophrenia. *Developmental Psychopathology* 11, no. 3 (1999): 525–43.

Kienzle, N., H. Braun-Scharm, and M. Hemme. Kognitive, Psychoedukative und familientherapeutische Therapiebausteine in der stationären jugendpsychiatrischen Versorgung. In *Integrative Therapiemodelle und Ihre Wirksamkeit,* edited by D Schön, 139–52. Regensburg: Roderer, 1997.

Kolvin, I., R. F. Garside, and J. S. H. Kidd. Studies in the Childhood Psychoses. Iv. Parental Personality and Attitude and Childhood Psychoses. *British Journal of Psychiatry* 118, no. 545 (1971): 403–06.

Kolvin, I., C. Ounsted, M. Humphrey, and A. McNay. Studies in the Childhood Psychoses. Ii. The Phenomenology of Childhood Psychoses. *British Journal of Psychiatry* 118, no. 545 (1971): 385–95.

Kolvin, I., C. Ounsted, L. M. Richardson, and R. F. Garside. Studies in the Childhood Psychoses. Iii. The Family and Social Background in Childhood Psychoses. *British Journal of Psychiatry* 118, no. 545 (1971): 396–402.

Kolvin, I., C. Ounsted, and M. Roth. Studies in the Childhood Psychoses. V. Cerebral Dysfunction and Childhood Psychoses. *British Journal of Psychiatry* 118, no. 545 (1971): 407–14.

Kraepelin, E. *Psychiatrie.* III Leipzig: Barth 1913.

Kremen, W. S., S. L. Buka, L. J. Seidman, J. M. Goldstein, D. Koren, and M. T. Tsuang. IQ Decline During Childhood and Adult Psychotic Symptoms in a Community Sample: A 19–Year Longitudinal Study. *American Journal of Psychiatry* 155, no. 5 (1998): 672–77.

Lay, B., B. Blanz, M. Hartmann, and M. H. Schmidt. The psychosocial outcome of Adolescent-Onset Schizophrenia: A 12–Year Followup. *Schizophrenia Bulletin* 26, no. 4 (2000): 801–16.

Leonhard, K. *Aufteilung Der endogenen Psychosen und Ihre Differenzierte Ätiologie.* Berlin: Akademie-Verlag, 1986.

Martin, M. *Der Verlauf der Schizophrenie im Jugendalter unter Rehabilitationsbedingungen.* Stuttgart: Enke, 1991.

Maudsley, H. *The Physiology and Pathology of Mind.* New York: Appleton, 1867.

Maziade, M., S. Bouchard, N. Gingras, L. Charron, A. Cardinal, M. A. Roy, B. Gauthier, G. Tremblay, S. Cote, C. Fournier, P. Boutin, M. Hamel, C. Merette, and M. Martinez. Long-Term Stability of Diagnosis and Symptom Dimensions in a Systematic Sample of Patients with Onset of Schizophrenia in Childhood and Early Adolescence. II: Postnegative Distinction and Childhood Predictors of Adult Outcome. *British Journal of Psychiatry* 169, no. 3 (1996): 371–78.

McKenna, K., C. T. Gordon, M. Lenane, D. Kaysen, K. Fahey, and J. L. Rapoport. Looking for Childhood-Onset Schizophrenia: The First 71 Cases Screened. *Journal of the American Academy of Child and Adolescent Psychiatry* 33, no. 5 (1994): 636–44.

Mehler-Wex, C., and A. Warnke. Klinik und Verlauf schizophrener Erkrankungen mit Beginn im Kindes- und Jugendalter. In *Schizophrene Erkrankungen Im Kindes-Und Jugendalter: Klinik, Ätiologie, Therapie Und Rehabilitation,* edited by H. Remschmidt, 41–50. Stuttgart Schattauer, 2004.

National Institute of Mental Health (NIMH). The NIMH Diagnostic Interview Schedule for Children. Rockville, MD: National Institute of Mental Health (1992).

Orvaschel, H. and Puig-Antich, J. Schedule for affective disorders and schizophrenia for school-age children: epidemiological version. Unpublished manuscript. Medical College of Pennsylvania, Eastern Pennsylvania Psychiatric Institute (1987).

Parry-Jones, W.L. Childhood Psychosis and Schizophrenia: A Historical Review. In *Schizophrenia in Children and Adolescents,* edited by H. Remschmidt. Cambridge: Cambridge University Press, 2001.

Rapoport, J. L., J. Giedd, S. Kumra, L. Jacobsen, A. Smith, P. Lee, J. Nelson, and S. Hamburger. Childhood-Onset Schizophrenia. Progressive Ventricular Change During Adolescence. *Arch Gen Psychiatry* 54, no. 10 (1997): 897–903.

Regier, D.A., W.E. Narrow, D.S. Rae, R.W. Manderscheid, B.Z. Locke, and F.K. Goodwin. The De Facto US Mental and Addictive Disorders Service System. *Archives of General Psychiatry* 50 (1993): 85–94.

Remschmidt, H. Early-Onset Schizophrenia as a Progressive-Deteriorating Developmental Disorder: Evidence from Child Psychiatry. *Journal of neural transmission* 109, no. 1 (2002): 101–17.

Remschmidt, H. *Schizophrenia in Children and Adolescents.* Cambridge: Cambridge University Press, 2001.

Remschmidt, H., B. Brechtel, and F. Mewe. Zum Krankheitsverlauf und zur Persönlichkeitsstruktur von Kindern und Jugendlichen mit endogen-phasischen Psychosen und reaktiven Depressionen. *Acta Paedopsychiatrica* 40, no. 1 (1973): 2–17.

Remschmidt, H, M. Martin, C. Fleischhaker, and E. Schulz. A 42–Year Follow-up Study of Childhood-Onset Schizophrenia. *Unpublished manuscript* (2005).

Remschmidt, H., M. Martin, C. Fleischhaker, F. M. Theisen, K. Hennighausen, C. Gutenbrunner, and E. Schulz. Forty-Two-Years Later: The Outcome of Childhood-Onset Schizophrenia. *Journal of Neural Transmission* 114, no. 4 (2007): 505–12.

Remschmidt, H., M. Martin, K. Hennighausen, and E. Schulz. Treatment and Rehabilitation. In *Schizophrenia in Children and Adolescents*, edited by H. Remschmidt, 192–267. Cambridge: Cambridge University Press, 2001.

Remschmidt, H., M. Martin, E. Schulz, C Gutenbrunner, and C. Fleischhaker. The Concept of Positive and Negative Schizophrenia in Child and Adolescent Psychiatry In *Negative Versus Positive Schizophrenia*, edited by A. Maneros, N.C. Andreasen and M.T. Tsuang, 219–42. Heidelberg: Springer, 1991.

Remschmidt, H., E. Schulz, M. Martin, A. Warnke, and G.E. Trott. Childhood Onset Schizophrenia: History of the Concept and Recent Studies. *Schizophrenia bulletin* 20 (1994): 727–46.

Remschmidt, H., and F. Theisen. Schizophrenia and Related Disorders in Children and Adolescents. *Journal of Neural Transmission Supplement*, no. 69 (2005): 121–41.

Remschmidt, H., and F.M. Theisen. *Schizophrenie. Manual Psychischer Störungen bei Kindern und Jugendlichen*. Heidelberg: Springer 2011.

Röpcke, B., and C. Eggers. Early-Onset Schizophrenia: A 15-Year Follow-Up. *European Child and Adolescent Psychiatry* 14, no. 6 (2005): 341–50.

Russell, A.T., L. Bott, and C. Sammons, The phenomena of schizophrenia occurring in childhood. *Journal of the American Academy of Child and Adolescent Psychiatry*, 28 (1989): 399–407

Rutter, M. Childhood Schizophrenia Reconsidered. *Journal of Autism and Childhood Schizophrenia* 2, no. 4 (1972): 315–37.

Rutter, M., D. Greenfeld, and L. Lockyer. A Five to Fifteen Year Follow-up Study of Infantile Psychosis. II. Social and Behavioural Outcome. *The British Journal of Psychiatry* 113, no. 504 (1967): 1183–99.

Rutter, M., and L. Lockyer. A Five to Fifteen Year Follow-up Study of Infantile Psychosis. I. Description of Sample. *The British Journal of Psychiatry* 113 (1967): 1169–82.

Schmidt, M., B. Blanz, A. Dippe, T. Koppe, and B. Lay. Course of Patients Diagnosed as Having Schizophrenia During First Episode Occurring under Age 18 Years. *European Archives of Psychiatry and Clinical Neuroscience* 245, no. 2 (1995): 93–100.

Schneider, K. *Psychischer Befund Und Psychiatrische Diagnose*. Leipzig: Thieme, 1939.

Schourfield, J., and P. McGuffin. Genetic Aspects. In *Schizophrenia in Children and Adolescents*, edited by H. Remschmidt, 119–34. Cambridge: Cambridge University Press, 2001.

Schulz, E. *Verlaufsprädiktoren schizophrener Psychosen in der Adoleszenz*. Göttingen Bern Toronto Seattle: Hogrefe, 1998.

Silverstein, M. L., G. Mavrolefteros, and D. Close. Premorbid Adjustment and Neuropsychological Performance in Schizophrenia. *Schizophrenia Bulletin* 28, no. 1 (2002): 157–65.

Strohmayer, W *Die Psychopathologie des Kindesalters*. München Bergmann, 1910.

Stutte, H. Psychosen des Kindesalters. In *Neurologie-Psychologie-Psychiatrie*, edited by F. Schmid, Asperger, H., 908–38. Berlin Heidelberg New York: Springer, 1969.

Towbin, K. E., E. M. Dykens, G. S. Pearson, and D. J. Cohen. Conceptualizing "Borderline Syndrome of Childhood" And "Childhood Schizophrenia" As a Developmental Disorder. *Journal of the American Academy of Child and Adolescent Psychiatry* 32, no. 4 (1993): 775–82.

Trott, G.E., H. Gold-Carl, and F. Badura. "Klinik, Verlauf Und Therapie Von schizophrenen Psychosen mit sehr frühem Krankheitsbeginn." In *Leponex - Pharmakolo-
gie und Klinik eines atypischen Neuroleptikums*, edited by D. Naber and F. Müller-
Spahn, 51–62. Berlin: Springer, 1999.

van der Gaag, R.G. Multiplex Developmental Disorder: An exploration of border-
lines on the autistic spectrum. Thesis, University of Utrecht, Netherlands 1993.

Werry, J. S, and J. M. McClellan. Predicting Outcome in Child and Adolescent (Early
Onset) Schizophrenia and Bipolar Disorder. *Journal of the American Academy of
Child and Adolescent Psychiatry* 31, no. 1 (1992): 147–50.

Werry, J. S., J. M. McClellan, L. K. Andrews, and M. Hamm. Clinical Features and
Outcome of Child and Adolescent Schizophrenia. *Schizophrenia Bulletin* 20
(1994): 619–30.

Werry, J. S, J. M. McClellan, and L. Chard. Childhood and Adolescent Schizophrenic,
Bipolar, and Schizoaffective Disorders: A Clinical and Outcome Study. *Journal of
the American Academy of Child and Adolescent Psychiatry* 30, no. 3 (1991): 457–65.

Wolff, S *Loners. The Life Path of Unusual Children*. London, New York: Routledge,
1995.

Ziehen, T. *Die Geisteskrankheiten im Kindesalter* Berlin: Reuther und Reichard, 1926.

8

Developmental Dyslexia

Andreas Warnke, Gerd Schulte-Körne, and Elena Ise

INTRODUCTION

History

Written language (script) was created when written symbols (graphemes) were used as signs/symbols for sounds (phonemes) of spoken language. The first known alphabetic writing system was invented about eighteen hundred years before Christ.

In the nineteenth century it was well known in neurology that brain injuries could result in reading and/or spelling disorders. These disorders were labelled "alexia" (acquired loss of reading ability) and "agraphia" (acquired loss of writing/spelling ability). Special attention was given to injuries of the regions gyrus angularis and gyrus supramarginalis of the left cerebral hemisphere, which were linked to alexia and agraphia (Kussmaul, 1877; he introduced the term "word blindness"). These observations gave Hinshelwood (1896, 1904; Hinshelwood et al., 1904) reason to postulate that "congenital word blindness" (dyslexia) could be caused by a constitutional dysfunction of the left angular gyrus. Most frequently cited is the impressive description of "congenital word blindness" published in 1896 by Dr. Pringle Morgan. Dr. Morgan's concept of "congenital word blindness," which cannot be explained by a general mental deficiency, poor academic education, a sensory disorder or any other illness, was highly stimulating to medical research and literature and its relevance keeps it in the focus of current scientific discussion. Hinshelwood (1917) mentioned the aspects of heritability, the possible negative psychosocial consequences, and that boys are more often affected than girls. Stephenson (1907) published "six cases of congenital word blindness affecting three generations of one family" and thus strengthened the congenital hypothesis. In the German literature Oswald Berkhan (1885, 1886), a general medical practitioner in Braunschweig, published some case studies of students with specific spelling disorders. He recognized an analogy to developmental language disorders and called it "language stammer" ("Sprachstammeln"). Continuing today, the assumptions of these pioneers are still guidelines in our clinical understanding and dyslexia research: 1) There is a specific developmental disorder in the human ability in learning to read and/or to spell written language and this impairment is independent from intelligence in its normal range; 2) This impairment is more obvious in boys than in girls; 3) In dyslexia there is a significant neurobiological aetiology with a significant congenital and especially genetic influence; 4) There are two roots—the visual system and the language system—which are supposed to be sources for the pathogenic pathways of developmental dyslexia (further literature with respect to history, see Miles, 1999).

THE CONCEPT OF "SPECIFIC" DISORDERS OF PSYCHOLOGICAL DEVELOPMENT

"Specific reading disorder" (ICD-10 F81.0) and "specific spelling disorder" (ICD-10 F 81.1) are classified in ICD-10 as "specific developmental disorders of scholastic skills" and as subtypes of the concept of "specific disorders of psychological development." This concept is based on three features:

(a) an onset that is invariably during infancy or childhood
(b) an impairment or delay in the development of functions that are strongly related to biological maturation of the central nervous system, and
(c) a steady course that does not involve the remissions and relapses . . . (WHO, 1996).

Diagnostic Guidelines and Operational Definition of "Specific Reading/Spelling Disorder"

Basic requirements for the diagnosis of reading and/ or spelling disorder as "specific" are:
The impairment

- in reading and/or spelling is of a significant degree and does not rapidly remit with increased scholastic help,
- is not explained by mental retardation,

- is developmental and is not acquired later in education (thus excluded: Acquired dyslexia/dysgraphia),
- is not explained by poor schooling (thus excluded: illiteracy, analphabetism). (WHO, 1996).

The operational definition is based on the discrepancy concept:

1. The severity of the reading and/or spelling impairment "may be expected to occur in less than 3% of schoolchildren" (WHO, 1996),
2. There is an unexpected discrepancy between insufficient reading and/or spelling ability and the significantly higher level of intelligence measured by standardized IQ test. The research criteria demand a 2-standard deviation between low reading/spelling level and higher IQ level. For routine clinical practice "the clinical guideline is simply that the child's level of attainment must be very substantially below the expected for a child of the same mental age." (WHO, 1996).

In DSM IV-TR (American Psychiatric Association, 2000) the "Reading Disorder" is classified under "academic skills disorder" and the diagnostic criteria are:

A. Reading achievement, as measured by individually administered standardized tests of reading accuracy or comprehension, is substantially below that expected given the person's chronological age, measured intelligence, and age-appropriate education.
B. The disturbance in Criterion A significantly interferes with academic achievement or activities of daily living that require reading skills.
C. If a sensory deficit is present, the reading difficulties are in excess of those usually associated with it.

Coding note: If a general medical (e.g., neurological) condition or sensory deficit is present, code the condition on Axis III. In contrast to ICD-10 the DSM definition no longer excludes individuals whose reading impairment is due to a neurological disorder.

The criticism of the discrepancy-based definition has to be kept in mind since there are strong arguments against it (Stanovich, 1992, 1996; Smythe and Everatt, 2004; Rispens et al., 1998) [see also chapter by Fung and Su in this book].

SYMPTOMATOLOGY

There are no reading or spelling errors which are specifically "dyslexic." The same kind of errors may be seen at the beginning of learning to read and write, as in students with mental retardation or any other learning handicaps. However, the difficulty in the normal development of the automation of word identification (reading) and /or spelling is characteristic.

Errors in reading aloud are:

(a) omissions, substitutions, distortions, or additions of words or parts of words;
(b) slow reading rate;
(c) false starts, long hesitations or "loss of place" in text, and inaccurate phrasing; and
(d) reversals of words in sentences or letters within words . . .
(e) an inability to recall facts read;
(f) inability to draw conclusions or inferences from material read; and
(g) use of general knowledge as background information rather than of information from a particular story to answer questions about a story read (WHO, 1996).

Errors in writing are:
Letter

- reversals (e.g., b for d; c for g; brick for brig),
- inversions (e.g., m for w),
- transpositions (e.g., gril for girl),

Word

- reversals (e.g., read for dear; god for dog)
- substitutions (e.g., tree for wood).

Obvious is a difficulty in alphabetic languages to learn the connection between letters and sounds and to convert sounds (phonemes: defined as the smallest discrete identifiable units of sound employed to form meaningful contrasts between utterances) to letter strings (words; graphemes, graphic characters) and vice versa. In non alphabetic scripts there are deficits to convert sounds to graphic characters and vice versa to convert graphic characters to word reading (phoneme processing). Often there is slow and poor quality of handwriting. Later on at a more advanced age the reading deficiencies are usually less obvious than the spelling difficulties.

EPIDEMIOLOGY

Dyslexia occurs in all known languages (Lindgren et al., 1985; McBride et al., 2008) and is one of the most common developmental disorders—

about 5 percent of school-aged children had a reading disorder (Shaywitz et al., 1990; Katusic et al., 2001). The National Assessment of Educational Progress (NAEP) in the USA estimated that 34 percent of fourth-grade children are significantly below normal range in reading skills (U.S. Department of Education, 2007).

A recent study found the prevalence of combined reading and spelling disorder is about 8 percent while that of spelling disorder alone is 6 percent and that of isolated reading disorder is 7 percent. It appears that different neurocognitive deficits underlie each of these disorders. However, as yet there are no valid research results on this (Landerl and Moll, 2009).

Studies involving large epidemiological samples have shown repeatedly that dyslexia is two to three times more common in boys than in girls. When differentiating between reading disorder and spelling disorder it was shown that boys exhibit spelling problems more frequently but are affected by reading disorder in similar numbers to girls (Landerl and Moll, 2009, 2010).

DYSLEXIA IN DIFFERENT LANGUAGES

Most research on dyslexia is done with alphabetic languages. But even the different alphabetic languages differ in transparency, that is, there is more or less relationship between phoneme and grapheme. German, Italian, Spanish and Finnish are significantly more transparent languages than English or French. Each language has its own regularities and irregularities and thus dyslexia manifests itself differently in different languages (Landerl, Wimmer, Frith, 1997; Landerl and Wimmer, 2000; Goswami, 1997, 2000; Smythe, Everatt, Salter, 2004). Paulesu et al., (2001) concluded from a positron emission tomography study (comparing scans from dyslexic readers of Italy, France and United Kingdom) "that there is a universal neurocognitive basis for dyslexia." Some examples for different languages may be mentioned.

Arabic orthography is also based on phonological decoding abilities. According to Abu-Rabia and Taha (2004) the limited research data reveal similar difficulties in dyslexic students as reported in literature: "poor phonological processing, poor working memory skills and poor syntactic skills."

Chinese languages have non alphabetic writing. The scripts are "logographic" and "morphographic." One character represents an individual phoneme. "This makes Chinese a morphographic script which means that the smallest pronounceable unit in a character is associated with a syllable" (Yin and Weekes, 2004). The basic unit in writing (the character) is a unit of meaning (morpheme) in the modern verbal language. Four different types of characters are said to be in use: (1), pictographic characters which represent a specific object; (2), indicative characters which represent abstract meaning; (3), associative characters which combine existing characters to produce a new meaning; and 4) phonetic-compound characters that combine semantic with phonetic component (Yin and Weekes, 2004). Here the prevalence of dyslexia was found to be 1.92 percent. Despite the significant differences between Chinese script and alphabetic Indo-European scripts there seem to be similar difficulties in dyslexia (Siok et al., 2009). One should expect deficits in the fine visual distinctions between the visually complex characters and high demands on the ability of a visual-spatial type of memory. Siok (2004) reported less activation of the left gyrus frontalis medialis in Chinese dyslexics, a brain region which correlates with the ability to analyze Chinese script characters. The available research points to deficiencies in Chinese dyslexics when "processing the phonetic and semantic radical components in the character" (Yin and Weekes, 2004). Similar problems occur in the Japanese language as Kanji also is a logographic script (see also the chapter by Fung and Su in this book).

In the Hebrew language morphological deficiencies appear to be prominent in reading and writing difficulties (Share and Leikin, 2004).

ASSESSMENT

The assessment is based on the multiaxial diagnostic system (WHO, 1996) and comprised of: psychiatric examination, psychological testing, anamnesis, and behavior analysis. The dyslexic child is most commonly referred because of severe problems at school and with homework conflicts as a reaction to the chronic severe failure in reading and/or spelling acquisition. Emotional, psychosomatic and behavioral problems are associated. Parent and teachers report a discrepancy between the unexpected failures in reading and spelling which are in obvious contradiction to strengths in other cognitive areas, i.e., math. As the operational definition of dyslexia is based on the discrepancy definition the disorder-specific assessment demands the use of standardised psychometric measures of IQ, and standardised reading and spelling tests. In widespread international use are the Wechsler Intelligence Scales for children and adults. The standardised reading and spelling tests include 1) phonetic and non phonetic words, 2) letter chains which screen for visual motor dysfunction, 3) simple word reading and writing of words and pseudo words, 4) reading speed and reading comprehension. The scores are converted to year (grade) group equivalents.

Further screening refers to neurological impairments (Coordination disorder—dyspraxia—, visual and auditory disorders), language skills (phonological abilities, developmental language disorder), attention deficit hyperactivity disorder (ADHD) and other emotional or behavioral difficulties (e.g., school anxiety, depression, conduct disorder).

The acquisition of reading and spelling skills is influenced by social and environmental factors. Thus the assessment of family and school background is important: school experience, literacy related support, lack of books at home, dyslexia in parents and/or siblings (risk of about 40 percent to become dyslexic if at least one parent also suffers from dyslexia). At risk children are those with dyslexic parents and/or dyslexic siblings, as well as preschoolers characterised by developmental language disorders. Specifically evidenced by deficits in phonological awareness, attention deficit, and less predictably developmental coordination disorder (visual-spatial difficulties, clumsiness). Significant to treatment is the assessment of individual strengths and family influences, as well as assessment of supportive social resources, (e.g., school programs, professional therapy).

ASSOCIATED EMOTIONAL AND BEHAVIORAL PROBLEMS

Children with severe school difficulties associated with dyslexia often reveal symptoms of (school) anxiety, depressed mood, abdominal pain, headaches, attention problems in scholastic learning conditions, sleep disorders, and finally educational problems at school and at home, especially, in the homework situation. Characteristically, all these complaints melt away or are diminished during holidays.

Dyslexic children are at increased risk of attention disorder, depression, anxiety disorder (school anxiety, school refusal) and conduct disorder (disciplinary problems). Dissocial problems are facilitated by attention deficits, while social adversities increase the risk of school failure and of antisocial behavior (Esser and Schmidt, 1993; Carroll, Maughan, Goodman, Melzer, 2005; Maughan, Rowe, Loeber, Stouthamer-Loeber, 2003; Maughan et al., 1996). Goldston et al. (2007) examined annually psychiatric disorders and functional impairment from mid- to late adolescence in samples with and without poor reading skills. "Adolescents with poor reading skills evidenced higher rates of current attention-deficit/hyperactivity, affective, and anxiety disorders, particularly social phobia and generalized anxiety disorder. Anxiety disorders, but not affective disorders, were related to reading status after controlling for attention-deficit/hyperactivity disorder." In a German follow-up study there was a significant correlation between level of performance in spelling and final school success (Haffner et al., 1998). Esser and Schmidt (1993) found a significantly higher number of psychiatric disorders (up to 43 percent) at ages eight, thirteen, eighteen, and twenty-four in a German epidemiological sample (birth cohort) of dyslexic individuals compared to a control sample. At age 18 the rate of juvenile delinquency was increased (25 percent). By age twenty-four, 25 percent of the dyslexic sample were unemployed compared to 4 percent of the control sample. The prognosis improves if there is qualified and continuous help and social support. In a twenty-year follow-up study of dyslexic children who had attended a special boarding school for children with dyslexia Schulte-Körne et al. (2003a) found no evidence of a significant number of psychiatric symptoms in the dyslexic adult sample. "The high IQ, the high socioeconomic status of these dyslexic adults and their parents, and the long lasting remedial work at the school all taken together might be relevant factors explaining this 'positive' development" (Schulte-Körne, 2004).

NEUROPSYCHOLOGY

Results from several decades of empirical research have identified cognitive processes that appear consistently associated with dyslexia. One of the major developmental problems is described as phonological processing deficits that have been found in three different areas: phonological awareness (e.g., Wagner and Torgesen, 1987), retrieval of phonological codes from long-term memory (e.g., Wolf et al., 1986), and verbal short-term memory (e.g., Catts, 1989). Phonological difficulties have been found to persist into adulthood (Shaywitz et al., 1999) and training phoneme awareness is an essential part of intervention and prevention for children with reading disabilities (Lyon and Moats, 1997).

Children and adults with dyslexia have also been found to have specific deficits in speech perception (Schulte-Körne et al., 1998; Bruder et al., 2011). They tend to have difficulties in discriminating speech signals that are characterized by spectral (e.g., formant transitions /da/-/ga/) (Kraus et al., 1996; Maurer et al., 2003; Schulte-Körne et al., 1998, 2001) or temporal transitions (e.g., voice onset time transitions /ga/-/ka/) (Bitz, Gust, Spitzer, and Kiefer, 2007; Cohen-Mimran, 2006) (for reviews, see Bishop, 2007; Schulte-Körne and Bruder, 2010). Recently evidence of impaired tuning to native language speech representations have been found in dyslexic children (Bruder et al., 2011).

Additionally, there is also some evidence for a more fundamental deficit in low-level auditory information processing. In particular, dyslexics may have problems processing short, rapidly presented and dynamic acoustic stimuli (e.g., Tallal, 1980; Farmer and Klein, 1995; McArthur and Bishop, 2001, 1998).

Many impaired readers are also characterized by deficits in naming speed (Wolf and Bowers, 2000). Extensive evidence from different paradigms now suggests that naming-speed deficits (NSD) may represent a second core deficit in reading disability (RD). Some researchers have described naming speed problems as largely independent of phonological skills (Clarke, Hulme, and Snowling, 2005; Wolf and Bowers, 1999; Cohen-

Mimran, 2006) and more predictive of reading disorder than phoneme awareness in transparent orthographies. Family studies have found that rapid naming (RN) deficits run in families, the heritability estimated for composites of numbers and letters being about 65 percent (Grigorenko, 2004). Specific neural correlates of RN objects and letters have been found in the fusiforme gyrus (Misra et al., 2004) at the temporal-occipital cortex (Schlaggar and McCandliss, 2007; Shaywitz et al., 2008).

A significant predictor of reading and spelling other than phonological processing and rapid naming is orthographic processing (Badian, 1998; Roman et al., 2009; Bekebrede et al., 2009). Orthographic processing has been defined as the ability to form, store and access orthographic representation (Stanovich and West, 1989). But orthographic knowledge has also been described as knowledge of the regularities of the visual and orthographic aspects of print (Roman et al., 2009). Since orthographically correct spelling often depends on knowledge of accepted patterns and accepted positions of letter patterns, the expectation is that orthographic knowledge is a more important predictor of spelling than reading performance. Research has shown that performance on an orthographic choice task correlates more strongly with spelling than reading performance in English-speaking undergraduate students (Stanovich and West, 1989). This result was replicated in Dutch, a more transparent language. Bekebrede et al. (2009) found that orthographic competence accounts for more unique variance in spelling (23 percent) than in reading (8 percent) performance. Twin studies have revealed a high heritability of orthographic choice of about 50–60 percent (Gayan and Olson, 2001) and molecular genetic studies have found orthographic processing to be associated to locus on chromosome 6p (Kaplan et al., 2002).

Working memory (WM) is a further cognitive ability that is correlated with reading and spelling development. Bradley and Bryant investigated an odd-one-out task in which the odd-one-out of a series of words presented aurally has to be detected (the child has to differentiate between the initial or last phonemes of spoken words, keep the odd-one-out word in their short-term memory, and then retrieve this memorized word from storage). This phonological memory task enables a prediction of reading development in preschool age (Bradley and Bryant, 1978). Several studies have shown that individuals with dyslexia have marked weaknesses in phonological working memory (Baddeley and Wilson 1993; Palmer, 2000; Swanson, 2006), and perform poorly in memory-related tasks as compared to age-matched controls. This quantitative measure is stable even in adults, and is thus considered to be a cognitive correlate within the complex dyslexia phenotype (Hulslander et al., 2004).

Molecular genetic studies suggest that loci in chromosomes 15 (Berninger et al., 2008) and 12 (Brkanac et al., 2008) might be associated with phonological memory in dyslexia. More recently a candidate gene,

GRIN2B, was identified as susceptibility of working memory and thus of a subtype of dyslexia (Ludwig et al., 2010).

NEUROBIOLOGY AND GENETICS

Family and twin studies clearly point to a genetic basis of this complex disorder. First candidate genes have been found (Fisher and Francks, 2006; Fisher et al., 2002; Smith et al., 1983). To date, linkage studies in dyslexia families have identified nine chromosomal regions—from DYX1 to DYX9—listed by the Human Gene Nomenclature Committee (HGNC). These regions are located in chromosomes 15q21 (DYX1), 6p21 (DYX2), 2p15-p16 (DYX3), 6q11-q12 (DYX4), 3p12-q13 (DYX5), 18p11 (DYX6), 11p15 (DYX7), 1p34-p36 (DYX8), and Xq27 (DYX9) (Scerri and Schulte-Körne, 2010). Furthermore, association studies within the mapped linkage regions have already led to the identification of dyslexia candidate genes. The most convincing findings have been reported within DYX2 at 6p21. Independent studies have identified the region by linkage analysis and association between dyslexia and genetic variants in the genes Doublecortin-Domain-Containing-Protein-2 (DCDC2) and KIAA0319 (Deffenbacher et al., 2004; Francks et al., 2004; Cope et al., 2005; Meng et al., 2005; Schumacher et al., 2006). A key function of these genes is their involvement in neuronal migration during the development of the neocortex. Studies on mice with knockdown condition of Dyx1c1 have revealed malformations including heterotopia in white matter, in the hippocampus and layer one of the neocortex (Rosen et al., 2007). Interestingly, these hippocampal heterotopias were correlated with impairments in learning (Threlkeld et al., 2007).

Investigating endophenotypes of dyslexia, the speech mismatch negativity (MMN or the frontocentrally negative component of the auditory event-related potential reflecting the accuracy of discrimination between different sounds) (Roeske et al., 2011) was found to be associated with *SLC2A3*, a gene in chromosome 12 which had not yet been associated with dyslexia or spelling disability. The functionality of *SLC2A3* renders it a compelling candidate for developmental disorders, as it is the predominant facilitative glucose transporter in neurons during child development. A reduction of glucose, or energy in the brain, might impact the development of speech sound discrimination skills and therefore may explain the attenuation of mismatch negativity (MMN) to speech sounds in children with spelling disability. In a subsequent study (Czamara et al., 2010) the MMN in children with spelling disability was associated with rare variants on the well known candidate genes for dyslexia *KIAA0319* and *DCDC2* both located in chromosome 6. Importantly, these findings suggest that the MMN to speech stimuli is influenced by genetics.

Socioeconomic status, family factors and reading exposure are known to influence the development of reading and spelling abilities, but are not causally related to dyslexia (Stevenson and Fredman, 1990; Vellutino et al., 2004; Harlaar, Dale, Plomin, 2007).

Imaging studies have clearly demonstrated an altered cortical network in dyslexic subjects that comprises left and right superior temporal cortices, left inferior temporal-occipital cortex and both left and right inferior frontal and posterior temporo-parietal cortices (for review see Schlaggar and Mc-Candliss, 2007).

Magnetic resonance studies have repeatedly identified brain regions and networks that are altered in children, adolescents and adults with dyslexia. One major finding is the underactivation in posterior regions of the left hemisphere, mainly in two different posterior networks: the temporo-parietal reading system, which is anatomically characterized as including the angular gyrus and supramarginal gyrus in the inferior parietal lobule, the posterior aspect of the superior temporal gyrus (Wernicke's area), the insula and supramarginal gyrus. This network is activated when mapping a letter of the visually presented word onto its phonological representation. This task reflects the typical word reading process of early readers. In dyslexic subjects an underactivation of this network has been reported and is associated with a phonological impairment (Rumsey et al., 1997; Paulesu et al., 2001; Kronbichler et al., 2006; Meyler et al., 2007). A meta-analysis found that the left inferior parietal cortex near the intra-parietal sulcus is under-activated, however the functional significance of this region is unclear.

The other posterior reading network is an occipito-temporal reading system comprising the posterior fusiform gyrus and the inferior temporal and medial temporal cortex. This network is mainly activated by fast and automatic processing of visual words, but also by letter strings and orthographic characteristics of the language. In dyslexic subjects delayed or lower activation in inferior temporal-occipital regions is seen as a correlate of deficient word recognition, especially when whole word recognition is required (Cao et al., 2006; McCrory et al., 2005; Paulesu et al., 2001). The under-activation of this network is also interfered with by disturbed connectivity between visual and auditory information processing, mainly the connectivity to higher cognitive processes of more basic sensory information (Price and Devlin, 2003). The under-activation of the medial temporal gyrus is more reflective of a deficient access to lexical-semantic information in dyslexic subjects.

A third region, the left inferior frontal region has been found to be overactive in subjects with dyslexia (Grünling et al., 2004; Hoeft et al., 2007; Kronbichler et al., 2006; Rumsey et al., 1997). The functional significance of this finding is unclear. Mostly, a compensation effect is associated with this finding. However, the results of a meta-analysis (Richlan et al., 2009,

2011), showed that the over-activation was found in the primary motor cortex and anterior insula. A compensatory over-activation of this motor cortical area as a correlate of articulatory based access to the phonological representation of a grapheme or word might be one plausible explanation. Right hemispheric regions are also correlated with compensation processes. Mainly right hemisphere temporo-parietal regions are more active in dyslexic subjects relative to left hemisphere regions (Démonet et al., 2004; Pugh et al., 2000; Shaywitz et al., 2004).

The cerebellum, which is activated in tasks requiring motor coordination under attention control, has been found to be less activated in dyslexic subjects (Nicolson et al., 1999). In several studies reduced gray matter density in the cerebellum of subjects with dyslexia have been replicated (Brambati et al., 2006; Brown et al., 2001; Eckert et al., 2005; Kronbichler et al., 2008).

INTERVENTION AND TREATMENT

Treatment consists initially of defining the disorder, advising the child with dyslexia and the parents, and possibly also advising teachers (e.g., Schulte-Körne, 2009; Reid, 2003). Subsequent treatment depends on the severity of dyslexia and clinical symptoms or comorbid disorders. Drug treatment is not beneficial for dyslexia. Only if a child with dyslexia also suffers from an attention deficit hyperactivity disorder (ADHD) can drug treatment for ADHD also improve reading and spelling abilities. Sometimes, as a consequence of the drug treatment, children and parents report significant improvement in handwriting as well.

Defining the disorder, explaining the causal factors, as well as the treatment options is usually a great relief to parents. Diagnosis often takes months to years, during which time parents, usually the mother, have tried to support their child via daily practice at home. Hours spent together every day on homework, regular (usually frustrating) dictation exercises, the child's unwillingness to study, paired with despair due to spelling errors in so many words in text writing and examination (despite so much practice), can lead to depressed mood in the child and feelings of failure in parents

In addition, parents often receive reports from teachers that their child would benefit from more practice at home. When the child and adolescent psychiatrist tells the parents that they have not failed, that their child finds it significantly harder than other children to learn to read and spell because of neurobiological deficits, parents find this as a great relief. Children themselves must also have the disorder explained to them and thereby have their stress relieved.

Advice for teachers serves to explain the diagnosis and the child's psychological stress and provides an opportunity to consider how the child can best be integrated at school. The dyslexia diagnosis must also be documented in the school records.

Dyslexia treatment has two major components: treatment of core problems with reading and spelling, and treatment of any concurrent psychological disorders (e.g., Schulte-Körne, 2009; Reid, 2003).

Reading support depends on an individual child's development. On the basis of a detailed analysis of developmental status in reading, reading support should be provided regularly, at least once a week for at least a year. In addition to this therapy, establishing a reading-friendly family environment with frequent reading sessions and reading together can also substantially boost reading development. Only a few types of reading support have been empirically investigated. A review by the National Reading Panel (2000) suggests training in phoneme awareness is most effective for word decoding. The review also emphasizes letter-sound association training. Combining word identification strategies with treatments based on improving phonological awareness is more effective than either treatment alone (Lovett, Steinbach, Frijters, 2000). Shaywitz et al. (2004) performed functional magnetic resonance imaging to study the effect of a phonologically based reading intervention on brain organization and reading fluency. After the year-long intervention children taught by the phonologically based intervention "had made significant gains in reading fluency and demonstrated increased activation in left hemisphere regions, including the inferior frontal gyrus and the middle temporal gyrus; one year after the experimental intervention had ended these children were activating bilateral inferior frontal gyri and left superior temporal and occipito temporal regions." The conclusion was that "the use of an evidence-based phonologic reading intervention facilitates the development of those fast-paced neural systems that underlie skilled reading." Temple et al. (2003) performed functional MRI on children with dyslexia during phonological processing before and after a remediation program focused on auditory processing and oral language training. The training improved the reading performance. After remediation "increases occurred in left temporo-parietal cortex and left inferior frontal gyrus, bringing brain activation in these regions closer to that seen in normal-reading children."

Spelling support must be given separately from reading support. As with reading support, the individual developmental status must be determined at the onset. Spelling support is then designed around this individual status. Beginning with support in phonics (spelling individual sounds), children learn regular trends in spelling. For example, in English the diphthong is usually spelled using the digraph *ou* (it is occasionally spelled *ow*, as in *fowl*, but more often *ou*, as in *found*). There are similar examples for double consonants, which in English words only follow short vowels (*filling* with *-ll-*, but *filing* with *-l-*). Children also learn how to use this knowledge. In a support program from the coauthors' working group (Schulte-Körne and Ise) a flowchart is used to show the systematic route to correct spelling, which consists of small steps (see Figure 8.1).

However, despite regular, intensive support most children with dyslexia achieve only slight improvement in their reading and spelling. The reasons for this are not well understood. Attempts are now being made to better understand the processes which are disrupted in these children by recording neurobiological correlates during treatment.

An essential part of treatment is therefore *psychotherapy*. Subjects with dyslexia learn how to handle their handicap. Children suffering from anxi-

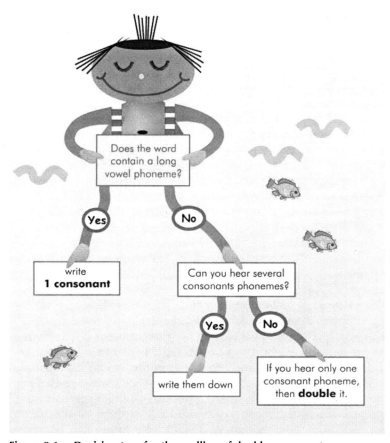

Figure 8.1.   Decision tree for the spelling of double consonants

ety and depression can be significantly helped by behavior therapy. ADHD comorbidity can be treated by stimulant medication

Treatment approaches for children with spelling disorder can be classified as either cause- or symptom-oriented. Cause-oriented programs target specific skills that are hypothesized to be the underlying causes of spelling disability (e.g., auditory or visual processing deficits). The idea behind cause-oriented programs is that eliminating a specific deficit enables children to overcome their spelling difficulties. Critics have argued that there is not a single cause of reading and spelling deficits, rather several factors seem to play a role (see also Vellutino et al., 2004). In summary: "cause-oriented" treatment approaches seem not to be helpful.

Symptom-oriented programs focus directly on reading and spelling skills and have repeatedly been found to significantly ameliorate reading and spelling abilities in dyslexic children (for a review see Ise, Engel, and Schulte-Körne, 2011). A meta-analysis of intervention studies with German-speaking dyslexic children (Ise, Engel and Schulte-Körne, 2011) found that symptom-oriented programs lead to significant benefits in reading and spelling, while the mean effect size for cause-oriented programs does not reach statistical significance.

As has been mentioned above, orthographic spelling is a major difficulty in dyslexic children. Because of the highly transparent German orthography, dyslexic children often master basic phonological decoding skills within the first years of formal schooling (Landerl, Wimmer, and Frith, 1997; Wimmer, 1993, 1996). However, difficulties in orthographic spelling remain (Landerl, 2001; Landerl and Wimmer, 2008). In contrast to English, orthographic spelling rules for German words are highly consistent. For example, in German words, a double consonant always marks a short vowel phoneme (e.g., *Bett* [engl. *bed*]), while English words may contain a double consonant either after a short vowel phoneme (e.g., *grass*) or after a long vowel phoneme (e.g., *ball*). Consequently, the majority of German words can be spelled correctly by applying orthographic spelling rules (in addition to phoneme-grapheme correspondence rules).

One of the most promising treatment approaches, at least in languages with consistent spelling rules, is to teach children how to spell words correctly by applying orthographic spelling rules. Rule-based spelling training therefore aims to enhance students' ability to effectively use explicit metacognitive knowledge of spelling rules. As an example of a rule-based training, the *Marburg Spelling Training* (*Marburger Rechtschreibtraining*, Schulte-Körne and Mathwig, 2009) depicts orthographic spelling rules graphically as yes/no decision-trees. Figure 8.1 depicts the decision-tree for the spelling of double consonants. Importantly, as children work with the decision-trees, they constantly verbalize spelling rules, which in turn strengthens their explicit memory of these rules. In addition, children learn how to use explicit knowledge of spelling rules effectively during spelling.

The *Marburg Spelling Training* implements recommendations derived from educational research. For example, children practice actively and receive direct feedback regarding their performance. The different spelling rules are introduced stepwise. That is, a spelling rule is practiced in a number of exercises with increasing levels of difficulty before the next spelling rule is introduced. Spelling rules that have already been learned are rehearsed on a regular basis. In addition, all training words can be spelled correctly by applying the rules that have already been learned. This was done to allow each child to give an errorless performance.

Three intervention studies have shown that the *Marburg Spelling Training* has a remedial effect on spelling and reading skills in children with spelling disorder. In a first study, the *Marburg Spelling Training* was conducted as a parent-child program (Schulte-Körne, Schäfer, Deimel, Remschmidt, 1997). After two years of supervised tutoring by a parent, children (n = 18) had significantly improved their spelling ability (Cohen's d = 0.53) (Schulte-Körne, Deimel, Remschmidt, 1998). A second intervention study investigated the effectiveness of the *Marburg Spelling Training* in a school setting (Schulte-Körne, Deimel, Remschmidt, 2003b). Twenty-one children with spelling difficulties were trained in small tutoring groups twice a week over a two-year period. The children significantly improved their reading (Cohen's d = 0.42) and spelling skills (Cohen's d = 0.59). A third intervention study (Schulte-Körne et al., 2001) used a pretest-intervention-posttest design with a treatment group (n = 10) and a delayed treatment control group (n = 10). During the first treatment period, children in the treatment group received phonological awareness training. Children in the delayed treatment group did not receive any training during the first training period, but were trained with the *Marburg Spelling Training* in the second training period. For both groups, training was conducted twice a week in individual sessions over a three month period. Consistent with previous evidence, phonological awareness training did not improve children's reading and spelling skills significantly (see also Wimmer and Hartl, 1991). The most likely interpretation of this finding is that the children had already mastered the alphabetic principle of the highly transparent German orthography. As expected, children in the delayed treatment group did not show a significant change during the first training period. However, their reading and spelling skills improved significantly during the second training period when they received the *Marburg Spelling Training* (Cohen's d = 0.50 for spelling improvement and Cohen's d = 0.74 for reading improvement).

The effectiveness of the rule-based spelling training for older students was evaluated in a recent intervention study (Ise and Schulte-Körne, 2010). The spelling training was provided to spelling-disabled children (grade 5-6) in a treatment group (n = 13) and a delayed treatment control group (n = 14). Analysis of spelling improvement revealed that gains in spelling were significantly greater in the treatment group (Cohen's d = 0.75) than in the control group (Cohen's d = 0.35). It was also found that the training program had a remedial effect on reading comprehension (Cohen's d = 0.60) and significantly improved children's explicit knowledge of orthographic spelling rules (Cohen's d = 1.10). This finding may not only be relevant for the treatment of German-speaking children, but also for treating dyslexic children learning to read and write other languages with transparent orthographies.

OUTCOME

The outcome depends on the severity of the dyslexia, comorbidity, the individual's general intellectual skills and the resources of the family's social background. Given appropriate educational support children with serious specific reading and spelling difficulties make slow progress. Nevertheless the subnormal level of achievement in reading and spelling will continue into adulthood in most cases (Maughan 1995; Klicpera et al., 1993). In total dyslexic individuals are finally less successful in their school career (Esser and Schmidt, 1994; Haffner et al., 1998). The risk for unemployment is significantly high in adulthood. But individuals with dyslexia who received continuous family encouragement and specialized support at school have found work in adulthood appropriate to their personal abilities (Maughan and Hagell, 1996; Schulte-Körne, 2004).

Furthermore educational failure is a risk of secondary antisocial behavior, attention problems, loss of self-esteem, and of emotional problems (anxiety) (Goldston et al., 2007; Esser and Schmidt, 1994; Heiervang et al., 2001; Klicpera et al., 1981; Maughan et al., 1996, 2003; Caroll et al., 2005; Klein and Mannuzza, 2000). Mediating factors are comorbid ADHD and low family support.

SOCIETIES

Worldwide there are national and international societies bringing together individuals with dyslexia, clinicians and researchers from different scientific disciplines to promote issues of common interest. The International Dyslexia Association (http://www.interdys.org/) and the European Dyslexia Association are examples of international societies. National associations are in nearly all countries of the European Union, in the United States, Canada, Australia, New Zealand, Brazil, Cyprus, India, Israel, South Africa, Singapore, Malta, and possibly several other countries in the world. The promotion of any scholastic and clinical support of individuals with dyslexia and the promotion of research and scientific knowledge is an important issue of IACAPAP. Dyslexia continuously is a main topic in the IACAPAP International Congresses and Research Group Meetings.

REFERENCES

Abu-Rabia, S. (2004). "Dyslexia in Arabic." 31–38. In Smythe, I., Everatt, J., Salter, R. (eds), *International Book of Dyslexia: A cross-language comparison and practice guide.* Chichester: John Wiley and Sons.

Abu-Rabia, S., and Taha, H. (2004). "Reading and spelling error analysis of native dyslexic readers." *Reading and Writing: An Interdisciplinary Journal, 17,* 65–689.

American Psychiatric Association. (2000). *Diagnostic and Statistical Manual of Mental Disorders (DSM IV TR).* Washington, DC: *American Psychiatric Association.*

Baddeley, A., Wilson, B. A. (1993). "A developmental deficit in short-term phonological memory: implications for language and reading." *Memory, 1*(1), 65–78.

Badian, N. A. (1998). "A validation of the role of preschool phonological and orthographic skill in the prediction of reading." *Journal of Learning Disabilities, 31*(5), 472–81.

Bekebrede, J., van der Leij, A., Share, D. L. (2009). "Dutch dyslexic adolescents: phonological-core variable-orthographic differences." *Reading and Writing: An Interdisciplinary Journal, 22,* 133–65.

Berkhan, O. (1885)"Über die Schriftsprache bei Halbidioten und ihre Ähnlichkeit mit dem Stammeln." *Arch. f. Psychiatr, 16,* 78–86.

Berkhan, O. (1886). "Über die Störung der Schriftsprache bei Halbidioten und ihre Ähnlichkeit mit dem Sprachgebrechen, 2. Stammeln und Stottern." *Arch. f. Psychiatr. 17,* 897–900.

Berninger, V. W., Raskind, W., Richards, T., Abbott, R., Stock, P. (2008). "A multidisciplinary approach to understanding developmental dyslexia within working-memory architecture: genotypes, phenotypes, brain, and instruction." *Dev Neuropsychol, 33*(6), 707–44.

Bishop, D. V. (2007). "Using mismatch negativity to study central auditory processing in developmental language and literacy impairments: where are we, and where should we be going?" *Psychol Bull, 133*(4), 651–72.

Bitz, U., Gust, K., Spitzer, M., Kiefer, M. (2007). "Phonological deficit in school children is reflected in the Mismatch Negativity." *Neuroreport, 18*(9), 911–15.

Bradley, L., Bryant, P. E. (1978). "Difficulties in auditory organisation as a possible cause of reading backwardness." *Nature, 271*(5647), 746–47.

Brambati, S. M., Termine, C., Ruffino, M., Danna, M., Lanzi, G., Stella, G., Cappa, S. F., Perani, D. (2006). "Neuropsychological deficits and neural dysfunction in familial dyslexia." *Brain Res, 1113,* 174–85.

Brkanac, Z., Chapman, N. H., Igo, R. P., Matsushita, M. M., Nielsen, K., Berninger, V. W., Wijsman, E. M., Raskind, W. H. (2008). "Genome scan of a nonword repetition phenotype in families with dyslexia: evidence for multiple loci." *Behav Genet, 38*(5), 462–75.

Brown, W. E., Eliez, S., Menon, V., Rumsey, J. M., White, C. D., Reiss, A. L. (2001). "Preliminary evidence of widespread morphological variations of the brain in dyslexia." *Neurology, 56,* 781–83.

Bruder, J., Leppänen, P., Bartling, J., Csépe, V., Démonet, J.-F., Schulte-Körne, G. (2011). "Children with dyslexia reveal abnormal native language representations: Evidence from a study of mismatch negativity." *Psychophysiology;* First published online: 17 Feb 2011, DOI: 10.1111/j.1469-8986.2011.01179.x.

Cao, F., Bitan, T., Chou, T. L., Burman, D. D., Booth, J. R. (2006). "Deficient orthographic and phonological representations in children with dyslexia revealed by brain activation patterns." *J Child Psychol Psychiatry, 47,* 1041–50.

Carroll, J., Maughan, B., Goodman, R., Meltzer, H. (2005). "Literacy difficulties and psychiatric disorders: Evidence for co-morbidity." *Journal of Child Psychology and Psychiatry, 46,* 524–32.

Catts, H. W. "Speech production deficits in developmental dyslexia." *Speech Hear Disord, 54*(3), (1989). 422–28.

Clarke, P., Hulme, C., Snowling, M. J. "Individual differences in RAN and reading: a timing analysis." *Journal of Research in Reading, 28*(2005). 73–86

Cohen-Mimran, R. "Temporal processing deficits in Hebrew speaking children with reading disabilities." *J Speech Lang Hear Res, 49*(1), (2006). 127–37.

Cope, N. A., Hill, G., van den Bree, M. "No support for association between Dyslexia Susceptibility 1 Candidate 1 and developmental dyslexia." *Molecular Psychiatry, 10*(3), (2005). 237–38.

Czamara, D., Bruder, J., Becker, J., Bartling, J., Hoffmann, P., Ludwig, K. U., et al. (2010). "Association of a rare variant with Mismatch Negativity in a region between KIAA0319 and DCDC2 in dyslexia." *Behav Genet.* Doi, 10.1007/s10519-010-9413-6.

Deffenbacher, K. E., Kenyon, J. B., Hoover, D. M. (2004). "Refinement of the 6p21.3 quantitative trait locus influencing dyslexia: linkage and association analyses." *Hum Genet, 115*(2), 128–38.

Démonet, J.-F., Taylor, M. J., Chaix, Y. (2004). "Developmental dyslexia." *Lancet, 363,* 1451–60.

Eckert, M. A., Leonard, C. M., Wilke, M., Eckert, M., Richards, T., Richards, A., Berninger, V. (2005). "Anatomical signatures of dyslexia in children: Unique information from manual and voxel based morphometry brain measures." *Cortex, 41,* 304–15.

Esser, G., Schmidt, M. H. (1993). "Die langfristige Entwicklung von Kindern mit Lese-/Rechtschreibschwäche." *Zeitschrift für klinische Psychologie, 22,* 100–116.

Esser, G., Schmidt, M. H. (1994). "Teilleistungsstörungen und Depression." *Kindheit und Entwicklung, 3.*

Farmer, M. E., Klein, R. M. (1995). "The evidence for a temporal processing deficit linked to dyslexia." *Psychonomic Bulletin and Review, 2,* 460–93.

Fisher, S. E., Francks, C., Marlow, A. J. (2002). "Independent genome-wide scans identify a chromosome 18 quantitative-trait locus influencing dyslexia." *Nat Genet, 30*(1), 86–91.

Fisher, S. E., Francks, C. (2006). "Genes, cognition and dyslexia: learning to read the genome." *Trends Cogn Sci, 10*(6), 250–57.

Francks, C., Paracchini, S., Smith, S. D. et al. (2004). "A 77-kilobase region of chromosome 6p22.2 is associated with dyslexia in families from the United Kingdom and from the United States." *Am J Hum Genet*, 75(6), 1046–58.

Gayan, J., Olson, R. K. (2001). "Genetic and environmental influences on orthographic and phonological skills in children with reading disabilities." *Dev Neuropsychol*, 20483–507.

Goldston, D. B., Walsh, A., Arnold, E. M., Reboussin, B., Daniel, S. S., Erkanli, A., Nutter, D., Hickman, E., Palmes, G., Snider, E. and Wood, F. B. (2007). "Reading Problems, Psychiatric Disorders, and Functional Impairment from Mid- to Late Adolescence." *J. Am. Acad. Child Adolesc. Psychiatry*, 46, 25–32.

Goswami, U. (1997). "Learning to read in different orthographies: Phonological skills, orthographic representations and dyslexia." In: Snowling, M. and Hulme, C. (eds), *Dyslexia: Biology, Identification and Intervention*. London: Whurr Publishers.

Goswami, U. (2000). "Phonological representations, reading development and dyslexia: Towards a cross-linguistic theoretical framework." *Dyslexia*, 6, 133–51.

Grigorenko, E. L. "Genetic bases of developmental dyslexia: A capsule review of heritability estimates." *Enfance* 3(2004). 273–87.

Grünling, C., Ligges, M., Huonker, R., Klingert, M., Mentzel, H.-J., Rzanny, R., Kaiser, W.A., Witte, H., Blanz, B. (2004). "Dyslexia: The possible benefit of multimodal integration of fMRI- and EEG-data." *J Neural Transm*, 1(11), 951–69.

Haffner, J., Zerahn-Hartung, C., Pfüller, U., Parzer, P., Strehlow, U., Resch, F. (1998). "Auswirkungen und Bedeutung spezifischer Rechtschreibprobleme bei jungen Erwachsenen–empirische Befunde in einer epidemiologischen Stichprobe." *Zeitschrift für Kinder Jugendpsychiatrie und Psychotherapie,*, 26, 124–35.

Harlaar, N., Dale, P. S., Plomin, R. (2007). "Reading exposure: a (largely) environmental risk factor with environmentally-mediated effects on reading performance in the primary school years." *Journal of Child Psychology and Psychiatry*, 48, 1192–99.

Heiervang, E., Stevenson, J., Lund, A., Hugdahl, K. (2001). "Behavior problems in children with dyslexia." *Nord J Psychiatry*, 55, 251–6.

Hinshelwood, J. (1896). "A case of dyslexia: a peculiar form of word-blindness." *The Lancet, Nov.* 21, 1451–54.

Hinshelwood, J. (1904). "A case of congenital word-blindness." *British Medical Journal*, 2, 1303–4.

Hinshelwood, J., Macphail, A., Ferguson, A. (1904). "A case of word-blindness, with right homonymous hemianopsia." *The British Medical Journal, Nov.* 12, 1304–7.

Hinshelwood, J. "Congenital word-blindness." London: Lewis, 1917.

Hoeft, F., Meyler, A., Hernandez, A., Juel, C., Taylor-Hill, H., Martindale, J. L., McMillon, G., Kolchugina, G., Black, J. M., Faizi, A., Deutsch, G. K., Siok, W. T., Reiss, A. L., Whitfield-Gabrieli, S., Gabrieli, J. D. E. (2007). "Functional and morphometric brain dissociation between dyslexia and reading ability." *Proc Natl Acad Sci*, 104, 4234–39.

Hulslander, J., Talcott, J., Witton, C., DeFries, J., Pennington, B., Wadsworth, S., Willcutt, E., Olson, R. (2004). "Sensory processing, reading, IQ, and attention." *J Exp Child Psychol*, 88(3), 274–95.

Ise, E. and Schulte-Körne, G. (2010). "Spelling deficits in dyslexia: evaluation of an orthographic spelling training." *Annals of Dyslexia, 60,* 18–39.

Ise, E., Engel, R. R., Schulte-Körne, G. (in press). (2011). "Was hilft bei der Lese-Rechtschreibstörung? Ergebnisse einer Metaanalyse zur Wirksamkeit deutschsprachiger Förderansätze. [How should dyslexia be treated? A meta-analysis on the effectiveness of German interventions of dyslexia]." *Kindheit und Entwicklung, 4.*

Kaplan, D. E., Gayán, J., Ahn, J., Won, T. W., Pauls, D., Olson, R. K., DeFries, J. C., Wood, F., Pennington, B.F., Page, G. P., Smith, S. D., Gruen, J.R. (2002). "Evidence for linkage and association with reading disability on 6p21.3–22." *Am J Hum Genet, 70*(5), 1287–98.

Katusic, S. K., Colligan, R. C., Barbaresi, W. J., Schaid, D. J., Jacobsen, S. J. (2001). "Incidence of reading disability in a population-based birth cohort." 1976–1982, Rochester, Minn. *Mayo Clinic Proc, 76,* 1081–92.

Klein, R. G., Mannuzza, S. (2000). "Children with uncomplicated reading disorders grown up: a prospective follow-up into adulthood," in *Learning Disabilities: Implications for Psychiatric Treatment.* Edited by Greenhill L. L. (*Review of Psychiatry Series*; Oldham, J. O. and Riba, M. B., eds.). Washington, DC: American Psychiatric Press, 1–31.

Klicpera, C., Schabmann, A., Gasteiger-Klicpera, B. (1993). "Lesen- und Schreibenlernen während der Pflichtschulzeit: Eine Längsschnittuntersuchung über die Häufigkeit und Stabilität von Lese- und Rechtschreibschwierigkeiten in einem Wiener Schulbezirk [Learning to read an write in compulsory education: A longitudinal study of the incidence and stability of reading and writing difficulties in a Vienna school district.]." *Zeitschrift für Kinder- und Jugendpsychiatrie, 21,* 214–25.

Klicpera, C., Warnke, A., Kutschera, G., Heyse, I., Keeser, W. (1981). "Eine Nachuntersuchung von verhaltensgestörten Kindern zwei bis zehn Jahre nach stationärer kinderpsychiatrischer Betreuung." *Nervenarzt, 52,* 531–37.

Kraus, N., McGee, T. J., Carrell, T. D., Zecker, S. G., Nicol, T. G., Koch, D. B. (1996). "Auditory neurophysiologic responses and discrimination deficits in children with learning problems." *Science, 273*(5277), 971–73.

Kronbichler, M., Hutzler, F., Staffen, W., Mair, A., Ladurner, G., Wimmer, H. (2006). "Evidence for a dysfunction of left posterior reading areas in German dyslexic readers." *Neuropsychologia, 44,* 1822–32.

Kronbichler, M., Wimmer, H., Staffen, W., Hutzler, F., Mair, A., Ladurner, G. (2008). "Developmental dyslexia: Gray matter abnormalities in the occipitotemporal cortex." *Hum Brain Mapp, 29,* 613–25.

Kussmaul, A. (2001). "Die Störungen der Sprache," 1–300. In: Ziemssen, H. v. (Hrsg.), Handbuch der speziellen Pathologie und Therapie." Bd. 12, Anhang, Leipzig: Vogel, 1877.

Landerl, K. "Word recognition deficits in German: More evidence from a representative sample." *Dyslexia, 7,* 183–96

Landerl, K., Moll, K. (2009). "Double dissociation between reading and spelling." *Scientific Studies of Reading, 13*(5), 359–82.

Landerl, K., Moll, K. (2010). "Comorbidity of learning disorders: prevalence and familial transmission." *J Child Psychol Psychiatry 51*(3), 287–94.

Landerl, K., Wimmer, H., Frith, U. (1997). "The impact of orthographic consistency on dyslexia: A German-English comparison." *Cognition, 63,* 315–34.

Landerl, K., Wimmer, H. (2000). "Deficits in phoneme segmentation are not the core problem of dyslexia: Evidence from German and English children." *Applied Psycholinguistics, 21,* 243–62.

Landerl, K., Wimmer, H. (2008). "Development of word reading fluency and spelling in a consistent orthography: An 8-year follow-up." *Journal of Educational Psychology, 100,* 150–61

Lindgren, S. D., DeRenzi, E., Richman, L. C. (1985). "Cross-national comparisons of developmental dyslexia in Italy and the United States." *Child Dev, 56,* 1404–17.

Lovett, M. W., Steinbach, K. A., Frijters, J. C. (2000). "Remediating the core deficits of developmental reading disability: A double-deficit perspective." *Journal of Learning Disabilities, 33,* 334–58

Ludwig, K. U., Roeske, D., Herms, S., Schumacher, J., Warnke, A., Plume, E., Neuhoff, N., Bruder, J., Remschmidt, H., Schulte-Körne, G., Müller-Myhsok, B., Nöthen, M. M., Hoffmann, P. (2010). "Variation in GRIN2B contributes to weak performance in verbal short-term memory in children with dyslexia." *American Journal of Medical Genetics Part B (Neuropsychiatric Genetics), 153B*(2), 503–11

Lyon, G. R., Moats, L. C. (1997). "Critical conceptual and methodological considerations in reading intervention research." *Journal of Learning Disabilities, 30*(6), 578–588.

Maughan, B. (1995). "Annotation: long-term outcomes of developmental reading problems." *Journal of Child Psychology and Psychiatry, 36,* 357–71.

Maughan, B., Hagell, A. (1996). "Poor readers in adulthood: Psychosocial functioning." *Development and Psychopathology, 8,* 457–76.

Maughan, B., Pickles, A., Hagell, A., Rutter, M., Yule, W. (1996). "Reading problems and antisocial behavior: Developmental trends in comorbidity." *Journal of Child Psychology and Psychiatry, 37,* 405–18.

Maughan, B., Rowe, R., Loeber, R., Stouthammer-Loeber, M. (2003). "Reading problems and depressed mood." *Journal of Abnormal Child Psychology, 31,* 219–29.

Maurer, U., Bucher, K., Brem, S., Brandeis, D. (2003). "Altered responses to tone and phoneme mismatch in kindergartners at familial dyslexia risk." *Neuroreport, 14*(17), 2245–50.

McArthur, G. M., Bishop, D. V. (2001). "Auditory perceptual processing in people with reading and oral language impairments: current issues and recommendations." *Dyslexia,7*(3), 150–70.

McBride-Chang, C., Lam, F., Lam, C., Doo, S., Wong, S. W., Chow, Y. Y. (2008). "Word recognition and cognitive profiles of Chinese pre-school children at risk for dyslexia through language delay or familial history of dyslexia." *J Child Psychol Psychiatry, 49*(2), 211–18.

McCrory, E. J., Mechelli, A., Frith, U., Price, C. J. (2005). "More than words: A common neural basis for reading and naming deficits in developmental dyslexia?" *Brain, 128,* 261–67.

Meng, H., Smith, S. D., Hager, K. (2005). "DCDC2 is associated with reading disability and modulates neuronal development in the brain." *Proc Natl Acad Sci, 102*(47), 17053–58

Meyler, A., Keller, T. A., Cherkassky, V. L., Lee, D. H., Hoeft, F., Whitfield-Gabrieli, S., Gabrieli, J. D. E., Just, M. A. (2007). "Brain activation during sentence comprehension among good and poor readers." *Cereb Cortex, 17,* 2780–87.

Miles, T. R., Miles, E. (1999). *Dyslexia: A hundred years on,* 2nd ed., Buckingham: Open University Press.

Misra, M., Katzir, T., Wolf, M., Poldrack, R. (2004). "Neural systems for rapid automatized naming in skilled readers: Unravelling the RAN-reading relationship." *Sci Stud Read, 8,* 241–56.

Morgan, W. P. "A case of congenital word-blindness." *British Medical Journal,* 2(1896). , 1378.

National Reading Panel. (2000). "Teaching children to read: An evidence-based assessment of the scientific research literature on reading and its implications for reading instruction." Reports of subgroups NICHD.

Nicolson, R. I., Fawcett, A. J., Berry, E. L., Jenkins, I. H., Dean, P., Brooks, D. J. (1999). "Association of abnormal cerebellar activation with motor learning difficulties in dyslexic adults." *Lancet, 353,* 1662–67

Palmer, S. (2000). "Phonological recoding deficit in working memory of dyslexic teenagers." *Journal of Research in Reading, 23*(1), 28–40.

Paulesu, E., Démonet, J.-F., Fazio, F., McCrory, E., Chanoine,V., Brunswick,N., Cappa, S. F., Cossu, G., Habib, M., Frith, C. D., Frith, U. (2001). "Dyslexia: Cultural Diversity and Biological Unity." *Science, 291,* 2165–67.

Price, C. J., Devlin, J. T. (2003). "The myth of the visual word form area." *Neuroimage, 19,* 473–81.

Pugh, K. R., Mencl, W. E., Jenner, A. R., Katz, L., Frost, S. J., Lee, J. R., Shaywitz, S. E., Shaywitz, B. A. (2000). "Functional neuroimaging studies of reading and reading disability (developmental dyslexia)." *Ment Retard Dev Disabil Res Rev, 6,* 207–213.

Reid, G. (2003). *Dyslexia: A Practitioner's Handbook.* 3rd ed., Chichester: Wiley and Sons.

Richlan, F., Kronbichler, M., Wimmer, H. (2009). "Functional abnormalities in the dyslexic brain: a quantitative meta-analysis of neuroimaging studies." *Hum Brain Mapp.*

Richlan, F., Kronbichler, M., Wimmer, H. (2011). "Meta-analyzing brain dysfunctions in dyslexic children and adults." *Neuroimage, 56*(3), 1735–42

Rispens, J. van, Yperen, T., Yule, W. (eds). (1998). *Perspectives on the Classification of Specific Developmental Disorders.* Dordrecht: Kluwer Academic Publishers.

Roeske, D., Ludwig, K. U., Neuhoff, N., Becker, J., Bartling, J., Bruder, J. (2011). "First genome-wide association scan on neurophysiological endophenotypes points to trans-regulation effects on SLC2A3 in dyslexic children." *Mol Psychiatry, 16,* 97–107.

Roman, A. A., Kirby, J. R., Parrila, R. K., Wade-Woolley, L., and Deacon, S.H. "Toward a comprehensive view of the skills involved in word reading in grades 4, 6, and 8." *Journal of Experimental Child Psychology, 102*(2009). 96–113.

Rosen, G. D., Bai, J., Wang, Y., Fiondella, C. G., Threlkeld, S. W., LoTurco, J. J., Galaburda, A. M. (2007). "Disruption of neuronal migration by RNAi of Dyx1c1 results in neocortical and hippocampal malformations." *Cereb Cortex, 17*(11), 2562–72.

Rumsey, J. M., Nace, K., Donohue, B., Wise, D., Maisog, J. M., Andreason, P. (1997). "A positron emission topographic study of impaired word recognition and phonological processing in dyslexic men." *Arch Neurol, 54*, 562–73

Scerri, T. S., Schulte-Körne, G. (2010). "Genetics of developmental dyslexia." *Eur Child Adolesc Psychiatry, 19*(3), 179–97.

Schlaggar, B. L., McCandliss, B. D. (2007). "Development of neural systems for reading." *Annu Rev Neurosci, 30*, 475–503.

Schulte-Körne, G. (2004). "Dyslexia Research in German-Speaking Countries." In: Smythe, I., Everatt, J., Salter, R. (eds), *International Book of Dyslexia: A cross-language comparison and practice guide* (93–104). Chichester: John Wiley and Sons.

Schulte-Körne, G., (2009). *Ratgeber Legasthenie.* München: Knaur.

Schulte-Körne G., Mathwig, F. (2009). *Das Marburger Rechtschreibtraining: Ein regelgeleitetes Förderprogramm für rechtschreibschwache Kinder (4. Aufl.).* [The Marburg Spelling Training: A rule-based treatment program for children with spelling difficulties (4th edition)]." Bochum: Winkler.

Schulte-Körne, G., Bruder, J. (2010). "Clinical neurophysiology of visual and auditory processing in dyslexia: A review." *Clin Neurophys, 121*(11), 1794–809.

Schulte-Körne, G., Deimel, W., Remschmidt, H. (1998). "Das Marburger Eltern-Kind-Rechtschreibtraining - Verlaufsuntersuchung nach zwei Jahren [The Marburg parent-child spelling training–follow up after two years]." *Zeitschrift für Kinder- und Jugendpsychiatrie und Psychotherapie, 3*, 167–73.

Schulte-Körne, G., Deimel, W., Remschmidt, H. (2003a). "Rechtschreibtraining in schulischen Fördergruppen - Ergebnisse einer Evaluationsstudie in der Primarstufe [Spelling training in school based intervention groups—Results of an evaluation trial in secondary school]." *Zeitschrift für Kinder- und Jugendpsychiatrie und Psychotherapie, 31*, 85–98.

Schulte-Körne, G., Deimel, W., Remschmidt, H. (2003b). "Nachuntersuchung einer Stichprobe von lese- und rechtschreibgestörten Kindern im Erwachsenenalter." *Zeitschrift für Kinder- und Jugendpsychiatrie und Psychotherapie, 31*(4), 267–76.

Schulte-Körne, G., Deimel, W., Bartling, J., Remschmidt, H. (1998). "Auditory processing and Dyslexia: evidence for a specific speech processing deficit." *Neuroreport, 9*(2), 337–40.

Schulte-Körne, G., Deimel, W., Bartling, J., Remschmidt, H. (2001). "Speech perception deficit in dyslexic adults as measured by mismatch negativity (MMN)." *Int J Psychophysiol, 40*(1), 77–87.

Schulte-Körne, G., Schäfer, J., Deimel, W., Remschmidt, H. (1997)"Das Marburger Eltern-Kind-Rechtschreibtraining [The Marburg parent-child spelling training program]." *Zeitschrift für Kinder- und Jugendpsychiatrie und Psychotherapie, 25*, 151–59.

Schumacher, J., Anthoni, H., Dahdouh, F. et al. (2006). "Strong genetic evidence of DCDC2 as a susceptibility gene for dyslexia." *Am J Hum Genet, 78*(1), 52–62

Share, D. L., Leikin M. (2004). "Developmental Dyslexia in the Hebrew Language" 113–21. In: Smythe, I., Everatt, J., Salter, R. (eds), *International Book of Dyslexia: A cross-language comparison and practice guide.* Chichester: John Wiley and Sons.

Shaywitz, S. E., Morris, R., Shaywitz, B. A. (2008). "The education of dyslexic children from childhood to young adulthood." *Annu Rev Psychol, 59*, 451–75.

Shaywitz, B. A., Shaywitz, S. E., Blachman, B. A., Pugh, K. R., Fulbright, R. K., Skudlarski, P., Mencl, W. E., Constable, R. T., Holahan, J. M., Marchione, K. E., Fletcher, J. M., Lyon, G. R., Gore, J. C. (2004). "Development of Left Occipito-temporal Systems for Skilled Reading in Children After a Phonologically-Based Intervention." *Biol Psychiatry*, 55, 926–33.

Shaywitz, S. E., Shaywitz, B. A., Fletcher, J. M., Escobar, M. D. (1990). "Prevalence of reading disability in boys and girls: Results of the Connecticut Longitudinal Study." *Journal of the American Medical Association*, 264, 998–1002.

Shaywitz, S. E., Fletcher, J., Holahan, J., Schneider, A., Marchione, K., Stuebing, K. (1999). "Persistence of dyslexia: The Connecticut Longitudinal Study at adolescence." *Pediatrics*, 104, 1351–59.

Siok, W. T., Perfetti, C. A., Jin, Z., Tan, L. H. (2004). "Biological abnormality of impaired reading is constrained by culture." *Nature*, 431, 71–76.

Siok, W. T., Spinks, J. A., Jin, Z., Tan, L. H. (2009). "Developmental dyslexia is characterized by the co-existence of visuospatial and phonological disorders in Chinese children." *Current Biology*, 19, 890–92.

Smith, S. D., Kimberling, W. J., Pennington, B. F. et al. (1983). "Specific reading disability: identification of an inherited form through linkage analysis." *Science*, 219(4590), 1345–47.

Smythe, I., Everatt, J. (2004). "Dyslexia: A cross-linguistic framework" 1–29. In Smythe, I., Everatt, J., Salter, R. (eds), *International Book of Dyslexia: A cross-language comparison and practice guide*. Chichester: John Wiley and Sons.

Smythe, I., Everatt, J., Salter, R. (2004). *International Book of Dyslexia: A cross-language comparison and practice guide*. Chichester: John Wiley and Sons.

Stanovich, K. E., (1992). "Discrepancy definitions of reading disability: Has intelligence led us astray?" *Reading Research Quarterly*, 26, 7–29.

Stanovich, K. E., (1996). "Towards a more inclusive definition of dyslexia." *Dyslexia*, 2(3), 154–166.

Stanovich, K., West, R. (1989). "Exposure to print and orthographic processing. *Reading Research Quarterly*, 24, 402–414.

Stephenson, S. (1907). "Six cases of congenital word-blindness affecting three generations of one family." *Ophthalmoscope 5*, 482–484.

Stevenson, J., Fredman, G. (1990). "The social environmental correlates of reading ability." *J Child Psychol Psychiatry 31*(5), 681–698.

Swanson, H. L. (2006). "Working memory and reading disabilities: Both phonological and executive processing deficits are important." In Alloway T. P., Gathercole S. E., (eds). *Working memory and neurodevelopmental disorders*. Hove, UK: Psychology Press. 59–88.

Tallal, P. (1980). "Auditory temporal perception, phonics, and reading disabilities in children." *Brain Lang*, 9, 182–198.

Temple, E., Deutsch G. K., Poldrack, R. A., Miller, S. L., Tallal, P., Merzenich, M. M., Gabrieli J. D. E. (2003). "Neural deficits in children with dyslexia ameliorated by behavioral remediation: Evidence from functional MRI." *PNAS*, 100, 2863.

Threlkeld, S. W., McClure, M. M., Bai, J., Wang, Y., LoTurco, J. J., Rosen, G. D., Fitch, R. H. (2007). "Developmental disruptions and behavioral impairments in rats following in utero RNAi of Dyx1c1." *Brain Res Bull*, 71(5), 508–14

U.S. Department of Education: National Center for Education Statistics. (2008). *National Assessment of Educational Progress (NAEP). The nation's report card, reading, 2007.* Washington, DC: Institute of Education Sciences, U.S. Department of Education. Retrieved August 15, 2008, from http://nces.ed.gov/nationsreportcard/pubs/main2007/2007496.asp

Vellutino, F. R., Fletcher, J. M., Snowling, M. J., Scanlon, D. M. (2004). "Specific reading disability (dyslexia). What have we learned in the past four decades?" *Journal of Child Psychology and Psychiatry, 45,* 2–40

Wagner, R. K., Torgesen, J. K. (1987). "The nature of phonological processing and its causal role in the acquisition of reading skills." *Psychological Bulletin, 101,* 192–212.

Wimmer, H. (1993). "Characteristics of developmental dyslexia in a regular writing system." *Applied Psycholinguistics, 14,* 1–33

Wimmer, H. (1996). "The early manifestation of developmental dyslexia: Evidence from German children." *Reading and Writing: An Interdisciplinary Journal, 8,* 171–188

Wimmer, H., Hartl, M. (1991). "Erprobung einer phonologisch, multisensorischen Förderung bei jungen Schülern mit Lese- und Rechtschreibschwierigkeiten [Evaluation of a phonological, multisensory remediation program in young students with reading and spelling difficulties]." *Heilpädagogische Forschung, 2,* 74–79

Wolf, M., Bally, H., Morris, R. (1986). "Automaticity, retrieval processes, and reading: A longitudinal study in average and impaired readers." *Child Devel 57,* 988–1000.

Wolf, M., Bowers, P.G. (1999). "The double deficit hypothesis for the developmental dyslexias." *J Educ Psychol, 91,* 415–438.

Wolf, M., Bowers, P.G. (2000). "Naming-speed processes and developmental reading disabilities: An introduction to the special issue on the double-deficit hypothesis." *Journal of Learning Disabilities, 33*(4), 322–324.

World Health Organization (WHO). (1996). *Multiaxial classification of child and adolescent psychiatric disorders: The ICD-10 classification of mental and behavioral disorders in children and adolescents.* Cambridge: Cambridge University Press,.

Yin, W., Weekes, B. (2004). "Dyslexia in Chinese" 39–45. In: Smythe, I., Everatt, J. and Salter, R. (eds), *International Book of Dyslexia: A cross-language comparison and practice guide.* Chichester: John Wiley and Sons.

9

The Effects of Child Maltreatment on the Developing Brain

Danya Glaser

INTRODUCTION

Most of the harm caused by child maltreatment is expressed in behavioural, emotional, cognitive and social difficulties, all of which must be assumed to have a neurobiological equivalent. There has been growing interest in the effects on the developing brain of different forms of child maltreatment, beyond the harm caused by trauma inflicted directly to the head. This interest has occurred in the context of greater accessibility of the results of neurobiological research. Brain structure, and precise timing and localisation of function can now be studied in a number of ways. A particular aspect is the possibility of simultaneous observation of brain functioning and mind—cognitive, emotional and behavioural—functioning (Nelson et al. 2002). The relationship between neurobiological and psychological processes is a complex one, as discussed among other by Marshall (2009).

It is important to recognize that while there is now clear evidence that maltreatment is associated with, and probably causes harmful neurobiological effects, there is both heterogeneity in these effects and not all children are equally affected. This chapter seeks to review the neurobiological evidence.

Why are possible neurobiological consequences of maltreatment of interest? One possibility is that if there is evidence of an effect on the brain, then child maltreatment must really be taken seriously. Another is that it may help to actually explain some aspects of the psychological harm, although this view has recently been challenged by Tallis (2011). A further reason is that studying effects of harmful experiences on the brain might further the understanding of the brain and its developments. Lastly, greater clarity of neurobiological effects of child maltreatment might open new avenues of physical or pharmacological treatment for the effects.

Since a previous publication of a similar review (Glaser 2000), there has been further reported research as well as a number of reviews of this subject (e.g., Teicher et al. 2003; De Bellis 2005; Anda et al. 2006; Marshall and Kenny 2009; and McCrory et al. 2010). Within an overall developmental perspective, some of the reported studies and reviews have focussed on brain structures thought to be particularly vulnerable to or associated with psychological difficulties, some on functional neurobiological equivalents of particular symptoms attributed to or following maltreatment—PTSD in particular, and others have studied the neurobiological associations or effects of particular forms of maltreatment—for example neglect. In a rapidly growing and developing field dealing with very complex mechanisms, it is inevitable that different studies are, at times, finding inconsistent or conflicting results. Moreover, many of the studies contain small samples; there is heterogeneity in the forms, duration and age at maltreatment; effects and outcomes have been studied in both child and adult populations with different results, for example, the size of the hippocampus following early abuse, with no reduction in children but consistent findings of reduction in adults following childhood maltreatment; many of the studies are cross-sectional rather than longitudinal and at least in theory, it is possible that the maltreatment was not causally related to the neurobiological changes. In this chapter, there is an attempt to place the information within an explanatory framework with some specific, but not exhaustive, examples of a number of postulated mechanisms.

The first three years of life are of great importance to the child's later development (e.g. Shonkoff and Phillips 2000). However, it is important to note that continuing and new experiences in childhood and adolescence also influence brain development and that neural plasticity implies that there is potential for change even after significant early disadvantage (Nelson 1999). Longitudinal study of the effects of child maltreatment, albeit not including neurobiological findings, has shown that adolescent maltreatment, both that which began in childhood and that with onset in adolescence, is associated with significant difficulties in adulthood including substance misuse, offending behaviour and suicidal thoughts (Thornberry et al. 2010). This may be related to particular changes in the adolescent brain during puberty. At the beginning of life, brain development is also strongly influenced by prenatal factors, including maternal alcohol (Fitzgerald et al. 2000) and drug abuse (e.g., Kosofsky and Hyman 2001; Mayes 1999) and significant maternal stress (Welberg et al. 2001). However, in the absence of a legal mandate to protect the foetus from maternal harm, there are only limited possibilities for protecting the vulnerable foetal brain from adverse circumstances. While the focus in this chapter is on the maltreating relationship between the primary caregiver(s) and the young child, sexual abuse is perpetrated equally commonly by non-primary caregivers. The relationships with the child are obviously nested within the family which is, in turn, significantly influenced by the social environment in which the family is located (Leventhal et al. 2000).

WAYS OF CAPTURING BRAIN STRUCTURE AND FUNCTIONING

Neurobiological functioning can be observed and measured in many ways, some of which have been utilized in the study of effects of child maltreatment. These include the measurement of:

1. Direct, electrical activity using event-related potentials (ERP) which record short, discrete, timed activity in m seconds, in response to discrete stimuli, but are poorer at localising the activity.
2. Indirect activity using functional magnetic resonance imaging (fMRI) which records deoxygenated haemoglobin levels in active sites (1cm localisation and timing in seconds).
3. Structure, in particular the size of particular regions (as well as lesions) using magnetic resonance imaging (MRI) and computerized tomography (CT) scanning.
4. Recently, diffusion tensor imaging (DTI) has been used to measure axonal white matter structure.
5. Levels of neuropeptides such as oxytocin and neurotransmitters, in particular the biogenic amines dopamine and noradrenaline (catecholamines) and serotonin (5HT) which are involved in regulation of emotions and behaviour. Their secretion and usage can be recorded by a variety of means including levels of the neurotransmitters or their metabolites in the blood and urine and cerebro-spinal fluid (CSF), and more localized neurotransmitter activity using labelled positron emission tomography (PET).
6. Stress hormones, especially cortisol, which is secreted in saliva in which levels follow closely changes in blood levels, and in urine from which 24 hour secretion levels can be measured.

FACTORS CONTRIBUTING TOWARDS EXPLANATORY MECHANISMS

There are a number of factors which contribute towards an understanding of the mechanisms leading to the harmful neurobiological effects of child maltreatment. They are:

- Aspects of child maltreatment
- The stress response
- Brain development
- Gene-environment interactions and resilience

While these factors are independent, their effects are often combined in the neurobiological outcomes.

ASPECTS OF CHILD MALTREATMENT

There are several forms of child maltreatment which may occur on their own, although more often different forms co-occur (Glaser, 2011). The commonest is neglect—lack of provision of basic care, lack of stimulation, emotional neglect and lack of supervision. Emotional abuse which takes many forms of persistent, non-physical harmful interactions with the child is also very common. Physical abuse/nonaccidental injury and sexual abuse are most likely to be traumatic experiences. The experience of maltreatment, including neglect, is stressful for the child and the harm exerted is wide-ranging (Gilbert et al. 2009).

THE STRESS RESPONSE

The body's response to stress is a physiological coping response necessary for survival, and involves several body systems. They include the sympathetic and parasympathetic (autonomic) nervous system, the hypothalamic-pituitary-adrenal axis (HPA) (Gunnar and Cheatham 2003), neurotransmitter systems and the immune system. There are individual variations in the threshold above which an individual perceives an experience to be stressful and in the response to the stress. These individual differences in stress responsiveness are partly genetically determined and partly based on prior experience. While mild stress leads to helpful "stress inoculation," early exposure to significant stress lays the foundation for later enhanced stress responsiveness. There are costs to the stress response and individual children who are innately more reactive to stress are therefore more vulnerable to its consequences.

The response of the sympathetic nervous system to stress results in secretion of adrenaline and noradrenaline by the medulla of the adrenal gland. The effects of these hormones include raising heart rate, blood pressure, sweating and activation of the fight or flight response. There is also an increase in neurotransmitter secretion in the brain in response to stress which includes noradrenaline and dopamine. The cerebellar vermis exerts strong modulatory effects on brain regions which produce noradrenaline and dopamine, including the locus coeruleus. Significantly raised levels of these neurotransmitters in the prefrontal cortex interfere with its functions (Arnsten, 1999), notably executive functions.

The HPA axis is regulated by a negative feedback loop. There is a diurnal variation in cortisol secretion with higher levels in the morning which fall in the late afternoon. Much has been written about the HPA axis response to stress (e.g., Sapolsky et al. 2000). One significant aspect of this is the increased secretion of cortisol. Regions in the brain with high density of glucocorticoid receptors are particularly vulnerable to the effects of stress; they include the hippocampus and cerebellar vermis. Cortisol acts in a number of different ways and on most tissues and organs. For example, cortisol suppresses glial cell division, reducing myelination (Lauder 1983). It has been found that during the first year of life, there is a progressive decrease in cortisol responsiveness to stress, returning to the subsequent normal stress response in early childhood. It is thought that this buffers the developing brain from the harmful effects of cortisol (Gunnar and Cheatham 2003). It has also been found that a sensitive parental responsiveness, which leads to secure attachment, is associated with a lower cortisol stress response (Albers et al. 2008).

Effects of Stress Due to Child Maltreatment

There are many aspects of child maltreatment which are stressful, although not necessarily traumatic. They include the stress of neglect and deprivation, the absence of external affect regulation, an unpredictable environment, exposure to frightening or traumatising experiences, physical pain, and emotional insults.

Sympathetic Nervous System

Several studies have found higher baseline levels of catecholamines in children who had been sexually abused (Bicanic et al. 2008).

In psychiatrically hospitalised boys who had experienced significant neglect with or without abuse in the first three years of life, an association has been found with reduced levels of plasma dopamine beta hydroxylase (D*b*H) levels, which correlate with cerebrospinal fluid (CSF) levels (Galvin et al. 1991). This enzyme is involved in the conversion of dopamine to noradrenaline. Galvin et al. postulated that the stress of early maltreatment led to an overstimulation of the noradrenergic system with subsequent reactive repression of enzyme activity. Similar findings have been reported by Rogeness and McClure (1996). Galvin et al. (1995) reported an association between low serum DbH and conduct disorder in a group of hospitalised boys who had a history of early maltreatment.

Effects of HPA Axis and Cortisol

Infants who have received insensitive and unresponsive caregiving, an aspect of child maltreatment, do not show the dampening of the cortisol stress response. Those infants who have negative emotional temperament and who are poorer at self-regulation are particularly vulnerable. Child maltreatment has been associated with dysregulation of the HPA axis diurnal cycle with varying patterns (Tarullo and Gunnar 2006) of low morning and high evening, raised overall and lowered overall levels of cortisol, even after cessation of the maltreatment. It is likely that the different patterns are related to different forms of psychopathology (Hawes et al. 2009).

Changes in Brian Function

Reduced cerebellar volume has been found in post institutionalised children adopted at least three years earlier, who had suffered severe neglect (Bauer et al. 2009). It is postulated that the stress of severe deprivation during a sensitive period (see below) led to the reduced cerebellar volume. This was associated with significantly poorer executive and memory functioning in comparison with a normal group of children. The cerebellar vermis, which has projections to the limbic system, has also been found to be functionally impaired following early stress and neglect (Teicher et al. 2003).

Hemispheric laterality has been found to be affected by maltreatment. The two cerebral hemispheres are specialized in their respective functions. Normally, the dominant, left hemisphere is concerned with language, and logical and analytical thought. The right hemisphere is concerned with the processing and expression of emotion, particularly negative or unpleasant. Clearly, for optimal functioning there needs to be close interaction between the two hemispheres which are connected through the corpus callosum and the anterior and posterior commissures. Reduced size of the corpus callosum has been shown to affect inter-hemisphere communication (Yazgan et al. 1995).

Hospitalised children who had been physically or sexually abused have been found to show left frontal and temporal EEG abnormalities. Furthermore, Ito et al. (1998) have found that in a group of children who had been abused, the left hemisphere was less developed relatively to the right in terms of ratio of grey to white matter and differentiation, a reversal of the normal pattern. Stress due to maltreatment during the age three to six years, when dendritic growth in the left hemisphere is at its highest, may account for this effect.

In an fMRI study of adolescents who had been adopted following prolonged experiences of early maltreatment and changes of caregiving, Mueller et al. (2010) showed prolonged reaction time in inhibiting and executing cognitive responses (executive function) with altered activation in inferior prefrontal cortex and striatum which are involved in cognitive inhibition and response control, as well as in primary motor and sensorimotor cortex. These changes are postulated to be related to stress.

Cerebral Volume

Using structural MRI, De Bellis et al. (1999) found that, in comparison to non-abused children, a group of maltreated children suffering from PTSD were found to have 7 percent smaller cerebral volumes; smaller areas in the corpus callosum, and larger total lateral ventricle and cortical and prefrontal cortical CSF volumes. The abnormalities were correlated with duration of abuse. Possible explanations discussed by the authors include increased catecholamine concentrations or raised cortisol levels related to the maltreatment. Lack of stimulation in the early lives of these children could also be contributing factors. As the authors show and discuss, there is a positive correlation between IQ measures and brain size.

SOME RELEVANT ASPECTS OF BRAIN DEVELOPMENT

The neurobiological effects of child maltreatment are, in part, related to the process of brain development so that the timing of particular forms of maltreatment may have particular effects. The growing understanding of the process and rate of early brain development lends support to the commonly held belief about the crucial importance of early experiences. However, it is important to emphasize also the potential for later development and to recognize particular changes in adolescence.

Most of the understanding of brain development emanates from studies of animals. The descriptions of aspects of brain development here are largely confined to the very complex human brain, about which much less is understood, and are necessarily simplifications.

The stepwise *sequence* of brain development is genetically predetermined and cannot be altered by environment and experience. It proceeds from lower to higher brain centres, from the brain stem to the cerebral cortex

(Nelson and Bloom, 1997). Areas of the brain subserving different functions mature at different times (Andersen 2003). Sensory centres serving vision and hearing are the earliest to mature. The process of brain maturation continues into adolescence, with the prefrontal cortex being the last to mature (Giedd 2004).

By birth, most of the brain's billions of neurons are formed and have migrated to their permanent position in the brain. Most post-natal brain growth occurs in the first 4 years, with the rate being highest in the first year. This post-natal growth is accounted for by a profuse, sequential proliferation and overproduction of axons, dendrites and synapses in the brain. During early childhood, the number of synapses reaches nearly double the number ultimately found in adulthood. It is accompanied by progressive myelination which increases the speed of neural impulse transmission, by the necessary proliferation of glial cells and of capillaries. The *timing* of synaptogenesis varies between different cortical regions (Huttenlocher 1979). Synaptogenesis allows initially for considerable plasticity and is responsive to a wide range of environmental stimuli.

Brain-Environment Interactions

Not all the synaptic connections survive, many being subsequently "pruned" due to lack of use (Singer 1995). It is environmental input, which includes sensory input, interactions between the primary carers and the child and child maltreatment, that determines which synapses will persist; to quote Courchesne et al. (1994) "neurons that fire together, wire together." A competitive process operates, determining which synapses and neurotransmitter receptors will survive. This enables the brain to conserve metabolic resources, ensure optimal speed of processing and match the brain's functioning to environmental circumstances. One aspect of the competition is for potential binding sites on the receiving neuron, with repeated stimuli reinforcing the synaptic connection.

Sensitive and Critical Periods

The periods of sequential synaptogenesis and pruning are termed sensitive or critical periods, during which the effects of particular experiences on the brain are unusually strong (Knudsen 2004). A sensitive period relies on evidence that "an experience (or the lack of) it during a given period in development has a more pronounced effect (positive or negative) on the organism than exposure to that same experience at any other time during the organism's development" (Bruer 2001). There are successive (and overlapping) sensitive periods in different parts of the brain, leading to the sequential development of different functions. Childhood is a prolonged process (compared to animals), the prefrontal cortex continuing to mature into adolescence. Until pruning occurs, the neural plasticity allows for a wide range of developmental opportunities. The price is a prolonged vulnerability to developmental insults. These individual experiences that contribute to brain development are an example of the non-shared environment (Plomin et al. 1994) to which even monozygotic twins are exposed. Some plasticity of function remains after the termination of the sensitive period but is then constrained by the synaptic connections previously established.

Greenough et al. (1987) postulated that, within the sensitive period paradigm, there are some experiences which are sufficiently species-typical to be expected and required by the developing organism. In humans, these experiences include handling of a young infant, responsive gaze, talking and responding to the infant particularly when the infant is alarmed or distressed. All these interactions need to be with a predictable and limited number of primary caregivers. This aspect of brain development was termed by Greenough et al. *experience-expectant*. Experience expectant development implies the existence of critical periods of development, which are regarded as a subset of sensitive periods. Examples of critical periods for aspects of development are found in animals, especially relating to perception of sensory modalities. The classical one is the work of Hubel and Wiesel (1979) who showed that by temporarily blocking the visual input to one eye of a kitten during a critical period of development, irreversible structural and functional changes are produced in the brain's visual cortex, leading to permanent impairment of vision in that eye. In humans, profoundly deaf children do not continue to vocalize in later infancy (Scarr, 1993) presumably because species-typical auditory experiences, which are required for the development of language, fail to reach the appropriate brain area. Young children who do not experience language during early life become unable to acquire and use the principles of language (Newport 1990). Irreversible reduction in visual acuity (amblyopia) occurs if an eye is deprived of visual input due to, for instance, a cataract or a squint beyond the age of 8 ± 10 years (Taylor and Taylor, 1979). According to this model of development, significant reduction in these experience-expectant stimuli carries several implications: 1) these effects would apply to all individuals in a species and therefore to all human infants; 2) their virtual absence leads to an elimination of the "expecting" synapses with structural modification which becomes irreversible beyond a certain age (Hensch 2004). The irreversibility appears to arise in at least some cases because a set of synapses had evolutionarily become committed to a particular pattern of organisation, while synapses that could have subserved alternative patterns have been lost. Subsequent more adaptive experiences would not reverse or entirely remediate the adverse developmental effects. However, in his review, Knudsen (2004) has shown that it is likely that some plasticity during a critical period can later be reinstated, with changes at molecular and cellular level later contributing to some change in function. It is also possible that later "working around" the deficit through learning (see below), which utilizes different parts of the brain might, to some extent, compensate for the deficit (Courchesne et al. 1994). Interestingly, enriched environments may prolong the critical period. In other words, the critical period is itself use-dependent. In human development, critical periods are rare, because even a little experience may be sufficient to lead to the "wiring" or establishment of synapses, albeit in a distorted pattern of normal development.

Experience-Adaptive Programming

An alternative view of what happens during sensitive periods has been termed by Rutter (2002) experience-adaptive programming, a mechanism denoting that the brain development of individual children is "designed" to be adaptive to the particular environment prevailing during the sensitive period. The adaptive nature of these neurobiological changes becomes redundant and maladaptive with a subsequent change of environment. Teicher et al. (2003) also postulate that the changes which they describe (see above) following stress due to maltreatment early in life are adaptive to that environment.

An interesting example of experience–adaptive programming is a study by Scott et al. (2007), in which they showed that, within the first year of life, there was a decline in visual discrimination for stimuli not found in an infant's environment. Specifically, while at the age of six months, infants showed novelty preferences for different monkey faces by spending longer looking at a new monkey face, neither nine-month-old infants nor adults continued to show evidence of such discrimination. While there were initially synapses which enabled the young infant to discriminate the monkey faces, as these were not part of the expectable environment, there was a (presumed) pruning of these (later-to-be-redundant) broadly-tuned synapses. If, however, the infants had been repeatedly exposed to pictures of different monkeys and the pictures accompanied by vocalized names, the capacity to discriminate was not lost. Lastly, while the behavioural capacity to discriminate the monkey faces was lost, there was ERP evidence of some continued activity, suggesting the retention of a capacity.

Child Maltreatment and Sensitive/Critical Periods/ Experience-Adaptive Programming

What is the relevance of sensitive and critical periods and experience-adaptive programming to child maltreatment? There is evidence both of effects of deprivation and neglect and of abuse leading to changes in brain functioning which are not, or only partially reversible even with a change of environment. Studying children who have experienced significant maltreatment at known ages and where the maltreatment is known to have been terminated have increased our understanding of the effects of maltreatment in relation to sensitive periods. For example, Rutter et al. (2007) in their longitudinal study of children adopted from Romanian orphanages, which were characterized by minimal care from a succession of staff, showed the persistence into adolescence of socially disinhibited and indiscriminate behaviour in children who had been moved after the age of six months. The phenomenon of social disinhibition and indiscriminate friendliness is also encountered with children who have experienced significant neglect by their biological parents in early childhood, although with good subsequent care, this behaviour has usually been amenable to change. There are a number of postulated neurobiological mechanisms to explain this finding, including the stress-related, early faulty programming of the oxytocin and vasopressin neuropeptide systems, which are critical for the formation of social bonds, associated with pleasurable social experiences (Marshall and Kenny 2009) and are protective against stress and anxiety. Wismer Fries et al. (2005) studied the oxytocin and vasopressin responses of adopted children (mean age fifty-four months) who had been living with their adoptive families for an average of three years following neglect in institutions. In comparison with birth children, some of the adoptees showed lower baseline urine arginine vasopressin (AVP) levels and lower oxytocin urine levels following thirty minutes of pleasurable joint play and physical interaction with their adoptive mothers. Behaviourally, there may well be an adaptive value to indiscriminate social approach in a depriving environment where the young child is seeking interaction with any available caregiver, an example of experience-adaptive programming.

A further example of the effects of maltreatment at certain sensitive periods has been provided by Andersen et al. (2008) in a study describing correlations between child sexual abuse at particular ages with reduced volume of different brain regions, measured in early adulthood (in women aged eighteen to twenty-two years). Specifically, using volumetric MRI scanning, they found that sexual abuse at preschool age was associated with reduced hippocampal volume; sexual abuse in middle childhood was associated with reduced corpus callosum volume; and abuse in mid-adolescence with reduced frontal lobe volume. This is presumably due to the reduced myelination due to high cortisol levels associated with the stress of maltreatment. These correlations correspond to recognized sensitive periods of development of these brain regions and may also explain the different psychological sequelae associated with a history of child sexual abuse.

EEG broad band frequency, specifically absolute and relative power of several frequency bands, is a marker of CNS maturation and norms have been standardized internationally in adequately reared children. In a longitudinal study of children born to high risk families in Mexico, characterized by no or poor parental literacy, large sibships, overcrowded home conditions, little stimulation and social interaction amounting to overall neglect, Otero et al. (2003) studied these EEG band frequencies repeatedly between eighteen months and six years of age. They found persisting significant differences between the neglected and normally reared comparison children in frontal and occipital region maturation.

The neurobiological effects of severe social deprivation have also been studied extensively by the Bucharest (Romania) Early Intervention Project (BEIP) of institutionalised children. One aspect has been an ERP study of neural circuitry subserving responses to facial processing at baseline, thirty and forty-two months (Parker et al. 2005; Moulson and Nelson 2009). They found that institutionalised children showed markedly smaller amplitudes and longer latencies for the occipital, parietal, temporal, frontal and central areas. In children who had subsequently been placed in foster care following institutional life there was some improvement which did not, however, reach the levels found in children who had never been institutionalised. Age at move to foster care did not determine magnitude of change. While the findings indicate a sensitive period, its length cannot be determined from these studies. Together with the findings by Chugani et al. (2001) of reduced metabolic activity in limbic and paralimbic regions, structural changes in brain connectivity from the amygdala to areas of the prefrontal cortex (Eluvathingal et al. 2006) and the work of Marshall et al. (2008) who showed altered patterns of EEG power and coherence in the institutionalised children compared with the children brought up in the birth families, these are clear indications of widespread cortical hypoarousal consequent on severe early deprivation.

A significant reduction in the size of the corpus callosum in children (mean age 12.9 years) who had been maltreated has been found by Teicher et al. (2004). For boys this reduction was associated with neglect and for girls, with sexual abuse. The postulated explanation for these different gender-related effects is that neglect by lack of stimulation decreases the rate of corpus callosum myelination which occurs early in life. The onset of marked neglect is usually early and boys have been noted to be more adversely affected by early neglect than girls (Kaufman and Cicchetti 1989). By contrast, myelination of the corpus callosum in girls continues later in childhood, a time when sexual abuse becomes more prevalent, and the associated stress then affects myelination of the corpus callosum in girls. Using diffusion tensor imaging, Choi et al. (2009) have recently shown white matter tract changes in young adults who had experienced verbal abuse including ridicule, humiliation in childhood, and postulate that these changes may underpin aspects of cognitive and emotional development.

Experience-Dependent Learning

Another aspect of neuroplasticity, the brain's ability to change its own structure in response to the environment and experience, is continual learning, termed by Greenough et al. (1987) *experience-dependent* development. This is associated with the formation of new synapses and continues into adulthood, although the rate of acquisition slows with increasing maturity. Learning is a sequential process which relies on the development of prior skills for the acquisition of new ones. Moreover, the *nature* of what has previously been learnt will either shape or interfere with subsequent learning. Unlike the experience-expectant process, here the nature of the experiences are not predetermined, and are particular to each individual child and carer-child relationship. The experience-dependent synapses that "wire together" following particular input, do not *anticipate* the experiences at any precise developmental stage, although learning (e.g. acquisition of languages) proceeds much more easily at the appropriate developmental stage, early in life. It is also possible that later experience-dependent synapse formation differs from that of early development in that it is localised to different, possibly higher cortical, regions from those specifically evolved for the task which were involved in earlier development of the same function. With appropriate change in environment and therapy, this allows for the possibility of some later recovery from the harmful effects or earlier maltreatment.

Children who have been physically abused in early life have been found to have larger P3b amplitude ERPs when looking at pictures of angry, rather than happy or fearful faces presented to them (Pollak et al. 1997; Pollak et al. 2001). Physically abused children have also been found to identify and preferentially discriminate as angry facial expressions from within a series of morphed faces ranging from sad to angry and from fearful to angry (Pollak et al. 2002). The implication is that being presented with negative affect carries a different meaning to maltreated children and elicits a physiologically and perceptually measurable different response. For a child living in an environment perceived as threatening, it is adaptive for their survival to identify anger preferentially. However, this predisposition becomes maladaptive when extended and used indiscriminately and outside abusive situations, over-interpreting or incorrectly interpreting facial expressions as threatening. These responses do not indicate conclusively whether they are to be regarded as falling within a sensitive period of development or are experience-dependant, meaning that they could follow exposure to repeated physical abuse and aggression at a later age in development but what is important is that they appear to be enduring.

The amygdala is important for learning about and monitoring the safety of the emotional environment for emotional significance, as a mediating agent between environmental stress and subsequent self-regulation difficulties, like anxiety and mood disorders. The amygdala undergoes early rapid development, rendering it vulnerable to early stressors. While stress is the stimulus for the enlarged amygdala, this can be regarded as an example of experience adaptive programming in that the amygdala is responding to a requirement for enhanced activity due to the unsafe environment. The cost is subsequent difficulty in self-regulation and modulations of arousal. In a study of children of mean age 8.5 years, adopted from institutions at a median age of fifteen months, larger amygdala volume was correlated with later adoption and longer time spent in institutional care and with difficulty in emotion regulation with increased sensitivity to negative stimuli (Tottenham et al. 2010). In a related, fMRI study, Tottenham et al. (2011) have shown that these children showed heightened amygdala activity relative to the comparison group in response to both fearful faces and distracter stimuli, suggesting that the post institutionalised children were less able to ignore the emotional content of the distracter stimuli. These children were found to show less eye-contact, mediated by the increased amygdala activity and were reported to show poorer social competence. As eye contact is related to amygdala activity, it is postulated that these children had adaptively reduced eye contact in order to reduce the aversive experience of eye contact with caregivers whom they found frightening, in order to reduce their arousal. However, reducing eye contact also militates against the formation of meaningful social relationships and, specifically, the necessary formation of attachment relationships which have been shown to be compromised in this population of children.

Gene-Environment Interaction: Genetic Vulnerability and Resilience

It is well recognized that children who have undergone apparently similar maltreatment experiences, and even when allowing for nonshared environments, do not share the same harmful outcomes. There is now growing evidence of both genetic vulnerability and resilience to the effects of maltreatment. Caspi et al. (2002) demonstrated that male carriers of the low-MAOA activity genotype who were maltreated in childhood were more likely to develop conduct disorders in adolescence than those with the high-MAOA activity genotype or than those who with the low-MAOA activity genotype who had not been maltreated. There have been several other examples of this interaction, summarized in McCrory et al. (2010). While these studies have demonstrated the effects of the presence or absence of alleles of single genes, it is likely that in many forms of child maltreatment there is a complex interaction between several genes and the harmful environment in bringing about neurobiological effects. Epigenetic effects, in which environmental, specifically significant aspects of intrauterine environment (Oberlander et al. 2008) and early caregiving affect gene expression without altering the genetic DNA sequence, are also being recognized as explaining enduring environmental effects which can be transmitted to the next generation (Groom et al. 2011).

CONCLUSIONS

Empirical evidence is accumulating about the considerable and multifarious effects of child maltreatment on the developing brain. In light of the very complex nature of brain development, structure and functioning combined with the heterogeneity of maltreatment experiences, and the fact of gene-environment interactions, it is not surprising that a very complex picture emerges without an overarching coherence.

Harm commonly follows from an enhanced stress response. Although there is evidence that some deficits of experience during critical periods can lead to the absence of development of some functions, this is rarely the case in human development. Sensitive periods are commoner but it is being recognized increasingly that particular neurobiological changes which may later be perceived as harmful, were developed as an adaptation to the particular maltreating environment at the time of maltreatment. Although later good caregiving will be incorporated and added on to past connections, it cannot undo established patterns, only modify them over time. Change requires significant improvement and protection in the interpersonal caregiving relationships with the child. The primary focus for early intervention therefore needs to be with the primary carers and the carer-child relationship. In cases where there is no indication of the caregivers' capacity to change within the child's timescales, consideration needs to be given to a permanent change in caregivers, in order to protect the developing brain from harmful trajectories. Later direct therapeutic work with the child who is in a more optimal environment will also be required. The most effective intervention is undoubtedly the prevention or very early recognition of inappropriate parent-child interactions when effects on the young child may not yet be apparent.

There is as yet little evidence of direct benefit to the child of the growing neurobiological understandings. However, in future it might be possible to identify very vulnerable children for early protection, although a Child Rights approach indicates the need for prevention of all child maltreatment.

REFERENCES

Albers, E., Marianne Riksen-Walraven, J., Sweep, F., and Weerth, C., "Maternal behavior predicts infant cortisol recovery from a mild everyday stressor." *Journal of Child Psychology and Psychiatry* 49 (2008): 97–103.

Anda, R., Felitti, V., Bremner, J., Walker, J. Whitfield, C., Perry, B., Dube, S., Giles, W., "The enduring effects of abuse and related adverse experiences in childhood: A convergence of evidence from neurobiology and epidemiology." *European Archives of Psychiatry and Clinical Neuroscience* 256 (2006): 174–186.

Andersen, S., "Trajectories of brain development: point of vulnerability or window of opportunity?" *Neuroscience and Biobehavioral Reviews* 27 (2003): 3–18.

Andersen, S., Tomada, A., Vincow, E., Valente, E., Polcari, A., Teicher, M., "Preliminary Evidence for Sensitive Periods in the Effect of Childhood Sexual Abuse on Regional Brain Development." *Journal of Neuropsychiatry and Clinical Neurosciences* 20 (2008): 292–301.

Arnsten, A., "Development of the cerebral cortex: XIV. Stress impairs prefrontal cortical function." *Journal of the American Academy of Child and Adolescent Psychiatry,* 38 (1999): 220–222.

Bauer, P., Hanson, J., Pierson, R., Davidson, R., Pollak, S., "Cerebellar Volume and Cognitive Functioning in Children Who Experienced Early Deprivation." *Biological Psychiatry* 66 (2009): 1100–1106.

Bicanic, I., Meijer, M., Sinnema, G., van de Putte, E., Olff, M., "Neuroendocrine dysregulations in sexually abused children and adolescents: a systematic review." *Progress in Brain Research* 167 (2008):303– 306.

Bruer, J., "A critical and sensitive period primer." In *Critical Thinking About Critical Periods.* Eds Bailey, D., Bruer, J., Symons, F., Lichtman, J., (2001) pp. 3–26 Brookes Baltimore.

Caspi, A., McClay, J., Moffitt, T., Mill, J., Martin, J., Craig, I., Taylor, A., Poulton, R., "Role of genotype in the cycle of violence in maltreated children." *Science* 297 (2002): 851– 854.

Choi, J., Jeong, B., Rohan, M., Polcari, A., Teicher, M., "Preliminary evidence for white matter tract abnormalities in young adults exposed to parental verbal abuse." *Biological Psychiatry* 65 (2009): 227–234

Chugani, H., Behen, M., Muzik, O., Juhasz, C., Nagy, F., Chugani, D., "Local brain functional activity following early deprivation: A study of postinstitutionalized Romanian orphans." *NeuroImage* 14 (2001): 1290–1301.

Courchesne, E., Chisum, H, Townsend, J., "Neural activity-dependent brain changes in development: Implications for psychopathology. *Development and Psychopathology* 6 (1994): 697–722.

De Bellis, M., "The psychobiology of neglect." *Child Maltreatment* 10 (2005): 150–172.

De Bellis, M., Keshavan, M., Clark, D., Casey, B., Giedd, J., Boring, A., Frustaci, K., Ryan, N., "Developmental traumatology Part II: Brain development." *Biological Psychiatry,* 45 (1999): 1271–1284.

Eluvathingal, T., J., Chugani, H., T., Behen, M., E., Juhasz, C., Muzik, O., Maqbool, M., et al. (2006). Abnormal brain connectivity in children after early severe socioemotional deprivation: A diffusion tensor imaging study. *Pediatrics, 117,* 2093–2100.

Fitzgerald, H., Puttler, L., Mun, E., Zucker, R., "Prenatal and Postnatal Exposure to Parental Alcohol Use and Abuse." In: Osofsky, J., Fitzgerald, H., (Eds) *WAIMH Handbook of Infant Mental Health. Vol. 4. Infant Mental Health in Groups at High Risk.* John Wiley and Sons: New York. 2000.

Fries, A. B. W., Ziegler, T. E., Kurian, J. R., Jacoris, S., Pollack, S. D. "Early experience in humans is associated with changes in neuropeptides critical for regulating social behaviour." *Proceedings of the National Academy of Sciences of the United States of America* 102 (2005): 17237–17240.

Galvin, M., Shekhar, A., Simon, J., Stilwell, B., Ten Eyck, R., Laite, G., Karwisch, G., Blix, S., "Low dopamine beta-hydroxylase: A biological sequela of abuse and neglect?" *Psychiatry Research* 39 (1991): 1–11.

Galvin, M., Ten Eyck, R., Shekhar, A., Stilwell, B., Fineberg, N., Laite, G., Karwisch, G., "Serum dopamine beta hydroxylase and maltreatment in hopitalized boys." *Child Abuse and Neglect,* 19 (1995): 821–832.

Giedd, J., "Structural Magnetic Resonance Imaging of the Adolescent Brain." *Annals of the New York Academy of Sciences* 1021 (2004): 77–85.

Gilbert, R, Spatz Widom, C., Browne, K., Fergusson, D., Webb, E., Janson, S., "Burden and consequences of child maltreatment in high-income countries." *Lancet* 373 (2009): 68–81.

Glaser, D., "Child Abuse and Neglect and the Brain—A Review." *Journal of Child Psychology and Psychiatry,* 41(2000): 97–116.

Glaser, D., "Child Maltreatment." In Skuse. D., Bruce. H., Dowdney, L., Mrazek, D., (eds) *Child Psychology and Psychiatry: Frameworks for Practice* (2nd Edition) pp.114–120. Oxford: Wiley-Blackwell. 2011.

Greenough, W., Black, J., Wallace, C., (1987) "Experience and brain development." *Child Development* 58 (1987): 539–559.

Groom, A., Elliott, H., Embleton, N., Relton, C., "Epigenetics and child health: basic principles." *Archives of Disease in Childhood* 96 (2011): 863–869.

Gunnar, M., Cheatham, C., "Brain and behaviour interface: stress and the developing brain." *Infant Mental Health Journal* 24 (2003): 195–211.

Hawes, D., Brennan, J., Dadds, M "Cortisol, callous-unemotional traits, and pathways to antisocial behaviour." *Current Opinion in Psychiatry* 22 (2009): 357–362.

Hensch, T., "Critical period regulation." *Annual Review of Neuroscience* 27 (2004): 549–579.

Hubel, D., Wiesel, T., "Brain mechanisms of vision." *Scientific American,* 241(1979): 150–162.

Huttenlocher, P., "Synaptic density in human frontal cortex—developmental changes and effects of aging." *Brain Research* 163 (1979): 195–205.

Ito, Y., Teicher, M., Glod, C., Ackerman, E., "Preliminary evidence for aberrant cortical development in abused children: a quantitative EEG study." *J Neuropsychiatr Clin Neurosci* 10 (1998): 298–307.

Kaufman, J., and Cicchetti D., "Effects of maltreatment on school-age children's socioemotional development: Assessments in a day-camp setting." *Developmental Psychology* 25 (1989): 516–524.

Knudsen, E., "Sensitive periods in the development of brain and behaviour." *Journal of Cognitive Neuroscience* 16 (2004): 1412–1425.

Kosofsky, B., Hyman, S., "No time for complacency: The fetal brain on drugs." *Journal of Comparative Neurology* 435 (2001): 259–62.

Lauder, J., "Hormonal and humoral influences on brain development." *Psychoneuroendocrinology* 8 (1983): 121–55.

Leventhal, T., Brooks-Gunn, J., "The neighbourhoods they live in: The effects of neighborhood residence on child and adolescent outcomes." *Psychological Bulletin*126 (2000): 309–337.

Marshall, P., "Relating Psychology and Neuroscience: Taking Up the Challenges." *Perspectives on Psychological Science* 4 (2009): 113–125.

Marshall, P., Kenny, J., "Biological perspectives on the effects of early psychosocial experience." *Developmental Review* 29 (2009): 96–119.

Marshall, P., J. Reeb, B., Fox, N., "Effects of early intervention on EEG power and coherence in previously institutionalized children in Romania." *Development and Psychopathology* 20 (2008): 861–880.

Mayes, L., "Developing brain and in-utero cocaine exposure: Effects on neural ontogeny." *Development and Psychopathology* 11 (1999): 685–714.

McCrory, E., De Brito, S., Viding, E., "Research Review: The neurobiology and genetics of maltreatment and adversity." *Journal of Child Psychology and Psychiatry* 51(2010): 1079–1095.

Moulson, M., Nelson, C., "Early adverse experiences and the neurobiology of facial emotion processing." *Developmental Psychology* 45 (2009): 17–30.

Mueller, S., Maheua, F., Dozier, M., Peloso, E., Mandella, D., Leibenluftd, E., Pine, D., Ernst, N., "Early-life stress is associated with impairment in cognitive control in adolescence: An fMRI study." *Neuropsychologia* 48 (2010): 3037–3044.

Nelson, C., "How important are the first 3 years of life?" *Applied Developmental Science* 3 (1999): 235–238.

Nelson, C., Bloom, E., "Child development and neuroscience." *Child Development* 68 (1997): 970–987.

Nelson, C., Bloom, F., Cameron, J., Amaral, D., Dahl, R., "An integrative, multidisciplinary approach to the study of brain-behavior relations in the context of typical and atypical development." *Developmental Psychology* 14 (2002): 499–520.

Nelson,C. Bosquet, M., "Neurobiology of Fetal and Infant Development : Implications for Infant Mental Health." Pp 37–59 in: Zeanah, C. (Ed.) *Handbook of Infant Mental Health*. 2nd Edition. New York: The Guilford Press 2000.

Newport, E., "Maturational constraints on language learning." *Cognitive Science* 14 (1990): 11–28.

Oberlander, T. F., Weinberg, J., Papsdorf, M., Grunau, R., Misri, S., Devlin, A., M., "Prenatal exposure to maternal depression, neonatal methylation of human glucocorticoid receptor gene (NR3C1) and infant cortisol stress responses." *Epigenetics* 3 (2008): 97–106.

Otero, G. F. B., Pliego-Rivero, T., Fernandez, J., Ricardo G. A. "EEG development in children with sociocultural disadvantages: A follow-up study." *Clinical Neurophysiology* 114 (2003): 1918–1925

Parker, S., Nelson, C., "The impact of early institutional rearing on the ability to discriminate facial expressions of emotion: An event-related potential study." *Child Development* 76 (2005): 54–72.

Plomin, R., Owen, M., and McGuffin, P., "The genetic basis of complex human behaviors." *Science* 254 (1994): 1733–1739.

Pollak, S. D., Cicchetti, D., Klorman, R., Brumaghim, T., "Cognitive brain event-related potentials and emotion processing in maltreated children." *Child Development* 68 (1997): 773–787.

Pollak, S. D., Kistler, D. J. "Early experience is associated with the development of categorical representations for facial expressions of emotion." *Proceedings of the National Academy of Sciences* 99 (2002): 9072–9076

Pollak, S. D., Klorman, R., Thatcher, J. E., Cicchetti, D., "P3b reflects maltreated children's reactions to facial displays of emotion." *Psychophysiology* 38 (2001): 267–274.

Rogeness, G., McClure, E., "Development and neurotransmitter-environmental interactions." *Development and Psychopathology* 8 (1996): 183–199.

Rutter, M., "Nature, Nurture, and Development: From Evangelism through Science toward Policy and Practice." *Child Development* 73 (2002): 1–21.

Rutter, M., Beckett, C., Castle, J., Colvert, E., Kreppner, J., Mehta, M., Stevens, S., Sonuga-Burke, E., "Effects of profound early institutional deprivation: an overview of findings from a UK longitudinal study of Romanian adoptees." *European Journal of Developmental Psychology* 4(3) (2007): 332–350.

Sapolsky, R., M. Romero, L., M., Munck, A. U. "How do glucocorticoids influence stress responses? Integrating permissive, suppressive, stimulatory and preparative actions." *Endocrine Reviews* 21(1) (2000): 55–89.

Scarr, S., "Biological and cultural diversity: The legacy of Darwin for development." *Child Development* 64 (1993): 1333–1353.

Scott, L. S., Pascalis, O., Nelson, C., "A domain-general theory of the development of perceptual discrimination." *Current Directions in Psychological Science* 16 (2007): 197–201.

Shonkoff, J., Phillips, D., "From Neurons to Neighbourhoods." Washington DC: National Academy Press. 2007.

Singer, W., "Development and plasticity of cortical processing architectures." *Science* 270 (1995): 758–764.

Tallis, R., "Aping mankind: neuromania, Darwinitis and the misrepresentation of humanity." Durham: Acumen Publishing. 2011.

Tarullo, A., Gunnar, M., "Child maltreatment and the developing HPA axis." *Hormones and Behavior* 50 (2006): 632–639

Taylor, V., Taylor, D., "Critical period for deprivation amblyopia in children." *Transactions of the Ophthalmological Societies of the UK* 99 (1979): 432–439.

Teicher, M., Andersen, S, Polcarib, A., Anderson, C., Navalta, C., Kim, D., "The neurobiological consequences of early stress and childhood maltreatment." *Neuroscience and Biobehavioral Reviews* 27 (2003): 33–44.

Teicher, M., Dumont, N. L., Ito, Y., Vaituzis, C., Giedd, J. N., Andersen, S. L. "Childhood neglect is associated with reduced corpus callosum area." *Biological Psychiatry* 56 (2004): 80–85.

Thornberry, T. P., Henry, K. L., Ireland, T. O., Smith, C. A., "The casual impact of Childhood-Limited maltreatment and adolescent maltreatment on early adult adjustment." *Journal of Adolescent Health* 46(4) (2010): 359–365.

Tottenham, N., Hare, T. A., Millner, A., Gilhooly, T., Zevin, J. D., Casey, B. J., "Elevated amygdala response to faces following early deprivation." *Developmental Science* 14(2) (2011): 190–204.

Tottenham, N., Hare, T. A., Quinn, B. T., McCarry, T. W., Nurse, M., Gilhooly, T., Millner, A., Galvan, A., Davidson, M. C., Eigsti, I.-M., Thomas, K. M., Freed, P. J., Booma, E. S., Gunnar, M. R., Altemus, M., Aronson, J., Casey, B. J., "Prolonged institutional rearing is associated with atypically large amygdala volume and difficulties in emotion regulation." *Developmental Science* 13(1) (2010): 46–61.

Welberg, L., A., Seckl, J., R. "Prenatal stress, glucocorticoids and the programming of the brain." *Journal of Neuroendocrinology* 13(2) (2001):113–128.

Yazgan, M. Y., Wexler, B. E., Kinsbourne, M., Peterson, B., Leckman, J. F. "Functional significance of individual variations in callosal area." *Neuropsychologia* 33(6) (1995):769–779.

10

Self-Harm in Adolescents

Dennis Ougrin, Troy Tranah, Eleanor Leigh, Lucy Taylor, and Joan R. Asarnow

DEFINITION

For the purpose of this chapter self-harm is defined as self-poisoning or self-injury, irrespective of the intent (Hawton, Zahl, and Weatherall, 2003). This broad definition commonly used in the UK as well as other countries (Carter, Reith, Whyte, and McPherson, 2005) includes self-harm with suicidal intent, non-suicidal, self-harm as well as those self-harm episodes with unclear intent. We will however, clearly state when the studies reviewed in this chapter apply to the adolescents with self-harm, suicidal attempts or non-suicidal self-injury where these distinction are clear.

PREVALENCE AND NATURAL HISTORY

Suicide is the second or the third leading cause of death in adolescents in the West (CDC, 2008; ONS, 2005) and an important cause of death in developing countries (Yip, Liu, and Law, 2008). Self-harm is one of the strongest predictors of death by suicide in adolescence, increasing the risk approximately ten-fold (Hawton and Harriss, 2007).

Self-harm is common among adolescents. A systematic review of 128 studies (including 513,188 adolescents) found that 13.2 percent (95 percent CI, 8.1–18.3) reported engaging in self-harm at some point in their lifetime (Evans, Hawton, Rodham, and Deeks, 2005).

In the Child and Adolescent Self-harm in Europe (CASE) study (Madge et al., 2008) 13.5 percent of females and 4.3 percent of males reported an episode of self-harm meeting the strict study criteria (based on the defini-tion above) by the time they finished school.

Prevalence rates of non-suicidal self-injury (NSSI) however vary consid-erably across epidemiological studies, with reported lifetime prevalence between 7.5 percent (Hilt, Nock, Lloyd-Richardson, and Prinstein, 2008) and 46.5 percent (Lloyd-Richardson, Perrine, Dierker, and Kelley, 2007). Whilst this variability in part reflects measurement error, it is also likely that there are differences in self-harm prevalence between countries (Madge et al., 2008).

An important minority of young people will self-harm more than once. Around 10 percent of adolescents will repeat self-harm in a year in clinical samples (Hawton and James, 2005), and about a third of the adolescents presenting with self-poisoning will have a further presentation with self-poisoning in adulthood (Harrington et al., 2006).

Recent epidemiological studies have moreover provided evidence of a significant association between NSSI (or non-suicidal self-injury) and actual suicidal behaviour (Lofthouse and Yager-Schweller, 2009). The characteristics of NSSI that appear to predict future suicidal behaviour include longer history of NSSI, use of a greater number of NSSI methods and absence of physical pain during NSSI (Nock, Joiner, Gordon, Lloyd-Richardson, and Prinstein, 2006). No study has as yet shown NSSI to be independently linked with a higher risk of competed suicide in adolescents.

BIOLOGICAL CORRELATES

There is evidence of a genetic contribution to suicidal behaviour with a higher concordance rate for suicide in monozygotic than dizygotic twins (24.1 percent vs. 2.8 percent) (Voracek and Loibl, 2007). Estimates of the heritability of suicidal behaviour range from 30 percent to 55 percent (Voracek and Loibl, 2007). Broadening the phenotype to include the more common suicidal ideation and attempts results in stronger additive genetic effects than when completed suicide is addressed. Heritability of the narrowly defined phenotype of suicide based on register-based twin studies is estimated between 21 percent and 51 percent (Voracek and Loibl, 2007).

The serotonergic system is the most consistently implicated neurotrans-mitter system in self-harm. Studies have shown there is a consistent asso-ciation between low concentrations of CSF 5–HIAA and suicidal behaviour (Asberg, 1997). More recently the role of the serotonin transporter gene has been highlighted. This gene is responsible for the reuptake of released sero-tonin from the synaptic cleft. Its promoter region contains a functional 44 bp insertion/deletion variant with two common alleles, short (s) and long (*l*): 5–HTT transcription and serotonin re-uptake are highest in individuals homozygous for the *l* (long) allele, whereas suicidal attempts are associated with the *s* (short) allele: a meta-analysis which pooled 1168 cases and 1371 controls found a significant association of the *s* (short) allele and suicide attempts (though not with completed suicide) (Anguelova, Benkelfat, and Turecki, 2003). Gene-environment interaction studies involving the serotonin transporter gene and its *s* allele have also been demonstrated, stressful life events predicting a diagnosis of depression, suicidal ideation and suicide attempts among carriers of the *s* allele but not among *l/l* homozygotes (Caspi et al., 2003).

Anomalies in the responsiveness of the central serotonin system have been further explored through the study of endocrinological responses to pharmacological serotonergic challenge, using drugs such as citaprolam or fenfluramine. This has documented a blunted neuro-hormonal (mainly prolactin) response in major depression and past suicidal behaviour, as well as blunting of the cortisol response in suicidal attempters. That this may have clinical implications is suggested by a recent study showing the blunting of cortisol response and worsening of mood after fenfluramine challenge to be predictive of future suicide attempts at two year follow up (Keilp et al., 2010).

Neuropsychological studies have indicated that selective attention and executive functioning are impaired among depressed individuals with suicidal behaviour. It may be that these impairments result in difficulty in shifting attention away from self-harm related stimuli onto more benign topics and in generating alternative solutions (Mann et al., 2009). Adolescents who self-harm have been found to be poorer in decision-making compared to those who *no longer* self-harm (Oldershaw et al., 2009), a finding that points to the state- rather than trait-dependent nature of the neurocognitive deficits.

Recent studies have also highlighted the importance of underlying emotional and behavioural dysregulation in self-harm, in particular impulsive aggression and affective dysregulation characterised by affect lability and intense emotional reactions (Mann et al., 2009). Early development of a mood disorder and impulsive aggression appear to predict early suicidal behaviour in children of parents with mood disorders (Melhem et al., 2007).

ENGAGEMENT WITH TREATMENT

There is growing evidence that poor treatment adherence is a marker of unfavourable psychosocial outcomes in adolescents presenting with self-harm (Pillay and Wassenaar, 1995) and that adolescents with disengaging coping styles tend to have worse psychosocial outcomes (Votta and

Manion, 2004). Disengagement from treatment is common in those who die of suicide (Ougrin, Banarsee, Dunn-Toroosian, and Majeed, 2010).

Studies indicate that older age, male gender (Piacentini et al., 1995), belonging to an ethnic minority (Goldston et al., 2003; Wilder, Plutch-nik, and Conte, 1977), low socioeconomic status (Pelkonen, Marttunen, Laippala, and Lonnqvist, 2000), being diagnosed with substance misuse and antisocial behaviour (Burns et al., 2008; Pelkonen et al., 2000) all predict poor engagement with aftercare. In addition time delays between the initial and the follow-up appointments (Clarke, 1988), delayed initial evaluation (Wilder et al., 1977) and the attitude of emergency department staff (Rotheram-Borus et al., 1996) all seem to influence engagement with treatment.

There is no evidence that offering a specific psychological treatment improves engagement in comparison with treatment as usual (Ougrin and Latif, 2011).

ASSESSMENT AND IMMEDIATE MANAGEMENT

When assessing young people presenting with self-harm clinicians should consider the following three categories of risk factors that might be linked to an increased risk of self-harm repetition and/or suicide: characteristics of the index event, proximal risk factors and distal risk factors.

Characteristics of the Index Event

The following four characteristics of the index episode are of particular importance: suicidal intent, motivation, lethality and method.

When assessing suicidal *intent* the following four factors may be considered (Brent et al., 1988): (1) The young person's belief about intent. Did they want to die? Are they relieved that they are still alive? Do they still want to die?; (2) Preparation before attempt. To what degree the episode was impulsive or planned? Did the young person select a significant date? How long before the event did they decide to self-harm? Had they been drinking or using drugs prior to self-harm? Did they give their possessions away?; (3) Prevention of discovery. Did they make efforts to avoid discovery? Where they alone? Did they resist help?; (4) Communication. Did the young person communicate their intention to self-harm to others? Did they leave a suicide note? Intent to die is not always black and white. Many young people will be ambivalent as to whether they live or die.

Motivation and intent are sometimes confused in psychiatric literature (Andriessen, 2006). These two concepts are closely linked and motivation (motives, reasons) is seen as a driving force underpinning intent (Hjelmeland and Knizek, 1999). Young people may present a range of motives for self-harm: to die, to escape thoughts and feelings, to feel better, to get help, or to replace emotional pain with physical pain.

Clinicians should distinguish between objective *lethality*, that is the actual degree of danger to life, and subjective lethality or the young person's anticipated consequences of self-harm. Did the young person require medical intervention? Did they attend hospital or their family doctor? Did they think they could die by holding their breath? There is often a low correlation between suicidal intent and objective lethality in children and adolescents (Brown, Henriques, Sosdjan, and Beck, 2004). This low correlation could be moderated by subjective lethality (Beck, Beck, and Kovacs, 1975).

Method refers to the way or the process that is used by the young person to self-harm. Method is closely linked with objective lethality, ranging from highly lethal behaviours like shooting and hanging at one extreme to cutting and burning on the opposite side of the spectrum (Skegg, 2005). One of the key questions in assessing risk is whether the young person has access to lethal agents like dangerous drugs or firearms.

Proximal Risk Factors

Proximal risk factors include recent changes of physical or mental state, substance misuse and recent stressful life events (Hawton et al., 2003). The latter could include self-harm precipitants like arguments with boyfriend/girlfriend or parents, recent "losses," e.g., bereavement, family break-up; school related stress, e.g., exams or being bullied; exposure to suicide/self-harm in friends and pregnancy in self or partner (Asarnow et al., 2008). Young people may report a recent episode of abuse (sexual or physical) or having been reminded of past abuse. There may be an impending court case or disciplinary action or the young person may be about to be placed in care or in a secure institution. Unavailability of an adult guardian is an important proximal risk factor which also influences immediate management of a self-harm episode. Subjective meaning attributed to the stressful event may be different from objective reality. For example some young people may feel devastated by relatively innocuous events and some might self-harm in anticipation of a perceived humiliating punishment.

Recent onset of physical or mental health problems (e.g., depression, bipolar disorder, schizophrenia, anxiety, conduct problems, substance misuse, being diagnosed with a life-threatening condition) and escalation of frequency and severity of suicidal thinking and self-harm have all been linked to increased risk of self-harm. Perhaps the most obvious indication may be that the young person is telling others of their intention to self-harm. This may be communicated directly to friends or parents or via blogs or through voluntary organisations that aim to help children in acute distress.

Distal Risk Factors

There are a number of known distal risk factors for self-harm (Bridge, Goldstein, and Brent, 2006). They can be divided into sociodemographic, psychiatric, and psychological variables.

Socio-Demographic Factors

Females are significantly more likely to self-harm compared to males though males are more likely to complete suicide (Hawton and James, 2005). Self-harm often starts in early adolescence and increases towards later teens (Hawton and James, 2005). Certain ethnic backgrounds such as Hispanic in the United States have been linked with increased risk of self-harm (CDC, 2009). A past history of physical or sexual abuse (Gratz et al., 2010) violence and/or forensic history (past police/court involvement) all seem to increase the risk of self-harm independently. A history of being bullied, recurrent interpersonal problems, self-harm behaviour in friends, being a child in a single-parent family, being in-care or in a secure institution, being an asylum seeker and socioeconomic deprivation are also linked to self-harm risk (King and Merchant, 2008). Family history of self-harm or suicide and family psychiatric disorders in general are consistent predictors of self-harm risk (Brent, Moritz, Bridge, Perper, and et al., 1996).

Psychiatric Factors

A previous history of self-harm is a key predictor of future self-harm. Diagnoses such as emerging borderline personality disorder, disruptive disorders, anxiety, mood disorders, eating disorders and psychosis are all associated with an increased risk of self-harm as are previous psychiatric admissions and substance misuse (Kyriakopoulos, 2010).

Psychological Factors

Low self-esteem, perfectionism, trait anger, impulsivity, poor decision making, hopelessness, neuroticism, non-heterosexual sexual orientation and poor emotional problem solving have all been cited to increase the risk of self-harm (Asarnow, Carlson, and Guthrie, 1987; Bridge et al., 2006).

Immediate Management

The priority in terms of immediate management is to ensure the safety of the young person. According to the National Institute for Health and Clinical Excellence (NICE) guidelines (NCCMH, 2004) all young people under the age of sixteen presenting with self-harm should be admitted to a paediatric unit overnight and be assessed by a specialist in child and adolescent mental health. There are no good quality trials showing that psychiatric in-patient admissions reduce the risk of self-harm, however common sense and clinical judgement dictate the necessity of an admission in some cases. That said, some young people may increase their self-harm behaviour once placed in an in-patient psychiatric unit (Huey et al., 2004) and it may also be difficult to discharge the young person back into the community. If in-patient care is deemed necessary then clinicians should be planning for discharge at the point of admission. Brief crisis admissions may help some young people deal with intolerable stress.

In all cases where there is a significant risk of self-harm and the young person is to be cared for in the community a crisis plan should be developed together with the patient and carers before they leave the initial session. This will include measures to be taken in a crisis e.g., friends they can phone, how to contact parent, therapist contact details, when to go to their family doctor and when to go to an emergency department. The young person may be asked to think of skills or activities that have helped in the past (e.g., listening to music, holding ice cubes). These activities could be used to combat self-harming urges as many young people find these urges subside as their distress diminishes over time. The therapist may provide the young person with some basic skills around emotional regulation or distress tolerance (Rathus and Miller, 2002). For example acting opposite to the current emotion (e.g., talking when the young person feels the urge to avoid conversation) and scheduling regular pleasant activities could teach the young person to self-regulate their emotions. Distress tolerance skills are designed to help young people endure those situations that cannot be solved like being stuck in traffic. They consist of learning to accept the current situation followed by learning how to self soothe using all five senses (e.g., having a box with five items that provide pleasant stimulation of all five senses). The assessor should also ask the young person and/or parent to remove all items that might readily be used to self-harm (razor blades, dressing gown cords or toxic tablets). The clinician should provide the young person and their carer with a clear indication as to the next steps (e.g., likely date of next appointment). The crisis plan should seek to identify and make use of any protective factors in the young person's life (e.g., friends, hobbies, distraction skills). The plan must be communicated to all those agencies involved in the young person's care.

INTERVENTIONS AIMED AT IMPROVING
ENGAGEMENT WITH TREATMENT

Older studies aimed at improving adherence to follow-up care (Rotheram-Borus, Piacentini, Cantwell, Belin, and Song, 2000; Zimmerman, Asnis, and Schwartz, 1995) using skills development, family therapy and staff training approaches, have shown modest results overall. However, there is good evidence that brief interventions could be beneficial in a range of adolescent psychiatric presentations such as acute alcohol intoxication (Colby et al., 2005; Goti et al., 2009; Moore and Werch, 2009; Spirito et al., 2004; Trent, Chung, Burke, Walker, and Ellen, 2009). A recent study of Therapeutic Assessment, a brief add-on to the initial assessment designed to promote understanding of self-harm behaviour as a vicious circle followed by mapping of the possible ways to break that cycle (Ougrin et al., 2011) replicated the results of a pilot (Ougrin, Ng, and Low, 2008) in significantly improving engagement with follow-up. These results have not been replicated independently.

PREVENTION INTERVENTIONS

Early prevention studies raised concerns about programmes being ineffective at best and dangerous (i.e., linked with iatrogenic increase in self-harm) at worst (Overholser, Hemstreet, Spirito, and Vyse, 1989; Shaffer, Garland, Vieland, Underwood, and Busner, 1991; Shaffer et al., 1990; Vieland, Whittle, Garland, Hicks, and Shaffer, 1991). Recent studies have reported short-term improvements in knowledge and more adaptive attitudes towards depression and suicidal behaviour in both young people and school staff, but no impact on self-harm repetition was shown (Kalafat and Elias, 1994; Portzky, van Heeringen, Portzky, and van Heeringen, 2006; Wyman et al., 2008; Wyman et al., 2010). The early concerns about iatrogenic impact of self-harm screening as part of a prevention programme have not been borne out when studied systematically (Gould et al., 2005). Furthermore a suicide prevention programme called Signs of Suicide (SOS) has been shown to reduce self-harm in two randomised trials (Aseltine, DeMartino, Aseltine, and DeMartino, 2004; Aseltine et al., 2007), although the trials had partially overlapping samples and the results have not yet been replicated independently. Nonetheless the SOS programme has been studied in a large and diverse sample of adolescents, which improves the generalisablity of the findings. The SOS programme includes raising awareness of suicide, highlighting its link with mental illness and substance misuse using a video dramatisation and a discussion guide, and a depression and suicidality screening using a self-report anonymised tool. The message given to the adolescents is this: suicidal thoughts are not a normal response to stress and if a pupil expresses suicidal thoughts one should ACT: Acknowledge the signs of suicide and take those signs seriously; show that the listener Cares and Tell a responsible adult.

An early non-suicidal self-injury (NSSI) prevention programme evaluation has recently been published. No significant reduction of NSSI has been reported post intervention (Muehlenkamp, Walsh, and McDade, 2010).

TREATMENT INTERVENTIONS

A recent systematic review (Ougrin, Tranah, Leigh, Taylor, and Asarnow, in press) included fourteen published RCTs of therapeutic interventions (TIs) in children and adolescents with the presenting problem of self-harm.

The trials included in this review reported the effects of the following TIs: specific problem-solving intervention designed to increase adherence to outpatient treatment (Spirito, Boergers, Donaldson, Bishop, and Lewander, 2002); skills-based, cognitive behaviour treatment targeting problem solving and affect management skills (Donaldson, Spirito, and Esposito-Smythers, 2005); home-based family therapy (Harrington et al., 1998); developmental group psychotherapy incorporating the techniques of problem-solving and cognitive-behavioural interventions, dialectic behaviour therapy and psychodynamic group psychotherapy (Green et al., 2011; Hazell et al., 2009; Wood, Trainor, Rothwell, Moore, and Harrington, 2001); individual cognitive analytic therapy (Chanen et al., 2008); attachment based family therapy (Diamond et al., 2010); Therapeutic Assessment for self-harm (Ougrin et al., 2011); emotion regulation group training (Schuppert et al., 2009), issuing tokens allowing readmission (Cotgrove, Zirinsky, Black, and Weston, 1995); and youth nominated support team (King et al., 2009; King et al., 2006)

None of the studies reviewed found an independently replicated statistically significant reduction in self-harm repetition compared with control treatment. The only intervention that demonstrated efficacy in at least one study was developmental group psychotherapy.

Developmental Group Psychotherapy

In a study by Wood et al., 2001, sixty-three participants (mean age fourteen years, range twelve to sixteen years, 78 percent female) were allocated to either developmental group therapy or standard care. Group therapy involved a minimum of six weekly sessions lasting one hour, after which participants were free to choose how much longer they remained in a long-term support group. At twenty-nine weeks' follow-up there was a significant difference favouring group therapy over standard aftercare with respect to reducing the likelihood of engaging in two or more episodes of self-harm (relative risk = 0.19; 95 percent CI 0.05 to 0.81). There was also a positive effect on a range of behavioural problems. These results were however not replicated in two subsequent trials (Green et al., 2011; Hazell et al., 2009).

SELF-HARM REPETITION IN DEPRESSION TRIALS

Depression is extremely common among young people presenting with self-harm and is an important predictor of repetition of self-harm and suicide (Kovacs, 1996).

In the Treatment of Adolescent Depression Study (TADS) (March et al., 2004) treatment with fluoxetine was superior to CBT and to placebo in terms of self-reported depression symptoms, whilst the combined treatment led to the greatest improvement. While suicidality reduced over the acute period with all treatments, there was significantly greater overall improvement in suicidal ideation with the combined treatment (Emslie et al., 2006). Suicide-related events were twice as common among those treated with fluoxetine alone compared to CBT or combined treatment, and only fluoxetine led to significantly more suicide-related events than placebo.

In the UK-based Adolescent Depression Antidepressant and Psychotherapy trial (ADAPT) (Goodyer et al., 2007) addition of CBT was not found to improve outcome at twenty-eight weeks, nor was it found to confer any protective effect against suicidality or frequency of self-harm. The study, however, was not powered to detect differences in suicidality and self-harm. In the Treatment of SSRI-Resistant Depression in Adolescents (TORDIA) trial (Brent et al., 2008) there was no reported benefit of CBT in terms of suicidal ideation or frequency of self-harm, in contrast to the findings of the TADS. A meta-analysis by Weisz and colleagues (Weisz, McCarty, and Valeri, 2006) found a significant, but small, effect of cognitive interventions on depression (average effect size = 0.35). This meta-analysis reported a small benefit of psychotherapy on suicidality, based on the six studies (five of which evaluated CBT) that reported this outcome (average effect size = 0.18, marginally different from zero, $p = .07$), although the effect of psychotherapy on self-harm was not reported. Another meta-analysis (Dubicka et al., 2010) recently concluded that the addition of CBT to medication provided only limited benefit in terms of depression symptoms or suicidality.

There has been considerable controversy regarding the use of antidepressant medication in young people with depression, and specifically whether SSRIs increase the risk of suicidal behaviours. A meta-analysis of twenty-seven trials of antidepressant medication (Bridge et al., 2007) revealed that although the benefits of medication with depressed young people were modest (number needed to treat = 10), these were far greater than the risks of suicidal ideation/attempt (number needed to harm = 112). The authors also reported that for children under twelve years, only fluoxetine was found to confer benefit over placebo. The Committee for Safety in Medicines (CSM, 2003) concluded that fluoxetine alone has a favourable risk-benefit profile in the treatment of depression in young people. Consistent with this, the antidepressant recommended by the NICE guidelines (NC-CMH, 2005) is fluoxetine, with consideration of citalopram and sertraline as second-line treatments.

OTHER TREATMENT STUDIES

Dialectical Behaviour Therapy (DBT)

Dialectical Behaviour Therapy (DBT) (Linehan, Armstrong, Suarez, Allmon, and Heard, 1991) is directed towards creating a "life worth living," primarily through stopping self-harm. Self-harm is seen as a maladaptive attempt to problem solve. Several trials have shown that DBT is particularly effective in reducing self-injurious behaviour and suicide attempts in adult women with a diagnosis of borderline personality disorder (BPD) (Linehan et al., 1991; Linehan et al., 2006; Linehan et al., 1999). DBT has also been found to be effective in improving treatment compliance and treatment drop-out rate (Linehan et al., 1991)

Despite the fact that for adults with self-harm, the NICE guidelines (NC-CMH, 2004) a Cochrane review (Hawton et al., 1998) and the American Academy of Child and Adolescent Psychiatry (AACAP, 2001) recommend DBT, to date only non-randomised trials of DBT in adolescents have been published in peer reviewed journals (Goldstein et al., 2007; James, Taylor, Winmill, and Alfoadari, 2008; Katz and Cox, 2002; Katz, Cox, Gunasekara, and Miller, 2004; Rathus and Miller, 2002). There is one pilot RCT, not published in a peer reviewed journal (Cooney, Davis, Thompson, Wharewera-Mika, and Stewart, 2010) describing early findings from an 18–month study comparing DBT with treatment as usual (TAU) in two speciality mental health services for youth in New Zealand. Results showed that DBT was acceptable to the adolescents, parents, caregivers and clinicians involved in treatment and that self-harm reduced in both conditions.

Multisystemic Therapy (MST)

MST is a treatment package that takes into account multiple systems that the family and the adolescents interact with. The main target of the therapy is effective parenting skills, primarily targeted at engaging young people with pro-social activities and disengaging with antisocial ones, removing potential methods of suicide and monitoring and support of the young people by responsible adults. In addition to the family, community, school and peer systems are targeted. The therapy is intensive (contact could be daily) and time limited (3–6 months). Contacts are made in adolescents' homes and the average caseload of the therapists is low (4–6 families).

MST was studied in a sample of adolescents referred to an Emergency Department and authorised for psychiatric admission (n = 156, age ten to seventeen, average age 12.9 years, 65 percent male, 65 percent African American). 51 percent of these young people were classified as suicidal (intense suicidal ideation or attempt); the rest had a variety of severe psychiatric problems. These young people were randomised to either MST or hospitalisation. Based on youth reports, MST was significantly more effective than hospitalisation at decreasing rates of attempted suicide at one-year follow-up. MST did not have any differential effect on depression, hopelessness or suicidal ideation.

Mentalization Based Therapy (MBT)

Mentalization could be defined as implicitly and explicitly interpreting the actions of oneself and others as meaningful on the basis of intentional mental states. In other words, having the awareness that all people have their own feelings and thoughts (mental states) that determine their actions while, by their very nature, mental states are opaque and can't be "read" directly.

MBT was developed primarily for adults with borderline personality disorder. A number of further therapeutic approaches to clinical work have been devised on the conceptual framework of mentalization. These include short-term mentalization and relational therapy (SMART) which is described as an integrative family therapy for working with children and adolescents.

Trials of MBT for partially hospitalised adults with borderline personality disorder have now reported eight-year follow-up showing significant improvements in suicidality and self-harm (Bateman and Fonagy, 1999, 2008). There are no published studies of MBT in adolescent literature.

Cognitive Behaviour Therapy

In a large open trial of adolescent suicide attempters with depression (n = 124) a specialised CBT for suicide attempting adolescents (n = 17), a medication algorithm (n = 14), or the combination (n = 93) were studied (Brent et al., 2009). At six-month follow-up 12 percent of the adolescents in the whole sample repeated a suicide attempt.

Another pilot study of a manualised CBT package (Taylor et al., in press) for adolescent self-harm (n=16) showed significant reductions in self-harm behaviour, depression symptoms and trait anxiety. These studies suggest that CBT should be studied further in adolescents with self-harm.

SUMMARY

Approximately 10 percent of adolescents will have self-harmed by the time they finish secondary school and 10 percent of those will repeat self-harm in a year. Different types of self-harm (i.e., sucidal, non-suicidal or with mixed intent) appear to be interlinked and practitioners should assess adolescents presenting with non-suicidal self-injury for suicidality and vice versa. The most clinically relevant findings of neurobiological and neuro-cognitive research include anomalies in the serotonergic system and related gene-environment interactions, as well as a significant association of self-harm with poor problem solving, impaired selective attention, impulsive aggression and emotional dysregulation.

At present there are no independently replicated findings of any inter-vention being effective in reducing or preventing self-harm in adolescents. There is limited evidence i) that the SOS programme designed to raise awareness and increase treatment seeking in adolescent with self-harm thoughts and behaviours is efficacious in the prevention of self-harm (two RCT by the same group with partially overlapping samples); ii) that the Therapeutic Assessment technique leads to improved engagement with after care (one unreplicated RCT); iii) that MST, an intensive community treatment package designed to optimise young people's function in the context of multiple social systems in comparison with hospitalization may lead to a statistically significant reduction in self-harm repetition in adolescents with a range of psychiatric emergencies (one unreplicated RCT). Positive results of non-randomized studies indicate that dialectic behaviour therapy and cognitive behaviour therapy require rigorous evaluation in RCTs. There is no evidence of any pharmacological interven-tion leading to secondary prevention of self-harm in adolescents. More research is urgently needed to establish effective treatment for self-harm in adolescents.

REFERENCES

AACAP. (2001). Summary of the Practice Parameters for the Assessment and Treat-ment of Children and Adolescents With Suicidal Behavior. *Journal of the American Academy of Child and Adolescent Psychiatry, 40*(4), 495–499.

Andriessen, K. (2006). On "intention" in the definition of suicide. *Suicide and Life-Threatening Behavior, 36*(5), 533–538.

Anguelova, M., Benkelfat, C., and Turecki, G. (2003). A systematic review of association studies investigating genes coding for serotonin receptors and the serotonin transporter: I. Affective disorders. *Molecular Psychiatry, 8*(6), 574–591.

Asarnow, J. R., Baraff, L. J., Berk, M., Grob, C., Devich-Navarro, M., Suddath, R., et al. (2008). Pediatric emergency department suicidal patients: two-site evaluation of suicide ideators, single attempters, and repeat attempters. *Journal of the American Academy of Child and Adolescent Psychiatry, 47*(8), 958–966.

Asarnow, J. R., Carlson, G. A., and Guthrie, D. (1987). Coping strategies, self-perceptions, hopelessness, and perceived family environments in depressed and suicidal children. *J Consult Clin Psychol, 55*(3), 361–366.

Asberg, M. (1997). Neurotransmitters and suicidal behavior: The evidence from cerebrospinal fluid studies. In *The neurobiology of suicide: From the bench to the clinic* (pp. 158–181). New York, NY: New York Academy of Sciences.

Aseltine, R. H., Jr., DeMartino, R., Aseltine, R. H., Jr., and DeMartino, R. (2004). An outcome evaluation of the SOS Suicide Prevention Program. *American Journal of Public Health, 94*(3), 446–451.

Aseltine, R. H., Jr., James, A., Schilling, E. A., Glanovsky, J., Aseltine, R. H., Jr., James, A., et al. (2007). Evaluating the SOS suicide prevention program: a replication and extension. *BMC Public Health, 7,* 161.

Bateman, A., and Fonagy, P. (1999). Effectiveness of partial hospitalization in the treatment of borderline personality disorder: a randomized controlled trial.[see comment]. *American Journal of Psychiatry, 156*(10), 1563–1569.

Bateman, A., and Fonagy, P. (2008). 8-year follow-up of patients treated for borderline personality disorder: mentalization-based treatment versus treatment as usual.[see comment]. *American Journal of Psychiatry, 165*(5), 631–638.

Beck, A. T., Beck, R., and Kovacs, M. (1975). Classification of suicidal behaviors: I. quantifying intent and medical lethality. *American Journal of Psychiatry, 132,* 285–287.

Brent, D., Emslie, G., Clarke, G., Wagner, K. D., Asarnow, J. R., Keller, M., et al. (2008). Switching to another SSRI or to venlafaxine with or without cognitive behavioral therapy for adolescents with SSRI-resistant depression: The TORDIA randomized controlled trial. *JAMA—Journal of the American Medical Association, 299*(8), 901–913.

Brent, D., Greenhill, L., Compton, S., Emslie, G., Wells, K., Walkup, J., et al. (2009). The Treatment of Adolescent Suicide Attempters Study (TASA): Predictors of Suicidal Events in an Open Treatment Trial. *Journal of the American Academy of Child and Adolescent Psychiatry, 26,* 26.

Brent, D., Moritz, G., Bridge, J., Perper, J., et al. (1996). Long-term impact of exposure to suicide: A three-year controlled follow-up. *Journal of the American Academy of Child and Adolescent Psychiatry, 35*(5), 646–653.

Brent, D., Perper, J. A., Goldstein, C. E., Kolko, D. J., Allan, M. J., Allman, C. J., et al. (1988). Risk factors for adolescent suicide. A comparison of adolescent suicide victims with suicidal inpatients. *Arch Gen Psychiatry, 45*(6), 581–588.

Bridge, J. A., Goldstein, T. R., and Brent, D. A. (2006). Adolescent suicide and suicidal behavior. *Journal of Child Psychology and Psychiatry and Allied Disciplines, 47*(3–4), 372–394.

Bridge, J. A., Iyengar, S., Salary, C. B., Barbe, R. P., Birmaher, B., Pincus, H. A., et al. (2007). Clinical Response and Risk for Reported Suicidal Ideation and Suicide Attempts in Pediatric Antidepressant Treatment: A Meta-analysis of Randomized Controlled Trials. *JAMA, 297*(15), 1683–1696.

Brown, G. K., Henriques, G. R., Sosdjan, D., and Beck, A. T. (2004). Suicide intent and accurate expectations of lethality: predictors of medical lethality of suicide attempts. *Journal of Consulting and Clinical Psychology, 72*(6), 1170–1174.

Burns, C. D., Cortell, R., Wagner, B. M., Burns, C. D., Cortell, R., and Wagner, B. M. (2008). Treatment compliance in adolescents after attempted suicide: a 2–year follow-up study. *Journal of the American Academy of Child and Adolescent Psychiatry, 47*(8), 948–957.

Carter, G., Reith, D. M., Whyte, I. M., and McPherson, M. (2005). Repeated self-poisoning: increasing severity of self-harm as a predictor of subsequent suicide. *British Journal of Psychiatry, 186*, 253–257.

Caspi, A., Sugden, K., Moffitt, T. E., Taylor, A., Craig, I. W., Harrington, H., et al. (2003). Influence of life stress on depression: moderation by a polymorphism in the 5–HTT gene.[see comment]. *Science, 301*(5631), 386–389.

CDC. (2008). *WISQARS Nonfatal Injury Reports.* Retrieved 20 December, 2008, from http://www.cdc.gov/ncipc/wisqars/nonfatal/definitions.htm#self-harm

CDC. (2009). *2009 State and Local Youth Risk Behavior Survey.* Retrieved 20 December, 2008, from http://www.cdc.gov/HealthyYouth/yrbs/pdf/questionnaire/2009HighSchool.pdf

Chanen, A. M., Jackson, H. J., McCutcheon, L. K., Jovev, M., Dudgeon, P., Yuen, H. P., et al. (2008). Early intervention for adolescents with borderline personality disorder using cognitive analytic therapy: randomised controlled trial.[Erratum appears in *Br J Psychiatry.* 2009 Feb;194(2):191]. *British Journal of Psychiatry, 193*(6), 477–484.

Clarke, C. F. (1988). Deliberate self poisoning in adolescents.[see comment]. *Archives of Disease in Childhood, 63*(12), 1479–1483.

Colby, S. M., Monti, P. M., O'Leary Tevyaw, T., Barnett, N. P., Spirito, A., Rohsenow, D. J., et al. (2005). Brief motivational intervention for adolescent smokers in medical settings. *Addictive Behaviors, 30*(5), 865–874.

Cooney, E., Davis, K., Thompson, P., Wharewera-Mika, J., and Stewart, J. (2010). *Database of New Zealand mental health research.* Retrieved 20 January, 2011, from http://www.tepou.co.nz/knowledge-exchange/research/view/listing/394/

Cotgrove, A. J., Zirinsky, L., Black, D., and Weston, D. (1995). Secondary prevention of attempted suicide in adolescence. *Journal of Adolescence, 18*(5), 569–577.

CSM, C. o. S. o. M. (2003). *Selective serotonin reuptake inhibitors (SSRIs): overview of regulatory status and CSM advice relating to major depressive disorder (MDD) in children and adolescents including a summary of available safety and efficacy data,* from http://medicines.mhra.gov.uk/ourwork/monitorsafequalmed/safetymessages/ssrioverview_101203.htm

Diamond, G. S., Wintersteen, M. B., Brown, G. K., Diamond, G. M., Gallop, R., Shelef, K., et al. (2010). Attachment-Based Family Therapy for Adolescents with Suicidal Ideation: A Randomized Controlled Trial. *Journal of the American Academy of Child and Adolescent Psychiatry, 49*(2), 122–131.

Donaldson, D., Spirito, A., and Esposito-Smythers, C. (2005). Treatment for Adolescents Following a Suicide Attempt: Results of a Pilot Trial. *Journal of the American Academy of Child and Adolescent Psychiatry, 44*(2), 113–120.

Dubicka, B., Elvins, R., Roberts, C., Chick, G., Wilkinson, P., and Goodyer, I. M. (2010). Combined treatment with cognitive-behavioural therapy in adolescent depression: meta-analysis. *Br J Psychiatry, 197*, 433–440.

Emslie, G., Kratochvil, C., Vitiello, B., Silva, S., Mayes, T., McNulty, S., et al. (2006). Treatment for Adolescents with Depression Study (TADS): safety results. *Journal of the American Academy of Child and Adolescent Psychiatry, 45*(12), 1440–1455.

Evans, E., Hawton, K., Rodham, K., and Deeks, J. (2005). The Prevalence of Suicidal Phenomena in Adolescents: A Systematic Review of Population-Based Studies. *Suicide and Life-Threatening Behavior, 35*(3), 239–250.

Goldstein, T. R., Axelson, D. A., Birmaher, B., Brent, D. A., Goldstein, T. R., Axelson, D. A., et al. (2007). Dialectical behavior therapy for adolescents with bipolar disorder: a 1-year open trial. *Journal of the American Academy of Child and Adolescent Psychiatry, 46*(7), 820–830.

Goldston, D. B., Reboussin, B. A., Kancler, C., Daniel, S. S., Frazier, P. H., Harris, A. E., et al. (2003). Rates and predictors of aftercare services among formerly hospitalized adolescents: a prospective naturalistic study. *J Am Acad Child Adolesc Psychiatry, 42*(1), 49–56.

Goodyer, I., Dubicka, B., Wilkinson, P., Kelvin, R., Roberts, C., Byford, S., et al. (2007). Selective serotonin reuptake inhibitors (SSRIs) and routine specialist care with and without cognitive behaviour therapy in adolescents with major depression: randomised controlled trial. *BMJ, 335*(7611), 142–.

Goti, J., Diaz, R., Serrano, L., Gonzalez, L., Calvo, R., Gual, A., et al. (2009). Brief intervention in substance-use among adolescent psychiatric patients: a randomized controlled trial. *Eur Child Adolesc Psychiatry*.

Gould, M. S., Marrocco, F. A., Kleinman, M., Thomas, J. G., Mostkoff, K., Cote, J., et al. (2005). Evaluating iatrogenic risk of youth suicide screening programs: A randomized controlled trial. *Journal of the American Medical Association, 293 (13)*, 1635–1643.

Gratz, K. L., Hepworth, C., Tull, M. T., Paulson, A., Clarke, S., Remington, B., et al. (2010). An experimental investigation of emotional willingness and physical pain tolerance in deliberate self-harm: the moderating role of interpersonal distress. *Compr Psychiatry, 52*(1), 63–74.

Green, J. M., Wood, A. J., Kerfoot, M. J., Trainor, G., Roberts, C., Rothwell, J., et al. (2011). Group therapy for adolescents with repeated self harm: randomised controlled trial with economic evaluation. *BMJ, 342*.

Harrington, R., Kerfoot, M., Dyer, E., McNiven, F., Gill, J., Harrington, V., et al. (1998). Randomized trial of a home-based family intervention for children who have deliberately poisoned themselves. *Journal of the American Academy of Child and Adolescent Psychiatry, 37*(5), 512–518.

Harrington, R., Pickles, A., Aglan, A., Harrington, V., Burroughs, H., and Kerfoot, M. (2006). Early Adult Outcomes of Adolescents Who Deliberately Poisoned Themselves. *Journal of the American Academy of Child and Adolescent Psychiatry, 45*(3), 337–345.

Hawton, K., Arensman, E., Townsend, E., Bremner, S., Feldman, E., Goldney, R., et al. (1998). Deliberate self harm: systematic review of efficacy of psychosocial and pharmacological treatments in preventing repetition. *BMJ, 317*(7156), 441–447.

Hawton, K., and Harriss, L. (2007). Deliberate self-harm in young people: characteristics and subsequent mortality in a 20-year cohort of patients presenting to hospital. *Journal of Clinical Psychiatry, 68*(10), 1574–1583.

Hawton, K., and James, A. (2005). Suicide and deliberate self harm in young people. *BMJ, 330*(7496), 891–894.

Hawton, K., Zahl, D., and Weatherall, R. (2003). Suicide following deliberate self-harm: long-term follow-up of patients who presented to a general hospital.[see comment]. *British Journal of Psychiatry, 182*, 537–542.

Hazell, P. L., Martin, G., McGill, K., Kay, T., Wood, A., Trainor, G., et al. (2009). Group therapy for repeated deliberate self-harm in adolescents: failure of replication of a randomized trial. *Journal of the American Academy of Child and Adolescent Psychiatry, 48*(6), 662–670.

Hilt, L. M., Nock, M. K., Lloyd-Richardson, E. E., and Prinstein, M. J. (2008). Longitudinal study of nonsuicidal self-injury among young adolescents: Rates, correlates, and preliminary test of an interpersonal model. *The Journal of Early Adolescence, 28*(3), 455–469.

Hjelmeland, H., and Knizek, B. L. (1999). Conceptual confusion about intentions and motives of nonfatal suicidal behavior: A discussion of terms employed in the literature of suicidology. *Journal.*

Huey, S. J., Jr., Henggeler, S. W., Rowland, M. D., Halliday-Boykins, C. A., Cunningham, P. B., Pickrel, S. G., et al. (2004). Multisystemic Therapy Effects on Attempted Suicide by Youths Presenting Psychiatric Emergencies. *Journal of the American Academy of Child and Adolescent Psychiatry, 43*(2), 183–190.

James, A. C., Taylor, A., Winmill, L., and Alfoadari, K. (2008). A Preliminary Community Study of Dialectical Behaviour Therapy (DBT) with Adolescent Females Demonstrating Persistent, Deliberate Self-Harm (DSH). *Child and Adolescent Mental Health, 13*(3), 148–152.

Kalafat, J., and Elias, M. (1994). An evaluation of a school-based suicide awareness intervention. *Suicide and Life-Threatening Behavior, 24*(3), 224–233.

Katz, L. Y., and Cox, B. J. (2002). Dialectical behavior therapy for suicidal adolescent inpatients. *Clinical Case Studies, 1*(1), 81–92.

Katz, L. Y., Cox, B. J., Gunasekara, S., and Miller, A. L. (2004). Feasibility of dialectical behavior therapy for suicidal adolescent inpatients. *Journal of the American Academy of Child and Adolescent Psychiatry, 43*(3), 276–282.

Keilp, J. G., Oquendo, M. A., Stanley, B. H., Burke, A. K., Cooper, T. B., Malone, K. M., et al. (2010). Future suicide attempt and responses to serotonergic challenge. *Neuropsychopharmacology, 35* (5), 1063–1072.

King, C. A., Klaus, N., Kramer, A., Venkataraman, S., Quinlan, P., and Gillespie, B. (2009). The Youth-Nominated Support Team-Version II for suicidal adolescents:

A randomized controlled intervention trial. *Journal of Consulting and Clinical Psychology, 77*(5), 880–893.

King, C. A., Kramer, A., Preuss, L., Kerr, D. C., Weisse, L., and Venkataraman, S. (2006). Youth-Nominated Support Team for Suicidal Adolescents (Version 1): A Randomized Controlled Trial. *Journal of Consulting and Clinical Psychology, 74*(1), 199–206.

King, C. A., and Merchant, C. R. (2008). Social and interpersonal factors relating to adolescent suicidality: A review of the literature. *Archives of Suicide Research, 12*(3), 181–196.

Kovacs, M. (1996). Presentation and course of major depressive disorder during childhood and later years of the life span. *Journal of the American Academy of Child and Adolescent Psychiatry, 35*(6), 705–715.

Kyriakopoulos, M. (2010). Psychosocial and Psychiatric Factors Relating to Adolescent Suicidality and Self-harm. In D. Ougrin, T. Zundel and A. Ng (Eds.), *Self-harm in Young People: A Therapeutic Assessment Manual* (pp. 59–79). London: Hodder Arnold.

Linehan, M. M., Armstrong, H. E., Suarez, A., Allmon, D., and Heard, H. L. (1991). Cognitive-behavioral treatment of chronically parasuicidal borderline patients. [see comment]. *Archives of General Psychiatry, 48*(12), 1060–1064.

Linehan, M. M., Comtois, K. A., Murray, A. M., Brown, M. Z., Gallop, R. J., Heard, H. L., et al. (2006). Two-year randomized controlled trial and follow-up of dialectical behavior therapy vs therapy by experts for suicidal behaviors and borderline personality disorder.[see comment][erratum appears in *Arch Gen Psychiatry*. 2007 Dec;64(12):1401]. *Archives of General Psychiatry, 63*(7), 757–766.

Linehan, M. M., Schmidt, H., 3rd, Dimeff, L. A., Craft, J. C., Kanter, J., and Comtois, K. A. (1999). Dialectical behavior therapy for patients with borderline personality disorder and drug-dependence. *American Journal on Addictions, 8*(4), 279–292.

Lloyd-Richardson, E. E., Perrine, N., Dierker, L., and Kelley, M. L. (2007). Characteristic and functions on non-suicidal self-injury in a community sample of adolescents. *Psychological Medicine, 37*(8), 1183–1192.

Lofthouse, N., and Yager-Schweller, J. (2009). Nonsuicidal self-injury and suicide risk among adolescents. *Current Opinion in Pediatrics, 21*(5), 641–645.

Madge, N., Hewitt, A., Hawton, K., de Wilde, E. J., Corcoran, P., Fekete, S., et al. (2008). Deliberate self-harm within an international community sample of young people: Comparative findings from the Child and Adolescent Self-harm in Europe (CASE) Study. *Journal of Child Psychology and Psychiatry, 49*(6), 667–677.

Mann, J. J., Arango, V. A., Avenevoli, S., Brent, D. A., Champagne, F. A., Clayton, P., et al. (2009). Candidate endophenotypes for genetic studies of suicidal behavior. *Biological Psychiatry, 65*(7), 556–563.

March, J., Silva, S., Petrycki, S., Curry, J., Wells, K., Fairbank, J., et al. (2004). Fluoxetine, cognitive-behavioral therapy, and their combination for adolescents with depression: Treatment for Adolescents With Depression Study (TADS) randomized controlled trial. *Journal of the American Medical Association, 292*(7), 807–820.

Melhem, N. M., Brent, D. A., Ziegler, M., Iyengar, S., Kolko, D., Oquendo, M., et al. (2007). Familial pathways to early-onset suicidal behavior: Familial and individual antecedents of suicidal behavior. *American Journal of Psychiatry, 164*(9), 1364–1370.

Moore, M. J., and Werch, C. C. (2009). Efficacy of a brief alcohol consumption reintervention for adolescents. *Subst Use Misuse, 44*(7), 1009–1020.

Muehlenkamp, J., Walsh, B., and McDade, M. (2010). Preventing Non-Suicidal Self-Injury in Adolescents: The Signs of Self-Injury Program. *Journal of Youth and Adolescence, 39*(3), 306–314.

NCCMH, N. C. C. f. M. H. (2004). *Self-Harm: The Short-Term Physical and Psychological Management and Secondary Prevention of Self-Harm in Primary and Secondary Care.Clinical Guideline 16*. London: Gaskell and British Psychological Society.

NCCMH, N. C. C. f. M. H. (2005). *Depression in Children and Young People: Identification and Management in Primary, Community and Secondary Care (CG28)*. London: The British Psychological Society.

Nock, M. K., Joiner, T. E., Jr., Gordon, K. H., Lloyd-Richardson, E., and Prinstein, M. J. (2006). Non-suicidal self-injury among adolescents: Diagnostic correlates and relation to suicide attempts. *Psychiatry Research, 144*(1), 65–72.

Oldershaw, A., Grima, E., Jollant, F., Richards, C., Simic, M., Taylor, L., et al. (2009). Decision making and problem solving in adolescents who deliberately self-harm. *Psychological Medicine, 39*(1), 95–104.

ONS. (2005). Deaths by age, sex and underlying cause, 2004 registrations. *Health Statistics Quarterly, 26*, 6.

Ougrin, D., Banarsee, R., Dunn-Toroosian, V., and Majeed, A. (2010). Suicide survey in a London borough: primary care and public health perspectives. *J Public Health (Oxf)*.

Ougrin, D., and Latif, S. (2011). Engagement with Specific Psychological Treatment versus Treatment As Usual in Adolescents with Self-Harm. Systematic Review and Meta-Analysis. *Crisis: The Journal of Crisis Intervention and Suicide Prevention*(epub ahead of print), 10.1027/0227–5910/a000060.

Ougrin, D., Ng, A. V., and Low, J. (2008). Therapeutic assessment based on cognitive-analytic therapy for young people presenting with self-harm: pilot study. *Psychiatric Bulletin, 32*(11), 423–426.

Ougrin, D., Tranah, T., Leigh, E., Taylor, L., and Asarnow, J. R. (in press). Self-harm in Adolescents: Practitioners' Review *Journal of Child Psychology and Psychiatry and Allied Disciplines*.

Ougrin, D., Zundel, T., Ng, A., Banarsee, R., Bottle, A., and Taylor, E. (2011). Trial of Therapeutic Assessment in London: randomised controlled trial of Therapeutic Assessment versus standard psychosocial assessment in adolescents presenting with self-harm. *Arch Dis Child, 96*(2), 148–153.

Overholser, J. C., Hemstreet, A. H., Spirito, A., and Vyse, S. (1989). Suicide awareness programs in the schools: effects of gender and personal experience. *Journal of the American Academy of Child and Adolescent Psychiatry, 28*(6), 925–930.

Pelkonen, M., Marttunen, M., Laippala, P., and Lonnqvist, J. (2000). Factors associated with early dropout from adolescent psychiatric outpatient treatment. *Journal of the American Academy of Child and Adolescent Psychiatry, 39*(3), 329–336.

Piacentini, J., Rotheram-Borus, M. J., Gillis, J. R., Graae, F., Trautman, P., Cantwell, C., et al. (1995). Demographic predictors of treatment attendance among adolescent suicide attempters. *Journal of Consulting and Clinical Psychology, 63*(3), 469–473.

Pillay, A. L., and Wassenaar, D. R. (1995). Psychological intervention, spontaneous remission, hopelessness, and psychiatric disturbance in adolescent parasuicides. *Suicide and Life-Threatening Behavior, 25*(3), 386–392.

Portzky, G., van Heeringen, K., Portzky, G., and van Heeringen, K. (2006). Suicide prevention in adolescents: a controlled study of the effectiveness of a school-based psycho-educational program. *Journal of Child Psychology and Psychiatry and Allied Disciplines, 47*(9), 910–918.

Rathus, J. H., and Miller, A. L. (2002). Dialectical Behavior Therapy adapted for suicidal adolescents. *Suicide and Life-Threatening Behavior, 32*(2), 146–157.

Rotheram-Borus, M. J., Piacentini, J., Cantwell, C., Belin, T. R., and Song, J. (2000). The 18–month impact of an emergency room intervention for adolescent female suicide attempters. *Journal of Consulting and Clinical Psychology, 68*(6), 1081–1093.

Rotheram-Borus, M. J., Piacentini, J., Miller, S., Graae, F., Dunne, E., and Cantwell, C. (1996). Toward improving treatment adherence among adolescent suicide attempters. *Clinical Child Psychology and Psychiatry, 1*(1), 99–108.

Schuppert, H. M., Giesen-Bloo, J., van Gemert, T. G., Wiersema, H. M., Minderaa, R. B., Emmelkamp, P. M., et al. (2009). Effectiveness of an emotion regulation group training for adolescents—a randomized controlled pilot study. *Clinical Psychology and Psychotherapy, 16*(6), 467–478.

Shaffer, D., Garland, A., Vieland, V., Underwood, M., and Busner, C. (1991). The impact of curriculum-based suicide prevention programs for teenagers. *Journal of the American Academy of Child and Adolescent Psychiatry, 30*(4), 588–596.

Shaffer, D., Vieland, V., Garland, A., Rojas, M., Underwood, M., and Busner, C. (1990). Adolescent suicide attempters. Response to suicide-prevention programs. *JAMA, 264*(24), 3151–3155.

Skegg, K. (2005). Self-harm. *The Lancet, 366*(9495), 1471–1483.

Spirito, A., Boergers, J., Donaldson, D., Bishop, D., and Lewander, W. (2002). An intervention trial to improve adherence to community treatment by adolescents after a suicide attempt. *Journal of the American Academy of Child and Adolescent Psychiatry, 41*(4), 435–442.

Spirito, A., Monti, P. M., Barnett, N. P., Colby, S. M., Sindelar, H., Rohsenow, D. J., et al. (2004). A randomized clinical trial of a brief motivational intervention for alcohol-positive adolescents treated in an emergency department. *The Journal of Pediatrics, 145*(3), 396–402.

Taylor, L. M. W., Oldershaw, A., Richards, C., Davidson, K., Schmidt, U., and Simic, M. (in press). Development and Pilot Evaluation of a Manualized Cognitive-Behaivoural Treatment Package for Adolescent Self-Harm. *Behavioural and Cognitive Psychotherapy*.

Trent, M., Chung, S. E., Burke, M., Walker, A., and Ellen, J. M. (2009). Results of a Randomized Controlled Trial of a Brief Behavioral Intervention for Pelvic Inflammatory Disease in Adolescents. *J Pediatr Adolesc Gynecol*.

Vieland, V., Whittle, B., Garland, A., Hicks, R., and Shaffer, D. (1991). The impact of curriculum-based suicide prevention programs for teenagers: An 18-month follow-up. *Journal of the American Academy of Child and Adolescent Psychiatry, 30*(5), 811–815.

Voracek, M., and Loibl, L. M. (2007). Genetics of suicide: a systematic review of twin studies. *Wiener Klinische Wochenschrift, 119*(15–16), 463–475.

Votta, E., and Manion, I. (2004). Suicide, high-risk behaviors, and coping style in homeless adolescent males' adjustment. *Journal of Adolescent Health, 34*(3), 237–243.

Weisz, J. R., McCarty, C. A., and Valeri, S. M. (2006). Effects of psychotherapy for depression in children and adolescents: a meta-analysis. *Psychol Bull, 132*(1), 132–149.

Wilder, J. F., Plutchnik, R., and Conte, H. R. (1977). Compliance with psychiatric emergency room referrals. *Archives of General Psychiatry, 34*(8), 930–933.

Wood, A., Trainor, G., Rothwell, J., Moore, A., and Harrington, R. (2001). Randomized trial of group therapy for repeated deliberate self-harm in adolescents. *Journal of the American Academy of Child and Adolescent Psychiatry, 40*(11), 1246–1253.

Wyman, P. A., Brown, C. H., Inman, J., Cross, W., Schmeelk-Cone, K., Guo, J., et al. (2008). Randomized trial of a gatekeeper program for suicide prevention: 1–year impact on secondary school staff. *Journal of Consulting and Clinical Psychology, 76*(1), 104–115.

Wyman, P. A., Brown, C. H., LoMurray, M., Schmeelk-Cone, K., Petrova, M., Yu, Q., et al. (2010). An outcome evaluation of the Sources of Strength suicide prevention program delivered by adolescent peer leaders in high schools. *American journal of public health, 100* (9), 1653–1661.

Yip, P. S., Liu, K. Y., and Law, C. K. (2008). Years of life lost from suicide in China, 1990–2000. *Crisis: Journal of Crisis Intervention and Suicide, 29*(3), 131–136.

Zimmerman, J. K., Asnis, G. M., and Schwartz, B. J. (1995). Enhancing outpatient treatment compliance: A multifamily psychoeducational intake group. In J. K. Zimmerman and G. M. Asnis (Eds.), *Treatment approaches with suicidal adolescents* (pp. 106–134). Oxford, England: John Wiley and Sons.

III

TREATMENT AND ADVOCACY

11

Integrating Medical and Psychological Therapies in Child Mental Health

An Evidence-Based Medicine Approach

Jeffrey J. Sapyta and John S. March

The combined efforts of molecular neuroscience and cognitive psychology are driving a revolution in how we understand the diagnosis and treatment of mental illness (Kandel and Squire, 2000). It is increasingly clear that psychotropic medications work by biasing specific central nervous information processes; but growing evidence suggests that even brief exposure to psychosocial treatments can also change neurocircuitry (Porto et al., 2009). Drugs and psychotherapy work because they act on the brain (Hyman, 2000), and it is becoming increasingly clear that they often work best in combination with each other. Therefore, when selecting a treatment strategy that is appropriate to the needs of a specific patient, pediatric clinicians must consider a wide variety of medications, psychosocial treatments, and protocols that carefully time the combination of the two.

In the complex world of clinical practice, selecting an appropriate treatment among available options is rarely straightforward. Even when a comprehensive assessment produces an unambiguous diagnosis and readily defined target symptoms, expected outcomes vary by disorder, treatment modality, and participant factors specific to the patient, doctor, and treatment setting. Depending on the theoretical underpinning and nature of the treatment, psychotherapeutic options are generally more narrowly defined than drug treatments, which often have a broader spectrum of action. Implementing two distinct treatments can be complicated when they differ in dose and time it takes to reach a desired outcome. Finally, doctors and patients and their families often differ in their preferences regarding choices among appropriate treatments. All of these factors complicate the choice of treatment strategy for many if not most patients.

As matching treatment(s) to clinical problems has become more complicated, yet more effective, child and adolescent psychiatry has moved away from non-specific interventions toward problem-focused treatments keyed to specific DSM-IV diagnoses (Kazdin, 1997). In particular, the past forty years have seen the emergence of diverse, sophisticated, empirically-supported pharmacological and psychosocial treatments that cover the range of childhood-onset mental disorders. Many clinicians and researchers now believe that the combination of disorder-specific medication and psychosocial treatment administered within an evidence-based, disease management model is the initial treatment of choice for many if not all children and adolescents with a major mental illness (J. March and Vitiello, 2009; J. S. March, Frances, Carpenter, and Kahn, 1997). And among psychosocial treatments, problem-focused cognitive behavioral therapy has been evidenced as the clear superior treatment over other forms of psychotherapy with little prospect of any serious contenders emerging soon (J. S. March, 2009). As evidence for the growing consensus advocating combined treatment, NIMH-funded trials such as the Multimodal Treatment Study of Children with ADHD (MTA; Swanson et al., 2001), the Study of Long-Term Methylphenidate and Multimodal Psychosocial Treatment in Children with ADHD, the Preschool ADHD Treatment Study (PATS; L. Greenhill et al., 2006), the Treatment for Adolescents with Depression Disorder (TADS; J. March et al., 2007), Treatment of SSRI-Resistant Depression In Adolescents (TORDIA; Emslie et al., 2010), Pediatric OCD Treatment Study (POTS; POTS, 2004), and the Child/Adolescent Anxiety Multimodal Treatment Study (CAMS; Walkup et al., 2008) have all helped to better understand the benefits, as well as the limitations of monotherapy.

Despite the evidence available from the aforementioned trials, most of these studies are explanatory trials, which don't generalize perfectly to clinical practice. Randomized trials have been broadly categorized as either having a pragmatic or explanatory attitude (Hollis and Campbell, 1999; Thorpe et al., 2009). Explanatory clinical trials ask, "Does the intervention work under ideal conditions?" Whereas, pragmatic clinical trials ask, "Does this intervention work under usual conditions?" With respect to clinical decision making, the field needs more and better studies in which the hypothesis and study design are developed specifically to answer the pragmatic and explanatory questions faced by decision makers at the various levels of the health care system, including patients, doctors, and public policy makers. Although navigating the rapidly expanding evidence base for research informing clinical practice is becoming increasingly difficult (Straus, Glasziou, Richardson, and Hayes, 2010), keep up we must, since new developments point toward the improved outcomes that we and our patients desire (Barlow, Levitt, and Bufka, 1999). Nowhere is this truer than when divergent treatment options, such as medication and psychosocial approaches, are among the choices for children with mental illness.

Within a stages-of-treatment model that emphasizes the practice of evidence-based medicine (EBM), this chapter provides a conceptual framework for how to integrate research devoted to pharmacological and psychosocial treatments for children with mental health issues. Readers interested in a deeper understanding of practicing and/or teaching EBM principles beyond what we will discuss should first begin with the recently updated text devoted to EBM (Straus et al., 2010). Also pertinent to this topic, a relatively recent research forum focused on the applicability of EBM to the care of mentally ill youths is also available (J. S. March et al., 2007). Finally, for the reader interested in how best to combine specific treatments for particular disorders would be well advised to consult the American Academy of Child and Adolescent Psychiatry practice parameters series (AACAP, 2010).

DISEASE MANAGEMENT MODEL

The current wealth of scientific evidence concerning the developmental psychopathology and efficacious treatment of mental illness owes its start from a reorientation to a biopsychosocial disease management model in pediatric psychiatry (Ludwig and Othmer, 1977). Specifically, the three features of the disease management model come into play in child mental illness as they do in the rest of medicine: the concept of disease and diagnosis, the concept of etiology and treatment, and the nature of the doctor-patient relationship. To the extent that symptom relief occurs, it can be assumed that improvement reflects concurrent changes (e.g., learning) in the CNS (Andreasen, 1997; Hyman, 2000). Thus, the treatment of pediatric OCD can be thought of as partially analogous to the treatment of juvenile-onset diabetes, with the caveat that the target organ, the brain in the case of major mental illness, requires psychosocial interventions of much greater complexity. The treatment of diabetes and OCD both involve medications, insulin in diabetes and in OCD a serotonin reuptake inhibitor. Each also involves an evidence-based psychosocial intervention that works in part by biasing the somatic substrate of the disorder toward more normal function (Hyman, 2000). In diabetes, the psychosocial treatment of choice is diet and exercise, and in OCD, CBT that includes elements of exposure and response prevention. Depending on the presence of risk and protective factors, not every patient has the same outcome. Bright youngsters from well-adjusted two-parent families typically do better with either diabetes or OCD than those beset with deleterious psychosocial adversity. Thus adversity, when identified, becomes an appropriate target for intervention, usually to increase compliance with treatment for the primary illness. Finally, not everybody recovers completely even with the best of available treatment, so some interventions need to target coping with residual symptoms, such as diabetic foot care in diabetes and helping patients and their families cope skillfully with residual symptoms (e.g., minimizing family accommodation of rituals) in OCD.

WHY ROUTINELY COMBINE TREATMENTS IN THE TREATMENT OF MENTAL ILLNESS?

Psychosocial treatments usually are combined with medication for one of three reasons. First, in the initial treatment of the severely ill child, two treatments provide a greater "dose" and, thus, may promise an improved and possibly more efficiently acquired outcome. For example, in pediatric OCD, treating a child with CBT alone is generally considered as effective as treating a child with only a selective serotonin reuptake inhibitor, except in patients with a first-degree relative with OCD (parent, sibling). In these cases, CBT will not work unless a combined approach is used (Garcia et al., 2010). Furthermore, adolescents with major depression may opt for combined treatment even though CBT or fluoxetine alone may *eventually* offer similar benefit (C. Kratochvil et al., 2006). Second, comorbidity frequently but not always requires two treatments, since different targets may require different treatments. For example, treating a teen who has both ADHD and major depression would be reasonably achieved with a psychostimulant and CBT (C. J. Kratochvil et al., 2009). Even within a single disorder, such as ADHD, important functional outcomes may vary in response to treatment. For example, hyperactivity may be more responsive to a psychostimulant and child oppositional behavior would be best addressed with parent training. Third, in the face of partial response, an augmenting treatment can be added to the initial treatment to improve the outcome in the symptom domain targeted by the initial treatment. For example, CBT when treated in combination with an SSRI for major depression can result in improved MDD-specific outcomes (Emslie et al., 2010). In an adjunctive treatment strategy, a second treatment can be added to a first one in order to positively impact one or more additional outcome domains. For example, an SSRI can be added to CBT for OCD to handle comorbid depression or panic disorder.

IMPLEMENTING CBT IN A MEDICAL CONTEXT

Most mental health clinicians are familiar with treatments that assume that psychological distress represents the product of both historical and present relationship problems that must be uncovered and addressed in therapy. In contrast to these more "story oriented" approaches to psychotherapy, CBT asks the clinician to adopt a problem-solving model in which he or she acts as a coach to teach the patient a set of adaptive coping skills, minimizing or unlearning ineffective coping behaviors, and orienting patients to viewing their symptoms that are associated with distress and impairment in the present tense (J. S. March, 2000). Thus, CBT, unlike most other psychotherapeutic approaches, fits beautifully into a disease management framework in which the symptoms of the illness and associated functional impairments are specifically targeted for treatment. The cornerstone of CBT is a careful functional analysis of problem behaviors that is governed by several important assumptions. First, behavior (including normal as well as problem behavior) is primarily governed by environmental contingencies (and in cognitive theory, by thoughts and emotions), such that the relationship between thoughts, feelings and behaviors is the primary focus of assessment and treatment. Second, the antecedents and consequences of target behaviors as well as target behaviors themselves must be operationally defined and accurately measured. Third, behavior may differ across settings so that multi-informant, multimodal, multi-domain assessment is critical. Fourth, treatment planning depends on careful assessment, including periodic reassessment of how behaviors have changed, with revision of treatment interventions as necessary. While these assumptions and procedures are not necessarily incompatible with pharmacological management, the level of specificity for functional outcomes is generally much greater for CBT than for medication management. On the other hand, the level of monitoring for change should be roughly equal for both pharmacological and psychosocial interventions as it is symptomatic change and improvement in functional outcomes that govern patient and clinician assessment of degree of improvement. Put experimentally, CBT lends itself to viewing the treatment of each patient through the lens of one of several possible single case designs (Hayes, 1981), which in turn makes combining pharmacological and cognitive-behavioral interventions relatively straightforward.

MULTIDISCIPLINARY PRACTICE IS BEST PRACTICE

Although cognitive-behavioral and pharmacological treatment strategies readily combine, psychology and psychiatry are often at odds over guild issues. We believe strongly that it is not possible to practice competent and ethical psychopharmacology in isolation, when practitioners of empirically-supported psychotherapy are available in your area. Similarly, it is not possible to practice competent and ethical psychotherapy in isolation, without the availability of empirically supported psychopharmacologists. Granting that patient preference may dictate starting a monotherapeutic approach at the start, physicians (who typically write prescriptions) and psychologists (who, for the most part, are typically are better versed in CBT) must collaborate in the care of individual patients if for no other reason than the complexity of modern mental health care is beyond the capacity of any one individual to master (J. S. March, Mulle, Stallings, Erhardt, and Conners, 1995). In this regard, the current generation of comparative treatment trials (e.g., CAMS, MTA, POTS, and TADS) nicely models both the benefits and the difficulties of multidisciplinary practice in which practitioners of both disciplines are stakeholders for the experiment (the research question) as well as the benefit of the individual patient (the clinical question). The evidence supplied by these trials is clear; without a clear commitment from clinicians to multidisciplinary practice, we shortchange our patients.

USING EVIDENCE-BASED MEDICINE (EBM) AS A FRAMEWORK FOR MAKING CLINICAL RESEARCH USEFUL TO CLINICAL PRACTICE

One of the common criticisms of the evidence-based approach in clinical practice is the notion that research applies very little to clinical practice. In other words, the external validity of many efficacy studies is suspect. External validity, which refers to the extent to which the results of the research are generalizable to clinical populations, is often contrasted to internal validity, which refers to the extent to which a study is methodologically sound. In any given study, there is always some level of tradeoff between external and internal validity. In order for a study to be methodologically sound, the experimenter must be able to manipulate or "control" the key variables of interest (e.g., train providers in manualized treatments, randomize patients to these treatments, and utilize data sources with established validity on the phenomena of interest). However, the more a study implements overt control of these variables, there is an increased likelihood that the patients recruited or the treatment provided will not resemble clinical practice, thus hurting the external validity of the findings. It is true that without any internal validity (e.g., your treatment implementation is not reliable), it is impossible to have external validity. However, many internally valid studies are not fully relevant to clinical practice. This is why the NIMH has largely moved away from funding efficacy trials conducted with patients with "relatively pure" diagnostic presentations toward effectiveness trials that utilize more representative clinical samples with co-occurring disorders and concomitant treatments (Norquist and Magruder, 1998). NIMH studies, such as TORDIA, TADS, and recently completed POTS-II (Freeman et al., 2011), are good examples of methodologically sound clinical trials, yet have the flexibility to utilize patients with heterogeneous presentations and/or various prior community treatment histories.

From the point of view of an individual practitioner hoping to conform to best-practice standards, it is critical therefore to decide whether and how the results of a particular study are both methodologically sound and clinically relevant. Instead of holding to a dogmatic adherence to an ill-defined "gold standard," EBM is simply a set of tools that allow the conscientious, explicit and judicious use of current best research evidence in making decisions about the care of an individual patient (Guyatt et al., 2000).

CHOOSING APPROPRIATE QUESTIONS AND STUDIES USING EBM

Whether approaching diagnosis, prognosis or treatment, EBM always begins with selecting a specific question among the scores of relevant questions presented by the care of a specific patient. The first step is in evaluating a treatment question is to frame the question as a P-I-C-O: What is the *P*opulation, the main *I*ntervention, the *C*ontrol or comparison condition, and the desired *O*utcome? A simple PICO might be: In children with ADHD, what is the evidence that bupropion is better than placebo in reducing symptoms of hyperactivity and impulsivity? Having framed the question as a PICO, the clinician then turns to the increasingly EBM-optimized resources available on the Internet, such as the clinical queries algorithm on PubMed available through the NIH website: (http://www.ncbi.nlm.nih.gov/sites/pubmedutils/clinical). In this regard, EBM provides a clear hierarchy of search strategies that move from EBM reviews on specific topics, to Critically Appraised Topics (CATs) which summarize one or two relevant articles, or, if none of these are available, doing a search and investigating the literature yourself. Full text articles for many journals are increasingly available, through open-access journals, subscription service or academic libraries. See Straus et al. (2010) for a more detailed discussion of search strategies and CATs.

STEPS IN EVALUATING THE CLINICAL USEFULNESS OF A TREATMENT STUDY

Having identified an article that is directly relevant to the question of interest, the next step is to evaluate the article for its validity and applicability to your patient. Four relatively commonsensical steps begin with a reasonably close reading of (1) the abstract to get an overall summary, (2) the methods section to assess validity and to identify the population studied and (3) the results section to understand the direction and clinical importance of the outcome. In the opposite of how many are trained, the introduction and discussion often can be skipped as an inefficient use of time. The four steps are as follows:

Step 1: Is the Study Valid?

Did the investigators use a randomized, controlled, blinded design in which all the patients were followed up at the end? Apart from intrinsic differences in the treatments themselves, were all the patients treated the same way? Without affirming these relatively straightforward parameters of internal validity, it is impossible to know whether differences in the outcome reflect true differences in the impact of the treatments or some other characteristic of the study.

Step 2: What Were the Results?

Ideally the results should be presented both dimensionally, using normed rating scales so that the reader can judge improvement toward or into the normal range, and categorically, to allow easy calculation of magnitude of clinical improvement. If the results are presented as a change score (the mean at post-treatment minus the mean at pre-treatment for each treatment group), the actual means scores for each treatment group at baseline should also be included so that the clinician can judge whether the amount of change moved the average patient into the normal range. If comorbidity is a factor, initial levels of comorbid symptomatology and changes in comorbidity over time should also be presented. Finally, the same questions that are asked about treatment effectiveness can be asked about harm to answer the critical question: "Is it safe?" (Levine et al., 1994).

Step 3: Are the Results Clinically Meaningful?

Traditionally in psychiatry and psychology (Weisz, 2000), the magnitude of the effect has been portrayed in terms of small (.3), medium (.5) or large (>.8) effect sizes in standard deviation units (Cohen, 1988). EBM uses a much simpler rubric, the "Number Needed to Treat" (NNT). In practice, the NNT represents the number of patients that need to be treated with the study intervention to produce one additional good outcome beyond that obtainable with the control or comparison condition. For example, an NNT of 10 means that you would have to treat 10 patients with the active treatment to find one that wouldn't have done just as well if assigned to the control treatment. A very small NNT (i.e., one that approaches 1) means that a favorable outcome occurs in nearly every patient who receives the treatment and in few patients in the comparison group. An NNT of 2 or 3 indicates that a treatment is quite effective. In contrast, NNTs above 30 or 40 fall in the realm of public health effects although they may still be considered clinically effective.

Step 4: Is the Result Applicable to my Patient?

Finally, even if a study has passed scrutiny of the previous steps, it is important to determine if a study has enough external validity to reasonably generalize to the particular clinical situation you are facing in your office. This can be accomplished quickly by asking the following questions. Is my patient represented in the research sample or were patients like mine excluded from the trial? Were there clinically important outcomes considered, such as functional (e.g., rate of children who return to school) and disorder-specific (e.g. less depression)? How were the outcomes measured, are they clinically meaningful, and can I apply these measures in my practice? Are the treatments worth the potential benefits, harms and costs? Can I and/or a colleague work together to provide the treatment in our treatment setting(s)? Will the patient accept the treatment? The answers to these questions bring the research study to the level of direct patient care.

CLINICAL EXAMPLES APPLYING EBM

Example One: Combined Treatment for Internalizing Disorders and School Refusal

The treatment of teenagers with severe anxiety, depression and associated school refusal provides an excellent example of how EBM can be used to guide combining medication and psychosocial treatments in clinical practice. Children with school refusal offer one of the most challenging clinical problems in pediatric psychiatry. These patients present with multiple behavioral and family problems and are often inappropriately thought of as treatment refractory even before treatment has begun (Bernstein, Borchardt, and Perwien, 1996; Bernstein, Warren, Massie, and Thuras, 1999).

In one study, Bernstein and colleagues (Bernstein et al., 2000) asked the following question (framed as a PICO): In school refusing teenagers with combined anxiety and depressive disorders (the population), is CBT plus imipramine (the intervention) more effective than CBT plus pill PBO (the control) in returning patients to school (the outcome) after eight weeks of treatment? They used a balanced randomized parallel group design, complete follow-up, an intent-to treat analysis, blind assessment and, gave pill PBO to balance the CBT alone condition, and ensured equal treatment characteristics in each group apart from the intervention. Over eight weeks, they found a statistically significant difference favoring combined treatment over CBT alone for patients returning to school. The magnitude of the NNT

(NNT = 3, CI 1–4) for this notoriously difficult-to-treat population were quite impressive in indicating that combined CBT and medication is better than CBT alone for anxious, depressed school refusers.

Example Two: Combined Treatment for Children with ADHD

A very large body of literature suggests that treatment with a psycho-stimulant is effective for externalizing symptoms in children with ADHD (Goldman, Genel, Bezman, and Slanetz, 1998). Another large body of literature suggests that behavior therapy, primarily in the form of parent training, is also effective as a treatment for children with ADHD (Wells et al., 2000). The combination of parent training and a psychostimulant has historically been recommended as the first-line treatment for ADHD by experts (C. Conners, March, Frances, Wells, and Ross, 2001).

For these reasons, we might wish to know (framed as a PICO) whether in the treatment of young children with ADHD (the population) combined treatment (the intervention) has an advantage over treatment with medica-tion or parent training alone (the comparison condition). We also might wish to know whether this is true for core ADHD outcomes as well as for non-ADHD outcomes, such as parent-child arguing, or in subgroups of ADHD children who are diagnostically more complex, such as those with a comorbid anxiety disorder.

A search of PubMed would identify the six-site NIMH collaborative Multimodal Treatment Study of Children with ADHD (MTA; Swanson et al., 2001). Parenthetically, while other trials also might emerge, assuming that the designs and outcomes are similar, the most recent and/or most powerful study likely is sufficient to construct a CAT. Conversely, where the literature is rich in randomized evidence, an up-to-date EBM review might be the most important source of information.

The MTA Study was designed to test both monotherapeutic and combined treatments for children, age seven to nine, with ADHD (Arnold et al., 1997). They used a balanced randomized parallel group design, complete follow-up, an intent-to treat analysis, blind assessment and, randomized some to a treatment-as-usual group to balance the various treatment conditions. It also serves as an excellent example of how CBT and medication can and should be combined in treating youth. Briefly, 579 children criteria for ADHD, combined subtype, were randomly assigned to either an intensive behavior therapy program, a titration-adjusted optimized medication management strategy, an interactive combination of the medication and behavioral treat-ment, or a comparison group that was assessed and then referred to local community care resources. The behavioral treatment consisted of fourteen months of parent training utilizing both group and individual parent ses-sions, four months of classroom behavioral management by a trained paraprofessional working with the teacher and an intensive eight-week summer treatment program (Wells et al., 2000). Optimal medication dosage was attained by acutely titrating medication (starting with methylphenidate and moving on as needed to other drugs) and subsequently adjusting the dose and timing of drug administration based upon teacher and parent symptom ratings over the course of the study (L. L. Greenhill et al., 1996).

As summarized by Jensen and colleagues (2001), children randomized to the optimized medication management strategy proved substantially improved compared to behavior treatment alone or treatment in the community, for primary ADHD symptoms. The differences between optimized medication management only or medication management combined with the intensive psychosocial treatment were not clinically meaningful, suggesting that the optimized medication management utilized in MTA was doing the heavy lifting for ADHD symptom reduction. Despite the fact that children randomized to community care were frequently medicated, the clinical benefit of the acute titration approach was clinically meaningful, with an NNT for combined treatment or medication management only relative to community treatment of two, indicating clearly that well-delivered treatment that includes medication is superior to less intensive community standard care. For other functioning domains (social skills, academics, parent-child relations, oppositional behavior, anxiety/depression), results suggested modest incremental benefits of the combined intervention over either monotherapy or community care (MTA, 1999). Secondary analyses also revealed that combined treatment had a significant incremental effect over medication management alone when categorical indicators of excellent response and when composite outcome measures were utilized. Finally, children with parent-reported comorbid anxiety disorders, particularly those with overlapping disruptive disorder comorbidities, showed additional benefits from including the psychosocial component to the interventions (J. S. March et al., 2000). Granted, the long term outcomes (six or more years from randomization) between treatment groups show few differences (Molina et al., 2009), these differences could be attributed to numerous reasons such as maturation of the child and study-wide reduction in assigned treatment adherence after such a long follow-up.

Example 3: Managing Partial Response to an SSRI in OCD

Many patients in clinical practice have already failed or had a partial response to one or more initial treatments, especially when treatment was unimodal. Though robust responses may still occur, on probabilistic grounds such patients may be expected to have a poorer response than naïve patients for another medication approach in the same class. For example, an OCD patient on his third SSRI trial may have as much as a three fold lower chance of responding than a treatment naïve patient (J. S. March et al., 1998). If your patient falls into this group, the NNT will be higher than the average research subject. The corresponding NNT from open trials in which CBT was added to medication is approximately two (Franklin et al., 1998). Hence, if full remission is the aim, the EBM informed clinician would likely opt for adding CBT to an SSRI early in the course of partial response in preference to switching to another SSRI.

LESSONS FROM THE CLINIC

Several important principles merit elaboration regarding combining medical and psychosocial interventions for children struggling with mental health issues.

Importance of Differential Therapeutics

In the context of medical treatment of psychiatric illness, differential therapeutics—identifying treatment interventions that are appropriate to various treatment targets is crucial for effective practice. Put in terms of the disease management model, current best-practice treatment requires clear specification of the behavioral/emotional syndrome (e.g., ADHD), within-syndrome problems (e.g., oppositional behavior), and functional impairments (e.g., refuses to go to bed) in order to decide on the best intervention. Both behavioral/symptomatic (doctor assigned) and functional (usually parent and child assigned) outcomes must be factored into the selection of psychosocial and drug treatments. Depending on the nature of the problem, some outcomes will be more easily approached with medication or psychosocial interventions.

Rating Scales are the Primary Assessment Tools for Psychiatric Practice

Regardless of diagnosis, most children present for mental health care because of problematic behaviors either in their relationships or in the school setting. Starting with the presenting complaint, the clinicians' task is to understand these behaviors in the context of the constraints to normal development that underlie them and in doing so to construct a differential diagnostic hierarchy that informs a thoughtfully constructed treatment regimen. Of all the assessment technologies available to us, gender, age and race normed rating scales perhaps offer the most efficient way to collect information regarding both internalizing and externalizing behavioral disturbances at home and school. Examples of excellent scales with good psychometric properties available for self-report include scales for externalizing disorders (C. K. Conners, Sitarenios, Parker, and Epstein, 1998), anxiety (J. S. March, Parker, Sullivan, Stallings, and Conners, 1997) and depression (Kovacs, 1985). Besides assessing an overall construct (e.g. anxiety), child self-report measures also provide useful information at the factor (e.g. physical anxiety symptoms) and item level (e.g., suffocation anxiety). Clinician administered ratings scales, such as the Children's Yale-Brown Obsessive-Compulsive Scale (Scahill et al., 1997) or the Childhood Autism Rating Scale (McDougle et al., 2000), also are de rigueur for some disorders. Using reliable and valid rating scales both makes the interview more efficient and initiates a dialogue between the doctor and the patient about the patient's most troubling symptoms. Such a procedure is consistent with medical evaluation procedures across other medical specialties, and meets goals for guidelines-based practice in managed care irrespective of whether a disease is conceptualized categorically (e.g., schizophrenia) or dimensionally (e.g., generalized anxiety).

Monitor Outcomes

Once treatment has started, the clinician inevitably will need to conduct additional assessments to collect detailed data on the patient's specific symptomatology and its impact on day-to-day functioning. Such data will serve as a basis for evaluating the progress and rate of treatment, and where possible for differentiating response to behavioral as contrasted to pharmacological interventions. Why evaluate outcome? First, tracking symptoms requires the clinician periodically to update the problem target list, minimizing the possibility that new or re-emerging symptoms will be missed. Second, child and parent ratings allow the clinician to address discrepant views of the child's progress or differential treatment response across different settings where they exist. Third, rating scales provide a detailed view of how the child is progressing in treatment. In this regard, disorder-specific rating scales, whether standardized or tailored to the patient's problems, provide a far richer source of information than global measures, which simply involve therapist ratings of general outcome. Using OCD as an example, patient symptomatology can be tracked with the CY-BOCS symptoms checklist, OCD symptoms with the CY-BOCS itself, specific CBT targets with a stimulus hierarchy and reductions in anxiety in response to successive exposure trials (e.g. habituation curves), using a fear thermometer.

Think Developmentally

As with academic skills, children normally acquire social-emotional (self and interpersonal) competencies via maturation. The failure to do so, relative to age, gender, and culture-matched peers, may reflect capacity limitations, individual difference in the rate of skill acquisition for specific competencies, environmental factors, and/or the development of a major mental illness. The task of the mental health practitioner considering how to combine drug and psychosocial treatment(s) is to understand the presenting symptoms in the context of constraints to normal development, and to devise a tailored target-specific treatment program that eliminates those constraints so that the youngster can resume a normal developmental trajectory insofar as is possible. Depending on the nature of the symptoms and the capacity of the child and family to make use of target-specific psychosocial interventions, the blend of treatments may vary within a developmental context. For example, irrespective of medication treatment, school avoidance in a separation anxious six-year-old will require dyadic CBT in which control is transferred from the therapist to the parent and then to the child, whereas a school avoidant teen with panic disorder likely will do best with individual CBT perhaps in association with behavioral family therapy (Silverman and Kurtines, 1996).

Emphasize Psychoeducation

Despite our best intentions, parents and children sometimes come away with only a limited appreciation for the complexity of their situation as we appreciate it at the end of the diagnostic process. In this context, one of the primary goals of the assessment stage is to use the diagnostic process as a vehicle for psychoeducation regarding the rationale for combining treatment for their particular situation. When initiating, or elaborating, treatment in the context of partial response the intention must always be to implement interventions that present a logically consistent and compelling relationship between the disorder, the treatment, and the specified outcome. This emphasis encourages a detailed review of the indications, risks, and benefits of proposed and alternative treatments, after which parents and patient generally chose a treatment protocol consisting of a monotherapy, typically either CBT or medication, or CBT in combination with an appropriate medication intervention.

Practice Guidelines

As a general rule, it is always best to use the simplest, least risky and most cost-effective treatment intervention available within a stages-of-treatment model that addresses selection of initial treatment, the management of partial response, maintenance treatment, treatment resistance and comorbidity. When the empirical literature and expert opinion agree regarding best practice (e.g., what treatment or combination of treatments likely will work best for most patients), it usually is not acceptable to substitute a less supported treatment than what is recommended, as doing so would rarely be in the patient's best interest. For example, initiating treatment for newly diagnosed OCD with a treatment other than the combination of CBT and SSRI would be difficult to justify (POTS, 2004). Since doctor, family and patient preference all come into play when choosing between CBT, SSRI, or combined treatment, any one of the three options could be acceptable as initial treatment, although the clinician ought to suggest that the probability of acute and long-term remission is greater if a combined treatment approach is implemented.

A LOOK AT THE FUTURE OF MEDICAL TREATMENTS IN PSYCHIATRY: ATTENTION BIAS MODIFICATION TRAINING

After twenty years of large comparative treatment trials evaluating treatments for specific diagnoses, the age of symptomatic diagnosis and with it the current generation of treatments is passing (Insel et al., 2010). The next generation of treatments will be informed directly from recent revolutionary advancements in neuroscience. Categorical diagnoses will likely be maintained minimally, but eventually the field is poised to move beyond the current DSM approach to a nosology based on intermediate phenotypes (reflecting CNS information processes) and linked circuit models of psychopathology (J. S. March, 2009). A prime example of this intervention revolution is recent developments in attention bias modification training (ABMT).

ABMT has been successful in addressing anxiety, depression, smoking, and alcohol abuse disorders (Browning, Holmes, and Harmer, 2010), but for brevity, we will focus on its implications for anxiety disorders. For example, it has shown that individuals, in both clinically anxious and nonclinical populations, selectively allocate attention toward threat-related information (Bar-Haim, Lamy, Pergamin, Bakermans-Kranenburg, and van IJzendoorn, 2007; Roy et al., 2008), and this fact has promising implications for treatments (Hakamata et al., 2010). Using methods such as the emotional Stroop task and the dot-probe detection task, subjects with varying degrees of trait anxiety and anxiety states can be shown to preferentially deflect attention away from negative information and toward positive information. Neuroimaging research on anxiety suggest that two neural systems are involved, a bottom-up amygdala-based system that assigns valence to threatening stimuli and a top-down cognitive control system involving the anterior cingulate cortex and lateral prefrontal cortex. Interestingly, interventions targeting anxiety disorders appear to modify at least one, and sometimes both of these systems. Serotonin reuptake inhibitors appear to bias attention away from threat via an effect on the amygdala-based appraisal system. Likewise, cognitive training interventions like CBT have shown a beneficial effect to both top-down and bottom-up processes (Porto et al., 2009), and ABMT interventions have too shown promise for affecting change in both systems in adults (Browning, Holmes, and Harmer, 2010; Browning, Holmes, Murphy, Goodwin, and Harmer, 2010). Although no treatment studies have yet been published for children with anxiety disorders, several clinical trials are now ongoing with results to be published in the near future (Bar-Haim, 2010).

CONCLUSION

Empirically supported unimodal treatments for children are now available for most disorders seen in clinical practice, including ADHD, OCD, Tourette's, major depression, schizophrenia, and anxiety disorders. In addition to the MTA Study, which set the standard for multimodal trials, POTS, CAMS, TADS, TORDIA are all now impacting clinical interventions. Taken together, these studies and others begin to approach the question of which treatment—drug, psychosocial or combination—is best for which child with what set of predictive characteristics. As our understanding of the pathogenesis of mental illness in youth increases, dramatic treatment innovations inevitably will accrue, including knowledge about when and how to combine treatments. Hence, the clinician facing the daunting task of keeping up with the rapid advances in evidence regarding the diagnosis and treatment of mental illness in children and adolescents would be well advised to acquire at least a basic understanding of the tools of evidence-based medicine. In the meantime, it is likely that the combination of targeted medication and psychosocial therapies skillfully applied across time affords the most plausible basis for sustained benefit in children and adolescents suffering from a variety of major mental illnesses.

REFERENCES

AACAP. (2010). AACAP Practice Parameters. Retrieved July 17th, 2011, from http://aacap.org/cs/root/member_information/practice_information/practice_parameters/practice_parameters

Andreasen, N. C. (1997). Linking mind and brain in the study of mental illnesses: a project for a scientific psychopathology. *Science, 275*(5306), 1586.

Arnold, L. E., Abikoff, H. B., Cantwell, D. P., Conners, C. K., Elliott, G. R., Greenhill, L. L., et al. (1997). NIMH collaborative multimodal treatment study of children with ADHD (MTA): Design, methodology, and protocol evolution. *Journal of Attention Disorders, 2*(3), 141.

Bar-Haim, Y. (2010). Research review: Attention bias modification (ABM): a novel treatment for anxiety disorders. *J Child Psychol Psychiatry, 51*(8), 859–870.

Bar-Haim, Y., Lamy, D., Pergamin, L., Bakermans-Kranenburg, M. J., and van IJzendoorn, M. H. (2007). Threat-related attentional bias in anxious and nonanxious individuals: A meta-analytic study. *Psychological Bulletin, 133*(1), 1.

Barlow, D. H., Levitt, J. T., and Bufka, L. F. (1999). The dissemination of empirically supported treatments: a view to the future. *Behav Res Ther, 37 Suppl 1*, S147–162.

Bernstein, G. A., Borchardt, C. M., and Perwien, A. R. (1996). Anxiety disorders in children and adolescents: A review of the past 10 years. *Journal of the American Academy of Child and Adolescent Psychiatry.*

Bernstein, G. A., Borchardt, C. M., Perwien, A. R., Crosby, R. D., Kushner, M. G., Thuras, P. D., et al. (2000). Imipramine plus cognitive-behavioral therapy in the treatment of school refusal. *Journal of the American Academy of Child and Adolescent Psychiatry, 39*(3), 276–283.

Bernstein, G. A., Warren, S. L., Massie, E. D., and Thuras, P. D. (1999). Family dimensions in anxious-depressed school refusers. *Journal of anxiety disorders, 13*(5), 513–528.

Browning, M., Holmes, E. A., and Harmer, C. J. (2010). The modification of attentional bias to emotional information: A review of the techniques, mechanisms, and relevance to emotional disorders. *Cognitive, Affective, and Behavioral Neuroscience, 10*(1), 8.

Browning, M., Holmes, E. A., Murphy, S. E., Goodwin, G. M., and Harmer, C. J. (2010). Lateral prefrontal cortex mediates the cognitive modification of attentional bias. *Biological psychiatry, 67*(10), 919–925.

Cohen, J. (1988). *Statistical power analysis for the behavioral sciences*: Lawrence Erlbaum.

Conners, C., March, J., Frances, A., Wells, K., and Ross, R. (2001). Treatment of attention deficit hyperactivity disorder: expert consensus guidelines. *Journal of Attention Disorders, 4*, 7–128.

Conners, C. K., Sitarenios, G., Parker, J. D. A., and Epstein, J. N. (1998). The revised Conners' Parent Rating Scale (CPRS-R): factor structure, reliability, and criterion validity. *Journal of abnormal child psychology, 26*(4), 257–268.

Emslie, G. J., Mayes, T., Porta, G., Vitiello, B., Clarke, G., Wagner, K. D., et al. (2010). Treatment of Resistant Depression in Adolescents (TORDIA): week 24 outcomes. *American Journal of Psychiatry, 167*(7), 782.

Franklin, M. E., Kozak, M. J., Cashman, L. A., Coles, M. E., Rheingold, A. A., and Foa, E. B. (1998). Cognitive-behavioral treatment of pediatric obsessive-compulsive disorder: an open clinical trial. *Journal of the American Academy of Child and Adolescent Psychiatry, 37*(4), 412–419.

Freeman, J., Sapyta, J., Garcia, A., Fitzgerald, D., Khanna, M., Choate-Summers, M., et al. (2011). Still Struggling: Characteristics of Youth With OCD Who are Partial Responders to Medication Treatment. *Child Psychiatry and Human Development*, 1–18.

Garcia, A. M., Sapyta, J. J., Moore, P. S., Freeman, J. B., Franklin, M. E., March, J. S., et al. (2010). Predictors and moderators of treatment outcome in the Pediatric

Obsessive Compulsive Treatment Study (POTS I). *Journal of the American Academy of Child and Adolescent Psychiatry*.

Goldman, L. S., Genel, M., Bezman, R. J., and Slanetz, P. J. (1998). Diagnosis and treatment of attention-deficit/hyperactivity disorder in children and adolescents. *JAMA: the journal of the American Medical Association, 279*(14), 1100.

Greenhill, L., Kollins, S., Abikoff, H., McCracken, J., Riddle, M., Swanson, J., et al. (2006). Efficacy and safety of immediate-release methylphenidate treatment for preschoolers with ADHD. *Journal of the American Academy of Child and Adolescent Psychiatry, 45*(11), 1284–1293.

Greenhill, L. L., Abikoff, H. B., Arnold, L. E., Cantwell, D. P., Conners, C. K., Elliott, G., et al. (1996). Medication treatment strategies in the MTA Study: relevance to clinicians and researchers. *J Am Acad Child Adolesc Psychiatry, 35*(10), 1304–1313.

Guyatt, G. H., Haynes, R. B., Jaeschke, R. Z., Cook, D. J., Green, L., Naylor, C. D., et al. (2000). Users' guides to the medical literature. *JAMA: the journal of the American Medical Association, 284*(10), 1290.

Hakamata, Y., Lissek, S., Bar-Haim, Y., Britton, J. C., Fox, N. A., Leibenluft, E., et al. (2010). Attention bias modification treatment: a meta-analysis toward the establishment of novel treatment for anxiety. *Biological psychiatry*.

Hayes, S. C. (1981). Single case experimental design and empirical clinical practice. *Journal of Consulting and Clinical Psychology, 49*(2), 193.

Hollis, S., and Campbell, F. (1999). What is meant by intention to treat analysis? Survey of published randomised controlled trials. *Bmj, 319*(7211), 670.

Hyman, S. E. (2000). The millennium of mind, brain, and behavior. *Arch Gen Psychiatry, 57*(1), 88–89.

Insel, T., Cuthbert, B., Garvey, M., Heinssen, R., Pine, D. S., Quinn, K., et al. (2010). Research domain criteria (RDoC): toward a new classification framework for research on mental disorders. *American Journal of Psychiatry, 167*(7), 748.

Kandel, E. R., and Squire, L. R. (2000). Neuroscience: Breaking down scientific barriers to the study of brain and mind. *Science, 290*(5494), 1113.

Kazdin, A. E. (1997). A model for developing effective treatments: progression and interplay of theory, research, and practice. *J Clin Child Psychol, 26*(2), 114–129.

Kovacs, M. (1985). The Children's Depression, Inventory (CDI). *Psychopharmacol Bull, 21*(4), 995–998.

Kratochvil, C., Emslie, G., Silva, S., McNULTY, S., Walkup, J., Curry, J., et al. (2006). Acute time to response in the Treatment for Adolescents With Depression Study (TADS). *Journal of the American Academy of Child and Adolescent Psychiatry, 45*(12), 1412–1418.

Kratochvil, C. J., May, D. E., Silva, S. G., Madaan, V., Puumala, S. E., Curry, J. F., et al. (2009). Treatment response in depressed adolescents with and without co-morbid attention-deficit/hyperactivity disorder in the Treatment for Adolescents with Depression Study. *Journal of child and adolescent psychopharmacology, 19*(5), 519–527.

Levine, M., Walter, S., Lee, H., Haines, T., Holbrook, A., and Moyer, V. (1994). Users' guides to the medical literature. IV. How to use an article about harm. Evidence-Based Medicine Working Group. *JAMA, 271*(20), 1615–1619.

Ludwig, A. M., and Othmer, K. (1977). The medical basis of psychiatry. *Am J Psychiatry, 134*(10), 1087–1092.

March, J., Silva, S., Petrycki, S., Curry, J., Wells, K., Fairbank, J., et al. (2007). The Treatment for Adolescents With Depression Study (TADS): long-term effectiveness and safety outcomes. *Focus, 64*(10), 1132–1143.

March, J., and Vitiello, B. (2009). Clinical messages from the Treatment for Adolescents With Depression Study (TADS). *Am J Psychiatry, 166*(10), 1118–1123.

March, J. S. (2000). Child psychiatry: Cognitive and behavior therapies. In B. Saddock and V. Saddock (Eds.), *Comprehensive Textbook of Psychiatry/VII* (pp. 2806–2812). New York: Williams and Wilkins.

March, J. S. (2009). The future of psychotherapy for mentally ill children and adolescents. *Journal of Child Psychology and Psychiatry, 50*(12), 170–179.

March, J. S., Biederman, J., Wolkow, R., Safferman, A., Mardekian, J., Cook, E. H., et al. (1998). Sertraline in children and adolescents with obsessive-compulsive disorder: a multicenter randomized controlled trial. *JAMA, 280*(20), 1752–1756.

March, J. S., Frances, A., Carpenter, L., and Kahn, D. (1997). Expert consensus treatment guidelines for obsessive-compulsive disorder: A guide for patients and families. *Journal of Clinical Psychiatry, 58*, 65–72.

March, J. S., Mulle, K., Stallings, P., Erhardt, D., and Conners, C. K. (1995). Organizing an anxiety disorders clinic. In J. March (Ed.), *Anxiety Disorders in Children and Adolescents* (pp. 420–435). New York: Guilford Press.

March, J. S., Parker, J. D. A., Sullivan, K., Stallings, P., and Conners, C. K. (1997). The Multidimensional Anxiety Scale for Children (MASC): factor structure, reliability, and validity. *Journal of the American Academy of Child and Adolescent Psychiatry, 36*(4), 554–565.

March, J. S., Swanson, J. M., Arnold, L. E., Hoza, B., Conners, C. K., Hinshaw, S. P., et al. (2000). Anxiety as a predictor and outcome variable in the multimodal treatment study of children with ADHD (MTA). *Journal of abnormal child psychology, 28*(6), 527–541.

March, J. S., Szatmari, P., Bukstein, O., Chrisman, A., Kondo, D., Hamilton, J. D., et al. (2007). AACAP 2005 research forum: speeding the adoption of evidence-based practice in pediatric psychiatry. *Journal of the American Academy of Child and Adolescent Psychiatry, 46*(9), 1098–1110.

McDougle, C. J., Scahill, L., McCracken, J. T., Aman, M. G., Tierney, E., Arnold, L. E., et al. (2000). Research Units on Pediatric Psychopharmacology (RUPP) Autism Network. Background and rationale for an initial controlled study of risperidone. *Child and adolescent psychiatric clinics of North America, 9*(1), 201.

Molina, B. S. G., Hinshaw, S. P., Swanson, J. M., Arnold, L. E., Vitiello, B., Jensen, P. S., et al. (2009). The MTA at 8 years: prospective follow-up of children treated for combined-type ADHD in a multisite study. *Journal of the American Academy of Child and Adolescent Psychiatry, 48*(5), 484–500.

MTA, T. C. W. G. (1999). Moderators and mediators of treatment response for children with attention-deficit/hyperactivity disorder: the Multimodal Treatment Study of children with attention-deficit/hyperactivity disorder. *Arch Gen Psychiatry, 56*(12), 1088–1096.

Norquist, G. S., and Magruder, K. M. (1998). Views from funding agencies. National Institute of Mental Health. *Med Care, 36*(9), 1306–1308.

Porto, P. R., Oliveira, L., Mari, J., Volchan, E., Figueira, I., and Ventura, P. (2009). Does cognitive behavioral therapy change the brain? A systematic review of neuroimaging in anxiety disorders. *Journal of Neuropsychiatry and Clinical Neurosciences, 21*(2), 114.

POTS, S. T. (2004). Cognitive-behavior therapy, sertraline, and their combination for children and adolescents with obsessive-compulsive disorder: the Pediatric OCD Treatment Study (POTS) randomized controlled trial. *JAMA, 292*(16), 1969–1976.

Roy, A. K., Vasa, R. A., Bruck, M., Mogg, K., Bradley, B. P., Sweeney, M., et al. (2008). Attention bias toward threat in pediatric anxiety disorders. *Journal of the American Academy of Child and Adolescent Psychiatry, 47*(10), 1189–1196.

Scahill, L., Riddle, M. A., McSwiggin-Hardin, M., Ort, S. I., King, R. A., Goodman, W. K., et al. (1997). Children's Yale-Brown obsessive compulsive scale: reliability and validity. *Journal of the American Academy of Child and Adolescent Psychiatry, 36*(6), 844–852.

Silverman, W. K., and Kurtines, W. M. (1996). *Anxiety and phobic disorders: A pragmatic approach*: Springer US.

Straus, S. E., Glasziou, P., Richardson, W. S., and Hayes, S. C. (2010). *Evidence-Based Medicine: How to Practice and Teach It* (4th ed.). London: Churchill Livingstone.

Swanson, J. M., Kraemer, H. C., Hinshaw, S. P., Arnold, L. E., Conners, C. K., Abikoff, H. B., et al. (2001). Clinical relevance of the primary findings of the MTA: success rates based on severity of ADHD and ODD symptoms at the end of treatment. *Journal of the American Academy of Child and Adolescent Psychiatry, 40*(2), 168–179.

Thorpe, K. E., Zwarenstein, M., Oxman, A. D., Treweek, S., Furberg, C. D., Altman, D. G., et al. (2009). A pragmatic-explanatory continuum indicator summary (PRECIS): a tool to help trial designers. *Canadian Medical Association Journal*, cmaj. 090523v090521.

Walkup, J. T., Albano, A. M., Piacentini, J., Birmaher, B., Compton, S. N., Sherrill, J. T., et al. (2008). Cognitive behavioral therapy, sertraline, or a combination in childhood anxiety. *The New England journal of medicine, 359*(26), 2753.

Weisz, J. R. (2000). Agenda for child and adolescent psychotherapy research: on the need to put science into practice. *Arch Gen Psychiatry, 57*(9), 837–838.

Wells, K. C., Pelham, W. E., Kotkin, R. A., Hoza, B., Abikoff, H. B., Abramowitz, A., et al. (2000). Psychosocial treatment strategies in the MTA study: rationale, methods, and critical issues in design and implementation. *J Abnorm Child Psychol, 28*(6), 483–505.

12

Learning Disorders

Daniel Fung and Liying Su

INTRODUCTION

The concept of learning is an evolving one. Schools only started in the last one hundred years. Before that, learning was through oral history, careful observation and imitation of seniors in the community. An apprentice model for education is an advance aspect of such education. Human societies evolved through such careful observations and avid learners found it important to seek out masters (or mentors) whom they can learn from. The experiences of the current generation needed to be transmitted to the next in a systematic fashion. Initially, this was done in families and subsequently in groups of families or tribes. Stories, legends, folklore, rituals, and songs were used to transmit the knowledge well before writing was even used. Starting about 3500 BC, writings were developed in the ancient civilizations in the East and Middle East. Over time, learning became more organized and the need to teach the next generation became an obvious necessity of communal life. Initially, academic learning and the transmission of knowledge were in the purview of the wealthy and important. Education was not accessible to all but with modern industrialized societies, this is no longer the case. Universal education is one of the basic rights of children articulated by the United Nations (United Nations, 2011). In modern meritocratic societies, education was the means of social mobility and with that, a way for every young person to achieve his or her potential.

LEARNING IN FORMAL EDUCATION

Education is a process by which children learn and this learning can be in the form of instruction by a teacher or tutor (Gopinathan, 1997). There are many forms of instruction or teaching and these can occur through various learning modalities or senses that the child is endowed with, namely visual, auditory and kinesthetic. Based on these modalities, some forms of teaching may be more effective than others depending on the child's natural inclinations. This is in fact the orthographic representation of the word for learning in Chinese. The Chinese character for learning shows a pair of hands reaching down to a child to transmit knowledge or experience. Learning is thus affected by two obvious domains, the basic intelligence of a child, as well as the adequate development of transmitting this to the child. Intelligence is a natural ability affected by brain development but it also has an environmental aspect. The act of transmission of knowledge is through the development of language, a template for the transmission of knowledge, affected somewhat by the sensory modalities. Both underlying cognitive abilities are intertwined and are fundamental to learning.

The importance of learning as a basic right of every child also brings with it inherent problems as not every child is born with a similar ability to learn. Previously, a child in an agricultural society may not have the need to endure the rigors of formal education. Today, every child is expected to enter into a number of years of formal education. With this comes a certain expectation from families, schools and society that every child should be able to learn. Research spanning at least forty years has provided much evidence that there are children who, despite having an average intellectual ability and normal sensory functions, continue to struggle in learning (Siegal, 1989). This has led to the development of the concept of a learning difficulty. These problems come in many forms and have many names depending on who is describing them.

Often, these children suffering from these learning difficulties are misunderstood by parents and teachers who might assume that they are simply stupid or lazy. In some countries, learning disabilities have been legislated and families can receive substantial support from the government. In countries where learning disabilities are not legislated, there is now a growing awareness among educators and parents of the needs of this special group of children. There is an increasing awareness and willingness to support these children in their learning needs (Fletcher, Fuchs and Barnes, 2007).

MODELS OF UNDERSTANDING DISABILITY

Before we describe the concept of learning disorders or disabilities, it may be necessary to discuss what disability actually entails. There are a number of models that can be used to understand disability. The medical model which many clinicians subscribe to defines disability as an individual pathology and assumes a view that etiology is well understood (Chappell, Goodley, and Lawthom, 2001). Learning pathology is through a defined, often brain based fault that results in learning difficulties. Such a linear model provides the practitioner with a simplistic approach to managing the difficulties by employing an intervention that corrects the abnormality.

The medical model is considerably weakened when etiologies are unclear, causative factors interact and multiple factors are involved in single learning deficits. The traditional understanding of learning is that it is the result of a specific language based deficit in a particular region of the brain. However, our brains have multiple neuronal systems of which there are parallel systems that can come into play if one system is not working well. These neuronal networks can reconfigure in the developmental process and allow for different pathways to work better when one pathway is affected by disease or injury. This complexity, both at the molecular genetic level as well as in global brain destruction caused by unfortunate accidents, is the basis for the term brain plasticity. Moreover, according to the social model, disabilities are "a fundamentally social, cultural, political, historical, discursive and relational phenomenon" and the services and support provided by the society could also interact and contribute to the learning deficits (Goodley, 2001).

INTELLIGENCE AND ITS TESTING

Discrepancy between achievement and intelligence has traditionally been of critical consideration in the definition of learning disabilities (Siegel, 1989). As such, it is essential to understand the history and nature of intelligence testing, which forms the basis to the learning disorders diagnosis.

Testing of the differential abilities of children has a long history in the East. In China, at around 1000 BC, systematic and routine testing occurred in the Imperial examinations as a means to select civil servants and government officials. Examinations were the key to education and the Chinese meritocratic system—in which anyone from all walks of life has the opportunity to rise to prominence—provided a summative examination focused on measuring what was achieved rather than formative in helping a child identify strengths and weakness for improvement. These summative examinations covered a variety of disciplines from art to military strategy. The studies of that period included scholastic arts, music, arithmetic, writing, and knowledge of the rituals and ceremonies in both public and private life, as well as militaristic skills such as archery and horsemanship. Other topics included military strategy, civil law, revenue and taxation, agriculture and geography, and of course, the Confucian classics. The strict examination system, aimed at supervising and controlling ideology and learning, started with the Western Zhou Dynasty (1027–771 BC), was sustained until its greatest prominence in the Ming Dynasty (1368–1644) and continued to the end of the Qing Dynasty in 1911 (Han and Yang, 2001).

The western history of testing is relatively shorter; it only began in the 19th Century and was more focused on providing equity of support to differential abilities in school. These included the "Mental Tests" of Cattell (1890) and Binet and Simon's "Mental Age" (Binet, 1905) for placement in special schools. Mental age refers to an age-normed level of performance on an intelligence test, and it became a popular way of referring to "mental level" as measured by the Binet-Simon Scale of 1908. The Binet-Simon Scale identified the academic skills typical of specific age groups. The goal of these tests in general was to identify the child's weaknesses and provide pointers in developing educational interventions. Today's widely used intelligence scales such as the Wechsler Intelligence Scale for Children are drawn mostly from these western concepts. It measures four main areas: perceptual reasoning, verbal comprehension, working memory and processing speed. These four main areas measure two main domains of general intelligence—the innate novel problem-solving skills and crystallized intelligence—accumulated, experiential language abilities.

Intelligence as a whole is a much more complicated concept than what can be assessed and documented through intelligence tests. It is important to realise that even though a child scores poorly on an intelligence test, there may be many other skills in which he may be competent. What we do know is that people who score well on intelligence tests tend to perform well in school settings. This predictive ability is one of the reasons why intelligence testing is so popular and its measurement a flourishing industry.

LANGUAGE AND LANGUAGE DEVELOPMENT

It is also essential to recognize that the template for learning is language. The development of language lies in three sensory domains: visual, auditory and kinesthetic. Languages are articulated, visualized and written down. All languages can have two main components; one is the structural component while the other is the functional aspect. In structure, a language can be divided into (1) the sound system called phonology, (2) a system of rules for its use called grammar or syntax and (3) the many different ways of naming and identifying things called vocabulary or semantics. The second aspect of language is how the three systems of phonology, syntax and semantics add up into its daily usage in a socially acceptable way called pragmatics. All languages have these two components of structure and function, and emphasize different aspects depending on culture, development and history of the language. The development of language encompasses anthropology, history and cultural development. With the invention of the written form, language became more complex and in its complexity, it became more difficult to learn. Depending on a child's background, exposure and specific cognitive skills, language learning presents a challenge in a personal and individualized manner.

Every written form of a language also has characters (or orthography) that can be described in two dimensions; (1) transparency of print-to-sound translation and (2) the size of the smallest orthographic unit that represents sound (also called granularity) (Wydell and Butterworth, 1999). Some languages are very transparent in that one sound is represented by one character while others are opaque in that one character may represent several sounds.

Phonology is but one of many different areas of challenges a child faces in mastering a language. We use the word mastery, as language and its acquisition is not a single ability but a constantly developing one. Phonological awareness is like the key that unlocks the use of the language. Let us take the English and Chinese language as examples. In English, most words are made up of two parts, onset and rhyme, which are the most important aspects of phonological awareness. For example, the word BAT is made up of the first part "B," the onset and "AT," the rhyme. Because English is encoded only at the phoneme level, its mastery is simpler. Unfortunately, English has rather unique semantic rules that add to its complexity, making it a more opaque language. In Chinese, phonological awareness is required at both the syllabic and subsyllabic levels which have their own onset and rhyme. This increased complexity makes phonological deficits only one aspect of poor readers of Chinese as the characters contain both semantic and phonetic aspects, so visual discrimination may also be needed.

READING AND DYSLEXIA

Reading is made up of three main components. There is a speech or phonological process which is juxtaposed against the print or orthographic process. When these two work in harmony, a child is able to discern the printed word and translate it into speech. But this is only the decoding aspect of reading. Reading also consists of putting the words into sentences and sentences into paragraphs and derives contextualized meaning for the reader. When we say that a child cannot read, we must be clear whether we are referring to the decoding part of reading or the understanding part (deriving meaning from context). Often this is not so easy to tease out and a connectionist model considers reading a series of learning and processing that are adjustable and interrelated. It assumes that the neural networks interact and adjusts the connections as a child learns (Foorman, 1994).

As early as 1877, Adolf Kussmaul described word blindness in an adult alexic patient with a parietal lobe lesion. James Hinshelwood, a Scottish ophthalmologist, studied and described an adult with word blindness in 1895 and an autopsy of this patient revealed abnormalities in the left angular gyrus immediately posterior to Wernicke's area. Pringle Morgan, an English general practitioner, published in 1896 the first case of a 14-year-old child with congenital word blindness who could not read but was in every other aspect like a normal youth. Rudolf Berlin, another ophthalmologist from Germany, coined the term "dyslexia." Hinshelwood was the first to characterize dyslexia, which he believed to be genetically transmitted and was associated with deficits in the visual memory for words and letters. He strongly advocated intensive, individualized personal instruction. Later this concept was expanded by Samuel Torrey Orton, an American neuropsychiatrist. Orton attributed dyslexia to a visual system dysfunction from "mixed cerebral dominance" which affects visual perception and memory and results in the reversal of words commonly seen in such children. Orton along with Anna Gillingham, an American educational psychologist, developed a multisensory language based training programme that transformed the educational intervention in children with learning disorders.

Dyslexia therefore refers to a disorder of reading. As we have described, reading has phonological, orthographic and contextualization aspects. Problems in any of those three areas can result in dyslexia. For many, phonological dyslexia is the most commonly described and studied but orthographic dyslexia (often called visual or surface dyslexia) may be understudied and less well known. This is largely due to the fact that research has been largely focused on European languages and less has been done in the Asian languages where orthographic elements are more prominent. The theories surrounding reading disorders are also not complete. Some argue that dyslexia is an either/or concept: a child can either have phonological dyslexia or the child may have orthographic dyslexia since both processes are distinct (Dual route model) (Foorman, 1994). A more integrated model (connectionist model) considers that all the various aspects, phonological, orthographic and contextualization are interlinked and contribute to the reading process which is disrupted when one aspect is problematic. This model is more attractive and has greater biophysiological basis in imaging studies that have emerged in the field (Pennington, 2009).

Reading fluency is a critical feature of reading acquisition. Fluency means the ability to read a passage effortlessly and is linked to the fundamental decoding process. Poor fluency is a key feature of dyslexia in adulthood; also poor fluency is a key feature of dyslexia in languages other than English (Bashir and Hook, 2009). Poor reading comprehension, on the other hand, often occurs in non-dyslexic children who have poor oral language development.

Wydell and Butterworth's (1999) concept of granularity and transparency can be used to predict the incidence of phonological dyslexia in different languages. Orthographies with fine granularity and opaque print-to-sound translation (e.g., English, Danish) would have a higher incidence of phonological dyslexia. In contrast, orthographies with coarse granularity (e.g., Japanese Kanji and Chinese) or transparent print-to-sound translation (e.g., Italian, Spanish) would have a low incidence of phonological dyslexia. This is generally supported in research.

DEFINITIONS OF LEARNING DISORDER

Reading disorders and dyslexia are but a subset of an even larger group of sometimes ill-defined problems associated with learning. There is no clear and widely accepted definition for a learning difficulty much like the well-known Asian fable of the blind men and the elephant (Saxe, 1873); in this story a group of blind men touch an elephant to learn what it is like, but each one feels a different part and when they compare notes they find that they are in complete disagreement. Not one definition gives a complete picture of this difficult issue. There are at least eleven definitions in the professional literature (Hammil, 1990) spanning both the educational and medical fields. For the sake of simplicity, we shall use the term learning disorder to describe the learning difficulties examined below.

The National Joint Committee on Learning Disabilities (NJCLD) gives a fairly wide-ranging definition stating that "learning disabilities" is a general term that refers to a heterogeneous group of disorders manifested by significant difficulties in the acquisition and use of listening, speaking, reading, writing, reasoning, or mathematical skills. These disorders are intrinsic to the individual, presumed to be due to central nervous system dysfunction, and may occur across the life span. Problems in self-regulatory behaviors, social perception, and social interaction may exist with learning disabilities but do not, by themselves, constitute a learning disability. Although learning disabilities may occur concomitantly with other disabilities (e.g., sensory impairment, mental retardation, serious emotional disturbance), or with extrinsic influences (such as cultural differences, insufficient or inappropriate instruction), they are not the result of those conditions or influences (NJCLD, 1990).

This wide-ranging definition is a good way to start in our understanding of learning disorders. In fact, it is anchored in five main constructs:

1. Learning disorders are heterogeneous, meaning that they are a mix of different difficulties that are both individualized and socioculturally affected.

2. Learning disorders result in significant difficulties in the acquisition and use of academic skills that are needed in school.
3. Learning disorders are intrinsic to the child and are related to brain developmental abnormalities.
4. Learning disorders may occur concomitantly with other disabilities that do not, by themselves, constitute a learning disorder.
5. Learning disorders are not caused by extrinsic educational influences such as inconsistent or insufficient instruction or a lack of instructional experience.

LEARNING DISORDERS AND MENTAL HEALTH DISORDERS

The traditional definition of a mental health disorder is that of a clinically significant behavioral or psychological syndrome or pattern that occurs in an individual. It should be associated with current distress or disability or have a significantly increased risk of suffering (Wakefield, 1997). However, this broad based definition does not take into account the multidisciplinary nature of the field. Children with learning disorders often see different professionals including mental health professionals, school and educational professionals, speech and language pathologists, and school psychologists as well as pediatricians specializing in developmental and neurological conditions.

Learning disorders is a term found in the American Psychiatric Association's Diagnostic Statistical Manual. The World Health Organization's International Classification of Diseases uses the umbrella term of disorders of psychological development, of which those of scholastic skills are a subcategory. Psychiatrists and other mental health professionals have described learning disorders as the most common of the psychiatric and developmental disorders that a clinician is likely to encounter (AACAP, 1998). Prevalence studies vary widely in determining the rate of learning disorders and can range from 2 percent to 20 percent depending on the diagnostic criteria and tests used. Some researchers have argued against the currently recognized 5 percent prevalence rate (Lyon, 1996) with estimates of 8–15 percent prevalence rates in the school population. Based on what we understand by the domains of intelligence and language acquisition as well as the three aspects of learning, it would be obvious to suggest that academic skills like reading, writing and arithmetic would be on a continuum rather than distinct entities. Interestingly, both the DSM and ICD use a categorical system to deal with learning disorders.

Both major psychiatric classification systems use the IQ achievement discrepancy to identify and diagnose learning disorders. By this we mean that a child is first given an IQ assessment using a standardized IQ test (assuming one is available in the community in which the child lives) and then followed up with an assessment of academic function in the domains of reading, mathematics and writing. The degree of discrepancy is thus used as the basis for a diagnosis.

Why then should mental health professionals be interested in learning disorders? Since learning disorders manifest themselves mainly in a school setting, it would make sense that it should be in the domain of educationists. The reasons why mental health professionals should be interested are several:

1. Mental health disorders can contribute to learning disorders. A common example is a child who misses school as a result of mental health disorders during critical developmental phases of learning may have difficulties acquiring the relevant vocabulary and the experiences of practice.
2. Learning disorders can lead to mental health disorders because children who do not succeed in school are less resilient, experience less success, become targets of bullying and have resultant stress and frustration. (Willcutt and Pennington, 2000; Miguel, Forness and Kavale, 1996).
3. There may be similar etiological factors for learning disorders and mental health disorders. An example is in schizophrenia in which premorbid non-verbal intellectual functioning appears to confer significant risk (Reichenberg et al., 2006).

PROBLEMS WITH CURRENT DEFINITIONS

A classical description of a reading disorder implies that it is a universal condition. It is dependent only on the ability to read and its discrepancy from expected abilities based on a test of cognitive function. However, recent research seems to indicate otherwise. First, tests of cognitive functions are limited to the context in which they are administered. These tests are dependent on the language in which it is administered, since languages differ greatly in terms of transparency and granularity. Secondly, cognitive abilities are variable across a range of functions and there is no universal understanding of an absolute intelligence. Intelligence tests are designed to do what they were designed to do. So if an IQ test is used to identify intellectual disabilities for special education, this is mostly what it is measuring. This is in stark contrast to a test that measures high abilities.

The achievement ability discrepancy model is thus inherently flawed and yet it is the basis of a diagnosis of a learning disorder in our traditional classification systems. In fact, there is little evidence to support the notion that a learning disorder must have substantial discrepancy between achievement and intellectual ability (Vellutino, Scanlon, and Lyon, 2000).

Nevertheless, our current systems of IQ and academic tests largely developed for Western populations are still useful for identifying and monitoring skills and skills deficits. It is the conceptualization of learning disorders that should be adjusted. By this we mean that testing should be used as means of identifying and continuing to monitor a child's progress and intervention. The diagnosis of learning disorder should not be cross sectional but a longitudinal one. Mental health professionals can find this quite comforting since it means that a child is not labeled for life once a diagnosis of learning disorder is made. They can improve. This is a more educational approach best exemplified in educational circles by the concept of Response to Intervention (RTI). Indeed, there is also basic science research that suggests this both in connectionist neural network theories as well as in functional imaging studies showing brain plasticity (Mangina and Beuzeron-Mangina, 2004; Kolb, Gibb, Robinson, 2003). The child's developing brain is a constantly changing one, not only with respect to its inherent genetic potential but also its response to the environment that is presented. This environmental influence can not only improve brain function, it may actually change the way the genes are expressed and therefore influence the final outcome (Walter, 2000; Isle and Humby, 2006).

CLASSIFICATION SYSTEMS AND FUTURE DIRECTIONS

The DSM-V, slated to be released in the summer of 2012, has proposed dramatic changes to categories of learning disorders. In fact, where previously there were no general criteria for learning disorders, it now stands as a category distinct from intellectual disabilities, which became the standalone category of Intellectual Developmental Disorder (with the removal of the term Mental Retardation). DSM-V is proposing that learning disorders interfere with the acquisition and use of one or more of the following academic skills: oral language, reading, written language, mathematics. These disorders will affect individuals who otherwise demonstrate at least average abilities essential for thinking or reasoning. The most significant change is that the diagnostic criteria will not depend upon overall IQ and achievement discrepancy. This is consistent with the change in the U.S. reauthorized IDEA regulations of 2004. Interestingly, dyslexia may be reinstated as a diagnostic category instead of reading disorder to match international use of the term and the new IDEA regulations. The relative importance of reading fluency compared to reading comprehension is emphasized in the new definitions.

Similarly, the ICD 11 is under consideration although a fixed date for its release has not been put forward as yet.

TREATMENT

Learning disorders could co-occur with other disorders such as Attention Deficit Hyperactivity Disorder (ADHD), emotional disorders and other mental health disorders. Intervention programmes are available to cater for the learning and social-emotional needs of these children. However, these programmes will not be effective without the collaboration of parents. When a child has been identified to have a learning disorder, it can be a period of great stress for the family. Parents often blame themselves or worse, deny that there is a problem leading to questioning the clinician's diagnosis in the first place. Clinicians must help families to stay positive and not give up on the child, and help families understand the child better and empathise with the difficulties that he or she is experiencing. Parent support groups are useful in this respect.

The challenge for the parent is to help their child overcome the psychological barriers that make learning a frustrating and traumatic experience. The first step is to give the child a sense of assurance that he is accepted and loved in spite of his poor achievement at school. The child needs to know that there are people who will journey or go along with him or her. Parents are key to creating a bond built on trust so that a child can derive a sense of "I am able—not disabled."

It is useful to have a framework for describing what to do once a child is identified (and we would rather use this term than "diagnosed") with a learning disorder. Such a framework should include a universally good general education system for all children which also identifies children with difficulties early. Such children should be streamed to appropriate classes for targeted small group interventions. A continuous educational assessment will also be in place such that the very weakest of such students should then receive intensive individual training.

The learning disorder framework should consist of the following evidence-based approaches:

- Highly structured training either in groups or individually.
- Skills based training, e.g., Phonics based approaches for reading disorders.
- School or community based teacher interventions in which teachers are given the teaching skills for helping such children.

- Work on interventions for other problems, e.g., Parent training for conduct, medications for ADHD and cognitive behavior therapy for emotional problems.
- Support and advocacy groups for parents and family.
- Appropriate accommodations such as time extensions during examinations.

Medications are not useful directly unless there is concomitant attention deficit hyperactivity disorder or ADHD. Even in such situations, stimulant or non stimulant medications tend to improve behavior rather than improve learning.

Taking a population based model, the treatment of learning disorders is probably best approached in a non-clinical setting. By labeling learning difficulties as a disorder and stigmatizing the child's development this can become a self-fulfilling prophecy. It is possible to identify children with learning difficulties early and since compulsory education is a modern phenomenon, it may be useful to screen them at school entry. Instead of just labeling the child as having a learning disorder, systematic interventions can be administered in appropriate doses. This assumes that at the very base is a universal quality educational system that provides good and individualized training, as well as specific small group interventions for children with specific weaknesses identified early. For the child with severe learning deficits, highly intensive individualized training can then be made available focusing not only on weaknesses but also on identifying potential strengths. By basing such a system in the school system but with support from mental health professionals, it would also remove the potential stigma that prevents children from receiving help early. Such a system would require mental health and educational services along with social service agencies to work together in a collaborative fashion resulting in a multi-sectoral, multidisciplinary team.

CONTROVERSIAL TREATMENTS

It is important for clinicians to consider the controversial treatments that are prevalent in the marketplace. Just as learning disorders are multidisciplinary in nature, and not limited to the medical field, medical regulatory bodies have little, if any, say in what is available to the consumer. The areas of educational interventions are varied and we would like to propose a simple approach for unsubstantiated treatments:

1. The theoretical basis for the treatment should be rationally considered. For example, it's unlikely that correcting visual defects will

significantly improve reading disorders if the cause of the reading disorder is a phonological decoding problem.

2. Promise of "cure" or "recovery" is an unlikely outcome for a developmental disorder. Any treatment purporting to do so must therefore be treated with skepticism.

3. Evaluate the scientific evidence of any novel treatment. Any treatment worth its salt should have been subjected to the gold standard of scientific evaluation, namely the randomized controlled trial. Even one such trial would suggest the possibility of at least considering the treatment as potentially effective or efficacious.

4. The objectivity of the proponent of the treatment should be evaluated. If the evidence for the treatment is based on personal case histories, case series and testimonials without a more unbiased account, one must suspect the veracity of this treatment. Be skeptical if the advocates of the treatment are unwilling to concede to criticism. Any treatment should only represent one of several options for the child. Any treatment should be individualized after assessment.

Current scientific evidence does not support the claims that visual training, muscle exercises, ocular pursuit-and-tracking exercises, behavioral/perceptual vision therapy, "training" glasses, prisms, and colored lenses and filters are effective direct or indirect treatments for learning disorders. There is no valid evidence that children who participate in vision therapy are more responsive to educational instruction than children who do not participate (Handler and Fierson, 2011).

PROGNOSIS AND OUTCOMES

The long term prognosis of learning disorders has been tracked in a number of longitudinal studies (Shaywitz et al.,1999; Maughan et al., 2009) which show two possible outcomes. Some poor readers when young could improve with time and compensate for their difficulties. Some others will stay persistently poor readers. An interesting study comparing normal readers with those that improve and those that stay persistently poor (Shaywitz et al., 2003) suggest that those who have learned compensatory mechanisms operate their brains differently. These findings suggest that children can learn compensatory techniques and there is a possibility of specifically training them. Such training needs to be investigated in the light of new functional imaging technology. With an RTI (Response to Intervention) approach in defining disorders within a dimensional rather than a categorical rubric, we will hopefully be able to help poor readers become reasonable ones who will be able to cope with the academic demands of our knowledge based economies. Such approaches should have universal appeal by being culturally relevant for all societies and in all languages.

REFERENCES

AACAP. (1998). Practice parameters for the assessment and treatment of children and adolescents with language and learning disorders. *Journal of American Child and Adolescent Psychiatry*, 37, 46S–62S.

Bashir, A. S., and Hook, P. E. (2009). Fluency: A key link between word identification and comprehension. *Language, Speech and Hearing Services in Schools*, 40, 196–200.

Binet, A. (1905). New methods for the diagnosis of the intellectual level of subnormals. *L'Année Psychologique*, 12, 191–244.

Cattell, J. M. K. (1890). V.–Mental tests and measurements. *Mind*, 15, 373–381.

Chappell, A. L., Goodley, D., and Lawthom, R. (2001). Making connections: the relevance of the social model of disability for people with learning difficulties. *British Journal of Learning Disabilities*, 29, 45–50.

Fletcher, J. M., Fuchs, L. S., and Barnes, M. A. (2007). *Learning Disabilities: From Identification to Intervention*. New York: The Guilford Press.

Foorman, B. R. (1994). The relevance of a connectionist model of reading for "The Great Debate." *Educational Psychology Review*, 6, 25–47.

Goodley, D.A. (2001). 'Learning Difficulties' the social model of disability and impairment: challenging epistemologies. *Disability and Society*, 16(2), 207–231.

Gopinathan, S. (1997). Education and development in Singapore. In Tan, J., Gopinathan, S., and Ho, W. K. (Eds.), *Education in Singapore: a book of readings* (pp. 33–54). Singapore: Prentice-Hall.

Hammil, D. D. (1990). On defining learning disabilities: An emerging consensus. *Journal of Learning Disabilities*, 23, 74–84.

Han, M., and Yang, X. (2001). Educational assessment in China: Lessons from history and future prospects. *Assessment in Education*, 8, 5–10.

Handler, S. M., and Fierson, W. M. (2011). Learning disabilities, dyslexia, and vision. *Pediatrics*, 127, 818–856.

Isle, A. R., and Humby, T. (2006). Modes of imprinted gene action in learning disability. *Journal of Intellectual Disability Research*, 50, 318–325.

Kolb, B., Gibb, R., and Robinson, T. E. (2003). Brain plasticity and behaviour. *Current Directions in Psychological Science*, 12, 1–5.

Lyon, G. R. (1996). Learning disabilities. *The Future of Children*, 6, 54–76.

Mangina, C. A., and Beuzeron-Mangina, J. H. (2004). Brain plasticity following psychophysiological treatment in learning disabled/ADHD pre-adolescents. *International Journal of Psychophysiology*, 52, 129–146.

Maughan, B., Messer, J., Collishaw, S., Pickles, A., Snowling, M., Yule, W., and Rutter, M. (2009). Persistence of literacy problems: spelling in adolescence and at mid-life. *Journal of Child Psychology and Psychiatry*, 50, 893–901.

Miguel, S. K. S., Forness S. R., and Kavale, K. A. (1996). Social skills deficits in learning disabilities: The psychiatric comorbidity hypothesis. *Learning Disability Quarterly*, 19, 252–261.

National Joint Committee on Learning Disabilities (NJCLD). (1990). Learning disabilities: Issues on definition. In: National Joint Committee n Learning Disabilities (1994). *Collective perspectives on issues affecting learning disabilities: Position papers and statements* (pp. 61–66). Austin, Texas: Pro-Ed.

Pennington, B. F. (2009). *Diagnosing Learning Disorders: A neuropsychological framework* (Second Edition). New York: The Guilford Press.

Reichenberg, A., Weiser, M., Caspi, A., Knobler, H. Y., Lubin, G., Harvey, P. D., Rabinowitz, J., and Davidson, M. (2006). Premorbid intellectual functioning and risk of schizophrenia and spectrum disorders. *Journal of Clinical and Experimental Neuropsychology*, 28, 193–207.

Saxe, J. G. (1873). The Blind Men and the Elephant. In: *The poems of John Godfrey Saxe, Complete edition* (pp. 77–78). Boston: James R. Osgood and Company.

Shaywitz, S. E., Fletcher, J. M., Holahan, J. M., Shneider, A. E., Marchione, K. E., Stuebing, K. K., Francis, D. J., Pugh, K. R., and Shaywitz, B. A. (1999). Persistence of dyslexia: The Connecticut longitudinal study at adolescence. *Pediatrics*, 104, 1351–1359.

Shaywitz, S. E., Shaywitz, B. A., Fulbright, R. K., Skudlarski, P., Mencl, W. E., Constable, R. T., Pugh, K. R., Holahan, J. M., Marchione, K. E., Fletcher, J. M., Lyon, G. R., and Gore, J. C. (2003). Neural systems for compensation and persistence: Young adult outcome of childhood reading disability. *Biological Psychiatry*, 54, 25–33.

Siegel, L. S. (1989). IQ is irrelevant to the definition of learning disabilities. *Journal of Learning Disabilities*, 22, 469–478.

United Nations. (2011). *Universal declaration of human rights*. Retrieved 20 June 2011, from http://www.un.org/en/documents/udhr/index.shtml.

Vellutino, F. R., Scanlon, D. M., and Lyon, G. R. (2000). Differentiating between difficult-to-remediate and readily remediated poor readers: More evidence against the IQ-achievement discrepancy definition of reading disability. *Journal of Learning Disabilities*, 33, 223–238.

Wakefield, J. C. (1997). Diagnosing DSM-IV–Part 1: DSM-IV and the concept of disorder. *Behaviour Research and Therapy*, 35, 633–649.

Walter, J. M. (2000). Genetic advances and learning disability. *British Journal of Psychiatry*, 176, 12–18.

Willcutt, E. G., and Pennington, B. F. (2000). Psychiatric comorbidity in children and adolescents with reading disability. *Journal of Child Psychology and Psychiatry*, 41, 1039–1048.

Wydell, T. N., and Butterworth, B. (1999). A case study of an English-Japanese bilingual with monolingual dyslexia. *Cognition*, 70, 273–305.

13

Advocacy for Child and Adolescent Mental Health

Gordon Harper

Throughout human history the young have been protected and nurtured by parents, the extended family, and neighbourhoods—a trait shared with other primates, indeed with other mammals. Aside from orphanages and the poorhouse, children had little protection outside of these "natural" supports. But in the last two centuries a new form of protection for children has arisen, outside the natural communities, in the form of *advocacy*. Especially in the West, the types of advocacy and the numbers of advocacy organizations have greatly increased and their areas of interest have diverged. "Child advocacy" no longer has a single meaning.

Child advocacy is one of those humanizing movements that have allowed adults to *see* and *act* on behalf of those, often invisible though in plain sight, who are unable to advocate for themselves. Among those movements, advocacy for child *mental health* speaks for those disadvantaged not just by age but by mental or emotional challenges as well. As such, advocacy always pushes professionals to think of *all* children at risk, not just those currently being seen. The improvements in children's lives attributable to such advocacy stand out as a major achievement of the modern age.

This chapter reviews the development and current status of advocacy for child and adolescent mental health (CAMH). The chapter is in three parts: *The Origins of Advocacy*, *Advocacy in the 20th Century*, and *Emerging Trends in Advocacy*.

THE ORIGINS OF CHILD ADVOCACY

In the last two hundred years, several factors led to the emergence of organized advocacy for children. These included:

- Recognition of *childhood as a distinct phase* of life with special needs (Aries 1962);
- Increased *knowledge* of child development, of the particular needs of children, and of the long-term consequences of adversity in early life;
- Increased *hardship* for many children and families associated with urbanization and industrialization;
- Increased awareness of such conditions, leading to a new sense of *public responsibility* for children, defining "our children" more inclusively;
- The emergence of *individuals* with knowledge about children's needs and the time and resources for advocacy.

Advocacy drew on the Enlightenment's belief in man's inherent good, on the political endorsement of universal rights in the French and American Revolutions, and on the insistence by the Romantics, especially Rousseau, that the established order stifled the human spirit. In the United States and Europe, starting in the early nineteenth century, new kinds of schools were established aiming to foster the development of the child as a whole person. In mid-century, some U.S. states and some European countries began to institute universal public education (Mondale 2001)

Such initiatives followed other movements on behalf of the powerless, notably those against slavery in Britain and the United States. In addition, many nineteenth-century Europeans believed that improving living conditions and the health of the poor was part of the fight for social and economic justice; as Virchow (1847) wrote, "the physician [is] the natural advocate for the poor."

Recognition of physical victimization led to the child protection movement. The public became aware of child abuse through highly publicized cases, like one in New York City in the 1870s that led to the founding of Societies for the Prevention of Cruelty to Children, then to laws outlawing physical maltreatment (Markel 2009). Child advocacy, for many, became equated with the fight against child abuse. Indeed, "child advocacy" is often used specifically for efforts on behalf of the abused (cf National Children's Advocacy Center).

The child protection movement extended society's oversight of the child into the home, the previously unchallenged domain of parents. Legal affirmation of children's rights followed legal recognition of their personhood, as happened also with slaves, women, and the disabled. Indigenous children are at particular disadvantage (Woolley 2009). The history of these developments in the the United States can be seen as a "timeline of children's rights" (2011.) The UN Convention on the Rights of the Child, adopted in 1989, extends these ideas worldwide. It has been ratified nearly universally. Non-ratifying countries include Somalia and, paradoxically in view of the establishment of children's rights in U.S. law, the United States.

Special education rights for all children in the United States. were established by federal law in several stages leading to the Individuals with Disabilities Education Act (IDEA) in 2004 (http://idea.ed.gov/). The law ensures services to children with disabilities through early intervention, special education and related services. It requires those responsible for education—in the U.S., the local towns and cities—to provide these services. This legislation created an entitlement and a new class of advocates ("educational advocates") to help children obtain the services. It perpetuated divided responsibility for children's services, which for many children are split between healthcare, special education, and child welfare, and necessitated the provision of adjudication to help settle disputes—between parents and town, between different agencies.

The first modern programs for children's *emotional and behaviour problems* came from what is now called youth corrections, in the form of "training" or "reform" schools for delinquent youth. Somewhat later, the first clinics for troubled children grew out of juvenile courts newly established in Australia, Europe, and the United States. Judges, recognizing that these "wayward youths" (Aichhorn 1951) needed to be treated as developing children, became early advocates for child mental health services. (Centers whose names recall those origins include the Institute for Juvenile Research in Chicago and the Judge Baker Center in Boston.) Along with support from youth courts, child advocacy drew on the developing field of social welfare, committed to document and attend to the needs of the underprivileged (Richmond 1995).

The development of mental health services for troubled children required shifts in how children were seen, specifically, recognition

- that children have emotional lives and that there is more to education than rote memorization (cf Rousseau, *Émile*; on Pestalozzi, see Silber (1960));
- that children vary in endowment and development;
- that they can suffer both immediate and long-term consequences if they don't get understanding and special help.

These new attitudes reflected a break with traditional responses to troubled children, including *non-recognition* (as in, "but you were happy yesterday"), *dismissal* ("just get over it"), *volitionalizing* ("can do it when he wants to"), *blaming* ("just doing it to get attention"), and *parent-blaming*.

With these changes in attitude and with new theories of how children develop, new services—instructional, behavioural, psychological, family-based, pharmacological—were developed. The emergence of those services led to advocacy for the *services themselves*, as if expanded services alone could be a proxy for improved child outcomes. In many countries today, disorder-specific and treatment-specific advocacy organizations flourish, calling, depending on the time and place, for more child guidance, applied behavioural analysis, the latest medication, or wraparound services. As a result, discussions of child advocacy must distinguish between:

- advocacy for child welfare in general
- advocacy for child mental health
- advocacy for specific child mental health treatments

Advocacy through literature also helped transform public attitudes to children. In the nineteenth century, public support for reform drew on portrayals by Dickens and the Brontës of children in hostile foster homes, proprietary orphanages, and workhouses. Those authors and their successors, like Stowe, Twain, Woolf, and Salinger, put a human face on children's suffering. Literary portrayals of children in the twentieth century have given voice to minority children (cf Richard Wright, *Native Son*; Toni Morrison, *The Bluest Eye*) and attempted, sometimes autobiographically, to represent the world as experienced by a severely disturbed child (Green, aka Greenberg, *I Never Promised You a Rose Garden*; Haddon, *The Curious Incident of the Dog in the Night-Time*). The record of modern media, especially motion pictures, in representing children's mental health treatment, has been mixed (Butler and Hyler 2005).

In *Children of Crisis*, Coles (1967, 1971a, 1971b, 1977a, 1977b) created a new form of advocacy, bridging qualitative epidemiology and literature, by living with, learning from, and giving voice to children facing historical and socioeconomic challenges.

ADVOCACY IN THE TWENTIETH CENTURY

The Many Forms of Advocacy

Just as the conditions in which children live and grow vary enormously around the world (UNICEF 2011), so the kinds of advocacy vary as well.

All organizations devoted to mental health identify advocacy as one of their aims. Such organizations include:

- national organizations (in the United States, the National Alliance on Mental Illness [NAMI]);

- international organizations (like the International Association of Child and Adolescent Psychiatry and Allied Professions [IACAPAP] and the World Federation for Mental Health);
- organizations of affected individuals and their family members (like the National Federation of Families for Children's Mental Health);
- those representing a specific profession (like the American Academy of Child and Adolescent Psychiatry [AACAP]); and
- those organized around a specific disorder or disease (like CHADD [Children and Adults with Attention Deficit/Hyperactivity Disorder]; The Child and Adolescent Bipolar Foundation; Asperger's Association of New England).

The aims of such organizations include:

- public education including efforts to decrease stigma;
- increased access to existing care; and
- appeals to insurers, legislators and administrators for more care.

The range of activities is well represented, for example, on the website of Young Minds in the UK (http://www.youngminds.org.uk). In the US, Ptakowski (2010) has described political advocacy from the point of view of the American Academy of Child and Adolescent Psychiatry (AACAP).

Institutionalized "Child Advocates"

"Child Advocates" in U.S. Community Mental Health

A new kind of "child advocate" was created in the United States in the 1960s and 1970s (Belfer 1976). The federal community mental health program called for new positions, called child advocates, to be filled by individuals without professional training from the community. These child advocates were to problem solve on behalf of individual children and families and help in program development through participation on the project board. This strategy reflected the theory that empowering members of the community served would help to make entrenched, professionally dominated services more client/patient-friendly.

While these programs did not outlive the political activism of the 1960s and early 1970s, child advocates of various backgrounds, including those self-styled advocates, continue to enter a crowded (and sometimes, confusing) field.

Offices of Child Advocate

A majority of U.S. states have created, by statute, an Office of a Child Advocate, charged with overseeing state efforts on behalf of children. These child advocates report either to the executive or to the legislature. The child advocate's role in state government is similar to that of the ombudsman in other organizations. Depending on the enabling legislation, the role may include responding to reported grievances and independently investigating state practice (Michigan Office of Children's Ombudsman, no date).

Advocacy and Civil Society

Where advocacy for child mental health gets located in each country depends on the degree to which civil society is developed, regardless of the level of economic development.

For instance, Singapore is highly developed in terms of income, education, sophistication of human services, and children's services. But voluntary organizations are much less developed than in the West. Some NGOs provide direct child and adolescent mental health services, but advocacy for developing more services occurs within the government departments themselves, not in outside agencies.

At the other extreme is the United States with *dozens* of nongovernmental organizations vying to advocate for mental health, including child mental health. These draw on the American history of advocacy for the disadvantaged (and on Americans' proclivity for forming associations). Those crowding into the tent of advocacy include public-spirited humanitarians, affected individuals and their family members, specialist professionals, and companies who sell products. The line between advocacy and advertising needs to be carefully drawn.

The UK occupies a middle position. While there are many advocacy organizations devoted to one disorder or another, one charity, Young Minds, predominates in advocacy for child mental health. It is supported by CAMH professionals, government agencies and lay public members. Activities include public education, organizing research, and preventive measures such as support for community parenting. Efforts to educate the public have included offering book prizes on issues related to CAMH.

When to Start Advocacy for Child Mental Health?

Many have argued that development of social and health supports, including child mental health, should not wait for a country to reach a certain level of economic prosperity. This argument has been made in contexts as diverse as Finland after World War II (Taipale 2011) and Brazil, looking back on the decades since the end of the military dictatorship (Paim et al.

2011, Victora et al. 2011). A similar spirit lies behind the World Health Organization's "mental health Gap Action Programme" (mhGAP). Omigbodun (2008), in reviewing mental health needs in the developing world, contrasts progress being made in reducing infant mortality with the need for action on behalf of mental health.

Once Established, Set Forever?

Gains in health and social policy are always subject to the vicissitudes of budget and the political process (Bogira 2009). For instance, in the United States, the federal Children's Bureau established early in the twentieth century helped individual states expand services for children, but was discontinued in 1946. The community mental health centers law started in 1963 was repealed in 1981 (Richmond and Eisenberg 1991). In Massachusetts, an Office for Children was established (Massachusetts State Office for Children no date), but in subsequent administrations its funding was gradually reduced, its functions dispersed, and the office terminated. On a larger scale, in Russia and China in the 1990s, the expansion of a market economy was accompanied by a reduction in accessible and affordable health services and deterioration in health status (on China, see Leonhardt 2010). Worldwide, an achievement of child advocacy, provision for separate judicial proceedings for defendants under eighteen, has been curtailed in many jurisdictions, usually in response to public outrage after a particularly egregious crime by a juvenile.

The great opportunity for CAMH professionals, as budgetary pressures and changing political tides move public policy to one side or the other, is to consistently ask about *outcomes* and *effectiveness*. The key questions are: What are we trying to achieve? How will we know whether we are getting there? Despite early calls for scientifically valid evaluations of service innovations (Hoagwood et al. 1996), progress has been slow (Zima and Mangione-Smith 2011).

One model of looking at outcomes, admirably simple, is the Triple Aim (health outcomes, consumer experience, costs per member) developed at the Institute for Healthcare Improvement in the United States (2011). Those who conceived of the Triple Aim recognized that structural fragmentation of services among different agencies in the public and private sectors, each with its separate responsibility (and separate data), make it hard to plan and develop in the coordinated way necessary for the Triple Aim. CAMH professionals, caring for children, need coordination among mental health, child protective, and educational services. They will recognize this challenge.

Another challenge encountered by advocates for CAMH, as in other fields, is the relative ease of gathering data on some variables—like participation and satisfaction—compared to others, like functional status over time. Those advocating expanded services, to be evaluated by such measures, must respond to the challenge from the Fort Bragg study, two decades ago, in which expanded services (of various kinds) resulted in greater parent satisfaction but no overall cost savings and no better health outcomes for the children (Bickman 1996).

Advocates will find it useful to keep in mind that desirable processes—like higher participation rates and better parent engagement—are meant to improve the other outcomes in the Triple Aim—health outcomes and costs per member. A logic model shows the relationship between the problem to be addressed, how it is measured, the goal sought, and how it is measured, the factors thought to contribute and the interventions chosen (see Figure 13.1, Logic Model).

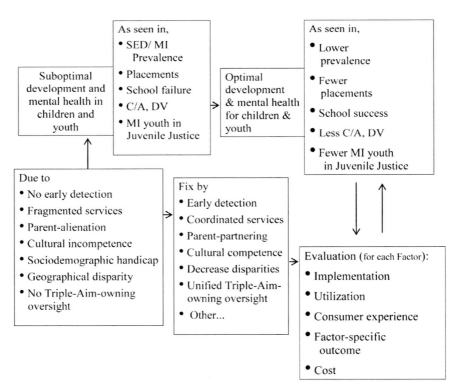

Figure 13.1.   Can we use a logic model in children's mental health?

Asking such questions is especially important because of the various aims, related but not equivalent, sought by advocates: increasing services, educating the public, reducing stigma.

Evaluation research, traditionally focused on clinical or functional outcomes, is being extended now by *economists*, analyzing the economic benefits of interventions—which favour interventions earlier in the child's life (Heckman 2008, Zechmeister et al. 2008).

Advocacy and Diversity

The divergent interests in modern societies confront each other in CAMH advocacy. Those advocating for children can expect to encounter these issues, such as:

- the rights of children vis-à-vis their parents;
- the protection of minority rights, whether based on ethnicity, sexual orientation, or gender identity;
- the right of youths accused of offenses to be tried as juveniles;
- pharmacological vs non-phamacological approaches to mental illness;
- the relationship of collaborative to coercive care; and
- the extent to which care should be driven by professionals, by patients or parents, or in collaboration.

EMERGING TRENDS IN CHILD MENTAL HEALTH ADVOCACY

CAMH advocacy in the twenty-first century is taking on new forms, all with the aim of improving children's lives. They can be grouped in categories suggested in a model of policy development (Richmond and Kotelchuk 1983) that emphasized the *interaction* among knowledge base, social, and political will.

New Knowledge

For much of the last two centuries, informal knowledge of children's condition, coupled with humanitarian impulses, sufficed to motivate advocacy. In the last fifty years, the development of epidemiology as a science (Verhulst and Koot 1992; Costello et al. 2005; Costello et al. 2006) has made it possible to replace impressions of prevalence with data, including the burden on children world-wide (Belfer 2008).

Public agencies have taken an expanded role in assembling, reviewing and disseminating new knowledge, as in publications from the United

States. These include reports on the importance of mental health in general health (Surgeon General's Report on Mental Health, 1999); a report calling for transformation of the entire mental health system, emphasizing participation by consumers (New Freedom Commission Report, 2003); and a report on prevention (Board of Children, Youth and Families 2009). The Institute of Medicine has drawn attention to the challenge of medical error, producing two reports, "To Err is Human: Building a Safer Health System" (2000) and "Crossing the Quality Chasm" (2001).

In the United Kingdom, the National Institute for Health and Clinical Excellence (http://www.nice.org.uk) and the Scottish Intercollegiate Guidelines Network (http://www.sign.ac.uk) have taken the lead in reviewing and disseminating new knowledge.

Not just the healthcare system, but the larger social field around the child is being examined using new computer-based methodologies like agent-based computer modelling (Hammond 2009, Hammond 2010). Such technology quantifies not just individual variables but relationships in the social network and larger social influences. Estimating the likely effect of a proposed intervention—modelling *in silico*—allows analysis and choice of options. These approaches are being applied to health problems like obesity and smoking and may be useful additions to advocacy in CAMH. A more concerted effort to coordinate clinical knowledge with emerging knowledge from other disciplines has been advocated under the rubric *transdisciplinary research* (Mabry et al. 2008).

Advocacy for CAMH will also benefit in coming years from the establishment in many universities and now at the U.S. National Institutes of Health (Collins 2011) of *Centers for Translational Research*, committed to studying the ways that new knowledge gets applied to benefit patients. It may take some advocacy to ensure that the Centers take on the challenges of CAMH.

Social Strategy

Every successful organization, even those founded to represent those lacking voice and power, over time can become the advocate of the status quo. Transforming change often has to come from outside, even in healthcare (Christensen 2003; Rae-Dupree 2009). Advocates in CAMH, using a variety of strategies, have in a similar spirit, shone light from outside on problems in the field. They have pointed out, for instance, that most troubled children receive no help, that the help available is often fragmented among agencies, that parents are excluded, that children often must leave home to get help, and, most important, that the care received is of uncertain benefit. A number of responses, mostly in the United States, may be noted.

Systems of Care

In the United States, a movement for wider access and better coordination of services was catalyzed by Knitzer's landmark work, "Unclaimed children: The failure of public responsibility to children and adolescents in need of mental health services" (Knitzer 1982). Knitzer showed that child mental health services were not reaching the most troubled children. What services they received were fragmented among education, social services, juvenile justice, and health services. Children's natural supports in family and community were not enlisted. As a result, troubled children were often sent, despite the lack of evidence for its effectiveness, to residential placement.

This work led to the "system of care" movement, advocating that services be provided earlier in a child's life, with more collaboration among serving agencies, and that parents be included—nay, empowered—in new ways: services were to be family focused, or even family driven. In states implementing systems of care, there has been a great increase in the numbers of troubled children recognized and served. Systems of care evaluations indicate greater participation and satisfaction among parents; evidence of effects on the child's functioning has been mixed (Bickman, 1996).

Legal Advocacy

A second new form of advocacy has been the use of the courts to advance protection and services for children. One approach uses a federal law requiring that States, when they enact health programs for low-income people, must provide what is called early and periodic screening, diagnosis, and treatment (EPSDT). This statutory right has allowed legal advocates, on behalf of troubled children, to argue in Court that the states are not following the law. In more than two dozen states the Courts have ordered sates to expand services and to offer new kinds of service. An example is the "Rosie D" suit and the resulting remedy in Massachusetts. Information from plaintiffs and the state is available online (Rosie D, CBHI).

Parent Engagement

A number of strategies are used to support, engage, and empower parents (Hoagwood et al. 2010). These include Family Group Conferencing (Mirsky 2003), the Let's Talk about Children program in Finland (Solantaus et al. 2010, Solantaus 2011), employment of parents with lived experience as aides (or "parent advocates") to parents of patients (Davis et al. 2010), and the Building Bridges Initiative (www.buildingbridges4youth.org) that aims to develop better ties between residential services and the parents of the children they serve. For some, the difference between "family focused" and "family driven" lies in having parents on the governing board.

New Coalitions

In Massachusetts, an effective coalition of providers, agencies and parent organizations, the Children's Mental Health Campaign, has succeeded in bringing together disparate stakeholders to maintain pressure on state government to maintain and expand children's services, even through times of fiscal retrenchment in state services in general, and to push for legislative changes on behalf of children (cf website).

Political Will

Public determination to do better by children and youth struggling with mental illness has been fostered by the media, by personal narratives by gifted writers who have struggled with mental illness, and by efforts to give voice to patients' experience.

The power of the media to mobilize public concern regarding child mental health has been evident in a recent spate of articles in the U.S. press.

A series in the *Boston Globe* (Wen 2010) on the large numbers of children obtaining federal disability payments on the basis of psychiatric diagnoses, and alleging that some were placed on psychoactive medications in order to qualify for those benefits, led to calls for federal investigation of the program. Considerable media coverage, sceptical to critical, of the increase in the prescription of psychoactive medications, especially second-generation antipsychotics, and especially to young children who are not receiving other services (Wilson 2010), has kept public interest in this subject high.

Patient experience has been conveyed by writers, recovered from serious illness, who choose to tell their stories publicly. In the spirit of Clifford Beers (1981), who used the story of his breakdown to launch the Mental Hygiene movement a century ago, writers like Elyn Saks (2007) and Brooke Katz (2004) have provided compelling narratives of their experience with serious mental illness, beginning in childhood, and the world of mental health services.

Patients' voices have also contributed, with unmatched immediacy, to the debate about the use of seclusion and restraint. In a video, "Behind Closed Doors." from a disability rights law centre, women describe their experience, as adolescents and young adults, in psychiatric facilities (Cain and Goss 2007). The spirit in which they recall painful experience resembles that expressed in the disability community, "Nothing about me without me" (O'Connor et al. 2005). These witnesses insist on being part of the debate.

CONCLUSION

In two centuries, advocacy for CAMH has moved from a few writers and educators to become a vast field encompassing patients and families, mental health professionals, attorneys expert in rights litigation, professional advocates, and researchers from the biological, behavioural, and social sciences. The challenge inherent in so rich a field is also its great asset: to speak for the historically voiceless, using methods not available even a generation ago, but in a way that still allows the voice of the child to be heard clearly.

ACKNOWLEDGMENTS

The author acknowledges the suggestions from Judy Ashton Esq, Myron Belfer, MD, Gail Garinger, Esq, Molly Harper, Moira O'Neill, and Tim Rivinus, MD.

REFERENCES

Aichhorn, A. (1951). *Verwahrloste Jugend (Wayward Youth: A psychoanalytic study of delinquent children: illustrated by actual case histories)*. Cleveland: World Publishing.

Aries, P. (1962). *Centuries of Childhood: a social history of family life*. New York: Knopf,

Beers, C. (1981). *A Mind That Found Itself*. Pittsburgh and London: University of Pittsburgh Press.

Belfer, M. (1976). The child advocacy concept: from a praiseworthy idea to practical demise. *Hospital and Community Psychiatry*, 27, 880–81.

Belfer, M. (2008). Child and adolescent mental disorders: the magnitude of the problem across the globe. *Journal of Child Psychology and Psychiatry*, 49, 226–36.

Bickman, L. (1996). A continuum of care: more is not always better. *American Psychologist*, 51, 689–701.

Board of Children, Youth, and Families of the National Research Council and the Institute of Medicine of the National Academies. (2009). *Preventing Mental, Emotional, and Behavioral Disorders Among Young People: Progress and Possibilities*. Washington: National Academies Press. Accessed at http://books.nap.edu/openbook.php?record_id=12480.

Bogira, S. (2009). Starvation diet: coping with shrinking budgets in publicly funded mental health services. *Health Aff (Millwood)*, 28, 667–75.

Butler, J. R., and Hyler, S. E. (2005). Hollywood portrayals of child and adolescent mental health treatment: implications for clinical practice. *Child Adolesc Psychiatr Clin N Am*, 14, 509–22.

Cain, L. and Gross, D. (2007) Film: *Behind Closed Doors: the Story of Four Women Trying to Reconcile Violence within the psychiatric system*. Maryland Disability Law Center. Described at http://behindcloseddoorsthefilmsite.com/index.html; copies available from Maryland Disability Law Center at: behindcloseddoors@mdlcbalto.org.

CBHI. State remedy available at: http://www.mass.gov/?pageID=eohhs2subtopican dL=4andL0=HomeandL1=GovernmentandL2=Special+Commissions+and+Initia tivesandL3=Children's+Behavioral+Health+Initiativeandsid=Eeohhs2

Children's Mental Health Campaign (Massachusetts). Website accessible at: http://www.childrensmentalhealthcampaign.org/index.cfm?andstopRedirect=1.

Christensen, C. M. (2003). *The innovator's solution: creating and sustaining successful growth.* Boston: Harvard Business Press.

Coles, R. (1967). *Children of Crisis: A Study in Courage and Fear.* Volume 1 of Children of Crisis. Boston: Atlantic-Little, Brown.

Coles, R. (1971a). *Migrants, Sharecroppers, Mountaineers.* Volume 2 of Children of Crisis. Boston: Little Brown.

Coles, R. (1971b). *The South Goes North.* Volume 3 of Children of Crisis. Boston: Little Brown.

Coles, R. (1977a). *Eskimos, Indians, Chicanos.* Volume 4 of Children of Crisis. Boston: Little Brown.

Coles, R. (1977b). *The Privileged Ones: The Well-off and the Rich in America.* Volume 5 of Children of Crisis. Boston: Little Brown.

Collins, F. S. (2011). Reengineering translational science: the time is right. *Sci Transl Med 6,* 90cm17.

Costello, J., Egger, H., and Angold, A. (2005). 10–Year Research Update Review: The Epidemiology of Child and Adolescent Psychiatric Disorders: I. Methods and Public Health Burden. *Journal of the American Academy of Child and Adolescent Psychiatry,* 44, 972–86.

Costello, J., Foley, D., and Angold, A. (2006). 10–year research update: The epidemiology of child and adolescent psychiatric disorders: II. Developmental epidemiology. *Journal of the American Academy of Child and Adolescent Psychiatry,* 45, 8–25.

Davis, T. S., Scheer, S. D., Gavazzi, S. M., and Uppal, R. (2010). Parent advocates in children's mental health: program implementation processes and considerations. *Adm Policy Ment Health,* 37, 468–83.

Hammond, R. A. (2009). Complex systems modeling for obesity research. *Prev Chronic Dis.* 6:A97. Epub 2009 Jun 15.

Hammond, R. A. (2010). Social influence and obesity. *Curr Opin Endocrinol Diabetes Obes,* 17, 467–71.

Heckman, J. J. (2008). The case for investing in disadvantaged young children. In *Big Ideas for children: Investing in Our Nation's Future.* Washington: First Focus, 2008.

Hoagwood, K., Jensen, P. S., Petti, T., and Burns, B J. (1990). Outcomes of Mental Health Care for Children and Adolescents: I: A comprehensive Conceptual Model. *J Amer Acad Child Adolesc Psychiatry,* 35, 1055–1063.

Hoagwood, K. E., Cavaleri, M. A., Serene, O. S., Burns, B. J., Slaton, E., Gruttadaro, D., and Hughes, R. (2010). Family support in children's mental health: a review and synthesis. *Clin Child Fam Psychol Rev,*13, 1–45.

Institute for Healthcare Improvement. *The IHI Triple Aim: Better Care for Individuals, Better Health for Individuals, and Lower Per Capita Costs.* Accessed 15 July 2011 at http://www.ihi.org/offerings/Initiatives/TripleAim/Pages/default.aspx

Institute of Medicine. (2000). *To err is human: building a safer health system.* Committee on Quality of Health Care in America. Washington: National Academy Press.

Institute of Medicine. (2001). *Crossing the quality chasm: a new health system for the 21st century.* Committee on Quality of Health Care in America. Washington: National Academy Press.

Katz, B. (2004). *I Think I Scared Her.* Bloomington, IN: Xlibris.

Knitzer, J. (1982). *Unclaimed Children: The Failure of Public Responsibility to Children and Adolescents in Need of Mental Health Services.* Washington: Children's Defense Fund.

Leonhardt, D. (2010). Life Expectancy in China Rising Slowly, Despite Economic Surge. *New York Times*: November 23.

Mabry, PL., Olster, DH., Morgan, GD., and Abrams, DB. (2008). Interdisciplinarity and systems science to improve population health: a view from the NIH Office of Behavioral and Social Sciences Research. *Am J Prev Med*, 35,(2 Suppl): S211–24.

Markel, H. (2009). *Case shined first light on abuse of children.* New York Times: December 14.

Massachusetts State Office for Children. *No date. The Office for Children: a New Approach to the Development of Children's Services in Massachusetts.* Accessed online at http://www.eric.ed.gov/ERICWebPortal/detail?accno=ED078894

Michigan Office of Children's Ombudsman. *No date. Ombudsman Reference List.* Accessed 15 July 2011 at http://www.michigan.gov/oco/0,1607,7–133–-11755–- ,00.html#ma

Mirsky, L. (2003). *Family Group Conferencing Worldwide: Part One in a Series.* Bethlehem, PA: International Institute for Restorative Practices. Accessed at http://www. iirp.org/article_detail.php?article_id=NDMz

Mondale, S. (2001). *School: The story of American Public Education.* New York: Beacon.

National Children's Advocacy Center. Accessed at http://nationalcac.org/

National Children's Alliance. Accessed at http://www.nationalchildrensalliance.org/ index.php?s=6#

New Freedom Commission. (2003). The President's New Freedom Commission on Mental Health. Dept of Health and Human Services.

O'Connor, L. A., Morgenstern, J., Gibson, F., Nakashian, M. (2005). Nothing about me without me: leading the way to collaborative relationships with families. *Child Welfare, 84,* 153–70.

Omigbodun, O. (2008). Developing child mental health services in resource-poor countries. *Int Rev Psychiatry,20,* 225–35.

Paim, J., Travassos, C., Almeida, C., Bahia, L., and Macinko, J. (2011). The Brazilian health system: history, advances, and challenges. *The Lancet, 377,* 1778–1797.

Ptakowski, K. K. (2010). Advocating for children and adolescents with mental illness. *Child Adolesc Psychiatr Clin N Am, 19,* 131–38.

Rae-Dupree, J. (2009). Disruptive Innovation, Applied to Health Care. *New York Times*: January 31.

Richmond, J. B. (1995). The Hull House era: vintage years for children. *Am J Orthopsychiatry, 65,* 10–20.

Richmond, J. B., and Eisenberg, L. (1991). Putting the "Public" back in Mental Health, and the "Mental" back in Public Health. *Biol Psychiatry, 30,* 427–29.

Richmond, J. B., and Kotelchuck, M. (1983). Political influences: rethinking national health policy. In McGuire, C.H., Foley, R.P., Gorr, A., Richards, R.W., (Eds.), *The handbook of health professions education*. San Francisco: Jossey-Bass.

Rosie D. Plaintiffs' information available at: http://www.rosied.org/Default.aspx?pageId=67061

Rousseau, J.-J. (1979). *Émile, or On Education*. Translated by Allan Bloom. New York: Basic Books.

Saks, E. (2007). *The Center Cannot Hold: My Journey Through Madness*. New York: Hyperion Books.

Silber, K. (1960). *Pestalozzi: The Man and his Work*. London: Routledge and Kegal Paul.

Solantaus, T., Paavonen, E. J., Toikka, S., and Punamäki, R. L. (2010). Preventive interventions in families with parental depression: children's psychosocial symptoms and prosocial behaviour. *Eur Child Adolesc Psychiatry, 19(12)*, 883–92. Epub 2010 Oct 2.

Solantaus, T. (2011). *Multisectoral health, social and educational services: Families with parental health issues, substance use and poverty in focus*. Presented at ESCAP Congress, Helsinki.

Surgeon General. (1999). Mental health: a report of the Surgeon General. Dept of Health and Human Services: US Public Health Service.

Taipale, V. (2011). *Welcome Address*. ESCAP Congress, Helsinki.

UNICEF (2011). *The State of the World's Children, 2011*. Accessed at http://www.unicef.org/sowc/

Verhulst, F. C., and Koot, H. M. (1992). *Child Psychiatric Epidemiology: Concepts, Methods and Findings*. Newbury Park, CA: Sage.

Victora, C. G., Barreto, M. L., Leal, M.doC., Monteiro, C. A., Schmidt, M. I., Paim, J., Bastos, F.I., Almeida, C., Bahia, L., Travassos, C., Reichenheim, M., Barros, F. C. and the Lancet Brazil Series Working Group on Health. (2011). Conditions and health-policy innovations in Brazil: the way forward. *The Lancet, 377*, 2042–53.

Virchow, R. (1847). *Der Arzt is der natürliche Anwalt der Armen*. Cited at http://www.ostdeutsche-biographie.de/vircru02.htm

Wen, P. (2010). *The other welfare*. Boston Globe. Accessed at http://www.boston.com/news/health/specials/New_Welfare/

Wikipedia. (2011). *Timeline of children's rights in the United States*. Accessed at http://en.wikipedia.org/wiki/Timeline_of_children%27s_rights_in_the_United_States

Wilson, D. (2010). Child's Ordeal Reveals Risks Of Psychiatric Drugs in Young. *New York Times*: September 2.

Woolley S. L. (2009). The rights of Indigenous children around the world—still far from a reality. *Arch Dis Child, 94*, 397–400.

World Federation for Mental Health. Accessed at http://www.wfmh.org/

World Health Organization. mental health Gap Action Programme (mhGAP). Accessed at http://www.who.int/mental_health/mhGAP/en/

Zechmeister, I., Kilian, R., McDaid, D., and the MHEEN group. (2008). Is it worth investing in mental health promotion and prevention of mental illness? A systematic review of the evidence from economic evaluations. *BMC Public Health, 8*, 20. Open Access at http://www.biomedcentral.com/1471-2458/8/20

Zima, B. T., Mangione-Smith, R. (2011). Gaps in quality measures for child mental health care: an opportunity for a collaborative approach. *J Amer Acad Ch Adolesc Psychiatry, 50*, 735–37.

Index

About the Contributors

Joan Rosenbaum Asarnow, PhD, is professor of psychiatry and biobehavioral Sciences at the UCLA David Geffen School of Medicine and a clinical psychologist. Dr. Asarnow's current work focuses on interventions and service delivery strategies for improving health and mental health in youth, with an emphasis on suicide/suicide attempt prevention and depression. She has led efforts to disseminate evidence-based treatments for child and adolescent depression and suicide prevention, working across multiple service settings including emergency departments, primary care, mental health, and school settings. Dr. Asarnow has received grants from the National Institute of Mental Health, Centers for Disease Control, Agency for Healthcare Research and Quality, American Foundation for Suicide Prevention, and MacArthur Foundation. At the UCLA Semel Institute for Neuroscience and Human Behavior, Dr. Asarnow directs the Youth Stress and Mood Program, a depression and suicide prevention program. This program provides clinical care for youth depression and suicidality, with an emphasis on cognitive-behavioral treatments, work with families, and community-based treatment and service strategies.

Thomas Bourgeron, MD, obtained his PhD in human genetics to study mitochondrial diseases after receiving a master's in the field of plant biology. He obtained a permanent position as professor at University Denis Diderot Paris 7 and joined the Institut Pasteur to study the role of the Y chromosome in male infertility. In 2003 he established a laboratory to study the genetics of autism spectrum disorders (ASD). His most recent results include the identification of one synaptic pathway associated with ASD. The causative genes code for cell adhesion molecules (NLGN3, NLGN4, NRXN1) or scaffolding protein (SHANK2 and SHANK3), which are crucial factors for appropriate synaptic function.

David Cohen, MD, PhD, is professor at the UPMC, head of the department of Child and Adolescent Psychiatry at La Salpêtrière hospital, and member of Institut des Systèmes Intelligents et Robotiques in Paris. His group runs research programs in the field of pervasive developmental disorder (autism) and learning disabilities, childhood onset schizophrenia, catatonia and severe mood disorder. He supports a developmental and plastic view of child psychopathology. His team proposes a multidisciplinary approach and collaborates with molecular biologist, experimental psychologist, sociologist and engineer. He has published more than one hundred research papers including some in high impact journals (see http://speapsl.aphp.fr).

Richard Delorme, MD, PhD, is assistant professor of child and adolescent psychiatry at the Robert Debré University Hospital, Paris, France. He obtained his MD at the medical school of Paris VII University in 1999 and acquired experience in clinics for child and adolescent neuropsychiatric patients of a broad range within the CNS. He is especially interested in autism spectrum disorders and anxiety disorders (especially obsessive compulsive disorder). Richard Delorme is also involved in several research programs and specifically in the search for vulnerability genes associated to developmental disorders such as ASD and OCD. He performed his post-doctorate in the laboratory of Human Genetics and Cognitive Functions directed by Thomas Bourgeron at the Institut Pasteur, Paris, France. He has published over forty articles in international peer-reviewed journals

Herman van Engeland, MD, PhD, is professor emeritus and chairman of the department of Child and Adolescent Psychiatry, University Medical Center Utrecht (1980–2008). He is past president of ESCAP and past vice president of IACAPAP. He published more than two hundred Pub Med articles and supervised more than sixty PhD projects. Currently his research interests are focused on KlineFeltersyndrome, schizophrenia, ADHD, and autism.

Daniel Fung is a psychiatrist and has been the vice chairman of the medical board at the Institute of Mental Health, Singapore, since 2009. He was formerly the chief at the Department of Child and Adolescent Psychiatry from 2006 to 2011. He is an adjunct associate professor with the Duke-NUS Graduate Medical School; National University of Singapore; and the Division of Psychology, School of Humanities and Social Sciences, at Nanyang Technological University. A recipient of the National Healthcare Group's

Distinguished Achievement Award in 2010, Dr. Fung is also the programme director of REACH (Response, Early Interventions and Assessment in Community Mental Health), a community-based mental health program that is part of the National Mental Health Blueprint. In his voluntary work, Dr. Fung is the secretary general of the International Association for Child and Adolescent Psychiatry and Allied Professions and the immediate past president of the Asian Society of Child and Adolescent Psychiatry and Allied Professions. He is also the president of the Singapore Association for Mental Health, an NGO that supports mentally ill persons and their families in the community. He volunteers with various NGOs in Singapore including the Singapore Children's Society and the Society of Moral Charities. Dr. Fung is also a member of the school board of Paya Lebar Methodist Girl's School. Dr. Fung has coauthored over forty research papers, more than ten books, and five book chapters.

M. Elena Garralda, MD, MPhil, FRCPsych, is professor of child and adolescent psychiatry at Imperial College London, UK, and honorary consultant child and adolescent psychiatrist with Central North West London NHS Foundation Trust in London. Her main research interests include the interface between physical and mental health in children, and measuring outcomes of child and adolescent mental health service use.

Danya Glaser, MB, BS, DCH, FRCPsych, Hon FRCPCH, is an honorary consultant child and adolescent psychiatrist at Great Ormond Street Hospital for Children, London. She is currently working on the early recognition of fabricated or induced illness. Previously a developmental paediatrician, at Great Ormond Street Hospital she was named doctor for child protection and for many years headed an integrated child protection service working respectively with the identification and treatment of emotional abuse; providing multidisciplinary assessments for Children Act proceedings as an expert witness and a post protection team working with children who have been seriously maltreated and their current, often new carers. She was a member of the Family Justice Council for six years. Dr. Glaser has taught, researched and written widely on various aspects of child maltreatment including sexual and emotional abuse, fabricated or induced illness; and the effects of child maltreatment on the developing brain. With her research team she is currently completing a follow-up study of maltreated children who have been subject to care proceedings and a study on the efficacy of training on emotional abuse. She is updating her coauthored book on the evidence base on attachment and attachment disorders. Dr. Glaser is past president of ISPCAN and visiting professor at University College London. She also chairs the Coram adoption panel.

Gordon Harper, MD, is an associate professor and a native of Rochester New York, trained in pediatrics, psychiatry, and child psychiatry. He has practiced and worked in Boston since the 1960s. His interests have been in the inpatient treatment of children with serious disorders, in the ways that treatment is organized (focal treatment planning), and in public policy regarding child/adolescent mental health. He has taught in IACA-PAP Congresses in San Francisco, Stockholm, Berlin, Melbourne, Istanbul, and Beijing. Outside the United States, he has also taught in Turkey, Egypt, Tunisia, Taiwan, Singapore, Finland, Korea, and China. He currently serves as Treasurer of IACAPAP.

Elena Ise, PhD, is post-doc at the Department of Child and Adolescent Psychiatry, Psychosomatics, and Psychotherapy, Ludwig-Maximilians-University of Munich. Her research interests include spelling development, orthographic knowledge, intervention, and treatment in dyslexia.

Miri Keren, MD, works as a child and adolescent psychiatrist; director of the first Community Infant Psychiatry Unit in Israel, created in 1996; and is affiliated to the Geha Mental Health Center. Since 1999, Dr. Keren has been the supervisor of a national project of infant mental health units implementation under joint sponsorship of the Ministry of Health and Sacta-Rashi Foundation. She also functions as a consultant of the Tel Aviv Residential nursery for infants waiting for adoption, consultant at the FTT Clinic, Schneider Children's Hospital, Petah Tiqva. She is lecturer at the Child Psychiatry Department of Tel-Aviv Sackler Medical School and is the head of a two-year early childhood psychiatry course in the faculty of Continuing Education, Tel-Aviv Sackler Medical School. She created the Israeli WAIMH Affiliate in 2000, has been its president from 2003 to 2007 and is now honorary president of the Israel WAIMH Affiliate, and president elect of the WAIMH. She is currently the editor of the WAIMH Newsletter *The Signal,* and consulting editor of the *Infant Mental Health Journal.* Her research domains are Infant mental health diagnostic classification, feeding disorders in infancy, symbolic play development, parent-infant dyadic and triadic relationships characteristics among clinic-and non clinic-referred families, abandoned babies and adoptive parents.

Luisa Lazaro, MD, is head of the child and adolescent inpatient psychiatric unit of Hospital Clínic of Barcelona. She is an associate professor of psychiatry in the Medicine Faculty of the University of Barcelona. She conducts research at the August Pi I Sunyer Biomedical Research Institute (IDIBAPS) and the Mental Health Research Network (CIBERSAM). She is also the coordinator of the clinical guidelines of OCD in the Hospital Clínic of Barcelona.

Eleanor Leigh, BSc, DClinPsy, is a chartered clinical psychologist at the South London and Maudsley NHS Foundation Trust and is affiliated to the Institute of Psychiatry, Kings College London. She works in the National and Specialist Child and Adolescent Mood Disorder Clinic and the Anxiety and Trauma Clinic, and provides teaching and training in cognitive behavior therapy (CBT).

John March, MD, MPH, is professor of psychiatry and psychology and director of the Division of Neurosciences Medicine at the Duke Clinical Research Institute. Dr. March develops, conducts, and facilitates research projects in adult and child neurology and psychiatry, which range from biomarker/biosignature development and validation, imaging genomics, Phase I-IV industry, and federal clinical trials, to outcomes research.

Marie Christine Mouren, MD, is head of the Department of Child and Adolescent Psychiatry at the Robert Debré University Hospital, Paris, France. Her interests focus on psychopharmacology and neuropsychiatric conditions in childhood, and her involvement with a number of important and influential research studies in these areas have informed European-level treatment guidelines. She has lectured extensively, specifically nationally, and published many books for parents and practitioners on hyperactivity, as well as written and contributed to more than one hundred scientific papers on hyperactivity, psychopharmacology, neuropsychiatry, and related topics.

Dennis Ougrin, MBBS, MRCPsych, PGDip(Oxon), graduated from a medical school in Ukraine in 1998. He completed his training in child and adolescent psychiatry at Guy's and Maudsley training scheme. At present Dr. Ougrin is a consultant child and adolescent psychiatrist at South London and Maudsley NHS Foundation Trust and is an honorary visiting lecturer at the Institute of Psychiatry, King's College London. Dr. Ougrin leads a program of information exchange between the United Kingdom and Ukraine and organizes annual conferences aimed at developing psychiatric services in Ukraine. His main professional interests include prevention of borderline personality disorder and effective interventions for self-harm in adolescents. Dr. Ougrin is the author of Therapeutic Assessment, a novel model of assessment for young people presenting with self-harm in emergency. Dr. Ougrin was the chief investigator of Trial of Therapeutic Assessment in London (TOTAL), a randomized controlled trial comparing Therapeutic Assessment and usual care. Dr. Ougrin teaches Therapeutic Assessment at a commercially successful annual training course at the Maudsley hospital. Workshops on Therapeutic Assessment form part of the academic programme of the American Academy of Child and Adolescent Psychiatry annual meetings and have recently been introduced into The International Association for Child and Adolescent Psychiatry and Allied Professions World Congress program. Dr. Ougrin is a mental health theme editor of *London Journal of General Practice* and also an honorary research and audit consultant at Brent Primary Care Trust.

Saskia Palmen, MD, PhD, completed her medical degree cum laude. In March 2005 she finished her PhD thesis "Structural brain abnormalities in autism," in which she investigated brains of children and adolescents with autism spectrum disorders both in vivo (structural MRI) and ex vivo (post-mortem). In March 2005 she started her residency in child psychiatry, which she finished in September 2010. Since then, she has been a staff member at the University Medical Center Utrecht where she works on a ward admitting first-episode psychotic adolescents and young adults. Her main research interest is in post-mortem research. As a result, she is busy in cooperation with the Netherlands Brain Bank to start a research program involving post-mortem research in psychiatric diseases in the Netherlands.

Jean-Philippe Raynaud, MD, is professor of child and adolescent psychiatry and head of department at Toulouse University Hospital (Centre Hospitalier Universitaire de Toulouse, France), member of the French National Institute of Health and Medical Research (INSERM UMR 1027), president of the scientific committee of French society for child and adolescent psychiatry (SFPEADA), and vice president of IACAPAP (International Society for Child and Adolescent Psychiatry and Allied Professions).

Helmut Remschmidt, MD, PhD, FRCPsych, was head of the Department of Child and Adolescent Psychiatry at Philipps-University, Marburg (Germany) from 1980 to 2006 and has been professor emeritus since October 2006. Previously, Dr. Remschmidt was special professor of psychiatry at the University of Birmingham/UK (1993–1996) and president of the European Society for Child and Adolescent Psychiatry (ESCAP) (1995–1999). He was also president of the International Society for Child and Adolescent Psychiatry and Allied Professions (IACAPAP) from 1998 to 2004 and scientific director of the WPA Global Presidential Program on Child and Adolescent Mental Health, carried out in cooperation with IACAPAP and WHO (2003–2005). Dr. Remschmidt's awards include the Hermann Simon-Award for outstanding research in social psychiatry (1990), Christina Barz Award for research regarding eating disorders (1994), Nilo Hallman-Medal of the Finnish Foundation for Pediatric Research (1998), Max Planck Award for International Cooperation (1999), and the Lilly Quality of Life Award (2006). His research interests include forensic child and adolescent psychiatry, developmental psychopathology, eating disorders, schizophrenia research, psychiatric genetics, therapy, and evaluation research. He has published more than six hundred articles in scientific journals and book chapters in several languages; is author, coauthor, and editor of more than fifty books in the field of child and adolescent psychiatry and mental health; and editor and coeditor of several scientific journals. In addition, Dr. Remschmidt is guest researcher and invited lecturer at universities in Europe, Israel, Africa, the united States, China, Chile, Brazil, Uruguay, Thailand, Korea, and Australia.

Jeffrey Sapyta, PhD, is assistant professor in the Department of Psychiatry and Behavioral Sciences at Duke University Medical Center. Dr. Sapyta's broad research interests are in the area of child and adolescent anxiety and mood disorders. His particular interests include improving treatment in obsessive compulsive disorder, youth suicidality, and developing clinical decision-making tools for mental health professionals.

Gerd Schulte-Körne, MD, is professor of child and adolescent psychiatry and psychotherapy at the Ludwig-Maximilians-University of Munich and director of the Department of Child and Adolescent Psychiatry, Psychosomatics, and Psychotherapy. His current interests include learning disabilities, depression, neuropsychology, neurophysiology, and genetics.

Philip Shaw, MD, PhD, is a research psychiatrist at the National Institute of Mental Health (Child Psychiatry Branch) in Bethesda, Maryland.

Liying Su, BA, is a research associate at the Department of Child and Adolescent Psychiatry, Institute of Mental Health, Singapore. She graduated from Nanyang Technological University with a BA (Hons) in psychology. Her honors thesis centered on parenting of children with special needs. Currently, she works closely with children and adolescents with disruptive behavior disorders, including attention-deficit hyperactive disorder, conduct disorder and oppositional defiant disorder. She administers assessments and facilitates social skills training interventions for this target population. Her work has also been presented in international conferences. Liying has a keen interest in educational psychology and is working towards this area of specialty.

Lucy Taylor, MPhil, DClinPsy, PGDip, is a practicing clinical psychologist with the Child and Adolescent Dialectical Behaviour Therapy Service, Maudsley Hospital. Her main areas of interest and specialism are cognitive behavior therapy (CBT), self-harm and adolescents. Prior to this, she worked in Croydon CAMHS, taking the lead research role in developing and piloting a CBT manual for young people who self-harm and their families. She also jointly set up a new mental health service offering input to all secondary schools in the Croydon area. She supervised on the CBT Child and Adolescent Postgraduate Diploma course at King's College London and has led supervision, teaching, and training program for child and adolescent mental health service teams nationally. She continues to teach and supervise the doctorate in clinical psychology course at the Institute of Psychiatry. Following completion of a psychology honors degree at Portsmouth University in 1992, she went to Cambridge University to study criminology as a master's degree. After DClin Psych training at the Institute of Psychiatry, she worked at the Bethlem Adolescent Unit as a Clinical Psychologist, and during this period she completed a postgraduate diploma in cognitive behaviour therapy (PGDip CBT). She is an accredited child and adolescent member of the British Association for Behavioural and Cognitive Psychotherapies (BABCP). Current research interests include the evaluation of dialectical behaviour therapy (DBT) in treating borderline personality disorder in adolescents and CBT treatment for self-harm in adolescents. Previous research work includes parental stress and "hard-to-manage" preschoolers, and the evidence base for offender profiling.

Frank Theisen, MD, is a child and adolescent psychiatrist and psychotherapist. He received his MD from the University of Bonn and worked as a physician at the Department of Psychiatry and Child and Adolescent Psychiatry at the University of Würzburg, Germany, 1996–1998. In 1999 and 2000 he was a research fellow of the German Research Association (DFG) at the Clinical Research Group "genetic mechanisms of body weight regulation," University of Marburg. He worked at the Department of Child and Adolescent Psychiatry, University of Marburg (head: Professor Remschmidt), between 2001 and 2007. In 2007 he completed his professorial dissertation ("Habilitation"), entitled "Weight changes under antipsychotics as exemplified by Clozapine and Olanzapine: Clinical, regulatory and genetic implications" at the University of Marburg. His publications include a variety of book chapters with clinical focus and original articles mainly concerning psychopharmacology, pharmacogenetics, and schizophrenia. His teaching specialties center on psychopharmacology and child and adolescent psychiatric disorders. Since 2007 he has been the head of the Department of Child and Adolescent Psychiatry in Fulda, Germany.

Josep Toro, PhD, is emeritus professor of psychiatry at the University of Barcelona. He was senior consultant and head of the Department of Child and Adolescent Psychiatry at Hospital Clinic of Barcelona. Eating disorders and obsessive-compulsive disorders are the principal subjects of his research and international publications.

Troy Tranah, BSc, MSc, PhD, is a consultant clinical psychologist and CAMHS CAG professional head of psychology for the South London and Maudsley NHS Foundation Trust. He is also an honorary lecturer at the Institute of Psychology, King's College London. Dr. Tranah completed a PhD at University of London on the topic of suicide and PTSD before commencing clinical psychology training at the Institute of Psychiatry. Since qualifying he has worked in a variety of clinical roles including adolescent and child in-patient units and in a variety of specialist out-patient services. More recently Dr. Tranah has developed a service for adolescents with recurrent self-harm and borderline personality disorder. Over the years Dr. Tranah has published numerous peer reviewed papers in a variety of areas including suicide, depression, PTSD, neuropsychology, sexual abuse, conduct disorder, and forensic psychology.

Sam Tyano, MD, FRCPsych, FAPA, HFWPA, was born in Israel in 1939; received a degree in medicine in Strasbourg, France; and trained in adult and child and adolescent psychiatry in Israel. Dr. Tyano was head of the Adolescent Psychiatric Department for twenty-five years before moving to infant psychiatry. He is currently professor emeritus in psychiatry at the Tel Aviv University, School of Medicine and is author and editor of four books on adult and child and adolescent psychiatry.

Andreas Warnke, MD, Psych, a professor of child and adolescent psychiatry and clinical psychologist. He is head of the Department of Child and Adolescent Psychiatry, Psychosomatics and Psychotherapy, University of Würzburg (Germany). He is the current vice president of the International Society for Child and Adolescent Psychiatry and Allied Professions (IACAPAP). His main research interests are developmental experimental psychopathology, genetics, psychotherapy, psychopharmacology, dyslexia, anorexia nervosa, obsessive-compulsive disorder, and attention deficit-hyperactivity disorder. Dr. Warnke's publications include more than 250 articles in scientific journals and book chapters in several languages. He is author, coauthor, or editor of more than twenty books in the field of child and adolescent psychiatry. He is the former section editor of biological child and adolescent psychiatry for the *Journal Neural Transmission*, coeditor of *Zeitschrift Kinder-und Jugendpsychiatrie und Psychotherapie*. He has received several awards, including the Hermann Emminghaus Award for outstanding research; "Excellent Teacher Reward" at the University of Würzburg; "Lotte-Schenk-Danzinger-Medal" for outstanding research and clinical engagement in developmental dyslexia; "Heinrich-Hofmann-Medal" of the German Society for Child and Adolescent Psychiatry, Psychosomatics, and Psychotherapy for outstanding merits to children in need of help; Medal of the Constitution of Bavaria; and Medal of the District Authority.

Lightning Source UK Ltd.
Milton Keynes UK
UKOW050021150312

188963UK00001B/2/P